On the Margins
of Citizenship

Allison C. Carey

On the Margins of Citizenship

*Intellectual Disability and Civil Rights
in Twentieth-Century America*

TEMPLE UNIVERSITY PRESS
Philadelphia

Temple University Press
Philadelphia PA 19122
www.temple.edu/tempress

∞ The paper used in this publication meets the requirements of the American National
Standard for Information Sciences—Permanence of Paper for Printed Library Materials,
ANSI Z39.48-1992

Library of Congress Cataloging-in-Publication Data

Carey, Allison C.
  On the margins of citizenship : intellectual disability and civil rights
in twentieth-century America / Allison C. Carey.
     p.   cm.
  Includes bibliographical references and index.
  ISBN 978-1-59213-697-1 (cloth : alk. paper)
  1. People with mental disabilities—Civil rights—United States. I. Title.
  HV3006.A4C367 2009
  323.3—dc22

                                                    2009003749

ISBN 13: 978-1-59213-698-8 (paper : alk. paper)

Contents

Acknowledgments

M any people and organizations assisted in the creation of this work. The research for this book was supported by grants from the Rackham Graduate School of the University of Michigan, by the Pennsylvania State System of Higher Education Faculty Professional Development Council, and by the Pennsylvania State System of Higher Education University Research and Scholarship Program.

Portions of the book have appeared or will appear in other publications, including *Disability and Society* (2003) and *Research in Disability and Social Sciences* (forthcoming). I thank the reviewers who served these journals for their insights. I also thank the reviewers for and staff at Temple University Press for offering many valuable suggestions.

Many other individuals, who assisted me in various stages of this project, deserve recognition. They include the members of my dissertation committee—Julia Adams, Renee Anspach, Mark Chesler, Martin Pernick, Margaret Somers, and James Trent—who encouraged me in my work and advised me in its development into a book; Deborah Schmitt, who provided editorial suggestions; and numerous other colleagues, including Barbara Denison, Carol Marfisi, and Richard Scotch, who offered feedback at every stage. In particular, I thank my husband, Blyden Potts, and my family, for providing both academic and emotional support throughout the process.

I

Introduction

Throughout American history, intellectual disability has challenged the popular images and legal boundaries of American citizenship and rights. While the storybook ideal citizen exudes intelligence, independence, and the ability to contribute to the national well-being through hard work, political participation, and bravery, people with intellectual disabilities tend to be characterized by their deficiencies. Difficulties performing tasks such as learning, processing information, communicating, caring for one's own basic needs, and attaining financial and social independence appear to impede the self-determination that is foundational to the exercise of rights. Thus, when judged by the standards of the ideal citizen, the person with an intellectual disability may appear unworthy, at best, and a threat to the nation and himself or herself, at worst.

At no point in our history have Americans reached consensus about the extent to which people with intellectual disabilities should be allowed to exercise rights. Rather, debates have raged for well over a century and have favored, at various times, views ranging from full exclusion to full equality. In part, the debates revolve around questions regarding the abilities and best interests of people labeled intellectually disabled, involving considerations such as whether they can make rational decisions and take full responsibility for these decisions or whether they require protection from their own limitations through restricted rights. More often, the debates reflect visions of the ideal national community, the standards for membership, and the way in which "difference" is to be treated within it.[1]

Although discrimination on the basis of race and gender has long been challenged and condemned as a form of irrational prejudice, we are only just beginning to question and de-naturalize the deprivation of rights from people with disabilities. The traditional legal model equated disability with incompetence and therefore assumed the inferior legal status of people with disabilities to be "an inevitable consequence of the physical and intellectual differences imposed by disability" (Funk 1987, 7). As such, exclusion on the basis of disability is still widely accepted and viewed as legally justified and even morally imperative.

Because intellectual disability represents such a traditional and well-accepted basis for exclusion, attempts to rethink the definition of intellectual disability and its relationship to rights call into question many of the fundamental assumptions about citizenship and raise key questions about the way in which we allocate rights, including the following: What are the abilities and character traits needed to exercise rights? Should rights be conferred based on ability, membership in a community, or other considerations? Does the state have an obligation to provide assistance or social rights to enhance citizens' well-being? What should happen to individuals who are denied rights? Does the state have any obligations to non-rights-bearing citizens? Throughout debates on intellectual disability and rights, these questions are raised over and over again, and Americans answer them very differently depending on the time and place in which they live and their relationship to intellectual disability.

Constructing the Exclusion of People with Intellectual Disabilities

To introduce some of the broad issues in these debates, we briefly consider the arguments for the exclusion of people with intellectual disabilities from rights, the arguments for inclusion, and the frequent movement between these positions. To first consider exclusion, the legal history of Americans with intellectual disabilities has been dominated by the formal deprivation of rights. At the time of their founding, almost all U.S. states developed constitutional and legal restrictions abrogating from "idiots," "incompetents," or "imbeciles" the rights to vote, to make contracts (and therefore to marry, as marriage is seen as a form of contract), and to serve on juries. In place of rights, legislators developed a series of legal protections. For example, people with intellectual disabilities could potentially receive exemptions from military obligations and have marriages and damaging contracts voided. While offering some degree of protection, the exclusion from rights simultaneously made individuals vulnerable to segregation, marginalization, and abuse.

Exclusion remained the driving force of disability policy throughout much of the twentieth century. In the early 1900s, institutionalization emerged as the primary policy for the treatment of intellectual disability and continued to guide national policy until at least the late 1960s (Trent 1994). People with intellectual disabilities rarely were given the opportunity to consent to their institutionalization, and the denial of their liberty could last any amount of time, potentially for their entire lifetimes. In addition to institutionalization, thirty-two states passed compulsory sterilization laws in the twentieth century and thirty-nine had restrictive marriage statutes at some time during that period. As recently as 1975, West Virginia enacted a sterilization law and promoted it by asserting the savings that it would provide for taxpayers (Reilly 1991). Moreover, prior to the passage of the 1975 Education for All Handicapped Children Act, children with disabilities frequently were excluded from public education.

Times have changed, but exclusion is not simply a matter of the past. People with intellectual disabilities continue to face tremendous marginalization in current times. Many states retain laws denying rights based solely on the diagnosis or legal adjudication of mental incompetence, regardless of the relevance of these medical and legal determinations to the ability to exercise specific rights. Moreover, due to the lack of accommodations and support, people with disabilities often cannot meaningfully exercise the rights that have been formally granted to them.

The deprivation of rights contributes to the broader lack of control that people with intellectual disabilities exercise over their lives. Pennsylvania data from 2003–2004 provides a glimpse into the current situation: 65 percent of adults receiving residential services through the state's Office of Mental Retardation reported that they had no input regarding where they lived, and of those who said they had input, the majority (66 percent) looked at no potential living situations outside their current residence; three-quarters (76 percent) of the respondents did not choose their housemates; only 31 percent had a key or a way to independently enter their residence; and almost half (45 percent) reported having no input regarding how they spent their day, regardless of whether they were employed or went to a "day activity" program (Feinstein et al. 2005). In Pennsylvania, as in many states, the receipt of services largely requires one to forfeit the right to select one's own housing, roommates, staff, daily activities, and schedule.[2]

Moreover, most services are currently provided in a manner that assumes and imposes asexuality on their recipients; sexuality, marriage, and parenting are largely incompatible with the dominant single-sex group home structure. Public transportation is infrequently available and, when it exists, remains largely inaccessible, leaving people with disabilities dependent on family, friends, staff, and separate and inferior systems of transportation provided specifically for people with disabilities. Segregation continues to dominate both the provision of public education for children and adult "programming" such as sheltered workshops and day activity centers. While not as blatant as compulsory institutionalization and sterilization, segregated services may prevent people with intellectual disabilities from participating meaningfully in mainstream society.

Several of the justifications used for excluding people with intellectual disabilities from rights are vividly demonstrated by the infamous 1927 Supreme

Court case *Buck v. Bell*. The case revolved around Carrie Buck, who was born out of wedlock to a woman committed to the Virginia State Colony for Epileptics and Feebleminded. At seventeen, she became a patient at this same institution. Carrie was pregnant and unmarried at the time of her commitment, and institutional physicians diagnosed her as "feebleminded," with a mental age of nine, and "sexually immoral" (Cynkar 1981). After Carrie gave birth, physicians waited only nine months before declaring her baby feebleminded, "proving" that hereditary feeblemindedness existed within Carrie's family and turning her into the embodiment of eugenic fears concerning genetic feeblemindedness and moral deviance (Gould 1984).[3]

Based on Carrie's diagnosis and presumed hereditary destiny to bear feebleminded children, her physicians ordered her to be sterilized, a legal option under Virginia's new sterilization law. Authorities from the Virginia State Colony argued that, as a "low-grade moron" whose family indicated a "very high frequency of feeble-minded persons," Carrie was a "potential parent of socially inadequate offspring" (Cynkar 1981). Not only did the authorities wish to sterilize Carrie but they also desired to use her case to test the new law, because she represented such an ideal candidate under the guidelines for eugenic sterilization. Sterilization had come under much legal fire, and they hoped Carrie's case would legitimate once and for all the state's right to prevent procreation in this way. Carrie's legal guardian approved of the sterilization, yet the superintendent of the State Colony asked her guardian to contest the procedure, setting in motion a legal "battle" in which everyone with power actually supported her sterilization. As the Virginia State Colony's authorities hoped, this case went all the way to the U.S. Supreme Court.

The denial of many basic rights actually went unquestioned in this case. Once institutionalized, inmates such as Carrie were denied rights to liberty and procreation through the enforced separation of the sexes as a matter of course. Hence, the lawyer representing the Virginia State Colony, Aubrey Strode, argued, "The state may and does confine the feeble minded, thus depriving them of their liberty. When so confined they are by segregation prohibited from procreation—a further deprivation of liberty that goes unquestioned" (Strode 1927). Carrie's own lawyer, I. P. Whitehead, simply agreed, noting, "We concede that the State has the right to segregate the feebleminded and thereby deprive them of the power to procreate. The State has exercised this right for a long time without question" (Whitehead 1927).

In addition to denying the right to procreate, though, forced sterilization violated the right to bodily integrity by surgically eliminating the biological potential of procreation. Hence, the matter under dispute in *Buck v. Bell* was not the right to procreate per se but, rather, the means available to the state to prohibit procreation. Would the state be allowed to violate an individual's bodily integrity and surgically eliminate the physical possibility of procreation? In his impassioned court decision, Justice Oliver Wendell Holmes Jr. gave unwavering support for the state's authority to deny basic civil rights, including the rights to privacy, parenthood, and bodily integrity, to people with intellectual disabilities:

> We have seen more than once that the public welfare may call upon the best citizens for their lives. It would be strange if it could not call upon those who already sap the strength of the State for these lesser sacrifices, often not felt to be such by those concerned, in order to prevent our being swamped with incompetence. It is better for all the world, if instead of waiting to execute degenerate offspring for crime, or to let them starve for their imbecility, society can prevent those who are manifestly unfit from continuing their kind. The principle that sustains compulsory vaccination is broad enough to cover cutting the Fallopian tubes. . . . Three generations of imbeciles are enough. (*Buck v. Bell* 1927, 207)

In this brief example, we see many of the justifications used to deny civil rights to people with intellectual disabilities. In his statement, Holmes judged people with intellectual disabilities to be "manifestly unfit" to exercise rights. His assessment was based on several criteria, including rationality, independence, economic productivity, and morality. First and foremost, people with intellectual disabilities were characterized as too incompetent or irrational to exercise rights responsibly. In this case, all parties, including institutional authorities, Carrie's lawyer, and the Supreme Court justices assumed that feeblemindedness involved the inherent and pervasive inability to make meaningful decisions and therefore to live a self-determined life. Carrie was deemed unable to provide informed consent, a key element in the exercise of civil rights. Thus, Aubrey Strode, the lawyer representing the Virginia State Colony, concluded without contest, "She cannot determine the matter for herself both because being not of full age her judgment is not to be accepted . . . and because she is further incapacitated by congenital mental defect" (Strode 1927).

More glaring, in Holmes's opinion, was the importance of Carrie's dependence on the government for her support. Holmes referred to the feebleminded as "those who already sap the strength of the State," highlighting their dependence on social programs for care and survival. According to Justice Holmes, without these programs they would "starve for their imbecility." By failing to meet the economic norms of society and depending on others for care, such "lesser citizens" implicitly forfeited their civil rights in exchange for care. Those dependent on others for economic and social support were legal children and lost their legal individuality to the expediency of their caregivers' needs. Those providing care, however, whether they be family or the state, were legally equivalent to parents or "masters," holding the power to determine the best interests of and make major life choices for their dependents.[4]

Deviance also played a central role in justifying the denial of rights. Failure to meet economic norms was certainly one form of deviance, but eugenicists at the times believed that feeblemindedness was associated with even more insidious character flaws, including promiscuity, criminality, alcoholism, and poverty (Reilly 1991; Trent 1994), explaining Holmes's belief that it was better to prevent feeblemindedness through sterilization than wait "to execute degenerate offspring for their crime." Regardless of social programs, charity, or upbringing, the feebleminded were destined to fall into lives of crime and delinquency because they had both a natural inclination for such degeneracy and lacked the wisdom to avoid it. Such deviants could not be trusted to uphold the precious rights of American citizenship.

The assumptions of incompetence, dependence, and deviance remain with us today and continue to be used as justification for the deprivation of rights. While this discrimination is not as blatant as it once was, people with intellectual disabilities are still assumed by many to be inherently different from and inferior to people without disabilities, and as such they remain one of the few groups against whom legal discrimination is still often viewed as appropriate.

Constructing the Inclusion of People with Intellectual Disabilities

Despite the long history of exclusion, the story of citizenship and intellectual disability is not one-sided. If people with intellectual disabilities were in fact naturally and categorically unable to exercise rights, we would see no significant debate about rights for this population. This is not the case, however; throughout the twentieth century advocates for people with intellectual disabilities and people with intellectual disabilities themselves engaged in many successful attempts to claim rights and support their active participation in society.

Even in the eugenics era, some professionals fought against the complete restriction of rights and advocated for some level of participation and inclusion, believing that at least some people with intellectual disabilities could marry, vote, bear children, receive education, and live in the community. For example, in the 1940s Oscar Kaplan (1944), a prominent psychologist specializing in mental disorders, supported the right to marriage based on his scientific findings showing that the majority of marriages among the feebleminded were successful. Phyllis Mickelson (1947, 1949), an academic in the field of social work, also provided support for parenthood by people with intellectual disabilities, finding in her research that some feebleminded parents could provide satisfactory care for their children and that factors such as marital harmony, income level, family size, and mental health often mattered more in successful parenting than intelligence.

In the 1960s and 1970s, the tide of national policy began to turn more clearly toward the recognition of people with disabilities as full citizens. Deinstitutionalization emerged as national policy; state-level courts and then Congress granted children with disabilities the right to a free and appropriate public education, including accommodations to ensure they could bene-fit from the curriculum; and the 1975 Developmental Disabilities Assistance and Bill of Rights Act stressed the importance of delivering services to people with intellectual disabilities in the least restrictive environments possible and granted them access to the same civil rights held by other citizens. Throughout the 1970s, national legislation was passed almost every year guaranteeing rights to people with disabilities. In 1990, President Bush signed the Americans with Disabilities Act (ADA), the most sweeping civil-rights legislation for people with disabilities to date, making discrimination in employment and exclusion from public services on the basis of disability illegal. If one looked purely at national political rhetoric and formal legal developments involving intellectual disability, it appeared that they had "made it."

In part, arguments for inclusion provided alternative portraits of intellectual disability, placing members of this population within the boundaries of rights bearer as typically defined. Narratives of disability and rights now argued that people with intellectual disabilities were—or, at least, *could be*—sufficiently independent, competent, productive, and moral to exercise rights. The narra-tive of the "special child," most often promulgated by parents, not only refuted the link between disability and immorality but also established people with dis-abilities as exceptionally moral, even as God's special gifts. They were viewed as unfailingly loyal, innocent, and selfless. While the "special child" narratives confronted stereotypes of moral deviance, narratives of the productive citizen established people with intellectual disabilities as "responsible, contributing citizens" (Robb 1952, 55), particularly if provided with the appropriate services and access to education and jobs. According to this narrative, people with intel-lectual disabilities remained dependent on others because society denied them the education, job training, and opportunity necessary to succeed. If provided with basic services, they could be "rehabilitated from a role of idleness and dependency to the status of full-fledged wage-earner and citizen" (President's Panel on Mental Retardation 1962, 100–101). Not only *could* people with intel-lectual disabilities be productive citizens; they had a *right* to the opportunities and services that would allow them to reach this potential.

These narratives exemplify the attempt to fit people with intellectual dis-abilities into popular conceptions of rights. More radical narratives attempted to re-frame the criteria established for the exercise of rights, questioning whether traits such as morality, dependence, and intelligence should be pre-requisites at all. Some scholars and activists argued that, unless the law could clearly demarcate the level or kind of morality, independence, or intelligence required for the exercise of rights and apply these standards to all American citizens, the law should not take these factors into account (e.g., "Editorial Note" 1979; Metcalf 1989).

In contrast with *Buck v. Bell*, the Pennsylvania court case *Pennsylvania Association for Retarded Children (PARC) v. Commonwealth of Pennsylvania* (1971, 1972) illustrates the change in both the perception of the abilities of children labeled "mentally retarded" (the label frequently used in the 1970s) and the prerequisites for exercising rights. In this case, PARC, an advocacy organization for people with mental retardation and their families, along with the parents of thirteen children, brought a class-action suit against the Commonwealth of Pennsylvania on behalf of all school-age children with mental retardation. The thirteen children had been excluded from public education, and evidence indicated that seventy thousand to eighty thousand additional children with retardation throughout the commonwealth also were being denied access to public education. Parents typically received neither notice of the decision to exclude their children nor the opportunity for a hearing to challenge the decision. "For example, the parents of David Tupi, a retarded child, were never officially informed of the decision to exclude him from school. Rather, they were only made aware of the situation when the school bus which regularly brought him to school failed to show up" (*PARC v. Pennsylvania* 1972, 293).

The commonwealth defended the school districts' actions on several grounds. Several Pennsylvania laws allowed the temporary or permanent denial of public education to children "who are found to be uneducable and untrainable," as well as to children "who have not attained a mental age of five years."[5] According to the commonwealth, this distinction was sensible in that

> a child who is uneducable and untrainable requires treatment different from those children of the other classifications. To place the retarded child in the public classroom is to subject such child to frustration since he cannot compete mentally with the other children, to subject him to ridicule by other students, to generally disrupt the classroom, albeit not intentionally and to impose upon the teacher a burden with which he is not trained to cope. There is therefore sound reason for the distinction. (*PARC v. Pennsylvania* 1972, 291)

The commonwealth also argued that hearings would delay immediate action at times needed to remove unruly and disruptive students from the classroom.

The court, however, overwhelmingly accepted the evidence provided by PARC. The court's opinion, written by Justice Thomas A. Masterson, provided a much different depiction of intellectual disabilities from the one offered by Justice Oliver Wendell Holmes Jr. in *Buck v. Bell*. Masterson depicted children with retardation as capable of citizenship or, at least, as capable of developing the skills necessary for citizenship. Masterson explained, first, that the distinction between "disabled" and "non-disabled" was difficult to make, citing evidence of questionable and even erroneous diagnoses. Second, the deficiencies associated with mental retardation were seen as resulting not solely from biological conditions but also from the stigma and exclusion imposed in part *by* the school. Third, Masterson argued that the "premise of the statute which necessarily assumes that certain retarded children are uneducable and untrainable lacks a rational basis in fact," citing expert opinion to conclude that "all mentally retarded persons are capable of benefiting from a program of education and training; that the greatest number of retarded persons, given such education and training, are capable of achieving self-sufficiency and the remaining few, with such education and training, are capable of achieving some degree of self care" (*PARC v. Pennsylvania* 1972, 296).

For Holmes, the "feeble-minded" individual stood in stark contrast to a rights-bearing citizen, too incompetent, dependent, and deviant to be entrusted with rights. In this case, however, Masterson explicitly referred to people with "mental retardation" as citizens and portrayed them as more like than unlike other American citizens, especially when given the same opportunities. Like other citizens, they had the right to a public education. Not only did this case re-envision people with intellectual disabilities as equal members of society; it also questioned the bases of granting rights. People receive rights because they are citizens, and perhaps because they are humans, not because they meet particular criteria of intelligence, productivity, or morality. Rather than insisting that individuals prove their worth before granting rights, Masterson's opinion for the court suggests that they develop their potential *through* the exercise of rights. Thus, the court set forth a "zero-reject" rule giving all children the right to a free public education regardless of competence, ability to benefit, or productivity.

This decision did not totally eschew the ideals of rationality, productivity, and morality; these were still held up as the goals for which rights were provided. Nor did it balk at all forms of segregation. Segregated public schools and classrooms remained viable options, although integration was "preferable" to segregation. That said, though, the re-conceptualization of the relationship between citizenship and intellectual disability that took hold in the fight for education would soon be applied and expanded to include all rights and all age groups.

Mixed Messages

While some cases clearly support or deny access to rights for people with intellectual disabilities, more common and intriguing are those that indicate the tension that exists between these positions. At no point in history has there been a clear resolution of the "problem" of intellectual disability as related to rights, toward either exclusion or inclusion. The ambiguity related to the position of people with intellectual disabilities in relationship to rights has resulted in several peculiar trends. First, throughout the twentieth century, this population has been granted, and even encouraged to exercise, some, but not all, rights, often resulting in contradictory laws and patterns of access. For example, federal legislation including the Developmental Disabilities Assistance and Bill of Rights Act and the Americans with Disabilities Act guarantees equal civil rights to people with disabilities, yet many states concurrently have legislation restricting the rights to vote, contract, and marry based on mental ability. Second, access to rights varies widely by time and by state. For example, while forty-one states at some point restricted marriage based on mental ability, others never did. Third, legislation has included assistance and accommodations as an integral aspect of some rights, but not all. For example, we have granted rights to accommodations in employment and education, but few supports exist for parenting or religious worship.

We can see the tension between inclusion and exclusion in the 1985 Supreme Court case *City of Cleburne, Texas, v. Cleburne Living Center*. The story of this case begins with the Cleburne Living Center (CLC), a provider of residential services to people with intellectual disabilities, which planned to lease a building in the city of Cleburne to provide twenty-four-hour supervised housing to thirteen "mildly retarded" men and women. The building was situated in a housing zone that permitted single-family residences as well as multiple-dwelling structures such as apartment houses, nursing homes, boarding homes, and hotels. However, the city required special permits for "hospitals for the insane or feebleminded, or alcoholic or drug addicts, or penal or correctional institutions." City officials determined that this group home was properly classified as a hospital for the feebleminded, and on this basis they denied the CLC the special use permit.

The CLC filed suit, alleging that the zoning ordinance violated the equal protection rights of both the organization and its potential residents; although a boarding house of similar size for people without disabilities would have been legal, the city council denied the CLC a permit to individuals with mental retardation, allegedly solely due to their disability. The city council, on the other hand, argued that a residence of this type would increase population concentration and congestion while potentially decreasing the serenity and safety of current residents, and therefore the denial of the permit was in the best interests of the city. Moreover, city officials argued that the denial of the building permit was in the best interests of the potential CLC residents. The CLC was planning to house thirteen residents, whereas new state standards urged group homes to house no more than six to eight persons. In addition, the home would be situated on a flood plain, raising the potential for physical harm. Neither of these conditions, the council argued, seemed beneficial for potential group-home residents.

Unlike in *Buck v. Bell*, scientific "evidence" no longer supported stereotypes of individuals with intellectual disabilities as deviant and dangerous; nor could the civil rights of this population be dismissed as unimportant. Housing within the community, typically in group homes rather than in large-scale institutions, had become national policy. Yet concerns still existed about the ability of people with intellectual disabilities to adapt and contribute to their communities, leaving many communities resistant to implementing the national rhetoric of inclusion.

The U.S. Supreme Court's decision illustrates the attempt to balance the inclusion and exclusion of people with intellectual disabilities by encouraging integration without making it an easily enforceable right or imposing it on other citizens. The court found that the city of Cleburne had violated the equal-protection rights of the CLC by discriminating unfairly against potential group-home residents based on fears related to mental retardation. However, the Supreme Court upheld the constitutionality of the City of Cleburne's zoning statute itself, which required a special permit for hospitals for the feebleminded. The court did not question the designation of a group home as a "hospital for the feebleminded"; nor did it require Cleburne to modify the statute, update or define its language, or justify the legitimacy of the interests it supposedly protected. Moreover, the court failed to define people with intellectual disabilities as a "suspect class," a status that would have given legal recognition to the history of discrimination experienced by people with intellectual disabilities and would have demanded increased scrutiny for all laws instituting differential treatment for this population.

The Supreme Court struck a precarious balance by protecting the rights of people with intellectual disabilities involved in this specific instance while doing little to advance the right to housing and community integration for the broader population of people labeled as intellectually disabled. In the eyes of the court, the application of Cleburne's zoning statute by town officials that distinguished between individuals with intellectual disabilities and those without disabilities served no legitimate interest of the city. Yet in failing to strike down or require review of this statute, the court assumed that it might at some point be in the legitimate interests of the city of Cleburne to require a group home to attain a special permit designated for hospitals for the feebleminded. In the future, others labeled as intellectually disabled could be forced to undergo the same challenges to their right to housing, and the decision might not be the same.[6]

The mixed messages evident in this decision are typical of modern law and rulings regarding intellectual disability. In many ways, the nation has come to support the legal equality of people with intellectual disabilities, yet fears and concerns about the best interests of people with disabilities and the communities in which they live make the commitment to equal rights questionable, at best.

An Overview

This book examines the history of intellectual disability and rights with several goals in mind. First, I examine various constructions of both concepts—intellectual disability and rights—throughout the twentieth century. For intellectual disability, I consider questions such as the following: How does this concept change through time? What are the key criteria for inclusion in this population? To what degree are people with intellectual disabilities perceived as similar or different to other citizens? What assumptions are made about the activities they can and cannot perform? For the concept of rights, I also consider its construction by asking questions such as the following: What are the assumed criteria for the exercise of rights? On what basis should rights be distributed? How should the state deal with the non-rights-bearing citizen? Ultimately, then, I problematize the various constructed relationships between these concepts, examining how, for instance, activists have drawn on various frameworks of rights to both include and exclude people with intellectual disabilities. As I engage in this analysis, I also examine who engages in these struggles regarding the rights of people with intellectual disabilities, who posits which ideas, why they might do so, and how and why activists come together and divide on this subject. Finally, I examine changes in formal law and policy to consider what rights people with intellectual disabilities have had through the twentieth century and why their access has varied.

Chapter 2 provides a theoretical discussion of relevant literature and puts forth the key theoretical arguments of this book. Because this book examines the twentieth century, Chapter 3 sets the stage, so to speak, with a brief discussion of the history of rights for people with intellectual disabilities in America prior to 1900. Chapter 4 examines the rise of eugenics and restrictive policies against people with intellectual disabilities, as well as competing notions of disability and rights found in the early twentieth century. Much of the historical work already published on intellectual disability concentrates on the rise of institutions and eugenics; therefore, this book gives greater weight to later events. Chapters 5 and 6 deal with events in the mid-twentieth century. Chapter 5 looks at the continued prevalence of eugenics and restrictive policies while also examining emerging shifts in professional thinking regarding rights, services, and intellectual disability. Chapter 6 then focuses on the rise of the parents' movement and the influence of the Kennedy family. Chapter 7 analyzes the rise of the civil-rights framework as applied to people with intellectual disabilities during the 1970s, and Chapter 8 describes the tremendous efforts needed to maintain and use the rights established during the 1980s. Chapter 9 presents current debates and issues and, in particular, focuses on the rise of the self-advocacy movement, recent understandings of intellectual disability, and the impact of the Americans with Disabilities Act. Finally, Chapter 10 concludes by offering a summary of the key lessons of this work and a brief discussion of some promising future directions.

2

A Theory of Rights and Disability

Work on citizenship and disability rights has burgeoned recently, yet intellectual disability has garnered little attention despite many lingering questions: Why have people with intellectual disabilities had access to some rights but not others? Why are some rights supported by accommodations and formal social support while others are not? Why is it that, even with the passage of rights legislation, people with intellectual disabilities still have limited control over their everyday lives?

This book examines debates throughout the twentieth century regarding the relationship between rights and intellectual disabilities—rather than focusing more heavily, for instance, on the intricacies of the various social movements, the internal workings of policy, or medical developments in this field. This chapter lays out the key theoretical arguments of this work and places these arguments within the broader literature on disability and rights in order to present the history and analysis in a way that is both interesting and understandable.

Theorizing the Relationship between Rights and Intellectual Disability

Intellectual disability is analyzed here as a contested social construction, not an objective biological condition. Activists draw on and construct various understandings of disability in their struggles to establish or restrict rights.

In general, "intellectual disability" is a label identifying a level of intelligence significantly lower than average that affects a person's ability to meet the cultural and social expectations of his or her contemporaries. The notion that intellectual disability, and disability more broadly, exist as contested social con-

---

Sections of this chapter are forthcoming in *Research in Social Science and Disability* 5.

structions rather than as "conditions" inherent in a person's biological or mental makeup is foundational to this project. The assertion of social construction does not preclude the possibility of a biological basis to low intelligence but suggests that labels shift in meaning through time and social context so that there is no clear or consistent demarcation between those of "normal intelligence" and those with "intellectual disabilities" (Bogdan and Taylor 1976; Davis 1997; Roth 1983).[1]

Throughout American history many terms emerged to refer to or include people considered to have sub-average intellectual functioning, including "idiot," "imbecile," "feebleminded," "mental deficient," "backward," "incompetent," "mentally retarded," "mentally handicapped," "mentally disabled," "developmentally disabled," "cognitively disabled," and "intellectually disabled." Each term, while loosely referring to a similar "condition," carried with it different assumptions about the characteristics and abilities of the population it identified. For example, the term "idiot" as used in early American law typically referred to people with levels of intelligence so low as to preclude *any* understanding or self-awareness, and therefore it presumed a severe level of disability. In comparison, the term "feebleminded," which became common in the early twentieth century, encompassed a wide range of individuals who were considered to have limited intellectual abilities as shown by their deviation from social norms. Feeblemindedness was understood as a condition related to and demonstrated by moral ineptitude, and many marginalized populations such as immigrants, people of color, single mothers, and poor people were subjected to this label. To compare another term, the current federal definition of "developmental disability" includes people with significant *physical and mental* disabilities who experienced the onset of their disability before the age twenty-two. The term "developmental disability" groups together individuals with diverse disabilities and is rooted in a functional rather than a moral model. Thus, the terms "idiot," "feebleminded," and "developmental disability" evoke very different images of disability and include different sets of people.

Not only do the understandings of intellectual disability vary. So, too, does the potential size of the population. A White House conference in 1930 defined the "feebleminded" as potentially including people with an IQ of 85 or below, meaning that 15 percent of the population could be diagnosed as feebleminded (U.S. Department of Labor 1930). In contrast, in 1962 the President's Panel on Mental Retardation defined as "mentally retarded" those individuals with an IQ of 70 or below and corresponding behavioral maladaptations and estimated that 3 percent of the nation fell within that classification. Due to changes in the definition alone, between 1930 and 1962 the number of people potentially labeled intellectually disabled dropped by roughly 30 million people.

As ideas of intellectual disability shifted over time, so, too, did the association of intellectual disability with rights. In the early twentieth century, eugenicists proclaimed the "menace of the feebleminded" and claimed that this condition caused many social problems, such as poverty, sexual deviance, and crime (Trent 1994). Based on this view, eugenicists promoted a range of restrictive measures, including institutionalization, sterilization, the prohibition of marriage, segregated education, and registration, to identify and control the feebleminded. Other narratives were more positive. Some professionals, for example, asserted an image of people with intellectual disabilities as potentially productive members of society who deserved rights and opportunities to develop their potential as humans and citizens. Parents created the image of the "special child," which portrayed people with intellectual disabilities as dependent, innocent, loyal, and loving eternal children in need of rights to lifelong care, guidance, and protection from society. In the 1970s, the civil-rights narrative emerged, depicting people with disabilities as equal citizens deserving of equal rights, including membership in the community; access to education; and opportunities for employment, marriage, and procreation. While a particular narrative might be dominant, at any given time multiple narratives are typically at play.

In these struggles, activists are forced to negotiate, often uncomfortably but sometimes to their advantage, the typical dichotomies by which intellectual disability and its relationship to rights are framed. These include, for example, whether intellectual disability is permanent or fluid; whether it is rooted in one's biology or in the social environment; and whether people with intellectual disabilities are similar to or different from other citizens.[2] As with most dichotomous thinking, the presumption that we can clearly locate people on the poles of such dichotomies is false, and therefore there is, and can be, no consistent or correct placement of people with intellectual disabilities. Thus, activists typically move between these poles as is helpful to them. For example, some institutional superintendents in the early twentieth century declared that feeblemindedness was a permanent condition that necessitated lifelong institutionalization yet in the next breath praised the transformative benefits of institutional life for inmates, thereby suggesting the dynamism of intellectual disability. More generally, we see that, because disability is a social construct, activists create and use various constructions in their political efforts to shape access to rights and the broader roles and opportunities afforded to people given these various labels.

In struggles over rights, activists typically draw on or contest liberal political philosophy, the dominant narrative guiding the American legal system. While liberalism constrains political opportunities to some degree, it is open to interpretation and can be used both to include and to exclude people with intellectual disabilities.

Citizenship serves as a means to demarcate who is a member of the national community and to establish the expectations for relationships among citizens, non-citizens, and the state. Rights constitute a resource of citizenship, providing a tool to be used to influence others, pursue one's interests, and mark one as a respected member of the community.[3] Yet not all citizens have access to the same package of rights or receive the same utility from them. The practices of rights are built on continuously shifting meaning systems that incorporate various, and at times conflicting, norms, values, and relational expectations. In building meanings, we draw on several narratives, or "political fictions," that offer overarching frameworks describing the moral rationales for rights, the required traits of rights bearers, and the expected social relationships among rights bearers, the state, and non-rights bearers (Joyce 1991; Somers 1992) While an assortment of narratives are available, liberal political philosophy, otherwise known as social contract theory, is the dominant narrative guiding American law on rights, and therefore activists must to some degree engage with it by relying on its ideas, reinterpreting them, or refuting them.

According to the narrative of liberal political philosophy, prior to the formation of government, humans existed as free and rational individuals. To protect themselves from chaos and tyranny by the strong, these individuals entered into a contract to create a government, establishing order by allowing themselves to be ruled to some extent, but also protecting themselves from the over-extension of such rule by providing fundamental rights to each citizen (Ackerman 1971; Rawls 1984). In this narrative, rationality and freedom are presented as essential prerequisites for the exercise of rights. Freedom, also referred to as autonomy or independence, is assumed to be vital to the act of entering the social contract because only a person with free will can truly make the independent decision to pursue his or her self-interest in a binding manner; if one has a gun to one's head, the ability to pursue one's self-interest would obviously be impaired, and any contract entered under such duress would be suspect. Rationality is also required, as only rational beings can understand the implications and consequences of a contract and thereby effectively pursue their self-interest. Thus, liberalism established the basis of legal equality for individuals who are deemed free and rational yet excluded those who are not (Fraser and Gordon 1992; Lister 1997; Okin 1989; Pedersen 1993). As Anne Phillips (1991, 24–25) states, "The individual had become the key to legitimate government—but not of course any old individual." The law developed in such a way to provide distinct legal tracks for "normal" (rational and autonomous) and "abnormal" (irrational and dependent) citizens, offering normal citizens a host of civil rights and abnormal citizens protection and care instead (Eisenberg 1982; Hahn 1983, 1987; Minow 1990).

Based on the criteria of rationality and autonomy, many groups have been denied equal rights. Feminist scholars were among the first to highlight the exclusionary assumptions of liberalism. Historically, women were depicted as irrational, their judgment impaired by hormonal fluctuations, intense emotions, and intimate connections with their spouse and children. Further, they were characterized as dependent because no money flowed from their roles as homemaker and mother. In response to these stereotypes, feminist scholars (e.g., Fraser and Gordon 1994; Okin 1989; Pateman 1988) criticized the way in which the criteria of rationality and autonomy are applied to women, arguing that women are no less rational or independent than men. Moreover, they deconstructed the very definitions and assumptions that underlie these criteria, claiming that all people are interdependent and emotional as part of their humanity (Benhabib 1992; Minow and Shanley 1997; Sevenhuijsen 2003).[4]

The assumption that disability naturally precludes rationality and autonomy is deep-seated and has posed a tremendous challenge for the Disability Rights Movement. For people with intellectual disabilities especially, this label seems to be predicated on some level of incompetence and dependence. Yet as feminist scholars have challenged the use of these terms as applied to women, disability scholars have also disputed the way in which these criteria have been applied to people with disabilities. With regard to rationality, activists and scholars with physical disabilities used their own lives and achievements to showcase their rationality. People with intellectual disabilities and their advocates faced a more difficult task in proving that they could meet the criterion of rationality. To do so, they fought to disconnect IQ and diagnostic labels from the concept of rationality, suggesting that a low IQ did not necessarily prevent someone from understanding and engaging in some specific activities. Moreover, they argued that the provision of support could assist people with intellectual disabilities in gaining the knowledge and experience required to make rational decisions reflecting their best interests.

People with disabilities also faced charges of dependence based on their need for assistance and support. To solve this dilemma, activists presented a new definition of autonomy, rooted in the mental activity of decision making rather than independent physical activity. Rather than serving as an indication of dependence, assistance merely supported their autonomy, similar to the use of an administrative assistant by an executive (Corbett 1997; Wendell 1996). The emphasis on decision making as the basis for autonomy, though, still potentially excluded people with intellectual disabilities. They asserted that with support, people with intellectual disabilities also could make self-directed decisions. Just as the receipt of physical assistance should not preclude one from being seen as autonomous, neither should assistance in processing information or learning.

The assertion that people with disabilities possess sufficient rationality and autonomy to exercise rights has been revolutionary, yet it leaves intact the importance of these concepts as criteria for the exercise of rights. It is far more revolutionary to subvert the very concepts of rationality and autonomy and re-imagine political systems based on different frameworks of justice (Kittay 2001; Reindal 1999). Michel Foucault (1965) was among the first theorists to question the distinction between rationality and irrationality, suggesting that irrationality was nothing more than deviance of thought and action, naturalized to hide the technologies of political regulation at work. In the area of intellectual disability, the legal scholar Steven Metcalf (1989) suggests, at least for the right to vote, that laws should remove the criteria of rationality (or "competence," its legal equivalent) because it is situational (not a permanent trait of the individual) and impractical to assess for all citizens. Similarly, wording within the *PARC* decision and the Education for All Handicapped Children Act of 1975 dismisses the use of rationality, competence, or "educability" as prerequisites for the right to a public education. According to this decision, all children, regardless of their abilities, should have the right to a public education. Rationality therefore is increasingly viewed as an outcome of situational and relational factors, and as such, blanket restrictions based on a diagnostic label are being challenged.

Attempts to deconstruct and invalidate the notion of autonomy have been even more widespread. As discussed by both feminist and disability scholars, the illusory "autonomous individual" is actually created through a reliance on a variety of support systems. As argued by Diana Pearce (1990, 275), "Are we really to assume that the ideal rational 'modern' subject (that is to say, an able-bodied male whose work is valued in the marketplace) is never needy and could . . . 'be independent' without the support system provided by the home or its surrogates?" Of course the answer is no. Men are available to perform their public-sphere activities due to the labor that women perform at home. Dependence is part of the human condition; we are not autonomous but, rather, interconnected, relational beings. Thus, self-determination can occur only within a relational context in which one's relationships and social context support individuals in the development of their potential.

Disability scholars (e.g., Lloyd 2001; Morris 1993) have drawn heavily on feminist literature to challenge the pretense of autonomy. When compared to an illusory autonomous ideal, people with disabilities appear dependent. Their potential need for care and assistance marks them as passive recipients of services and excludes them from the role of self-directing citizen without acknowledging that people in relationships often exist as both caregivers and as recipients of care. Like feminist scholars, disability scholars have moved toward a rejection of autonomy in favor of notions of interdependence and relationality. Exposing the interconnectedness of all people reveals the myth of independence and positions dependence as the "normal" state of being in which all people require support and assistance (Galvin 2004; Linton 1998; Marks 1999; Watson 1998).

Much of the historical debate concerning intellectual disability and citizenship centers on the merits of these criteria and the way in which intellectual disability relates to them. Whereas eugenicists tended to present the "feebleminded" as naturally lacking rationality and competence and cast a wide net in terms of who should be defined as such, today's self-advocates have attempted to reconstruct these notions in a manner more inclusive of people with various abilities and needs. In the end, regardless of who is included or not, the dominance of the liberal narrative leads to a fixation on individual-level abilities rather than encouraging a discussion about social justice and the type of society we want to create.

> *While it may be the dominant narrative of rights, liberalism is not the only one available. Activists draw on and intermingle other narratives of rights with liberalism, including civic republicanism, human rights, and ascriptive traits. Thus, the narratives of citizenship become "free-floating resources," open for interpretation to be used by activists in fights for and against rights for this population.*

Despite the attention liberalism receives in scholarship and activism, it is not the sole narrative of importance in these debates. Civic republicanism provides one alternative. Derived from Aristotle's work, the good citizen of civil republicanism is one who has the intellect, time and power to engage in public affairs—one who, in essence, is both "ruler and ruled" (Pocock 1992). Rather than entering the public sphere as an already formed citizen vested with certain rights, individuals become citizens through the activity of public participation, creating and reinforcing a national identity based on shared values. Participation is not simply about performing one's duties but also about connecting to the heart and morality of the nation and creating a unified citizenry. This framework posits as an ideal an active citizenry working together to form a morally cohesive society (Burchell 1995; Riesenberg 1992; Walzer 1991).

Civic republicanism offers a framework that, like liberalism, can be used to include or exclude. Civic republicanism imagines a citizen who is created and fulfilled through his or her participation rather than a pre-formed citizen who must have particular traits prior to entering a social contract. As such, it potentially encourages all people to participate in their communities and to exercise rights and envisions participation as an opportunity through which people with intellectual disabilities can develop themselves into better citizens. Yet it has a more exclusionary side, as well. The ideal of the active citizen is premised on a level of economic and political independence, as well as, possibly, knowledge and intelligence, which may be difficult for many people to attain (Burchell 1995). As discussed by Helen Meekosha and Leanne Dowse (1997) as well as by Len Barton (1993), citizens are called on to participate, yet people with disabilities may live in isolation or have their access to mainstream participation mediated by caregivers unconcerned with their development as citizens; they are called on to contribute to the nation, yet legislation continues to place people with disabilities in a "category of individual burdens"; they are expected to volunteer and give of themselves, yet people with disabilities are cast in the role of charity recipient. Thus, current social practices, stereotypes and legislation hinder and devalue participation by people with disabilities.[5]

Despite liberalism's emphasis on equality, Americans have also clung to and used ascriptive traits such as race, ethnicity, and gender to define the boundaries of citizenship and rights bearer. According to Rogers Smith (1997, 2–3):

> Many of the restrictions on immigration, naturalization, and equal citizenship seemed to express views of American civil identity that did not feature either individual rights or membership in a republic. They manifested passionate beliefs that America was by rights a white nation, a Protestant nation, a nation in which true Americans were native-born men with Anglo-Saxon ancestors.

Smith argues that ascriptive traits are built into the American legal system as a way to create and maintain a particular national identity.[6] They have been fused with the narratives of liberalism and republicanism in ways that define marginalized populations as irrational or dependent, but Smith shows that these appeals to other narratives often conceal "core political identities" shaped by ascriptive traits. In other words, the exclusion of particular populations may or may not rely on liberal or republican rationales, but at its core are often deeply held views regarding superior and inferior traits involving class, race, gender, religion, and so on.

Smith's argument can be applied to debates about citizenship for people with disabilities, and more specifically for people with intellectual disabilities. Opinions about controversial topics such as institutionalization, educational segregation, euthanasia, and procreation by people with intellectual disabilities often provoke "gut" responses about the moral status of people with intellectual disabilities. Martin Pernick's (1996) work on euthanasia, for example, showcases the "aesthetics" of exclusion, or, in other words, the desire to remove from sight, through institutionalization or euthanasia, infants who were deemed hideous and ugly. In addition to expecting autonomy and rationality, American society imposes a "moral order of the body," demanding a particular appearance and specific physical capabilities in exchange for resources and rewards (Davis 1997; Hahn 1997; Thomson 1997).

As with other ideals such as rationality and autonomy, the "normal body" is illusory. The aesthetic ideal of the young, athletic, white, fully able, productive male excludes most of the population yet still is embedded throughout American culture, media, architecture, and legislation. The normal body, argues Rosemarie Garland Thomson (1997, 45), is unimpeded by architectural barriers, by stares from those who pass by, by uncoordinated and shaky movements or unarticulated patterns of speech, whereas the disabled body represents a body susceptible to external forces, "property badly managed, a fortress inadequately defended, a self helplessly violated." While connected to liberalism, aesthetic judgments exist independent of assessments of rationality and autonomy. Thus, Bill Hughes and his colleagues (2005) call for a theory of embodied citizenship that recognizes and problematizes the experiences of people with "abnormal" corporeality in a society that expects bodily conformity and uniformity. The concept of embodied citizenship may not be inclusive enough for people with mental and intellectual disabilities, however. In addition to having a potentially deviant physical appearance, they are marked as mentally different while existing in a world which assumes a "normal" IQ range, a standard developmental process, typical ways of processing and retaining information, and a relatively uniform set of outlooks and understandings of the world. As Foucault argues, regulation subsumes even expected mental processes. Failure to meet these expectations or a rejection of the ideal marks one as inferior, dangerous, or even monstrous.

A final narrative to be considered is that of human rights. Human-rights theories begin with the presumption that all human beings are worthy of dignity and that rights are a means to recognize and secure that dignity (Nussbaum 2006). Unlike liberalism, human-rights theories do not presume that rights rest on rationality or autonomy; nor do they require active participation or particular ascriptive traits. They are inclusive of all humans and recognize all humans as interdependent, diverse, and in need of basic resources and opportunities to experience worthwhile lives. According to the United Nations Universal Declaration of Human Rights of 1948, "All human beings are born free and equal in dignity and rights." As such, all people regardless of country, age, religion, or other differences, are entitled to various rights and freedoms. While the proposed list of human rights varies, they may include rights such as life, liberty, and bodily integrity; freedoms of thought, self-expression, and assembly; opportunities to receive a basic education, health care, protection within the criminal justice system, and some minimum of economic security; the opportunity to participate in one's government; and employment, the opportunity to join a union, and the receipt of fair remuneration for one's work.

Human rights have often been invoked by disability activists. In the "special child narrative," parents have argued that all humans deserve care and respect simply on the basis of their humanity (e.g., Rogers 1953). Contemporary activists working for community inclusion similarly argue that all humans should have basic rights, including the right to grow up and reside in the community of one's choice with appropriate support, regardless of medical diagnosis or political or economic cost–benefit analyses.

Because of the inclusivity of human-rights approaches, they represent a powerful tool in the fight to secure rights for people with disabilities. Human-rights approaches have their limitations, though. They, as with any other kind of right, must actually be established and enforced through legal and political institutions, and America lacks a strong tradition of respecting human rights. Moreover, human-rights theories tend to set forth the minimum that should be available to all people, such as minimal economic security and health care, and therefore they may not be useful in achieving greater levels of inclusion, participation, or resources as desired by some activists. And finally, the provision of positive rights (those that require active intervention by the state or other citizens such as the provision of education or health care) requires the creation of social institutions that monitor the needs of citizens and deliver access to resources if needed. These systems, which may support citizens, can instead serve to stigmatize, regulate, and segregate those who are "in need" from other citizens, so that the implementation of human rights may actually subvert its inclusive philosophy.

These narratives—liberalism, civil republicanism, ascriptive myths, and human rights—include ideals, language, and imagery that can be manipulated by activists to define people with intellectual disabilities as either worthy or unworthy of bearing rights. As such, they represent resources to be used in contestations over rights rather than rigid or mutually exclusive philosophical systems.

> *The processes of constructing, claiming, and exercising rights are active practices, subject to interpretation, negotiation, and contestation. As such, access to rights varies by "relational settings," including one's state, local residence, and social network, and it is rarely self-evident whether an actual person in a particular situation and setting will be able to claim and exercise a right or not.*

Citizenship is typically seen as a legal status in which one either has access to rights or not, yet this approach to citizenship fails to adequately explain the history of rights for people with intellectual disabilities (as it fails to address the experience of rights for other populations). Status approaches emerged out of the seminal work *Citizenship and Social Class* (Marshall and Bottomore 1992 [1950]), in which T. H. Marshall examined the evolution of citizenship from a traditional system of rights based on one's ascriptive position in society (e.g., race, class, gender) to a modern system in which all citizens receive equal rights regardless of their social position. According to Marshall, the modern state grants individuals the legal status of citizenship and confers an identical package of rights to all citizens, providing them with the power to call on the state to protect them from and offer redress for civil and political abuses.

History provides ample evidence that citizenship is "messier" than Marshall's status approach suggests (Mann 1993). He assumed that one is either a citizen—with the same set of political, civil, and social rights as other citizens—or one is not, yet between these poles many shades of gray exist. People with intellectual disabilities may hold U.S. passports documenting their citizenship yet may be denied a host of rights offered to fellow citizens, such as the rights to vote, contract, or marry. Not only is the "package" of rights incomplete but the power of its contents is also ambiguous; the conditions under which rights claims will be upheld or denied are variable. For example, the right to a free and appropriate public education for children with disabilities was formally established in 1975, yet litigation and informal struggles regarding this right proliferate. Numerous issues remain open to interpretation, such as who should determine the "least restrictive environment," how reasonable accommodations should be determined, and how the rights of other children should enter into placement and funding decisions. Given the number of children with disabilities who receive their education in segregated settings and who never receive appropriate assistive technology or support services, access to the right to education in the least restrictive environment seems limited, at best, for many children with intellectual disabilities.

Recent analyses of the Americans with Disabilities Act, including those by Fiona Kumari Campbell (2005), David M. Engle and Frank W. Munger (2003), Leslie Pickering Francis and Anita Silvers (2000), and Ruth O'Brien (2004), highlight the active negotiation of rights. Rather than offering firm guarantees of protection from discrimination, the rights granted by the ADA provide a set of resources that can potentially be harnessed by people with disabilities to shape identity, discourse, and interaction between themselves and others (Bérubé 2003). When formal claims are made, it is by no means certain that the right in question will actually be upheld. Moreover, most negotiation of rights occurs in informal interpersonal settings without even explicitly referencing, let alone enacting, formal laws or legal processes.

As experiences with the ADA illustrate, rights are *practices* and must be understood as dynamic resources or discourses that are constantly revised and negotiated both in formal legal settings and in informal micro-settings (Turner 1990, 1993). Margaret Somers (1994, 79), one of the earliest scholars to articulate citizenship and rights as practices, argues:[7]

> Rather than being a category of social status, the rights of citizenship comprise a bundle of enforceable claims that are *variably and contingently* appropriated by members of small civil societies and differentiated legal cultures. . . . [R]ights are free-floating cultural and institutional resources that must be appropriated and in turn given meaning only in the practical context of power and social relations.

One of the primary advantages of a practice approach is that, whereas a status approach fails to account for the contradictory and ambiguous patterns that characterize access to rights for people with intellectual disabilities, a practice approach assumes the dynamic construction of rights that occurs in particular social contexts (Turner 1993). The relationship between intellectual disability and rights is not fixed; nor is it necessarily logical or consistent. Rights are continually constructed and reconstructed both formally and in everyday practice, and therefore we cannot say simply that people with intellectual disabilities "have" rights or do not.

To analyze the impact of relationality on the practice of rights, Somers (1993) developed the concept of relational setting. A relational setting is a set of expected relational patterns embedded within social institutions. Relational settings such as residences, workplaces, and schools are characterized by both formal and informal relational practices and expectations that affect the likelihood that rights will be claimed and how they will be negotiated across relationships. For people with disabilities, many of the settings in which they live and work are characterized by tremendous asymmetry in power. Disability-specific settings, including special education, nursing homes, group homes, segregated workshops, and day facilities, typically endorse a rhetoric of rights, yet often simultaneously encourage formal and informal restrictions of rights guided by state demands for accountability, limited funding, liability issues, professional views of the "best interests" of people with disabilities, and professional concerns related to their own quality of working conditions and income. Though not always the case, segregated facilities often assume a power structure in which staff members make major (and minor) decisions while residents exercise little control over their daily lives (Drinkwater 2005; Yates 2005). Within this context, then, it may be difficult or even meaningless to assert one's rights.

Particularly for individuals who require extensive care and support, families may also have a tremendous impact on their access to rights, structuring their access to such things as recreation, intimate relationships, work, and liberty. The impact of the family is particularly variable as it exists within the "private sphere," outside the reach of much government regulation and civil-rights law (Okin 1989). The ADA cannot demand that a family make its home accessible or that it provide accessible transportation or equal opportunities. Thus, the family has tremendous leeway to shape access to rights, and relational expectations vary widely from family to family. Of course, some families may choose to be restrictive, and others may fully support their family member in exercising his or her rights. The point here is not that families—or any other setting, for that matter—are necessarily restrictive or empowering but, rather, that one's access to rights will be shaped in part by the expectations and typical patterns of interaction established within a setting.

Many people participate in some settings that assume their subordinate status and hinder their likelihood of claiming and exercising rights. For people with intellectual disabilities, though, all or almost all of their relationships and relational settings, including their families, educational systems, places of employment, and places of worship, may institutionalize social practices and values enforcing their inferior social position. Thus, when we talk about rights as a social practice, there may be few or no relational settings in which people with intellectual disabilities are presumed able to exercise rights and supported in doing so. They may also have fewer opportunities to leave settings characterized by inequality and to find or create more egalitarian settings. The pervasiveness of practices supporting their inferior position, their continued exclusion from some settings, and their heightened need for accessibility and support may leave them with few options.

Access to rights for people with intellectual disabilities is inherently tied to their position in the stratification system and to the relational configuration of other groups in the stratification system.

An additional advantage of a relational-practice approach is that it recognizes not only variation across time and place but also the impact of power on access to rights. According to Bryan Turner (1993, 2), a practice approach "places the concept [of citizenship] squarely in the debate about inequality, power differences and social class, because citizenship is inevitably and necessarily bound up with the problem of the unequal distribution of resources in a society."

When rights are conceived as individual rather than relational actions (e.g., I vote, I go to worship, I own a gun), then biological limitations seem to constrain the autonomous action of individuals with disabilities (e.g., people with disabilities are not able to vote because they cannot get into the voting booth). In these instances, people with disabilities seem different from, and potentially inferior to, supposedly autonomous citizens. Their exclusion is seen as rooted in their disability and has no parallel to populations marginalized for social reasons. However, a relational approach argues that rights are necessarily practiced in relationship with other people and that the practice of rights is socially mediated for all citizens. Therefore, the practice of voting, for example, is potentially limited for all citizens. If one's family discourages voting, one's employer does not provide time off for voting, or officials promote the use of equipment and materials that are difficult to comprehend, then one's right to vote is constrained. One's social context serves as a de facto arbiter of rights for all individuals.

Because people with intellectual disabilities tend to hold a social position on the lower rungs of the stratification system, they face particular vulnerabilities in exerting influence within their social context. Max Weber's three dimensions of stratification—status, class, and party—may be useful here. To consider status first, people with intellectual disabilities typically garner little respect or honor in American society. For a host of cultural and structural reasons, they have traditionally been defined as "unproductive" or "non-contributing" (Carey 2003; Trent 1994). This perception of non-contribution is reified by their relatively poor economic, social, and political position. In a vicious cycle, they are seen as inferior and denied opportunities by which to contribute, and this lack of valued contributions then reinforces the image of their inferiority. To exercise rights, they must be able to convince at least some people within relevant relational settings that they have the potential to understand, demand, and enact rights. If other people refuse to accept them in the role of rights bearer and instead view them only as the receivers of care, it can be extremely difficult for them to enact that role and pursue rights (Fraser and Gordon 1992; Galvin 2004). Conversely, when they can highlight their contributions, such as employment or self-advocacy, their ability to demand rights may increase.

For Weber (1978 [1968]), "class" refers to a group of people with a shared relationship to the market that leads them also to share economic interests and similar life chances. Just as not all people with intellectual disabilities share a similar level of status, they do not all share the same class. However, demographic data indicate that people with intellectual disabilities tend to be among the poorest and least well educated in society and therefore tend to lack the economic, human, and social capital that promote the exercise of rights. Even when they have wealth, they tend not to control it and therefore may not gain the influence that typically flows from wealth. However, even when individuals with intellectual disabilities lack their own economic resources or control over these resources, they may be connected to families and organizations that will devote significant resources to secure rights for them.

These possible sources of social capital lead to Weber's third concept regarding stratification: party, or, in other words, access to and involvement in organizations that attempt to achieve some goal in an organized manner. Historically, people with intellectual disabilities have had little participation in or control over civic or political organizations. The rise of parents' and professional organizations beginning in the 1950s devoted to the improvement of the life chances and opportunities for people with intellectual disabilities marked an important change in their access to rights. So, too, the rise of their own self-advocacy organizations potentially will bring about additional improvements in their access to rights. Self-advocacy organizations represent the first time historically that people with intellectual disabilities have organized as a group to consider their group goals and pursue them. In doing so, they have struggled to wrest the claim of expertise in intellectual disability away from professionals and parents and instead secure recognition of themselves as the experts. Through their efforts, they not only gain political power but also increase the respect accorded to them by the people with whom they interact.

Thus, as individuals invoke, practice, and contest rights on both the macro- and micro-levels, they bring various resources to the fore, including the images and narratives of disability and citizenship; symbolic power such as claims to expertise, moral standing, or identity and group membership; wealth and economic resources; and organizational and relational support. These factors shape whether a claim is deemed legitimate and for whom or whether it is to be enforced or invoked at all (Das and Addlakha 2001; Engle and Munger 2003; Somers 1994) Over time, as access to status, economic resources, and political organizations has increased, so, too, has their access to rights. Yet the simultaneous persistence of the devaluation they experience, high rates of unemployment and poverty, and marginalization in political and organizational activities also continue to undercut their attempts to establish and to informally and formally claim their rights.

Laws and policies regarding rights for people with intellectual disabilities are related not solely to their own social position but also to the overall system of stratification and the position of other groups. In other words, the history of intellectual disability intertwines with the histories of other populations as communities have created and modified their stratification structures. The most obvious example, perhaps, is the tremendous impact of the Civil Rights Movement on access to rights and, more broadly, visions of social justice for all marginalized groups. As African Americans successfully resisted their oppression, they opened opportunities for all other oppressed groups to also resist.

We see other intersections through history that are less obvious. For example, an understanding of variations in the social-stratification structure by setting can help to explain the late development of institutional segregation in the South as compared with the North (Larson 1995; Noll 1995). In the late 1800s and early 1900s, many professionals in northern states believed "feeblemindedness" led to the pressing problems of the day, including poverty, immigration, and crime, and therefore they advocated institutionalization as an appropriate solution to these problems. At this same time, southern communities were recovering from the Civil War, suffering from a lagging economy, and focusing on stabilizing race relations. In this context, the issue of disability went relatively unnoticed. Moreover, because of strict expectations of racial segregation, institutions for the insane and feebleminded typically excluded African Americans, thereby excluding the primary population believed to be dangerous enough to warrant social control. Therefore, although some southerners promoted eugenics and the establishment of institutions for the feebleminded, few policymakers made this issue a priority. Whereas the low social, economic, and political power held by people with disabilities throughout the United States resulted in their general vulnerability to marginalization, their position in the stratification system and their perceived interconnections with other marginal populations varied by locality and state and led to different patterns of inclusion and exclusion.

The politics of rights are principally centered on attempts to create a particular pattern of relationships within society. Each of the groups engaged in rights-related political struggles has particular interests that emerge from its relationship to intellectual disabilities within a specific social context, and each group chooses to fight for or against rights because it sees rights as serving a particular role in the creation of its desired relational patterns.

Rights are relational, and like other forms of power they are meaningful only in a relational context. We assert a right in order to influence or alter the actions of someone else, and therefore rights mediate and transform our relationships, at times establishing individuals as equals and other times drawing on insider–outsider distinctions to reinforce differences (Benhabib 1992; Kittay 2001; Sevenhuijsen 2003).

The relationality of rights is perhaps most clearly seen when conflicts arise. Because rights are relational, the exercise of our "individual" rights influences those around us and may be perceived as conflicting with the rights of others. For example, a woman's right to privacy in reproductive matters may be seen as conflicting with a man's right to protect and gain access to his potential offspring or with a fetus's right to live. One cannot understand the conflict between a woman, man, and fetus without examining the relationship between all three parties, including the perceived expectations and obligations of each party to the other and to society. Any resolution will have an impact on these relationships and the way power is exercised in them.

The perception of conflict is particularly common when people within marginalized populations exercise their rights. Because people with disabilities historically have faced tremendous marginalization and segregation from the mainstream community, their demands for integration appear to conflict with the rights of other citizens. Citizens without disabilities are accustomed to a life without regard for disability, yet new civil-rights laws demand that they change their culture, physical environment, behavior, and attitudes to provide equal access for people with disabilities. For example, in *Voices from the Edge* (O'Brien 2004), a storeowner resists a customer's demands for handicapped parking and suggests that the customer is infringing on his rights to private property. As individuals with disabilities attempt to secure supposedly guaranteed rights, they are pitted against other citizens—including storeowners, employers, and school-board members—who consider their own rights to be violated by these new relational expectations (Johnson 2003; O'Brien 2004).

For people with intellectual disabilities, the exercise of rights is similarly fraught with conflict. Conflict may arise with community members who believe that integrated education negatively affects their own children or that the establishment of a group home decreases their property values. The conflict may take on broader dimensions, as well: The exercise of rights by people with intellectual disabilities may be constructed as threatening the rights of society. For example, eugenicists claimed that the rights exercised by the feebleminded created a direct threat to the health and well-being of American society.

Although conflict makes relationality more obvious, the relationality of rights is not solely about conflict. Rights establish a broad set of relational expectations and obligations. Therefore, the politics of rights are principally centered on attempts to create a particular pattern of relationships within society. Each of the groups engaged in rights-related political struggles expresses particular interests that emerge from their relationship to people with intellectual disabilities within a specific social context. They choose to fight for or against rights because they imagine that rights will serve a particular role in the creation of their desired relational patterns. Thus, activism is rooted not simply in beliefs about the abilities or inabilities of people with disabilities but, rather, in the desire to create particular patterns of relationships in society.

We can therefore examine various constituencies to see how their constructed relationship to people with intellectual disabilities shapes their vision of desired relational patterns and the role of rights in this vision. Here I give two examples, the first of which draws on institutional superintendents who supported the expansion of institutions in the early twentieth century. Rooted in the medical perspective dominant at the time, these men tended to believe that both people with disabilities and society would benefit from the professional supervision of people with intellectual disabilities. They imagined a world in which they held the power necessary to decide who would be segregated and how to treat those who were segregated, and people with disabilities held basically no power in this process. In their vision, the exercise of rights by the "feebleminded" only hindered professional attempts to improve society and effectively improve the condition of the feebleminded. Of course, not all superintendents were engaged in selfless acts of social improvement. The establishment of institutions served many interests for them. Institutions brought increasing numbers of people under medical supervision; created a relatively autonomous professional site where superintendents had almost complete control; enhanced their political influence; secured a population and other resources required for the conduct of research; and enhanced their own image as heroes rescuing society from a dangerous disease (Trent 1993). Whether we see superintendents as self-serving, idealistic, or both, they sought to create a society that channeled power to them as professionals and away from the "feebleminded," with the assumption that segregation of the feebleminded would certainly benefit "society" (defined by superintendents of the time as people without disabilities), themselves as superintendents, and potentially those with disabilities, as well.

Parents in the 1950s offered a very different view of rights rooted in a different relational vision. Parent activists in this time tended to see their primary role in relation to people with intellectual disabilities as the providers of love, care, and protection. As such, they tended to advocate for both rights and rights restrictions that supported their perceived roles and the provision of long-term care for and protection of their children. They created a family model of rights in which parents (rather than or alongside professionals) were acknowledged as the experts in the care of people with intellectual disabilities. They believed that parents should be empowered to make choices for their children (including adult "children") and demanded that the state support their empowerment through the establishment of community-based services as well as the expansion of institutional care so that they actually had choices to make regarding the development and care of their children. They fought to modify guardianship laws to make it easier for parents to secure the official authority to guide and protect their adult offspring. When parents could not adequately perform their role due to death, illness, or other causes, they asked the state to step in as a substitute parent, with both authority over and obligations to its dependents. Thus, parents in the 1950s created a very different vision of the relationships across people with disabilities, families, the state, profession-als, and other citizens. Whereas superintendents had primarily sought rights restrictions, parents' perceived role as caretakers led them to seek both rights and rights restrictions to support the long-term care of their children.

Constituencies, which form and re-form over time and construct and re-construct their interests and agenda over time, participate in rights struggles based on a desire to alter relational patterns in accordance to their perceived relationships to people with intellectual disabilities, their desired relationships, and their broader concerns regarding the social-stratification structure. In these examples, superintendents and parents never came completely together as cohesive groups unified in their interests; nor did their perceived interests remain constant over time. Rather, they constructed their interests and practi-cal goals in specific social contexts, allowing for diversity within any given con-stituency and changes across time.

Because the negotiation of rights is ultimately a negotiation of power within and across relationships, it is inherently a political activity. According to Doug McAdam's (1982) political opportunity model, any given political structure creates opportunities and constraints for social movements. For the establish-ment of rights for people with intellectual disabilities, among the most impor-tant of these opportunities/constraints across time has been the compatibility between the desired rights change and the direction of the broader disability policy. Rights typically have been granted or restricted because they were per-ceived as necessary for the effectiveness of broader policy initiatives. For exam-ple, as the nation moved toward segregation, rights for people with disabilities were seen as an impediment to effective treatment and control; therefore, a broad set of rights restrictions was used to complement the goal of institution-alization. However, when the national goal of community-based employment was impeded by discrimination, policymakers expanded rights to include anti-discrimination in employment (Scotch 1984). Because rights are often used as a means to an end, rather than ends in and of themselves, not all rights receive the same level of support; nor is the support offered by policymakers necessar-ily adamant. They may, for example, want to promote the right to live in the community as part of deinstitutionalization yet maintain some level of institu-tionalization as they deem bureaucratically and politically efficient.

Opportunities also arise from the internal dilemmas and tensions inherent in any single policy paradigm. For example, the policies of institutionalization and rights restrictions led to practical concerns about the control of such large numbers of people; ultimately, the segregation of all people with intellectual disabilities simply proved too costly. The realistic limits of segregation created a tension in restrictionist policies and thereby opened opportunities for new ways to think about and handle intellectual disability both in social policy and with regard to rights.

Opportunities may also be created by specific political actors, as in the case of the Kennedy family, who exerted tremendous influence over national policies regarding intellectual disability during the 1960s. Other politicians also played important roles, such as Congressman John Fogarty, who had a close friend affiliated with the Parents' Movement, and Mary Switzer, director of the Office of Vocational Rehabilitation during the 1950s, whose sister served as executive director of Connecticut's Association for Retarded Children. Thus, as activists tried to assert their power and bring to fruition their desired visions for society, they worked within a political context that in some ways encouraged their activities and in some ways discouraged them.

In practice, rights can both empower individuals with intellectual disabilities and bring them into systems of regulation and control.

The absence of rights typically signifies marginality and helplessness. Indeed, in the absence of rights, people with disabilities have been subjected to euthanasia, institutionalization, and brutality against which they had little recourse. The opposite, then, is also assumed to be true: The acquisition of rights indicates an increase in power regarding relational expectations and obligations. However, rights embedded within asymmetrical relationships can at times fail to offer power for marginalized populations and may even create new technologies of power over them. A relational-practice approach highlights that rights discourse can be used for many purposes, including to claim membership, impose relational demands, or establish the outsider status of others (Lister 1993). Works by Rebecca Barnes and her colleagues (2004) and by Ravina Rapp and Faye Ginsburg (2001), for instance, show how rights for one population may be tied to the restriction of rights for others, as with zoning laws that recognize the rights of the non-disabled to live in communities free from group homes while denying the right of people with disabilities to choose the communities in which they live. More subtly, Foucauldian analyses indicate that the provision of rights to marginalized populations may be structured to provide inclusion only in exchange for conformity (Tremain 2005). In essence, inclusion may provide a technology of regulation greater than exclusion.

In the late 1960s, Isaiah Berlin (1984 [1969]) argued that the lack of material resources could undercut an individual's abilities to effectively use his or her rights. In a society with vast differences in wealth and opportunities, equal rights do not guarantee equality of outcome and can, in effect, mask oppression because all people appear to be treated equally when in fact they have access to very different levels of opportunity.

Berlin's argument is important to consider in examining the issue of rights for people with intellectual disabilities. When people with intellectual disabilities are given rights, they are often not provided with corresponding social support to make the exercise of those rights feasible. Time and time again, rights are formally established with little attention to the material and relational existence of many people with intellectual disabilities. For example, in *Cleburne v. Cleburne Living Center* (1985), the U.S. Supreme Court debated the right of people with intellectual disabilities to live in the community of their choice without recognition that the current system of service provision reduces their choice of residence by tying services to particular living situations and by determining the availability of these residential services through bureaucratic policies of eligibility rather than need. In their actual experiences, people with intellectual disabilities usually do not get to choose their living situation.

Yet there is another, subtler argument about the way in which rights may actually disempower and mask oppression. While Berlin argues that rights may not be exercised due to the lack of resources, Foucauldian analyses (Drinkwater 2005; Foucault 1979; Tremain 2005) suggest that rights are at times structured in ways that create technologies of social control. In his examination of power, Foucault suggested that in modern society, social control has transformed from brutal confrontations among individuals into a subtle, impersonal, invasive system designed to rehabilitate and transform the individual to conform to particular norms. As part of the regime of normalization, rights have become a way to support those people with disabilities who are most able to contribute to and participate in society in prescribed ways while still exerting control over most of this population by granting access only to supervised settings such as education, developing narrow legal applications, using ambiguous wording, instituting categorical requirements that divide the population, and demanding compliance to prescribed norms prior to accessing rights. In this context, rights become a mechanism of control rather than (or, at least, as well as) a tool for liberation.

Many of the rights and rights restrictions for people with intellectual disabilities passed thus far have been justified as a way to encourage self-sufficiency and productivity. On one hand, the government historically has supported the segregation and restriction of people with intellectual disabilities, in part at least to reduce the cost and "burden" of disability for the larger society. However, systems of segregation are costly to maintain, and a tension emerges between the desire to exclude this population and the recognition that some members of this population can contribute to their self-care and to society. Rights then help to ensure that people with disabilities will receive opportunities to contribute to society. As Marta Russell (1998) argues, "We got our 'civil rights' in exchange for getting disabled people off entitlements."[8] However, not everyone is considered to have the contributory potential sufficient to warrant the economic and social costs of integration, nor is everyone deemed worthy to exercise the control and autonomy that come with rights. To resolve this tension, legislators and the courts often have attempted to encourage contribution from people with disabilities while maintaining relational asymmetry and, as a result, denying them control over their own lives.

Attempts to deal with this tension result in "controlled integration." Controlled integration is attained in part by offering rights to people with disabilities based on their ability or potential to contribute. A cost–benefit analysis seems always to occupy the forefront of thinking about rights for people with disabilities. How expensive or culturally demanding would accommodation be? Will the economic benefit of inclusion outweigh the economic and social burdens placed on family, employers, and society? Jerome E. Bickenbach (1993) argues that it is not always clear whether the policy goal of reducing the cost of disability (the typical primary goal in disability policy) is best served by providing people with disabilities with a "ticket in" or a "ticket out" of the labor market. Most government funding provides a ticket out, yet to increase productivity, a smaller portion of funding is used to promote the employability of people with disabilities in "appropriate" cases.

Because of the perceived benefit to society, education and employment tend to receive some degree of support. Other rights are ignored, at best, and discouraged, at worst, because the exercise of them by people with disabilities is perceived to have too great a cost or too little benefit. Rights to privacy, sexual activity, and procreation in particular have suffered in this cost–benefit analysis. Procreation by people with intellectual disabilities often is perceived as creating an addition burden on family and society with children who cannot be supported socially or economically by their already dependent parents. While policies no longer encourage sterilization, social services still support segregated housing, supervised interaction between the genders, and the denial of privacy while also encouraging the use of birth control for individuals who are sexually active.

Controlled integration is also achieved through the use of rights to channel people with intellectually disabilities into structured, supervised settings. The rights that are most sought and encouraged for this population—rights to education, accommodated work, and treatment—are rights that place people with disabilities within structured and supervised environments that encourage conformity to the rules and expectations of society (Drinkwater 2005; Simons and Masschelen 2005). In these cases, the line between rights and restrictions become precariously thin, as the right to treatment typically requires one to forfeit many other rights, and the right to education often places children with disabilities in segregated settings where they learn their devalued status in the broader society. Not all rights can be so conveniently structured (for mainstream society, that is); the rights to vote and to privacy in reproductive decision making provide no back door through which control of people with intellectual disabilities may be ensured. Policymakers and non-disabled advocates are therefore even less likely to encourage these rights. The prevalence of controlled integration provides evidence that few of those fighting for rights for the intellectually disabled have had an interest in maximal autonomy or self-determination for this population (Drinkwater 2005).

Even when rights are provided formally, ambiguous legal language allows flexibility in determining to whom the law applies. For example, the legal terminology embedded in the ADA, such as the definitions of "disability," "equally qualified," and "reasonable accommodations," provide the flexibility to extend accommodations and protections to some while excluding others. Other forms of legal ambiguity, such as retaining restrictions rooted in eugenics alongside antidiscrimination laws and remaining vague on the measures for enforcement, have similarly diminished the power of rights for people with disabilities.

Controlled integration is further supported by the construction of disability rights as "special" rights tied to specific diagnoses, eligibility requirements, or cost–benefit analyses (Francis and Silvers 2000; O'Brien 2004; Prince 2004). The ADA offers a perfect example: While people with intellectual disabilities are typically defined as "too" disabled to seem equally qualified, those with carpal-tunnel or back problems are defined as not sufficiently disabled to have the right to accommodations. Only a small subset of well-qualified, significantly disabled people with the correct diagnoses are able to claim successfully the accommodations that the law provides. Similarly, only a subset of children with intellectual disabilities has had access to inclusive educational practices, despite advances in civil rights in this area. In determining educational placement and support, children must qualify as disabled, and inclusive settings must be determined to be the most appropriate one for the provision of education, a determination that involves weighing the advantages and disadvantages not only for the child with a disability but also for his or her classmates.

Moreover, by relying on rights rhetoric without formally extending rights and failing to provide adequate enforcement for rights, policymakers promote the illusion of justice without a practical commitment to it. In every era, state actors and organizations write up symbolic documents that espouse rights yet lack real enforcement measures. For example, the 1975 Developmental Disabilities Assistance and Bill of Rights Act guaranteed all people with development disabilities the right to appropriate treatment in the least restrictive setting, yet the U.S. Supreme Court (*Halderman v. Pennhurst* 1981) found that the Bill of Rights Act "does no more than express a congressional preference for certain kinds of treatment." As such, its power is reduced to symbolic support of inclusion without providing to people with disabilities the means to demand it.

Controlled integration allows legislators to promise equality yet holds this promise on the end of a long stick. Integration has been offered as a reward for contribution and attaining "normality" and provided to those who can overcome their disability and participate in mainstream society in typical ways (Titchkosky 2003). Thus, as stated by Henri-Jacques Striker (2000, 152), "The disabled person is integrated only when disability is erased."

Conclusion

The deprivation of rights for people with intellectual disabilities has largely been "naturalized," or assumed to be determined by biological difference and inferiority.[9] Yet the history of intellectual disability is far from that simple. Characterized by shifting and often contradictory patterns of access, category labels, and justifications, an analysis of this messy, complex history requires far more than an understanding of the biology of intellectual disability. It can be best understood through an examination of rights as they are embedded within relational contexts. Rather than assuming that rights should simply be given or denied on the basis of individual characteristics, a relational-practice approach presupposes and focuses attention on the dynamic and contested nature of rights. It assumes that groups of actors will form, disaggregate, and reconstitute in new ways, reimagining their agendas concerning rights based on their perceived relationship to people with intellectual disabilities, their perceived interests, and the political context. It allows for an understanding of rights as both a form of empowerment and a technology of control. It also examines the processes involved in claiming and using a right even after it has been legally established. This approach does not offer neat, simple answers to the question of whether at any given time people with intellectual disabilities "have" a particular right. It does, however, provide a set of tools and concepts with which to analyze history and the practice of rights in all of its complexity and ambiguity. It also serves to place people with intellectual disabilities in the same theoretical context as other citizens, as citizens embedded in a relational context that provides various levels and types of support or barriers for the claiming and exercise of rights. Human interdependence and vulnerability to social constraints are not solely issues for people with intellectual disabilities, or for people with disabilities more broadly. They are the crux of the exercise and value of rights for all people.

Setting the Stage

Early Tensions in Citizenship

E very story is rooted in a prior story, a foundation that escapes detailed attention. This is certainly true for this story. The tensions and controversies surrounding citizenship, rights, and disability in the twentieth century were shaped by the earliest understandings of American citizenship. This chapter provides a glimpse of the "prequel" to our story by briefly examining the development of American rights as they related to intellectual disability prior to 1900.

As the concept of American citizenship developed, "good" citizenship was identified in part through a contrast with "idiocy."[1] While the good citizen was seen as rational, autonomous, and morally upright, the "idiot" was depicted as incompetent, dependent, and deviant and on these bases received protections and faced rights restrictions. However, being labeled a person with an intellectual disability did not automatically preclude one from exercising rights. Legal restrictions provided options to be used when needed, not mandates to be applied systematically to all individuals perceived to have a low level of intelligence. Individuals in early America perceived little threat from intellectual disability and saw little need for extensive control mechanisms (Ferguson 1994; Trent 1994). More important, although *individuals* at times gained from the restrictions placed on disabled *individuals*, no groups such as physicians, psychologists, educators, and elites had yet developed an agenda of pursuing personal gain or "social well-being" through the systematic categorization and control of people with intellectual disabilities.

Rather than or along with restriction, the label "intellectual disability" could also at times lead to protection or even privilege, depending on many factors, including the resources, motivations, and politics at play in each individual case. Given the multiple characteristics required for the exercise of rights and the contradictory goals of American laws and treatment, access to rights for people with intellectual disabilities proved to be ambiguous and tremendously variable.

The Potential Irrelevance of
Intellectual Disability

In colonial and post-revolutionary America, many people labeled simple or slow never encountered formal restrictions based on their disability. Children with intellectual disabilities at times attended school alongside their non-disabled peers; local schoolmasters made decisions about admissions based on many factors, such as the family's ability to pay tuition, the family's status, and a student's educational skills. As adults, many people with intellectual disabilities lived successfully in their communities. In her study of family life and developmental disability in mid-nineteenth-century America, Penny L. Richards (2004, 67–68) records the following instance (among others) of community participation by a person with an intellectual disability: "In the 1830's, Thomas Cameron held a visible job, attended weddings and other social events, and voted regularly. He had responsibilities on the plantation and enjoyed riding his horse between the family properties without supervision, often carrying written messages back and forth." In his history of intellectual disability, Trent (1994, 7) makes a similar point:

> All postrevolutionary Americans knew feebleminded people. As members of their families and their communities, feeble minds were an expected part of rural and small-town life. Physically able simpletons found no great obstacles to day-to-day living, and obviously disabled idiots received care from various members of what were usually extended families. . . . Feebleminded people might be teased, their sometimes atavistic habits might disgust, but unlike the mad and the criminal, they were not feared.

Court cases offer more examples of people with intellectual disabilities who lived successfully within the community. For example, a case in West Virginia in 1885, *Knight, Committee, & C. v. Watts's Adm'rs et al.*, involved a man named William D. Littlepage, whom the court described as "very dull" at school. According to the court, "He tried to study reading, spelling, writing and arithmetic but he made a very poor out in studying them. . . . His mind did not improve any as he grew old." The court concluded, "He was not an idiot but was a boy and man of weak mind," and based on this weakness of mind the court appointed a committee to manage his estate. Yet despite adjudication, Littlepage served in the Confederate Army, married and fathered several children, and attended to business on the farm "such as having fences put up and buying calves." Adjudication for Littlepage did not lead to his total exclusion; rather, it seems to have supported his activities within the community.[2]

Institutional settings such as almshouses existed, yet most people with intellectual disabilities resided in communities. In 1855, a statistician named Edward Jarvis reported the presence of 1,087 "idiots" in Massachusetts, 60 percent of whom lived in the community (compared with only 42 percent of those identified as insane living in the same period).[3] Given that the term "idiot" referred to people with severe intellectual disabilities, presumably those with less severe disabilities were even more likely to reside in the community.

Early American Restrictions

Although early American communities made little effort to systematically identify and restrict "incompetents," states did enact laws enabling intervention when deemed necessary. These laws drew on three defining characteristics of citizenship: competence, independence, and morality.

Competence and Incompetence

Early American definitions of citizenship drew heavily on liberal political philosophy; therefore rationality was assumed to be of grave importance in the exercise of rights. The assumptions of this philosophy created a dilemma when individuals appeared to lack rationality. The state relied on three strategies for dealing with such individuals. First, as already discussed, many of the "incompetent" were simply left to participate in citizenship as feasible given their abilities, social support, and exposure to informal social control without state intervention.

Second, states developed narrow legal restrictions and protections that disqualified individuals from participation in specific activities but allowed participation in others. These legal restrictions most commonly concerned the rights to contract, to marry, and to engage in the political process (e.g., voting, serving on juries) and either prohibited the exercise of these rights outright or attempted to minimize the potential negative consequences of exercising these right by making marriages and contracts "voidable" if necessary. For example, in their first set of laws published in 1641, Massachusetts colonists granted the right to dispose of property to "all persons which are of the age of 21 yeares, and of right understanding and meamories," thereby presumably excluding individuals who were seen as lacking "right understanding."[4] As states formed and created their body of law, many state legislatures developed similar laws (following in the footsteps of English law) and made contracts "void" or "voidable" if entered into by "[those] entirely without understanding," "persons of unsound mind," "idiots," "the insane," or those adjudicated incompetent. Some states made marriage void or voidable on similar grounds. The underlying principle for such restrictions was summarized by U.S. Supreme Court Justice William

Strong in *Dexter v. Hall* (1872) when he stated that a contract required "the assent of two minds. But a lunatic, or a person non compos mentis, has nothing which the law recognizes as a mind, and it would seem, therefore, upon principle, that he cannot make a contract which may have any efficacy as such."

As a third strategy, state legislatures created the legal process of adjudication, through which the courts could define individuals as incompetent and prohibit their exercise of a broad array of rights. The adjudication process assumed incompetence to be a permanent and pervasive trait of the individual (rather than a potentially shifting product rooted in the social context). In lieu of autonomous decision making, the state provided the "incompetent" with a guardian or committee to oversee his or her rights and activities. Of course, the guardian was supposed to care for and protect the ward; however, few channels existed to challenge the guardian's decisions or the quality of care provided.

One might imagine that the use of these strategies might correlate with the level of incompetence, such that competent individuals would be allowed full access to rights, individuals with limited competence would be exempted from exercising specific rights if necessary, and individuals with severely limited competence would be placed under guardianship and would therefore be subjected to the greatest degree of restriction. However, restrictions were never applied in such a systematic manner. In fact, a stricter standard of incompetence was typically required to void a specific right than for adjudication. To void a contract based on idiocy, the courts typically required proof that an individual lacked *any* understanding and that this condition could be traced back to infancy (Andrews 1998). Courts recognized that a very small portion of people who potentially had intellectual disabilities would fit this stringent definition, and they commonly allowed individuals with less severe intellectual disabilities to exercise rights. For example, in 1852, Justice John Allen of the Virginia Supreme Court wrote that "mere weakness of understanding is no objection to a man's disposing of his own estate" (*Greer v. Greers* 1852). Similarly, in *Ward v. Dulaney* (1852), the court decided that marriages of those with "mere weakness of intellect" should not be declared void if both parties understood the nature of marriage and the duties involved.[5] According to these precedents, only those who completely lacked understanding would be denied the specific rights to contract or marry (Scheerenberger 1983).

Adjudication, by contrast, required only evidence that an individual showed poor decision making due to disability or old age such that his or her best interests would be served by the assignment of a guardian. Adjudication hearings did not even systematically assess a broad range of decision-making abilities. Because adjudication processes were often initiated by relatives with concerns regarding an individual's ability to manage his or her money or estate, the assessment of skill in adjudication hearings often focused on an individual's business acumen, defined by the "mental capacity to transact one's business with intelligence" or to provide for the "care and management" of property (Nielsen 2006). Although such an assessment might have been relevant for the management of one's financial estate, it commonly served as the basis for a broad declaration of legal incompetence and therefore affected a vast range of rights.[6] Ironically, then, the courts required evidence of a complete lack of understanding shown from childhood to restrict a specific right but used a far less stringent definition, often rooted in one's business skills, to remove almost all rights. This was seen in the case of Littlepage: Although the court did not consider him to be an "idiot," he experienced adjudication based on weakness of mind.

Why use more stringent criteria when removing fewer rights? Voiding an already established contract or marriage had the potential to harm parties other than the disabled individual. Therefore, the stringent standard to void a contract or marriage served, at least in part, to protect the individuals who had entered into a contract with a person with a disability. In contrast, adjudication was presumed to be a protective measure that would be in everyone's best interests; the person with a disability would presumably be protected from his or her own poor choices, and other individuals would be protected from the harmful results of these choices. Although the complete restriction of rights appears to be more extreme, the courts imagined that adjudication caused little direct harm and therefore allowed for a more liberal definition of incompetence. Thus, the strategy used to deal with incompetence involved more than an assessment of an individual's abilities and took into account the potential harm to and interests of various parties, including people with and without disabilities.

Regardless of which formal legal process was used, both had to be initiated. Typically, initiation of these costly and complex legal processes would be pursued by people without disabilities who perceived some serious concern or interest warranting it. At times these concerns reflected the best interest of the person with a disability and sometimes they did not; regardless, though, adjudication and the restriction of specific rights were almost always initiated by people without disabilities and therefore relied on their perceptions. Not surprisingly, perhaps, few concerns provoked the use of these formal legal processes more than money. While access to money often supported the exercise of rights, it also heightened one's vulnerability to adjudication. In her research on incompetence hearings, Nielsen (2006) found elderly female widows who had inherited money to be among the most frequent targets for adjudication, as relatives, most commonly adult sons, sought to establish themselves as the guardians of the newly inherited property. Presumably, the competence of these women did not change dramatically with widowhood; rather, their roles and control over money changed, sparking an interest among others in pursuing formal adjudication.[7] Whereas concerns about money often led to formal proceedings, attempts to exercise other rights, such as the right to vote, rarely sparked formal court disputes. Few people saw potential for gain by preventing an individual from voting or any great harm done by allowing an individual to cast a vote.

Both adjudication and the voiding of specific rights are characterized by a set of contradictory goals: to protect people with disabilities from exploitation and their own poor decision making and to protect others and "society" from the potentially harmful consequences of incompetence. While we may imagine that the same law can protect both people with and people without disabilities, these interests cannot always be reconciled. In win–loss situations, the legal system tended to favor the perceptions of people without disabilities. Formal legal processes were complex and costly and required the ability to articulate one's cause, each of which tended to advantage people without disabilities. Moreover, it was difficult for individuals with disabilities to successfully initiate proceedings for their own protection, as the ability to pursue legal channels indicated some level of understanding and therefore disqualified them from the "protections" offered to "idiots." Thus, the level of restriction experienced typically was determined not by the level of competence, but instead by the motivations and personal interests of others, as well as the disabled person's support system and resources.

The case of *Miller v. Rutledge* (1887) provides an example of several of the points under discussion, including the different standards for incompetence used in adjudication versus the voiding of specific rights, the use of both types of formal restrictions by interested parties for their own personal gain, and the failure of these processes to protect people with intellectual disabilities. In 1866, the family of Joseph Rutledge successfully pursued his adjudication. The court described Rutledge as "illiterate and of weak intellect, delicate physical condition, and indolent habits" and placed him under guardianship with a committee to manage his affairs. In a surprising twist, in 1871 Rutledge went to court to remove a member of his committee, and the court deemed him competent to resume management of his own affairs (his use of the legal process itself contributing to an assessment that he was competent). During this period of self-management, Rutledge sold a piece of land to purchase two mares, a wagon, and a harness. In 1881, his family members again initiated adjudication, and the court again appointed a committee to manage Rutledge's affairs. His brother (a member of the committee and prospective heir) then pursued legal action to void the sale of land by claiming that his brother had been unable to contract due to idiocy. The court found that Rutledge did not meet the stringent standards of idiocy required to void a contract, deemed him capable of managing his own affairs during the ten-year period when he did not have a committee, upheld the validity of the sale, and actually indicated his probable competence while under guardianship. Justice Robert A. Richardson suggested that Rutledge's brother had pursued "ill-conceived and unnecessary litigation" to protect the estate of which he was heir, in essence accusing him of using the law to void his brother's rights and further his own financial interests. Despite Justice Richardson's criticisms, the case merely upheld the sale of the land and did not reverse Rutledge's status as incompetent. Hence, depending on the legal process (voiding a contract or adjudication), the courts differentially assessed his competence, usually in a process initiated by people other than himself. His committee members mixed their own interests with the protection of his interests and used the legal designation of incompetence to pursue their own gain. One might imagine that if Rutledge had not owned an estate, adjudication would not have been considered necessary by his family.

As argued by Martha Minow (1990), the American legal system established a dual track in which "competent" citizens received civil rights and "incompetents" received protections and restrictions. Yet the definition of incompetence was not clear; nor was the process of designation and restriction evenly applied. The legal designation of incompetence resulted not solely from one's actual abilities but also from legal contestation, usually initiated by someone with a concern significant enough in their eyes to warrant formal action. Thus, many people who could have been subjected to formal exclusion never were, while others lost rights due to the interests and concerns of people without disabilities. Furthermore, in the case of most rights, informal restrictions probably occurred far more often than formal restrictions, as families and community members decided for themselves who they would treat as incompetent regardless of what the law allowed. Informal restrictions varied significantly, as family members and others held different views of incompetence and different resources and motivations for either supporting or restricting participation in rights by people with disabilities. Given their potential limitations in cognitive capacity and potential economic and social dependence, many people with disabilities probably accepted informal restrictions without much resistance.

Independence and Dependence

In early America, most people with disabilities lived in varying states of independence with little intervention from the state. The family held primary responsibility for the care of its dependents, including children, people with disabilities, and the elderly. Communities stressed the importance of maintaining the family unit and offered relief directly to families that had difficulties supporting their dependents rather than encouraging institutional care for the dependents (Ferguson 1994). Families, of course, were expected to use relief wisely, but they did not necessarily face stigma or formal social control based on their receipt of assistance.

When the family could not or would not fulfill its role as caretaker, and individuals caused problems in the community such as vagrancy and petty theft, communities turned to more formal mechanisms of care and control. One of the earliest poor laws, the 1693 Act for the Relief of Ideots and Distracted Persons, passed by the Massachusetts Bay Colony, provided "relief and safety . . . as long as such person shall live" to idiots (defined as "any person to be naturally wanting of understanding so as to be uncapable to provide for him or her self") in the absence of family members to provide for them (Wickham 2001). This law authorized town authorities to "dispose the Estate of such Impotent or Distracted Person to the best improvement and advantage towards his or her support as also the person to any proper work or service he or she may be capable to be imployed in."[8]

Wards of the community were usually either placed with other families (referred to as "placing out") or institutionalized. The system of placing out, the forerunner of today's foster-care system, delegated the care of the dependent to a local individual or family who received a small sum of money in compensation (Scheerenberger 1983). Ideally, placing out supported the creation of a new, substitute family that offered personalized, community-based assistance to people with disabilities. However, these families held tremendous power over the lives and livelihoods of people with disabilities and encountered few rules and even less enforcement regarding the quality of care they offered. Thus, placing out created relatively private relationships that offered people with disabilities varying social, emotional, and economic benefits.

Alternatively, institutions, including almshouses and hospitals, housed "dependents," including the poor, disabled, widowed, orphaned, and sick, collectively in a relatively undifferentiated manner. Institutional solutions emerged first in urban centers that lacked the community bonds prevalent in smaller towns. Even in urban centers, though, almshouses and hospitals initially served as places of last resort, reserved for the poorest and most seriously disabled and sick (Ferguson 1994; Rothman 1971). Throughout the 1800s, institutional solutions grew in popularity. According to Philip M. Ferguson, "The almshouse went from an unpopular last resort in a few large cities and towns to the common practice of counties and cities across the Northeast and Midwest."[9] Supporters of the almshouse claimed that a formal system of institutional care would provide the worthy poor (those who were perceived as unfit for paid employment such as idiots and the insane) with superior care while deterring the unworthy poor (those who could work) from needless dependence and idleness; however, these goals proved inherently contradictory. To deter the unworthy poor, conditions in almshouses had to be sufficiently inhumane and abusive to motivate anyone who could work to do so, making compassionate care of the worthy poor impossible.[10] Thus, abusive custodial situations emerged as the preferred means of "caring" for people with disabilities because these conditions served the interests of the emerging capitalist system, which demanded wage work of all able-bodied people and the stigmatization of those unwilling or unable to do so (Ferguson 1994; Foucault 1965; Scull 1977). The conditions soon got to be so terrible that they attracted national attention. Dorothea Dix (1850), after conducting an extensive investigation into the living conditions for the insane and idiotic throughout the United States, described the wretched conditions that had become typical for thousands of people with disabilities:

> I have myself seen more than nine thousand idiots, epileptics, and insane, in these United States, destitute of appropriate care and protection; and of this vast and most miserable company sought out in jails, in poor-houses, and in private dwellings, there have been hundreds, nay, rather thousands, bound with galling chains, bowed beneath fetters and heavy iron balls, attached to drag-chains, lacerated with ropes,

scourged with rods, and terrified beneath storms of profane execrations and cruel blows; now subject to gibes, and scorn, and torturing tricks— now abandoned to the most loathsome necessities, or subject to the vilest and most outrageous violations. These are strong terms, but language fails to convey the astounding truths.

Again we see a connection between economic resources and rights. While some individuals were targeted for adjudication because they possessed wealth, others were institutionalized and adjudicated incompetent because they lacked a means of self-support. Once institutionalized or placed out, they were forced to relinquish control over their estate and their person. They could be beaten, chained, and forced into labor. As with the laws regarding competence, these laws and policies also embody the competing goals of protecting people with disabilities and protecting other individuals. Certainly some institutional administrators hoped to help and protect their wards, and certainly some people benefited from the assistance they received. Yet formal systems of care granted guardianship to community members and almshouse administrators whose interests were often in direct opposition to the interests of their wards. People with intellectual disabilities needed food, shelter, employment, and assistance to succeed in the community, yet almshouse directors catered to the desires of community leaders to use the almshouse as a deterrent for laziness and offered only the barest essentials for survival in the most horrid conditions. Once placed in these new situations, people with disabilities had little means by which to protect themselves, and therefore a relationship supposedly established to protect them easily became abusive.

Freedom from formal intervention did not leave people with disabilities free to exercise their rights, either. Within their own families, "dependents" were at the mercy of the head of household who assumed the cost of their care and responsibility for their behavior, as well as the right to manage their affairs as he saw fit (Okin 1989). "Dependents" were not necessarily the passive recipients of care; some people with disabilities provided care to their family members, performed work in or outside the home, and otherwise contributed to the household and society. In a hierarchal world that stigmatized physical and mental difference, though, people with disabilities could be defined as dependents regardless of their contributions. While Thomas Cameron's family supported his ability to exercise numerous rights, other families hid, abused, or sold their dependents into bondage as apprentices or indentured servants (Deutsch 1949). For those people with intellectual disabilities who did not have families or community support, life could be extremely difficult and dangerous. Communities engaged in "passing on," in which community members loaded unwanted vagrants into a cart and dropped them off in another community or in the middle of nowhere. Communities also "warned out," informing newcomers they were not welcome to stay (Minnesota Governor's Council on Developmental Disabilities 1996; Scheerenberger 1983). People perceived to be deviant or dependent could wander from town to town without any access to the basic necessities of survival. Thus, dependence threatened one's access to rights. Moreover, individuals with similar levels of dependence could have very different access to rights based on their living residence in a family, a community placement, or an almshouse.

Morality and Deviance

Deviance served as the third characteristic used to protect and restrict people with intellectual disabilities. Of the three characteristics, the laws related to deviance were perhaps the most clearly intended to protect. Legal tradition back to the tenth century granted leniency to those who committed crimes but lacked intent, free will, or an ability to understand the difference between right and wrong (Andrews 1998; Wickham 2001). Explaining the rationale behind leniency for those groups, Justice Lemuel Shaw wrote in 1844 (*Commonwealth v. Abner Rogers, Jr.*): "In order to constitute a crime, a person must have intelligence and capacity enough to have a criminal intent and purpose; and if his reason and mental powers are either so deficient that he has no will, no conscience, or controlling mental power, or if, through the overwhelming violence of mental disease, his intellectual power is for the time obliterated, he is not a responsible moral agent, and is not punishable for criminal acts." Given the harsh sentences common in early America, including corporal punishment and execution, leniency due to idiocy or insanity "could mean the difference between life and death" (Scheerenberger 1983, 9).

Although early American law mitigated punishments for criminals with idiocy, laws against vagrancy and begging criminalized poverty, and therefore people with intellectual disabilities were often imprisoned and denied their rights anyway. Prisons served an explicit role in warehousing the poor, as in the authorization of a Connecticut house of correction in 1727 intended to house "all rogues, vagabonds and idle persons going about in town or country begging . . . as also persons under distraction and unfit to go at large, whose friends do not take care of their safe confinement" (Deutsch 1949, 52, quoted in Scheerenberger 1983, 95). Thus, as with restrictions based on incompetence and dependence, the legal system supposedly designed to protect people from the criminal justice system also served to subject people to it.

Intersections

The experience of disability cannot be considered separate from intersecting identities such as race and gender. For example, although Richards records that Thomas Cameron voted regularly, women in this era, disabled or not, had yet to attain suffrage or many other rights that men took for granted. To talk about political rights in this era for people with disabilities, then, is to talk about political rights for disabled men. For women with disabilities, integration hinged on their access to accepted female roles, including those of wife and mother. Often, women with intellectual disabilities were deemed unfit and denied access to these roles. Without the potential for marriage, disabled girls could face abandonment or lifelong responsibilities to serve in their parents' home. However, the traits associated with intellectual disability, such as dependence, passivity, and incompetence, were not necessarily deemed incompatible with feminine roles, as women were generally expected to be dependent and irrational. Access to such roles depended not solely on one's competence but also on the perception of an individual's abilities, the family's interests and resources, and the interests of others. For women with disabilities, their lives were largely bound by "private" relationships outside the context of civil rights—parent–daughter, husband–wife—and their opportunities were negotiated within those relational contexts.

Race also intertwined in complex ways with intellectual disability. On one hand, African Americans were widely assumed to have lower levels of intelligence than whites. Thomas Jefferson (cited in Gossett 1965, 510) wrote, "I advance it, therefore, as a suspicion only, that the blacks . . . are inferior to the whites in the endowment of body and mind." While it was only a suspicion for Jefferson, others claimed to have scientific proof of lower levels of intelligence and mental stability among blacks. Secretary of State John C. Calhoun, for example, infamously used 1840 Census data to argue that "the African is incapable of self-care and sinks into lunacy under the burden of freedom. It is a mercy to give him the guardianship and protection from mental death" (cited in Thomas and Sillen 1979, 17).[11]

While ideologies of mental and moral inferiority were used to justify slavery, slaves were not simply assumed to be "idiots." On the contrary, a body of law arose specifically regarding mentally disabled slaves. Some states provided a "warranty of slaves" to protect purchasers from defective merchandise, which held that "craziness or idiocy is an absolute vice; and, where not apparent [at time of purchase], will annul the sale." States also enacted laws obligating owners to provide basic necessities for all of their slaves, including the elderly, disabled, and otherwise unproductive, throughout their lives (Goodell 1853). Such legislation was designed to protect communities from the burden of providing for slaves or former slaves who were disabled rather than to protect slaves per se. By the 1820s, states had begun to limit owners' rights to manumission (i.e., the freeing of slaves) to ensure that owners were not offering freedom to avoid their economic responsibility for unproductive slaves. The "Black Code" of Louisiana (1724) ordered "slaves disabled from working by old age, sickness, or otherwise, to be provided for by their masters, otherwise they shall be sent to the nearest hospital, to which the masters shall pay eight cents a day for each slave, and the hospital shall have a lien on the plantations of the masters" ("Black Code" of Louisiana 1724; Goodell 1853). Of course, despite laws, not all owners were so benevolent, and slaves at times were killed or freed if they were economically unproductive. In a heart-wrenching story, for example,

Afi-Tiombe A. Kambon (1993) tells of a physically disabled baby born into slavery who was killed by her master due to her economic worthlessness.

Free African Americans with disabilities and slaves with disabilities whose masters could not or would not care for them were either left to their own devices or housed in public facilities such as the almshouse, jail, or hospital. According to the social historian Vanessa Jackson (2001, 10), "If conditions in the facility were poor for white patients, conditions were completely inhumane for African-American patients. For instance, one of the first African-American patients admitted to the South Carolina Lunatic Asylum in 1829 was a fourteen-year-old slave named Jefferson. Jefferson's name was not recorded in the admission book and he was reportedly housed in the yard."

The experiences of free and enslaved blacks illustrate yet another dimension of the history of rights. Disability may actually have protected free blacks from being sold into slavery or may have helped one attain freedom if a slave. Similarly, being African American may have protected people with disabilities from the experience of being warehoused in a public institution such as an almshouse, since whites were hesitant to support dependent African Americans. However, disability among slaves could jeopardize their very life, and access to treatment was rare. African Americans could be denied assistance in almshouses and hospitals, and if they were institutionalized, they could be exposed to the harshest of treatment. Hence, as with gender, a marginalized racial status could at times protect people with disabilities and vice versa, but the combination probably increased the danger and marginalization experienced.

To summarize, in early America the state did not systematically attempt to identify and exclude people with mental or intellectual disabilities; nor was there any concerted movement to criminalize, stigmatize or exclude people with intellectual disabilities as a group. Yet the state did provide mechanisms to achieve the contradictory goals of protecting people with intellectual disabilities and protecting society from them. Given the contradictory goals of these mechanisms and the fact that they were employed in the context of unequal relationships, they frequently benefited people without disabilities more than they did people with disabilities. Moreover, the state sanctioned private control over dependents, including women, children, slaves, and people with disabilities. Thus, the rights available to these groups depended on their personal resources and relationships; the family and community mediated rights for incompetents and dependents, allowing some rights for some people while restricting rights for others.

Seeds of Social Change

By the mid-nineteenth century, systems of "care" were transforming into the more expansive, specialized systems that would come to dominate policy in the early twentieth century. These transformations were propelled by the spread of capitalism, the increasing reliance on institutions for the management of social problems, the medicalization of intellectual disability, and the rise of eugenics.

The growth of capitalism slowly and fundamentally transformed American understandings of citizenship and rights. Growing capitalist markets required a vast pool of mobile and free workers, and traditional systems of charity seemed to undermine the work ethic and encourage dependence. Of course, not everyone could work. Thus, capitalists advanced different agendas for the able-bodied poor and the disabled poor. The able-bodied were to be inculcated with the proper work ethic and "motivated" to work either by the complete denial of assistance or the provision of assistance in conditions wretched enough to make paid labor seem attractive. Those incapable of work, those "worthy" of assistance, would be identified and provided with custodial care and institutional segregation, but their care would also be inhumane, as they would serve as an example of the horror of dependence. Thus, capitalism required the differentiation of able-bodied and disabled, productive and non-productive. While some of the "non-productive" were easily identified, differentiation based on mental and intellectual disability proved more challenging. Medical, psychological, and educational professionals took on the task of sorting the productive from the unproductive (the unworthy from the worthy) and their appropriate treatment. Thus, Foucault (1965, 46) wrote, "Before having the medical meaning we give it, or that at least we like to suppose it has, confinement was required by something quite different from any concern with curing the sick. What made it necessary was an imperative of labor."

In addition to the imperative of separating the able-bodied population from the disabled population, capitalism also created widespread social dislocation, and reformers looked to the institution as a remedy for this new social chaos (Rothman 1971). Reformers of the day believed that the combination of industrialization and modern citizenship promoted disorder and deviance; in such a highly mobile society, people could imagine themselves as anything, forget the boundaries of their lives, and easily fall into insanity or deviance in their efforts to meet their desires. Within the walls of the institution, experts could create an environment that exemplified the principles of a well-ordered society and teach the proper work ethic, thereby curing inmates of insanity, deficiency, and deviancy. Of course, if treatment failed, the institution also offered social control and segregation, protecting society from the chronically deviant.

The growing popularity of almshouses, hospitals, and prisons throughout the 1800s reflects these trends; yet, it was the specialized institution that emphasized sorting, labeling, and differential care that emerged as the dominant model for the treatment of people with significant disabilities. In his analysis of early institutional care for people with intellectual disabilities, Ferguson (1994) stresses the similarities between the almshouse and the specialized institution for people with intellectual disabilities. Both pursued contradictory goals (to care for people with disabilities and to deter unnecessary dependence), were characterized by abhorrent conditions, and ultimately failed to care for people with significant disabilities. The difference lay in the ability of the specialized institution to create an increasingly complex system of diagnosis and classification, in effect professionalizing the care and study of intellectual disability in a way that the almshouse never did.

It should be noted that the creators of the earliest specialized institutions believed that specialization would be a vast improvement over the almshouse, leading to the cure—or, at least, the enhancement of skills—of people with intellectual disabilities. Beginning in the eighteenth century, the work of European physicians and educators, including Jean-Marc Gaspard Itard, Edward C. Seguin, Johann Guggenbuhl, and Maria Montessori, transformed the understanding of idiocy from an incurable, immutable product of sin or state of animalism into a sensory and intellectual disability that could be improved with education and training. For example, Seguin (1866), one of the most influential leaders in re-conceptualizing mental deficiency, argued that mental deficiency was caused by sensory isolation or deprivation. To treat this condition, he developed a system of intensive sensory stimulation focusing on three areas of training: physical, intellectual, and moral. Seguin believed that all people, regardless of the level of disability, could benefit from training and become increasingly productive and well-adjusted. Building on this tradition, Samuel Gridley Howe opened the first publicly funded American school for idiots in 1847, housed in a wing of the Perkins Institution and Massachusetts Asylum for the Blind. In his report to the Massachusetts legislature to secure funding, Howe advocated the right of the "poor idiot" to an education and affirmed the tremendous benefits to be reaped by the disabled individual and by society through education:

> Massachusetts admits the right of all her citizens to a share in the blessings of education; she provides liberally for all her more favoured children; if some be blind or deaf, she still continues to furnish them special instruction at great cost—and will she longer neglect the poor idiot,—the most wretched of all who are born to her,—those who are usually abandoned by their fellows,—who can never, of themselves, step up upon the platform of humanity, will she leave them to their dreadful fate, to a life of brutishness, without an effort on their behalf? . . .
>
> The benefits to be derived from the establishment of a school for this class of persons, upon humane and scientific principles, would be very great. . . . [I]t would be demonstrated that no idiot need be confined or restrained by force; that the young can be trained to industry, order, and self-respect; that they can be redeemed from odious and filthy habits, and that there is not one of any age, who may not be made more of a man, and less of a brute, by patience and kindness, directed by energy and skill. (Howe 1958 [1848])

Similarly indicating the hope of successful outcomes from education, in the earliest years of the New York State Asylum for Idiots the board of trustees purposefully limited their first students to those capable of being "moulded and trained." In their first annual report, in 1852, they wrote with confidence that, "in a large majority of cases, idiots may be so trained and instructed as to render them useful to themselves and fitted to learn some of the ordinary trades, or to engage in agriculture," and they recommended keeping the school small to allow each student an appropriate education. These initial efforts promoted the belief that intensive training could develop a person's abilities and that people with intellectual disabilities could be transformed into contributing citizens.

To obtain funding, though, superintendents such as Howe and Hervey B. Wilbur had to convince politicians of their successes. At first, they spoke of their triumphs in transforming idiots into productive citizens, a task at which the almshouse had clearly failed. However, reformers quickly realized the limitations of claiming "curability." Even those patients who improved significantly faced difficulties in the new industrial labor market that demanded fast-paced and standardized work, particularly given competition from increasing numbers of immigrants and other workers willing to accept low wages. Ferguson (1994, 55) notes, "As economic utility became the distinction between success and failure, the ranks of failures inevitably swelled." As optimism about the schools' ability to cure faded, superintendents began to emphasize the cost-effectiveness of specialized institutions for the lifelong custodial care of idiots. Thus, the mission of the specialized institution quickly changed, offering the provision of "care" in a segregated setting at the lowest cost to the community, with little reason for education and little hope of a return to the community (Noll and Trent 2004; Trent 1994). By the dawn of the twentieth century, the specialized custodial institution had become the dominant model of care and control supported by professionals and policymakers. Despite the growing prevalence of the institution, though, most people with intellectual disabilities continued to live with their families, in their communities, or in almshouses, hospitals, or jails. In 1890, the "federal census identified only 20 public and 4 private asylums for idiots, housing a total of 5,254 inmates" (cited in Ferguson 1994).

At the close of the nineteenth century, intellectual disability still garnered little national attention. However, the rising pseudo-science of eugenics would radically change the national perception of intellectual disability. Francis Galton, credited with founding eugenics in the late 1800s, defined this new science as "the study of the agencies under social control that may improve or impair the racial qualities of future generations either physically or mentally" (Galton 1907). Galton believed that through scientific inquiry society could discover the factors that promoted positive and negative characteristics within the human race, and that knowledge could then be used to design policies for the improvement of population quality (Forrest 1974). As is discussed in the next chapter, very different groups with very different agendas sought to use eugenics to improve the population, but eugenics came to be known primarily for its efforts to avert "race suicide" by controlling immigration and preventing the reproduction of people considered to be unfit. As eugenics grew in influence, intellectual disability took on an unprecedented significance in debates concerning the welfare of the nation. No longer seen as a product of individual sin, a local burden for a community, or a condition treatable within institutions, "feeblemindedness" was viewed by eugenicists as a biological and hereditary condition leading to the downfall of society. Eugenics, with its reliance on science and heredity, would further cement a biological understanding of intellectual disability, an individualized notion of incompetence, the importance of segregation and social control, and the vulnerability of those who were labeled feebleminded.

Conclusion

Early Americans identified the "idiot" as potentially unfit for the exercise of rights and developed a variety of social-control mechanisms—including the law, the almshouse, and informal restrictions imposed by family and community members—to protect and restrict people with intellectual disabilities. However, access to rights for people with intellectual disabilities was highly variable, dependent on their abilities, relationships, resources, and intersecting statuses. Many people who had sufficient ability and support simply lived their lives as best they could without experiencing formal challenges or restrictions. Rights were typically negotiated within "private" relationships so that one's family greatly affected one's access to rights. Formal restrictions were reserved for people with disabilities whose actions or situation concerned someone enough to warrant the use of formal legal controls and were initiated by people without disabilities based on their own perceptions and interests (including their potential interest in protecting someone with a disability) more so than an effort to systematically exclude a whole category of people. Thus, although intellectual disability increased one's vulnerability to restrictions, the connection between disability and access to rights was highly variable, with little systematic application.

4

The Feebleminded
versus the Nation

1900–1930s

Prior to 1900, intellectual disability received little attention from society and caused minimal alarm. In the early 1900s, though, a radical shift in the nation's understanding of intellectual disability took place, and the "feebleminded"[1] emerged as one of the principal enemies in the nation's war against population degeneracy and "race suicide." An odd assortment of bedfellows, loosely united under the umbrella of the eugenics movement, called for institutional segregation and rights restrictions for the feebleminded. They achieved considerable success. Institutions grew at an astounding rate: From 1904 to 1910, the institutionalized population increased by 44.5 percent, and from 1910 to 1923, it increased another 107.2 percent (U.S. Department of Commerce 1926). In 1890, fourteen states had institutions for the feebleminded, and by 1923, forty states had at least one institution, and several states supported multiple institutions. By 1930, thirty states had passed sterilization laws, and the U.S. Supreme Court had upheld the constitutionality of compulsory sterilization. Forty-one states had passed laws restricting marriage based on mental disability. Although most states already had restricted voting and contracting based on mental disability, eighteen states passed additional restrictions on voting, and six passed additional restrictions on contracting (Scheerenberger 1983). "Imbeciles" and the "feeble-minded" were added to the list of people, which already included "idiots," who could be deported according to immigration regulations, and supporters of the 1924 Immigration Act justified additional restrictions for people of certain races, ethnicities, and

Sections of this chapter were originally published in *Disability and Society* (2003).

nationalities in part by arguing that such restrictions would reduce the prevalence of feeblemindedness (Baynton 2001).

This chapter analyzes the emerging perception of feeblemindedness as a pressing problem, the push to restrict the rights of the feebleminded, and the justifications offered to support these restrictions. In this era, a very diverse set of constituencies, including eugenicists, institutional superintendents, feminists, educators, social workers, and others, advanced their interests through policies that imposed social control on the feebleminded. Of particular importance, rights restrictions for the feebleminded enabled two pursuits: the attempt to increase the prestige and jurisdiction of those professionals charged with the control of the feebleminded, and the preservation of the social-stratification system through the control of a broader set of people deemed unfit who could be labeled feebleminded. I begin the analysis with an overview of eugenics and then analyze why eugenicists and others focused attention on feeblemindedness as a social problem and how they constructed the relationship between feebelmindedness and rights.

Eugenics and the Threat of the Feebleminded

Eugenics and its corresponding restrictions of the feebleminded emerged during a time of great social dislocation (Kevles 1985; Paul 1995; Reilly 1991; Rothman 1971; Trent 1994). Post–Civil War reconstruction, rapid industrialization and urbanization, growing disparities of wealth, tremendous immigration, and the crippling of traditional social-support systems created disorder and anxiety among people of all classes. As a result of these changes in society, some of America's historically marginalized groups appeared to be making gains in their social and economic positions, and these gains worried those who benefited from the prevailing system of social stratification.

One of the most disturbing changes to many Americans was the great influx of immigrants, especially "new wave" immigrants from non–Western European backgrounds. The number of new immigrants rose from 225,000 in 1898 to 1.3 million in 1907, alarming both laborers who feared for their economic security and elites who worried about increasing poverty, crime, and the deterioration of Anglo-Protestant culture (Baynton 2001; Reilly 1991).[2] Racial tensions were also high. During Reconstruction, race relations improved in the North, and fourteen states passed antidiscrimination laws. By 1900, though, "The issue was not whether Negroes would continue to experience improvements in basic civil and human rights, but whether they would be able to retain the few rights and privileges they had attained during the previous three decades" (Wilson 1978, 63; see also Woodward 2001 [1955]).[3] Better job opportunities and more favorable political climate in northern cities encouraged black migration; in the 1920s, the net black migration from south to north was 872,000, an increase of more than 250,000 from the last decade (Wilson 1978). As competition between white and black workers grew fierce, the racially charged situation erupted into interracial riots in more than twenty cities in 1919. In addition to keeping their jobs, white men also worried about maintaining exclusive access to white women; between 1875 and 1924, several states established restrictions against miscegenation or strengthened their existing restrictions (Dorr 1999).

Women, too, were actively reconstructing their roles in work, family, and politics. Between 1890 and 1920, women's participation in the paid workforce increased by 226 percent, while men's participation increased by only 78 percent (Mattaei 1982). Women entered college in record numbers, further expanding their opportunities within the workplace. New levels of economic independence and social freedoms combined with increasing access to sexual education and birth control led to unprecedented sexual freedom for women; studies indicated that from 1890 to 1930, the number of women engaging in premarital sex doubled (D'Emilio and Freedman 1988). College-educated women married less often, later in life, and had fewer children. Women also entered the political sphere as never before, and women's organizations emerged dedicated to issues ranging from women's suffrage to child labor and housing.

While many people applauded these shifts as indications of progress, others foresaw "race suicide," the term frequently used to describe the deteriorating moral and racial order and the ostensible corresponding rise of degeneracy, deviance, and chaos. In the political turmoil of this age, the new science of eugenics quickly became a tool to preserve traditional gender and race roles (Leonard 2005). From its creation, eugenics assumed the superiority of Anglo-Saxon stock. Francis Galton, who is credited with coining the term "eugenics," suggested that the races could be classified by level of intelligence, ranking British citizens above Africans and Australian aboriginals (Galton 1962 [1869]). Eugenicists vigorously gathered evidence to "prove" that new-wave immigrants brought with them inferior cultures and defective biological stock. In 1907, Henry Goddard administered the newly imported Binet intelligence test on immigrants entering the nation at Ellis Island and reported that 40–50 percent of them were feebleminded. Edward Ross (1914), author of *The Old World and the New: The Significance of Past and Present Immigration to the American People*, criticized the physical traits of immigrants, as well, linking perceived physical defects with moral defects. For eugenicists, unchecked immigration allowed entry of the world's unfit into the land of opportunity, and would lead to its destruction.

According to eugenicists, interracial procreation also posed a grave threat to the quality of the population. Madison Grant and Lothrop Stoddard, two of the most explicitly racist eugenicists, both preached against miscegenation. Grant (1916, 18) argued, "The cross between a white man and an Indian is an Indian; the cross between a white man and a Negro is a Negro." Therefore, any mixing of the races diluted the quality of the population. Pushing this argument further, Stoddard (1922, 165–166) warned that the product of miscegenation was even worse than the "lesser" race, producing "a mongrel—a walking chaos, so consumed by his jarring heredities that he is quite worthless."

Much of the blame for race suicide was placed squarely on the shoulders of women, including women of supposedly superior stock who ignored their social obligation to bear children responsibly with men of good stock, as well as women of supposedly inferior stock who were believed to reproduce often and indiscriminately with inferior men. Eugenicists stressed that superior, "old stock" Europeans and Americans were fueling their own decline by limiting their birthrate while allowing inferior populations to breed at higher rates. In *The Rising Tide of Color against White World-Supremacy*, Stoddard (1922, 162) warned, "It was precisely those peoples of highest genetic worth whose birth rate fell off most sharply," whereas "the lower types were gaining ground." According to Stoddard, if left unchecked, this "disgenic trend" could only lead to the downfall of the white race and civilized society.

Wendy Kline's (2001) historical analysis of the eugenics movement in California reveals that, although its advocacy of white male superiority may seem extreme, the eugenics movement actually tapped into a very popular view that babies should be born into families that possessed the intellectual, moral, and financial capacities to raise children well and that other families should be discouraged from having children. To encourage larger and stronger families, eugenicists urged a return to traditional gender roles, valorizing women's role as mothers. Paul Popenoe, the "father of marriage counseling," for example, insisted that married women should bear at least four children and warned that failure to do so placed the white race "in danger of losing ground" (Popenoe and Johnson 1918, 134).[4]

While eugenicists criticized superior women for ignoring their social duties, they portrayed "inferior" women (e.g., women who were poor, non-white, or single and sexually active) as over-sexed and depraved. Unchecked procreation among the unfit supposedly swamped the nation with dependents and incompetents, the care of which drained the pocketbooks of responsible taxpayers. For example, in advocating the establishment of the first institutions for feebleminded women, Josephine Shaw Lowell claimed that "one of the most important and most dangerous causes of the increase of crime, pauperism, and insanity [i.e., mental weakness] is the unrestrained liberty allowed to vagrant and degraded women" (Lowell 1879, 189). The political discourse supporting the passage of Virginia's 1924 Racial Integrity Act, which forbade whites from marrying outside their race, showed similar concerns about women's sexuality. According to the historian Lisa Lindquist Dorr (1999, 150), "To Southerners, feebleminded women, because they were 'irrational' and genetically controlled by powerful sexual desires, could not appreciate the need to maintain racial purity; thus, they could not be trusted to avoid any sexual liaisons, including those between races." Thus, the success of white America hinged on the differential control of women's sexuality so that procreation was encouraged among "fit" women and restricted among the "unfit."[5]

These broad concerns related to the decline in population quality fueled the rhetorical transformation of feeblemindedness from a condition of little consequence to a pressing national epidemic. In the late 1800s, scientists "discovered" a tremendous increase in the number of the feebleminded. Isaac Kerlin, medical director at the Elwyn Institute in Pennsylvania, used census data to show that between 1870 and 1880 the general population grew by 30 percent, but idiocy grew by 200 percent. In addition, Kerlin suggested that the census probably vastly undercounted idiocy (Reilly 1991). Frederick Wines, a consultant for the U.S. Census Bureau, further studied the prevalence of feeblemindedness within the community and found the rate of feeblemindedness identified in 1880 was two and a half times the rate identified in 1870 (Trent 1994). One of the first American sociologists to study intellectual disability, Stanley Davies (1923, 43), noted that "there was a rather rapid multiplication in the numbers of known mental defectives and these additions to the ranks of the feebleminded were found not in the institutions for the most part but in the very midst of the community."

At first, eugenicists portrayed feeblemindedness as simply one among many forms of degeneracy plaguing the nation. In *The Jukes* (Dugdale 1877), the first of many family-lineage studies examining the intergenerational transmission of character traits, R. L. Dugdale documented a few instances of feeblemindedness but gave the condition little importance in his overall interpretation of the Jukes' lineage. In his work, Dugdale traced the ancestry of six prisoners back five generations and documented a remarkably high rate of dependence, deviance, and illegitimacy. Creating the fictitious name the "Jukes," Dugdale estimated that the twelve hundred members of the family line spanning five generations had cost the nation $1.308 million in relief, arrests, court proceedings, maintenance in jail, drugs and medical treatment, wages lost, property damaged, and other costs. In explaining the concentration of social inadequacy within a given family, Dugdale viewed most intergenerational characteristics as "inherited" but denied that they were transmitted solely through genetics or biology. Instead, he argued that the interplay between biology and the social environment caused traits such as poverty and deviance—the social problems of principal concern to Dugdale—to perpetuate themselves across generations.

As the eugenics movement grew, however, its proponents portrayed feeblemindedness as a *direct cause of* poverty, crime, sexual deviance, and moral degeneracy. Family studies after *The Jukes*, including *The Hill Folk* (Danielson and Davenport 1912), *The Nam Family* (Estabrook and Davenport 1912), *The Kallikak Family* (Goddard 1912), "The Pineys" (Kite 1913), and *The Family of Sam Sixty* (Kostir 1916), became more adamant about the danger of feeblemindedness and its causal connection to other forms of degeneracy.[6] For example, Arthur H. Estabrook and Charles B. Davenport (1912, 1) began *The Nam Family* by proclaiming the importance of hereditary feeblemindedness in explaining social deficiency: "The rural community of 'degenerates' usually have this in common: an unusual lack of industry, retardation in school work, and a failure to observe the conventionalities in sex-relationships. There is reason for concluding that the first and second traits are hereditary, and are, in measure, the raison d'être of the foundation of such communities."

In the well-known study *The Kallikak Family*, Henry Goddard also positioned feeblemindedness at the center of his analysis.[7] Whereas Dugdale began his study with male criminals, Goddard began his study with a female patient institutionalized for feeblemindedness named Deborah. In tracing her lineage back six generations, Goddard found a specific point at which her family line diverged, taking two very different paths. One man, Martin Sr., produced two lines of descendants, each with very different characteristics. With his wife, whom Goddard characterizes as a morally upstanding Quaker woman, Martin Sr. produced a line of "fine" citizens. According to Goddard, "All of the legitimate children of Martin Sr. married into the best of families of their state, the descendents of colonial governors, signers of the Declaration of Independence, soldiers, and even the founders of a great university. Indeed, in this family and its collateral branches, we find nothing but good representative citizenship" (Goddard 1912, 30). However, prior to marriage Martin Sr. had had an affair with a feebleminded woman, producing a child born out of wedlock and a subsequent line of descendants, of which Deborah was one. Of the 480 people descended from the affair, Goddard identified 143 as feebleminded and only 43 as "normal." Goddard concluded that "the best material out of which to make criminals, and perhaps the material from which they are most frequently made, is feeblemindedness" (Goddard 1912, 54). Without intelligence or will, all "instincts and appetites are in the direction that would lead to vice."

Because these traits were hereditary, Goddard claimed that social change and environmental uplift could not significantly alter the destiny of individuals with defective genes; for Goddard, the "whole family was a living demonstration of the futility of trying to make desirable citizens from defective stock" (Goddard 1912, 78). Education would be lost on "defectives," as they "had neither the will nor power to learn anything out of books." Economic assistance also would be useless: "If all of the slum districts of our cities were removed tomorrow and model tenements built in their places, we would still have slums in a week's time, because we have these mentally defective people who can never be taught to live otherwise than as they have been living" (Goddard 1912, 71).

Adding to the perceived threat, evidence suggested that the feebleminded were "the most prolific and potentially the most dangerous [class of people] from the standpoint of race standards" (Nebraska Board of Examiners of Defectives 1922 [1916]). With rising numbers and no chance for environmental modification, the only solution perceived to be feasible was to prevent feeblemindedness by shutting down the two avenues by which the unfit increased their numbers: immigration and procreation. To handle the threat of immigration, eugenicists advocated restrictive immigration legislation. To prevent procreation, they advocated institutionalization of the feebleminded during at least the childbearing years, marriage restrictions, and compulsory sterilization.

By 1922, when the eugenicist Harry Laughlin created the Model Eugenical Sterilization Law, the feebleminded topped the long list of types of people
to be subject to compulsory sterilization. The list included the

> (1) Feeble-minded; (2) Insane, (including the psychopathic); (3) Crim-
> inalistic (including the delinquent and wayward); (4) Epileptic; (5) Ine-
> briate (including drug-habitués); (6) Diseased (including the tubercu-
> lous, the syphilitic, the leprous, and others with chronic, infectious and
> legally segregable diseases); (7) Blind (including those with seriously
> impaired vision); (8) Deaf (including those with seriously impaired
> hearing); (9) Deformed (including the crippled); and (10) Dependent
> (including orphans, ne'er-do-wells, the homeless, tramps and paupers).
> (Laughlin 1922, 446–447)

To understand the attention accorded to feeblemindedness and the success
of rights restrictions, though, we must move beyond an examination of the key
ideas of eugenics to consider the relational interests motivating the pursuit of
restrictions. In contrast with the early period of American history, in this era
several groups perceived the control of the feebleminded to be in the best interests of society and a way to advance their personal and professional interests.

Relational Interests and Rights Restrictions

Eugenics provided much of the ideological framework for legislation supporting compulsory sterilization and marriage restrictions, as well as the growth of
institutions for the feebleminded. However, many activists and organizations
drew on eugenics selectively, using portions of eugenic ideology as suited the
advancement of their own, unique interests. In fact, part of the power of eugenics was the flexibility it provided to individuals to advocate very different political positions (Hasian 1996; Paul 1995; Pernick 1997; Trent 1993). Institutional
superintendents, social workers, women's organizations, social elites, and legislators each dissected the ideology of eugenics to pursue their own goals. The
pursuit of rights restrictions for the feebleminded served two primary interests: It enhanced the prestige and expanded the jurisdiction of the professionals charged with the control of those labeled feebleminded, and it stablilized
the social-stratification system through the control of a broader set of people
deemed unfit.

The principal constituency of the eugenics movement consisted of middle-
class, white, Protestant, well-educated professionals (Kevles 1985; MacKenzie 1976). For these individuals, eugenics provided a scientific legitimization of
middle- and upper-class culture, "proving" that middle-class norms were essential to the well-being of the nation and that deviation from such norms could be
socially and economically devastating. By putting forth a biological argument of
morality and deviance, eugenics naturalized the power and privilege of the mid-

dle and upper classes; the middle class did not merely do good things but consisted of good people from good stock whose social position resulted from their naturally superior abilities. In contrast, those who failed or refused to conform to social norms did so because they were personally and biologically defective. The perceived threat of increasing deficiency legitimated and demanded the intervention of professionals, who emerged as the protectors of the nation. Eugenics justified and even glorified the professional mission of social control, a very appealing perspective for professionals (Kevles 1985; MacKenzie 1976; Paul 1995; Rafter 1988). Some professionals had more to gain by the exertion of social control than others, and therefore some professions were more active in the politics of rights restrictions than others. Institutional superintendents in particular had clear interests in restricting the rights of the feebleminded. Reformers had begun their efforts to establish institutions for the care of "idiots" in the mid-1800s, but they faced difficulties in securing funds and proving the importance of their mission, especially when cure rates turned out to be low. Eugenicists dramatized the problems caused by the feebleminded and applauded the institution for protecting society and saving the public money by preventing the birth of new generations of the unfit. Although superintendents might not reliably cure feeblemindedness, they could save the nation from grave peril. Indeed, spreading fear regarding the "threat" of the feebleminded produced far more public and political interest in and financial support for institutions than the promise of transforming idiots into citizens ever had.

Institutional expansion was key to the professional growth and prestige of superintendents because institutions served as centers for research, treatment, and funding (Trent 1993, 1994). Within institutions, additional rights restrictions such as sterilization also served the interests of superintendents. In a compelling analysis, James Trent (1993) shows that superintendents' support of sterilization transformed over time depending on how and whether they considered it useful in meeting institutional demands. Sterilization was first used as a tool of behavior modification for troublesome inmates, especially male inmates. Later, superintendents saw that sterilization might help them manage the problem of overcrowding; rather than using institutionalization as a prophylactic, certain patients could be sterilized and released back into the community, reserving space in the institution for people with more severe disabilities or with additional problems (such as delinquency or lack of family support). As the use of sterilization shifted, so, too, did the population targeted, from troublesome male inmates to high-functioning females (Carey 1998).

Ideally, institutions also provided opportunities for superintendents to use their professional expertise in the community (Trent 1993). Superintendents could work with the public schools to identify and oversee the appropriate placement of feebleminded children. Moreover, they looked to develop a system of community-based mental-health clinics connected to the institution so they could guide the treatment of the feebleminded still residing in the community. Thus, institutions gave superintendents both a centralized site of professional authority and the power to position themselves as central to the health of communities.

Other types of professionals supported rights restrictions for the feebleminded, as well, including educators and social workers. These individuals were attracted to eugenics for some of the same reasons that medical professionals and elites found it compelling: Eugenics supported the place of professionals in society and their control over other populations (Seldon 1999). However, community-based professionals typically sought to remove the feebleminded from the community rather than to expand their professional base by serving them. The profession of social work expanded rapidly in the early twentieth century because of progressive reforms, and social workers criticized the feebleminded for clogging their systems of care and hindering their success rates in community reform (Wenocur and Reisch 1989). For example, Herman Newman (1915, 121), a social worker associated with the Illinois Children's Home and Aid Society, related the story of a feebleminded woman who had been served by seventeen different agencies: "The best social service talent in Chicago has given much time to the case and today, so far, as we can see, we are no nearer a solution than when we started. All this futile effort, because the state of Illinois has no institution for the care of, nor adequate laws for dealing with its feebleminded." For social workers, the idea that feeblemindedness was a permanent and significant disability led them to blame the feebleminded themselves for the failure of social-work services and to advocate their removal from society to achieve social improvements for other populations. Thus, while social workers used eugenics to justify their control over the feebleminded, many preferred to hand "chronic cases" over to institutions.

The field of education also underwent rapid growth after the passage of compulsory education laws, and educators tended to view the feebleminded as hindering their success. Educators often argued that the presence of feebleminded children in the public schools wasted the teacher's time and diverted energy away from other students. According to Bruce B. Robinson (1928, 367–368), director of child guidance for the Board of Education in Newark, New Jersey, "Children who can be recognized as markedly dull stigmatize the special class," making learning more difficult for all children. While slow learners could be accommodated within public education, feebleminded children needed to be segregated in special classrooms, their homes, or institutions. Robinson defended this position, stating, "The public schools are training for citizenship, and a child who, because of very poor learning ability, will never be self supporting or able to participate in civic life is an institutional, and not a public school, problem." Like social workers, community-based educators looked to the institution to handle cases of feeblemindedness so that they could concentrate on children perceived as more likely to be successful.[8]

While these professions had specific interests in institutionalizing and restricting the rights of the feebleminded, elites and other professionals had a more general interest in stabilizing the social-stratification structure by controlling the "unfit," as broadly defined. Scholars have documented considerable support of eugenics among the elite, including prominent individuals such as Mrs. E. H. Harriman, John D. Rockefeller, and Andrew Carnegie. The factors that motivated elites to support eugenics are a matter of debate. In his work *War against the Weak*, Edwin R. Black (2003) argues that elites used eugenics to pursue an agenda of white supremacy and to advance the notion of a "master race." In contrast, many scholars suggest that elites were more concerned with preserving the social order to advance their class interests than with trying to create a master race (Allen 2004; Kevles 1985; Scott 2005). For example, in his study of the funding offered by John D. Rockefeller Jr. in support of eugenics, Nicholas Scott (2005) argues that Rockefeller's principal aim was to ensure an orderly society in which labor and capital could thrive. Rockefeller believed that, at times, the attainment of social order required social uplift of the poor, and at other times, it required restrictive measures to prevent their deviance, dependence, and family instability. Of course, even if their support was primarily intended to preserve social order more broadly, social order as perceived by elites was largely premised on racial, as well as gendered and ablist, hierarchies.

In addition to professionals and elites, a broad range of other groups supported restrictions—most notably, women's organizations. Considering that eugenicists often blamed middle- and upper-class women for neglecting their social duties and targeted "unfit" women for social control, it may seem peculiar that women played a prominent role in supporting eugenic measures. However, middle-class female activists found eugenics to be useful for promoting various political initiatives, including mother's pensions (aid for poor and widowed women with children), access to birth control, access to education, and even the right to vote (Paul 1995). Typical of feminist politics of the day, female reformers valorized women's roles as mothers and housekeepers and claimed that women needed rights and support (such as access to education and mother's pensions) to best perform them (Boris 1991; Skocpol 1992). In their efforts to create state support and recognition of women based on their traditional roles, activists drew sharp distinctions between "worthy" and "unworthy" women. Individuals who met the criteria for responsible, capable, moral womanhood were worthy of support and control over their own lives, while those who failed to meet such criteria would be subject to continued control (Davis 1983; Gordon 1974; Mink 1990). In her analysis of sterilization policies, Molly Ladd-Taylor (2004, 289) shows that, "mothers' pensions might not have been instituted for widows and 'deserving' mothers had not more punitive programs continued for the rest." Thus, feminists argued for the advancement of middle- and upper-class women and denied access to these same advancements to "unfit" women.

This trend is particularly evident within the birth-control movement. Activists, including Margaret Sanger and Marie Stopes, drew clear lines between women who deserved control over their bodies and women whose bodies needed to be controlled (Davis 1983; Gordon 1974; Kennedy 1970; Soloway 1995). For middle- and upper-class women, access to birth control would free them from the burden of unwanted children while improving their ability to parent wanted children. For women from the lower classes, however, birth control could be used to prevent procreation. Speaking at the American Birth Control Conference in 1921, Sanger promoted the use of birth control to stop procreation among "those irresponsible and reckless ones having little regard for the consequences of their acts, or whose religious scruples prevent their exercising control over their numbers. Many of this group are diseased, feebleminded, and are of the pauper element dependent on the normal and fit members of society for their support. There is no doubt in the minds of all thinking people that the procreation of this group should be stopped." Eugenic rhetoric helped substantiate the lines between fit and unfit women, justify greater freedom for the fit, and legitimate continued control of the unfit. By connecting their movement to eugenic circles, feminists also connected it to the powerful scientific and medical communities that enhanced their prestige and legitimacy, even if this alliance came at a cost (Gordon 1974).

In sum, although eugenics had only a small core constituency, restrictions for the feebleminded found support among many diverse groups who used parts of the eugenic ideology to promote and legitimize their own goals. While diverse, each group promoted a hierarchical vision of society and defined the best interests of society from its own perspective. Not surprisingly, each group believed that it played a key role in improving the nation, a mission that depended on defining others as unfit and gaining the power to intervene in their lives.[9] Although these groups' interests were not unified, and at times conflicted, they intersected to promote the "menace of the feebleminded" mythology and rights restrictions.

The Power of the Label "Feebleminded"

The label "feeblemindedness" proved quite effective for establishing social control over a broad range of groups. As intellectual disability became defined as a medical condition with a relatively flexible definition, it had the potential to bring many people under medical control. In addition, feeblemindedness offered a basis for establishing legal restrictions that was still considered well justified at a time when legal justifications for restricting other marginalized groups such as women and African Americans increasingly faced challenges. Finally, the label "feeblemindedness" activated the potential not only for medical and legal control but also for a host of other social-control systems, including the education system, social welfare, and the family.

A Scientific yet Malleable Definition

In the early twentieth century, the diagnosis of intellectual disability simultaneously became more technical and broader and vaguer, allowing for the appearance of scientific objectivity while enabling eugenicists to label many "unfit" people "feebleminded." Evaluations of mental deficiency came to rely on an evaluation of both intelligence and social adaptation. Goddard (1914, 8), for example, defined feeblemindedness as "the state of mental defect existing from birth or from an early age and due to incomplete or abnormal development in consequence of which, the person affected is incapable of performing his duties as a member of society in the position of life to which he is born." To measure intelligence, professionals came to rely on the IQ test, introduced in the United States by Goddard in 1908 (Brown 1992).[10] The IQ test provided the appearance of scientific objectivity while incorporating tremendous measurement biases that disadvantaged those with minimal English-language skills or little education or who came from non-Anglo-Saxon or lower-class backgrounds. Even more ambiguous, the measurement of social adaptation included an assessment of characteristics such as social failure, deficient personal character, and poor judgment. So strong was the emphasis on social adaptation that the scientist Karl Pearson wrote, "It appears to me that the term 'mental defective' ought to be replaced by some such term as 'social inefficient'" (as quoted in Berry and Gordon 1931, 24).

With the creation of these new "objective" measurement tools came more elaborate classification systems. In 1910, the American Association for the Study of the Feeble-Minded established a tripartite schema to differentiate levels of development, dividing the feebleminded into idiots, imbeciles, and morons ("Report of the Committee on Classification of the Feeble-Minded" 2004 [1910]).[11] Idiots were described as individuals on the lowest functional level, whose mental age was that of a one- to two-year-old and who could not learn basic self-care and communication skills. Imbeciles were believed to attain the mental age of a three- to seven-year-old. They were able to care for some of their basic needs and to communicate but were thought to be unable to benefit from education and work. Morons were the largest (approximately 85 percent) and highest-functioning subpopulation. They attained a mental age of between seven and twelve, were able to benefit from education and work, could potentially support themselves, and were not easily identified as disabled; however, they were believed to lack direction, solid judgment, and emotional control.

The criteria for feeblemindedness were so broad and malleable that some estimates identified 30–40 percent of the nation as feebleminded (Paul 1995).[12] Individuals within marginalized groups, especially poor sexually deviant women, were particularly likely to be labeled feebleminded. Eugenicists connected the negative stereotypes associated with both feeblemindedness and womanhood to make the feebleminded woman a representative of the worst of each; she was without the ability to reason, unable to protect herself, and guided purely by her emotions, uncontrolled sexuality, and animal instinct (Katz and Abel 1984; McLaren 1986; Rafter 2004). George Bliss (1919, 12), superintendent of the Indiana School for Feebleminded Youth, described the feebleminded woman as "the most needy of God's creatures, the woman of weak mind, no will, and strong animal instincts, who for centuries has been the prey of mankind." Feebleminded women were thought certain to bear illegitimate children and thereby spawn generations of deficiency. In presenting the "looming problem" of the feebleminded female, Joseph Byers (1916, 225–226), secretary of Pennsylvania's Committee on Provision for the Feeble-Minded, wrote:

> We know that the feeble-minded mother is more prolific in the bearing of children than the normal mother. We know that the feebleminded lack in judgment and resistance to evil influences and that they are therefore unable to adjust themselves to normal life in the community. We know that the social evil is fed from the ranks of feeble-minded women.

In his President's Address to the National Conference of Charities and Correction, Amos Butler (1907, 2) warned that "the debasing and demoralizing influence of an unrestrained feebleminded woman in the community is beyond the comprehension of the uninformed. . . . It is not difficult to get some idea of the expense a feebleminded woman can entail on a community. Aside from this are the evils of her life and the seeds that are sown, of which no one can count the cost. Feeblemindedness bears with it a vast train of woes." Preventing pregnancy among feebleminded women became a primary tool in the fight against degeneracy, poverty, and vice. With the establishment of mothers' pensions and the onset of the Depression, concerns about poor women and their sexuality grew, as did the notion that they were "moral obligated" to limit their family size (Gordon 1974; Skocpol 1992).

Race and ethnicity likewise were linked with feeblemindedness, and again stereotypes of both feeblemindedness and racial and ethnic minorities combined to reinforce the negative image of the feebleminded person of color. Both the feebleminded and ethnic and racial minorities were believed to lack intelligence, the ability to distinguish wrong from right, and civilized sexual impulses. Offering evidence of this point, Lewis Terman (1916), a psychologist at Stanford University, expert on intelligence testing, and author of *The Measurement of Intelligence*, argued that black children and children of other minority backgrounds were "uneducable beyond the nearest rudiments of training. No amount of school instruction will ever make them intelligent voters or capable citizens in the sense of the world." New-wave immigrants were also "proven" to have high rates of mentally defects. Goddard (1917a, 1917b) found that 40–50 percent of recent immigrants were feebleminded, and Harry Hamilton Laughlin (1922) argued that a "high percentage of inborn social inadequacies [were] found within recent immigrants."

Similarly, the poor were associated with feeblemindedness. Nicole Rafter's work in particular highlights the focus of eugenicists on poor, white, rural individuals who were considered as violating middle-class codes of morality and civility. Much of the family-lineage genre focused on poor whites, accusing them of causing the degeneration of the white race and establishing them as the "white other" (Frankenberg 1993).

Thus, the label "feebleminded" supported the control of marginalized groups, while racial and gender stereotypes were used to reinforce the necessity of controlling the feebleminded. As the political scientist Rogers Smith (1997) points out, American citizenship has always contained ascriptive elements. To be American was thought by some to be white, middle class, Anglo-Saxon, and intelligent. For a time, it seemed that everyone who did not conform to the ideal of American citizenship would simply be lumped into the category "feebleminded."

Medical Control

Once defined as feebleminded, individuals could be subjected to medical control based on their presumed mental disability. The rising power of medical institutions offered an important alternative to other systems of control—most notably, the criminal-justice system. Whereas the criminal-justice system offered certain protections to the accused and the prisoner, such as due process during the trial and sentencing procedures, a sentence of a specified duration, and protection against cruel and unusual punishment, medical institutions allowed the compulsory admittance of patients against their will based on only a medical diagnosis, an indefinite time of commitment, and "treatments" that were both painful and harmful to the patients, such as extended periods of isolation, physical restraints, and electric-shock "therapy." In general, the government and the public assumed that medical "treatment" was in the best interests of both the patient and society, and great autonomy was given to physicians to determine the best course of treatment (Conrad and Schneider 1992; Goffman 1961; Snyder and Mitchell 2006; Szasz 1974). On admittance, patients lost all civil rights and almost all means by which to protect themselves or protest their confinement or treatment.[13]

For eugenicists, institutions were to serve as the backbone of the system of control. Their importance for eugenicists lay in their ability to mitigate the negative impact of defectives on society and to prevent the transmission of feeblemindedness to the next generation (e.g., Butler 1907; Byers 1916; Doll 1929a; English 1931; Weidensall 1917). As already discussed, institutions also played an important role in the advancement of professionals concerned with the feebleminded, as they centralized treatment, research, and funding. For parents, institutions "represented both a resource and a restriction" (Brockley 2004, 132). For parents who could not care for a child or who desired that a child receive professional treatment, the institution was often their only option. Parents, recognizing their limited options, often resisted institutionalizing their children or tried to influence institutional authorities to provide better care; however, authority figures disproportionately held power due to the long waiting lists for placements, laws granting them control over patients, and lack of effective monitoring of institutional conditions (Brockley 2004; Dwyer 2004; Ladd-Taylor 2004).

Transforming the Criteria of Liberalism

LIBERALISM AND THE LEGAL VULNERABILITY OF THE FEEBLEMINDED: INCOMPETENCE

Most scholarship has emphasized the importance of the category of feeble-mindedness as a link to medical control, but it also held importance as a legal justification to deny civil rights, even for individuals outside the institution. When eugenics emerged, legal precedent had already existed for restricting the rights of people labeled idiotic or mentally deficient. Yet prior to the twentieth century, courts did not consider a label of mental disability as a clear indication of legal incompetence. In the early twentieth century, eugenicists sought to strengthen the association between legal incompetence and the diagnosis of feeblemindedness while simultaneously eliminating the court's role in evaluating an individual's level of understanding and skills. According to eugenicists, the feebleminded might appear to possess the necessary degree of understanding and skills to exercise rights, but this was only an illusion; feeblemindedness was a profound and hereditary disability that undermined people's judgment and ability to assess rationally their self-interest and the interests of society, and therefore they should not be granted rights.

Henry Goddard's *The Kallikak Family* (1912) illustrates this reasoning. In his study, Goddard focused attention on a female institutional patient named Deborah, whom Goddard claimed was born out of wedlock at an almshouse and came to live at an institution for the feebleminded at age eight. Institutional records characterized Deborah as "high-grade" feebleminded, and Goddard admitted that she possessed significant abilities: "can run an electric sewing machine, cook, and do practically everything about the house. She has no noticeable defect. She is quick and observing, has a good memory, writes fairly, does excellent work in wood-carving and kindergarten" (Goddard 1912, 12). From this description, it seems that Deborah would not have met the early American legal standards for idiocy and that she might have gotten along fairly well in the community, working as a domestic or marrying. Goddard strongly countered this view:

> This is a typical illustration of the mentality of a high grade feeble-minded person, the moron, the delinquent, the kind of girl or woman that fills our reformatories. They are wayward, they get into all sorts of trouble and difficulties, sexually and otherwise, and yet we have been accustomed to account for their defects on the basis of viciousness, environment, or ignorance. . . . [T]oday if this young woman were to leave the Institution, she would at once become prey to evil men or women and would lead a life that would be vicious, immoral, and criminal, though because of her mentality she herself would not be responsible. (Goddard 1912, 12).

Because of her feeblemindedness, and regardless of her apparent skills, Deborah threatened her own and society's well-being. Goddard recommended segregation through her childbearing years to protect society from her and her potential offspring.

In fact, individuals identified as "high-grade" or "morons" became a primary target for eugenic restrictions. Whereas individuals with severe disabilities rarely exercised rights and were readily identified and prevented from doing so if they tried, high-functioning feebleminded individuals often "passed" as normal and thereby gained access to rights and participation in the community. According to eugenicists, with this access they then wreaked havoc on society in the present and perpetuated their deficiency through their offspring.[14] Seth Humphrey (1913, 461), a strident eugenicist, explained the danger of the high-functioning feebleminded person:

> The helplessly idiotic and the insane are fairly taken care of, but the numerous class variously known as "high-grade imbecile," "defective delinquent," "moron" "borderliner" is left in the community,—the man, shifty, alcoholic, thieving, unworkable, habitually in jail; the woman, with enough wit to make a dissolute living but not enough wit to avoid child-bearing, the prolific mother of incapables,—what of her? . . . Society does its very best for her at the particular moment when she is doing her very worst for society—and then turns her adrift again, because "she can take care of herself!"

George Bliss (1916) bemoaned the difficulty of distinguishing between the high-grade feebleminded and the normal person, arguing that this difficulty too often led professionals to allow "morons" to remain in the community. As a result, according to Bliss, communities were left to deal "with an individual with the mind of a child of from eight to twelve years; an individual incapable of mental growth beyond this point, no matter what you do for him in an educational line. This individual, in fact, has even less of responsibility than a normal child of an age similar to the mental age of this person" (Bliss 1916, 263).

In addition to that fact that feeblemindedness was considered a pervasive disorder that was difficult for the untrained eye to detect, the issue of heredity was used to justify the prioritization of medical diagnosis rather than a court assessment of skill or understanding. According to Mendel's theories of recessive traits, even those who appeared healthy and intelligent could be genetically tainted with feeblemindedness and pass on defective genes if allowed to procreate. Genetic taint could be identified only through a professional assessment of lineage and social adaptation, not through an evaluation of an individual's specific level of skill. Thus, in advocating marriage restrictions and compulsory sterilization, Walter Fernald (1915, 297), an institutional superintendent and president of the American Association for the Study of the Feeble-Minded during the 1920s, argued, "The most important point is that feeble-mindedness is highly hereditary, and that each feeble-minded person is a potential source of endless progeny of defect. No feeble-minded person should be allowed to marry or become a parent." Regardless of one's apparent skills, the professional diagnosis of feeblemindedness alone would be sufficient to restrict a person's right to marry.

Institutional policies further reinforced the notion of blanket legal incompetence based on diagnosis regardless of skill level. Entering an institution served as a declaration of complete legal incompetence, which was somewhat paradoxical, since superintendents relied heavily on the labor of inmates for tasks that ranged from cleaning and caring for severely disabled inmates to secretarial work (Trent 1994). Yet no significant challenge arose related either to the state's power to institutionalize or to the assumption of legal incompetence for the institutionalized.

Thus, eugenicists reshaped the connection between incompetence and feeblemindedness. They tended to be most successful where legal precedent restricting rights based on incompetence already existed, and they attained early success in promoting institutional segregation and marriage restrictions because these measures were justifiable within existing law. However, compulsory sterilization generated substantial debate. Little legal precedent existed that allowed the state to violate bodily integrity, and many people resisted the establishment of such a precedent (Larson 1995; Reilly 1991). To justify compulsory sterilization, the U.S. Supreme Court ultimately relied on the precedent of compulsory vaccination, which established the state's right to violate bodily integrity to protect the health and safety of its population from the spread of disease (*Buck v. Bell* 1927). Still, several states never passed sterilization laws, and only a few states ever developed well-funded, expansive sterilization programs. Regional variations also highlight the role of legal precedent. In his study of eugenics in the Deep South, Edward Larson (1995) documented higher levels of resistance to marriage restrictions where there was less historical precedent for such restrictions based on incompetence. Of the states in the Deep South, only Georgia, Mississippi, and South Carolina passed restrictions on marriage related to feeblemindedness, and these states had pre-existing laws invalidating marriage by "lunatics" and "idiots."

Rather than creating the association among feeblemindedness, incompetence, and rights restrictions anew, eugenicists expanded and strengthened the already established connection between incompetence and the denial of rights. At the same time, they drew on emerging ideas about heredity, the medicalization of feeblemindedness, and the expansion of institutionalization to reshape this association and make the identification of feeblemindedness based on eugenic evaluation and medical diagnosis instead of an assessment of skill. By doing so, they greatly expanded the number and type of people who potentially could be denied rights.

LIBERALISM AND THE LEGAL VULNERABILITY OF
THE FEEBLEMINDED: DEPENDENCE

Eugenicists also manipulated notions of dependence. According to liberalism, autonomous citizens possessed the free will necessary to participate in government and the economy. In contrast, eugenicists emphasized that the feebleminded were "weak-willed" and susceptible to influence. For example, Charles Davenport (1913), a biologist and prominent leader of eugenicist thought, argued that the decision-making processes of the mentally deficient were determined purely by their instinctual response to the stimuli around them and that they therefore required an institutional environment filled with positive stimuli in which they would be protected from their own poor judgment and bad external influences.

In addition to mental dependence, eugenicists built their case for institutionalization and rights restrictions around the economic dependence of the feebleminded. With the growth of institutions and the welfare state, the feebleminded no longer depended solely on their families or local communities for support. They had become a tax burden, and eugenicists used this status to push for further exclusion. Unlike good citizens who held jobs and contributed to society, the feebleminded were depicted as a "burden" (Byers 1916; Wack 1913; Wallin 1916), a "dead load" (Humphrey 1913), and a "social encumbrance" (Goddard 1912). Amos Butler entitled his 1907 presidential address to the Conference of Charities and Correction "The Burden of Feeble-Mindedness" and concluded that "feeble-mindedness produces more pauperism, degeneracy, and crime than any other force. It touches every form of charitable activity. It is felt in every part of our land. It affects in some way all our people. Its cost is beyond our comprehension" (Butler 1907, 10).

Eugenicists argued, in the name of the taxpayer, that individuals receiving support from the state should be subjected to additional regulation. According to Franklin Kirkbridge (1912, 1838), a trustee of a New York institution for the feebleminded called Letchworth Village, a cost–benefit analysis indicated the economic error of allowing the feebleminded to exercise rights: "We as a people are awakening to a better realization of the fact that from the standpoint of the taxpayer, if from no other, it is good business to seek out the causes of human waste and stem the tide of degeneracy." In his article "The Imbecile and Epileptic versus the Tax-Payer and the Community," Martin Barr (1902, 163–164), chief physician at the Pennsylvania Training School, claimed that every taxpayer should be interested in the affairs of the feebleminded: "He [the taxpayer] may be willing to contribute to the support of one set of imbeciles, but even the father of a family would be justified in resenting acts which required him to do it twice." From this point of view, the segregation of the feebleminded was the most cost-effective and therefore the best solution for the taxpayer. Eugenics rhetoric emphasized that institutionalization was not the only cost to the taxpayer. Left to their own devices in the community, the feebleminded, due to their high fertility and lack of productivity, cost the nation dearly. In *Buck v. Bell*, Supreme Court Justice Oliver Wendell Holmes Jr. called on those who "sap the strength of the state" to sacrifice their rights "in order to prevent us from being swamped with incompetence," reinforcing the idea that dependence justified the loss of rights.

THE LEGAL VULNERABILITY OF THE FEEBLEMINDED: DEVIANCE AND MORAL CONFORMITY

Eugenicists also built on and transformed the relationship between incompetence and criminal justice. In early America, "idiots" were potentially granted leniency if caught committing crimes because they were assumed to be incapable of adequately understanding right and wrong, a foundation of the criminal-justice system. Eugenicists, however, asserted that the feebleminded were certain to become criminals and should therefore be treated as such. Many studies in this period connected feeblemindedness with crime and delinquency. J. Harold Williams (1915), director of research at the Whittier State School, found that of the nearly sixty thousand children institutionalized for delinquency, one-third were "definitely" feebleminded. A report regarding New York State's Sing Sing prison claimed that 59 percent of inmates had some mental abnormality and 80.6 percent of recidivists were "intellectually defective" (Davies 1923). Dr. V. V. Anderson (1919, 257–258), medical director for the National Committee for Mental Hygiene, declared, "At least 50 per cent of the inmates of state prisons throughout the country are suffering from some form of nervous or mental disease and defect. . . . These individuals furnish a substantial nucleus to that most expansive body, the recidivists who clog the machinery of justice, who spend their lives in and out of penal institutions and furnish facts for the astonishing facts of recidivism." Not only was feeblemindedness connected to crime but it also led to the worst kind of criminality: the recidivist who could not be rehabilitated within the prison system.

Even when no evidence of deviance was apparent, eugenicists argued that the potential for deviance among the feebleminded was so great that they all should be subjected to restrictions. Thus, the Training School at Vineland, New Jersey, held as an early principle that "every feeble-minded child is a potential criminal" (Goddard 1932). Ideally, segregation would occur early in life and at the time of diagnosis to prevent deviance rather than after a crime had already been committed. Anderson (1919, 259) argued that "proper institutional provision for the feebleminded at a time when all these antisocial problems are preventable is an idea that the State can most profitably set itself to achieve."

Like criminals, the feebleminded could be restricted because they posed a threat to the nation's security (O'Brien 2006). Unlike criminals, because they lacked competence and autonomy, they were established as a separate class to be dealt with in a parallel system that allowed for proactive control *before* a crime was committed.

Conflicts between the Rights of the Feebleminded
and the Protection of Society

Liberalism frames the denial of rights as a result of individual incapacity, but it also recognizes relationality. In other words, the rights of one individual can be removed, at least temporarily, when in conflict with the rights of another individual. In the eugenics era, the rights of people with disabilities were constantly positioned as antagonistic to the rights of people without disabilities. For example, Edgar A. Doll (1929b, 25), director of research at the Vineland Training School, justified the removal of disabled children from public schools by showing the conflict between the presence of disabled children and the rights of non-disabled children, stating that "normal children have a right to expect that their school progress should not be retarded because of the presence of subnormal children in their classes." Similarly, the attorney J. Kenyon (1914, 466–467) argued that procreation by the feebleminded violated the rights of other citizens: "It is a well-known principle of law that a person owning real estate . . . cannot use this property in such a way as to be a nuisance to his neighbor. Is it less true that the faculty of procreation is the gift of nature, a right in every human being, but nevertheless a right that must be exercised in a way that it will not interfere with the rights of neighbors? Will not these rights be interfered with if procreation be permitted by the adjudged criminal, the adjudged insane, idiot or degenerate?"

More broadly, proponents of rights restrictions depicted the rights of the feebleminded as an impingement on the rights of "society." This was especially true for procreation by the feebleminded. Whether or not the feebleminded understood the nature of procreation or could support their children, procreation supposedly weakened the genetic pool and burdened the state and therefore stood in conflict with the best interests of society. For Kenyon, procreation by the feebleminded undermined the very promises of the Constitution for the American citizenry. Writing in defense of voting restrictions, Mary Wolfe (1924, 132), superintendent of the Laurelton State School in Pennsylvania, similarly positioned the rights of the feebleminded against the rights of society: "The presence of these defectives in the electorate is a danger to our Country. Each one of these votes is capable of neutralizing the vote of an intelligent citizen." Jessie Spaulding Smith (1914, 370), a special educator, explained that "we are rapidly coming to the realization that it is not only our right, but our duty to protect the future from the evil of the past and present." The presence of people with disabilities—and, indeed, their very existence—seemed to conflict with the rights of other citizens to live peaceably in a well-ordered, harmonious society.

To note, while drawing on liberalism, eugenicists did not by any means abide strictly by this political philosophy. Instead, they used ideas of race, ethnicity, gender, and ablism to define a "good" member of society in such a way that "competence" and "independence" became code words for moral and racial conformity. While courts may have wanted justifications for the denial of rights couched in liberalism, the masses tended to be just as content with, or even more energized by, messages that were simply racist, classist, sexist, and ablist.

Eugenicists portrayed all three characteristics—incompetence, dependence, and deviance—as inherent in the feebleminded and therefore as traits that would be passed through the generations if the feebleminded were allowed to reproduce. In addition, the deficiency of the feebleminded made it impossible for them to exercise their rights without impinging on the rights of other citizens and on society. These arguments did not derive simply from new understandings of feeblemindedness but relied heavily on meta-narratives of citizenship and rights that accepted incompetence, dependence, and immorality as legitimate reasons for exclusion. In many ways, the feebleminded individual came to epitomize the "unfit citizen," and his or her exclusion went largely unquestioned. But because of the loose definition of feeblemindedness and the intersection of stereotypes and exclusions, individuals within other marginalized groups could be labeled feebleminded and similarly restricted.

Additional Mechanisms of Control

In addition to medical and legal control, the feebleminded were subjected to several other community-based systems that could exert varying levels of control, including the education system, the social-service system, and the family. Ideally, social control as imagined by eugenicists would involve a broad range of professional and nonprofessional systems that would infiltrate almost all areas of life.

Within the community, the family served as one of the most important sources of control, both before and after medicalization. Traditionally, parents held responsibility for determining the best interests of their children until those children reached adulthood. For the feebleminded, however, the continued need for support and questions about competence often extended parental control into adulthood. Due to their interest in and responsibility for the well-being of their children, parents could at times secure formal guardianship over their disabled adult offspring simply by showing that it would be in their offspring's best interests. More often, this level of formality was not even required. Guardianship of disabled adult offspring was largely assumed until the 1930s, at which time newly emerging parental organizations began seeking better laws and formal processes to formally establish their authority and designate guardians to take care of their offspring after their own death (Bruggeman 1980; Jost 1980).

Professionals such as Edward Seguin, the first president of the Association of Medical Officers of American Institutions for Feeble-Minded and Idiotic Persons, hoped that professionals could guide parents to replicate the kind of care found in institutions in their home (Brockley 2004). However, families could not be easily regulated by professionals and usually did not provide the methodical approach that professionals desired. Professionals criticized families for spoiling their disabled children through their "misguided attempts to make up to the child through physical means that which is mentally lacking" (Smith 1922, 60). Moreover, professionals worried that mothers would exhaust themselves in the care of their disabled child and neglect their responsibilities to their other children, spouse, and housework, leading to overall family dysfunction. In addition, as feeblemindedness came to be seen as a hereditary disorder, professional distrust in the abilities and moral worth of parents grew. When aligned with professionals' wishes, though, authorities seemed to give great weight to parental wishes, at least compared with the significance given to the wishes of the person with a disability. For example, parents were frequently allowed to consent to sterilization procedures, and parental opinion was taken into account in institutionalization proceedings (Woodside 1950). Yet parents and professionals, especially institutional superintendents and social workers, often found themselves in conflict, disputing diagnoses, treatment options, and appropriate parenting styles (Abel 1996; Brockley 2004; Dwyer 2004).

The education system served as another locus of community control—one that was far more amendable to adhering to professional standards and working with institutional colleagues. As the community organization responsible for educating all children, the public school represented an ideal site for the early diagnosis, labeling, tracking, supervision, and channeling of individuals into institutions, if necessary. Jessie Taft (1918, 547), a member of the Mental Hygiene Committee of New York State's Charities Aid Association, argued that "the school and the ungraded class give us the nucleus for a system of supervision which could be worked in so simply that it would not only *not* meet with opposition but would be welcomed by the children and by the parents." Similarly, according to Edgar A. Doll (1929a, 172), "Special classes for the feebleminded constitute one of the most important means for the control of feeblemindedness as a community problem. . . . They receive children at an age when training and habit formation are most effective. They assist in stabilizing these children while of school age in the community, thereby anticipating their adjustment in the community as adults." For eugenicists, public schools ideally would implement a multilayered approach in which they would educate those with mild disabilities while channeling those with greater needs into institutions. In the public schools, children would be effectively supervised while also taught the norms of society and, one hoped, given the tools necessary for self-sufficiency.

Social-service agencies played their own, unique role in regulating home life. For people with disabilities and their families who needed public assistance, social workers held tremendous power, as they could approve or withhold access to services and financial assistance, recommend sterilization or institutionalization, or begin procedures to remove children from the home. Many forms of assistance allowed social workers access to clients' homes, and they could use this access to impose moral and social rules on the recipients of assistance. Moreover, as social workers were linked with other systems of control, including institutions, they could potentially channel people into more restrictive settings (Carey 1998; Ladd-Taylor 2004; Woodside 1950).

Most people labeled feebleminded resided in the community, where regulation proved to be far more difficult than in the institution. Therefore, eugenicists relied on a range of social structures, including the law, education, social services, and the family, to control those labeled feebleminded and restrict their access to rights. These structures functioned at least somewhat independently from the medical profession. Within each sphere of activity, "competent" professionals or family members had the authority to assert specific types of control over the feebleminded and to offer differential and limited access to rights. Thus, the label "feebleminded" subjected people to a pervasive, multi-layered system of control.

This diverse system of control parallels the experience of other marginal populations. Women faced restrictions within the family, regulation by social service, and protections within the workplace. African Americans faced harsh restrictions within almost all social institutions, as well as extensive violence. In some ways, though, the system of social control was very different based on the label "feebleminded." Although women and slaves were defined as dependents, their productive and reproductive roles were typically considered very important to the functioning of society. People with mental and intellectual disabilities, however, were perceived as having little to contribute to society and were largely seen as "surplus" (Farber 1968). Their status as a medicalized population also legitimated the use of specific forms of restriction in the name of treatment. Because the diagnosis of feeblemindedness was vague, and the corresponding system of social control was multifaceted, the label "feebleminded" could be used to differentiate those unworthy of rights from other citizens (Scull 1977; Stone 1984).[15] Middle-class, morally "fit" women could be granted greater access to civic participation, while poor or sexually deviant women could continue to be classified as feebleminded and restricted from exercising their rights. Immigrants who assimilated to Anglo norms and values could be successfully integrated and allowed full participation in society, while those who were perceived as failing or refusing to assimilate could be labeled feebleminded and denied full citizenship. Increased integration could be granted to those within marginalized groups who met certain criteria, while those who failed to meet particular standards could be labeled feebleminded and denied rights.

Strains on Exclusion

Criticisms of Eugenics: Science, Faith, and Liberalism

Eugenics always had its critics. Just as eugenicists exploited liberal notions to pursue their goals, others wielded the same concepts for the advancement of their own, opposing interests. Although people in this time period rarely defended the feebleminded as upstanding citizens, critics of eugenics stressed that the problem was not as great as eugenicists claimed; the problem could not be solved through the imposition of restrictions; and the restrictions themselves posed problems as they potentially opened the door to totalitarian control.

Developments in the sciences cast grave doubts about the merit of the research conducted by eugenicists. As the study of genetics diverged from eugenics, geneticists stressed the complexities of heredity (compared with the simplistic assumptions made by eugenicists), as well as the rigorous scientific methods required to uncover such complexities (compared with the family and pedigree studies so lauded by eugenicists). Raymond Pearl (1927), a geneticist at Johns Hopkins University, compared the two fields and saw eugenics falling far short of scientific standards: "In preaching as they do, that like produces like, and that superior people will have superior children and inferior people will have inferior children, the orthodox eugenicists are going contrary to the best established facts of genetic science, and are, in the long run, doing their cause harm." In 1935, the geneticist Hermann Muller declared that eugenics had become "hopelessly perverted" into a pseudoscientific façade for "advocates of race and class prejudice, defenders of vested interests of church and states, Fascists, Hitlerists, and reactionaries generally" (quoted in Kevles 1985, 164).

Other scientific fields also took part in the growing schism concerning heredity and biological determinism. In 1938, the American Neurological Association formed a committee, chaired by Dr. Abraham Myerson, to study eugenic sterilization. In a landmark scientific treatise against compulsory eugenic sterilization, the committee dismissed many of the key tenets of eugenics. Myerson's committee found no threat of race suicide or reasons for extraordinary alarm about the feebleminded; it claimed that "all the actual statistics on the matter and the biological trends as indicated by the marriage rate, birth rate, death rate, divorce rate, and fertility rate indicate that these groups are not increasing and, if anything, are declining; that while the problem is huge, there is nothing new or increasingly alarming about it" (Myerson 1938, 254; see also Trent 2001). Furthermore, the committee found significant problems with the common methodologies used by eugenicists, including their use of small sample sizes and hearsay to constitute evidence and their failure to study the psychopathic constitution of the general population. The committee concluded, "Any law concerning sterilization passed in the United States under the present state of knowledge should be voluntary and regulatory rather than compulsory" (Myerson 1938, 256).[16]

Criticism also came from the fields of psychology, sociology, and anthropology. Franz Boas, a leading scholar in cultural anthropology, was among the earliest and most fervent academic critics of eugenics within the social sciences. By the 1930s, cultural studies such as those by Margaret Mead lent substantial support to the importance of environment in determining behavior and social adaptation. Even eugenicists began to rethink the scientific bases of their theories. For example, in 1919, Walter Fernald, a leading American eugenicist, found that the feebleminded had a low marriage rate and birthrate, challenging his own, earlier assertions of pending race suicide. As some professionals identified with eugenics because it supported their role as experts, scientists increasingly distanced themselves from it because it lessened respect for their fields.

The Catholic church also offered sustained and heated criticism of eugenics.[17] In his study of sterilization laws, Philip R. Reilly (1991, 118) found that "by the mid-twenties, representatives of Catholic dioceses and lay Catholic groups were often the most important opponents of eugenic sterilization bills." The papal encyclical *Casti Connubi* of 1930 took a clear stand against sterilization, encouraging strong resistance from lay organizations to sterilization bills so that, by the 1940s, the Catholic church coordinated a "sustained drive" against sterilization (Reilly 1991). Unlike the scientific community, the Catholic church developed a strong grassroots campaign against pro-sterilization legislation, rallying its members to engage in political struggles to defeat such bills. Moreover, more than just hard scientific evidence, the church offered an ideology that debunked the moral assumptions of eugenics, presented the danger of state intervention for democracy and faith, and offered an alternative vision of justice and humanity.

Practical Problems of Managing Control and Contribution

Rights are not granted or denied solely due to scientific evidence, ideologies of justice, or the "best" interpretation of liberalism; money and politics influence decisions about rights, as well. Politicians and the public had hoped that rights restrictions would lower the economic and social costs of feeblemindedness and its "related" conditions, such as poverty and crime; however, the eugenic plan for total restriction of the feebleminded, including identification, registration, segregation, marriage restriction, and sterilization for upward of three hundred fifty thousand people, by some estimates, required the commitment of a remarkable quantity of resources (Barr 1915). The institutionalized population expanded rapidly, but still there was not nearly enough room for those who "required" institutionalization, and waiting lists continued to grow. States did not commit the funds necessary even to maintain their institutions according to standards of decency, let alone to develop an efficient system of total exclusion (Trent 1994). Total segregation and exclusion of all people labeled feebleminded came to be seen as political and financially impractical.

This led superintendents and other interested parties to debate who *really* needed to be controlled, for what period of time, and to what degree. One of the first lines of demarcation was based on the individual's level of functioning. As discussed, eugenicists and institutional superintendents had stressed the need to control all "feebleminded" people, and especially "morons," a goal designed to solidify the importance of trained diagnosis and to expand their potential patient base. However, the public typically wanted to reserve segregation for the lowest functioning, the multiply handicapped, and delinquent individuals, as they were seen as most burdensome to the community. Growing waiting lists and pressure to admit people with severe disabilities intensified debates concerning whom to institutionalization and the duration of institutionalization (Dwyer 2004). Although some superintendents had depicted feeblemindedness as a pervasive disorder requiring lifelong segregation, they increasingly began to acknowledge (in the tradition of the earliest founders of schools for the feebleminded) that many feebleminded individuals could participate in society, especially if sterilized or otherwise infertile. Sterilization emerged as a way to solve the dilemma of institutional overcrowding; rather than segregating the highly functioning, they could be sterilized and paroled, thereby increasing space for inmates with more severe disabilities (Trent 1993). To make the argument for sterilization as a means of managing overcrowding, however, superintendents now had to define a segment of the feebleminded as otherwise able to participate in the community. Examining Kentucky's institutional population, George Skinner claimed in 1934 that 35 percent of Kentucky's inmates "could safely be released in good times, and could make their own way" (Skinner 1934, 174). Similarly, Doll (1929b, 23) argued that "not all feeble-minded require permanent custodial care. Many of them are found in homes where they can be cared for by their own relatives without menace to the state. Still others are sufficiently stable and industrious so that they can make a fair living under favorable conditions."

The growing acknowledgment that some of the feebleminded could live and succeed in the community exacerbated debates about other rights, such as the right to marry. Although the eugenics movement had staunchly supported marriage restrictions, now, with the growing acceptance that some feebleminded individuals would remain in the community, professionals increasingly pointed out the positive functions of marriage in the lives of the sterilized feebleminded. Once the potential for childbearing had been eliminated, marriage contributed to the normality of the feebleminded, provided them with a social support system and potentially two incomes, and enhanced their ability to contribute to society. Paul Popenoe (1928, 70), an early advocate of sterilization, conducted research on marriage among sterilized feebleminded individuals living in the community and found that it increased their ability to "make a useful adjustment to society, lead a relatively normal and happy life, relieve the state of the burden of support, and make room for patients needing custodial care at the state institution." Similarly, in his presidential address to the American Psychiatric Association, Walter English (1931, 8) showed the great likelihood that sterilized female parolees could marry, maintain "comfortable homes," and become "worthy citizens."

Professionals also returned to the idea, common among superintendents in the late 1800s, that the feebleminded could work in their communities. While admission to an institution stripped inmates of their right to make contracts, professionals showed little interest in restricting the right to contract for feebleminded individuals in the community. Professionals rarely argued that the feebleminded should not work because they were incompetent to understand the contractual relationship between employer and employee. On the contrary, superintendents increasingly offered examples of successful parolees who held jobs and supported themselves in the community. In a study of New Hampshire parolees, B. W. Baker (1939) concluded that "85% are adjusted in the community," a conclusion based primarily on rates of economic self-support. In his study of special-education graduates, Charles Berry (1925, 442) similarly concluded that "80 percent of the special-class children possess the possibilities of developing into self-supporting, law-abiding citizens." Indeed, professionals even spoke of the advantages of the feebleminded as laborers. For example, George Bliss (1919, 14) recommended feebleminded men for manual work in the military, noting, "While the feeble-minded should be eliminated from the active service of a soldier, there is a class of war work the moron can do just as well, if not better, than the normal human being. The manual work of building camps, ditching, grading and rough labor of all description can be done as well by this class as by laborers receiving from $3.00 to $4.00 dollars a day."

The renewed focus on keeping the feebleminded in the community also brought about a renewed emphasis on access to education, both in the institution and in the community. Special education in the community could serve both to control and to prepare children for self-sufficiency and citizenship. As discussed, special education was seen as key to community control. In addition, a "minor narrative" emerged in the professional literature suggesting that children with disabilities had a "right" to education, albeit in segregated settings. In his proposed plan for Missouri's state care of the feebleminded, J. E. Wallace Wallin (1916), a leading psychologist and early advocate of special education, recommended the creation of a mandatory special-education law to ensure that disabled children received an education, which would then benefit society through their productivity and adaptation. William Hodson (1919, 211), director of the Children's Bureau of St. Paul, suggested that education for feebleminded children was an obligation of the state. "The education and training of the higher grade defective children," he wrote, "is an obligation no less compelling than that of educating normal children, and there should always be room to receive such children." Of course, this "right" had many limitations, including that education would be offered primarily in segregated settings and only to individuals of a "higher grade," but it still represents an early conceptualization of rights for this population.

In this era, the overriding concern was social control of the feebleminded; however, participation by the feebleminded was allowed in some spheres of life, and even encouraged at times, to provide community-based supervision and to encourage productivity and moral conformity. In this light, providing limited access to education and work seemed logical to many professionals and policymakers, as both enhanced the likelihood of productivity and offered physical sites where professionals could supervise the feebleminded. Moreover, neither work nor education, particularly if segregated, gave the feebleminded much opportunity to have a negative impact on their communities. Even marriage among the infertile was seen as promoting normalcy and productivity. However, procreation was almost never encouraged, even by individuals who opposed compulsory sterilization, as it was seen as too costly for society. In other words, rights were subjected to a cost–benefit analysis in which the benefits of supervision and contribution were weighed against the potential harm to society (Dwyer 2004; Ladd-Taylor 2004).[18]

The balancing of exclusion and inclusion can be vividly illustrated by the report of the 1930 White House Conference on Children in a Democracy. The report proposed a five-stage "attack" on the growing problem of mental deficiency, including state registration of the feebleminded, community supervision, institutionalization, and sterilization. Immediately following this plan, however, came the "Bill of Rights for the Handicapped Child," which proposed to ensure for each child the right "to an education so adapted to his handicap that he can be economically independent and have the chance for the fullest life of which he is capable" and "to be brought up and educated by those who understand the nature of the burden he has to bear and consider it a privilege to help him bear it." This odd juxtaposition shows that control was the centerpiece of the era, but it was later combined with a growing recognition of the importance of participation in the community, particularly in education and work for the individuals who would remain in the community.

Variations in Access

Access to rights for the feebleminded continued to vary tremendously in this era by state, setting, and demographic factors. Although we tend to talk of trends as if they are national, legislation affecting rights was passed and implemented on a state or even on a local level. Some states established expansive institutional and sterilization programs, while others did very little to formally restrict or segregate the feebleminded. California and North Carolina illustrate the variation by state found in this era. Reports at the time indicated that California had one of the highest rates of mental disability, presumably due to the influx of pioneers, immigrants, and people seeking their fortunes, and its legislature showed an early interest in supporting mental-health initiatives. By 1905, California had five mental-health hospitals and a home for the feebleminded. The state's system of mental health at the time was directed by the general superintendent of the Commission on Lunacy, a position held by F. W. Hatch. Hatch was a committed eugenicist and used his influence to expand institutionalization, win passage of one of the nation's earliest sterilization laws (passed in 1909 and amended in 1913 and 1917), and develop the nation's largest sterilization program. In the first twenty years of legal sterilization, California sterilized more people than all other states combined. In addition to Hatch, an active eugenics community, including the Human Betterment League, the Eugenics Society of Northern California, and many influential elites, also lent support to eugenics in California (Stern 2005).

By contrast, at the beginning the twentieth century, North Carolina had no institution specifically for the feebleminded, and it placed little importance on feeblemindedness as a problem because it lacked all of the following: strong professional and academic communities that created and promoted eugenic research and rhetoric, leaders who effectively pursued eugenics as a key political issue, and abundant state-level resources to dedicate to resolving social problems.[19] North Carolina did not establish its first institution for the feebleminded until 1914, did not pass a sterilization statute until 1929, and failed to use its sterilization statute for several years after it was passed. According to the historian Mark Smith (2005, 897), "Although economic *thought* facilitated eugenicist ideas, economic *realities* in the Depression-era South hampered the actual implementation of eugenics as medical and social practice."[20] This brief comparison illustrates that one's state of residence could greatly affect one's likelihood of institutionalization, sterilization, or other restrictions.

Demographic factors such as race, gender, and economic standing also continued to have a complex relationship with intellectual disability and rights restrictions. As seen prior to the twentieth century, being a minority could potentially increase one's likelihood of being labeled feebleminded and experiencing institutionalization and sterilization (Stern 2005). For example, in their study of sterilization in California, Ezra Gosney and Paul Popenoe (1929) found that immigrants, African Americans, and Mexicans all experienced disproportionately high rates of sterilization. However, racial and ethnic minorities in other places were often denied services given to people with disabilities, and this exclusion actually served to protect them from these mechanisms of social control.

A look at sterilization by race in North Carolina can provide a brief example of the complex interconnections between race, gender, and feeblemindedness. From 1934 to 1942, African Americans made up 25 percent of those sterilized in North Carolina, roughly equivalent to their proportion of the population (North Carolina Eugenics Board 1942). If this figure is broken down by gender, though, African American men were twice as likely to be sterilized as African American women, a surprising statistic given that, among whites, women were far more likely to be sterilized than men (Carey 1998). The African American men subjected to sterilization overwhelmingly came from the institutional population, where sterilization was used to control their "disruptive" behavior within these institutions. By contrast, women who underwent sterilization were largely recruited from the community and were usually returned to the community following the procedure. Because African American women were typically denied access to public assistance, social workers did not have the same access to them as they did to poor white women; nor did social workers necessarily consider it "appropriate" to offer such "services" to African American women (Woodside 1950). To add to the complexity, the denial of sterilization could also be seen as a hardship and form of exclusion. While in many cases, including the famous Carrie Buck case, sterilization was performed either against the wishes of the individual or without her knowledge, some poor women permitted themselves or even asked to be labeled feebleminded in order to be sterilized, a birth-control procedure that they could not otherwise have afforded (Ladd-Taylor 2004). These programs would have been largely out of reach for poor African American women.

Rates of institutionalization show similar variations by race, which can be differentially interpreted whether one sees institutionalization as a privilege (access to treatment) or as a form of control (segregation). The 1923 U.S. Census of Institutions (U.S. Department of Commerce 1926) indicates that 7.4 per hundred thousand whites had been admitted to institutions for feeblemindedness, whereas only 2.5 per hundred thousand African Americans had been admitted; twenty states with institutions did not provide any institutional "services" for African Americans. A decade later, whites were still disproportionately over-represented. Analyzing data from 1933, the Census Bureau reported that "the ratio for Negroes is very low, as compared with that for whites, mainly because a large proportion of the Negroes live in the South, where the provision for caring for Negro mental defectives and epileptics in special State institutions is small" (U.S. Department of Commerce 1935, 22).

As in early America, social class also played a role in the relationship between feeblemindedness and rights restrictions. On one hand, states continued to use segregation and rights restrictions as a means to deal with "problem" individuals in the community, including the poor and deviant. In her study of the first institution for feebleminded women, Rafter (2004) shows that of 414 residents, almost all had come from poorhouses, and many were institutionalized because they were poor women who were potentially sexually active. On the other hand, families with means could at times pay for private institutional care and, in a time of long waiting lists, may have had greater success in placing their children. Under such circumstances, it is unclear whether such placement should be viewed as a privilege or a restriction, or both, as families were purchasing a service in high demand, yet the individual being institutionalized usually had little say in the initial decision and no recourse after the decision was made.[21] The differential exposure to institutionalization and sterilization thereby calls into question the whole interpretation of these measures as "services" versus "restrictions."

Hence, despite the dream of eugenicists to create a pervasive and methodical system of social control for all of the feebleminded, access to rights varied by the right in question and by the individual's ability level, location, gender, race, and other contextual factors. The popularity of eugenic ideas fueled a growing institutionalized population; however, the majority of people with intellectual disabilities remained outside institutions, despite eugenicists' great efforts. In general, people with intellectual disabilities faced significant formal mechanisms of exclusion, but for some people there were opportunities to participate in some spheres of life, especially spheres of life that encouraged self-support and a contribution to society and that offered professional supervision.

Conclusion

The desire of professionals to advance their interests through the control of the feebleminded and the desire of elites to control marginal populations coalesced in the eugenics agenda to restrict the rights of those labeled feebleminded. In doing so, this movement drew on and expanded the legal precedent for denying the feebleminded rights based on incompetence, dependence, and deviance. In conjunction, eugenicists created a flexible definition of feeblemindedness that potentially enveloped a diverse set of marginalized populations and subjected them to a pervasive system of control via the medical institution, legal restrictions, the family and guardianship, and the special-education and social-welfare systems. Despite enthusiasm about the merits of social control, legislators in the end pushed to institutionalize only individuals with severe disabilities, a history of deviance, or a lack of social support rather than everyone who might be labeled feebleminded. Those who could reside with their families and contribute to their own support were usually expected to do so. But for people with disabilities to remain in the community, they needed at least to have some opportunity to participate in typical activities. Thus, occasionally towns and states encouraged participation in spheres of life that allowed the feebleminded to make a positive contribution and provided supervision for them. Participation was granted not as a right but, rather, because one "passed" as a person without a disability or proved one's potential for contribution. Therein, policymakers secured some positive contribution while offering individuals labeled feebleminded little control over their own lives and little power over society.

5

Professionals and the
Potentially Productive Citizen

Histories tend to examine the early and late twentieth century to illustrate the dramatic change that has occurred in the politics of intellectual disability but gloss over the years between the 1940s and early 1960s, depicting them as an uneventful time *between* the eugenics era and the civil-rights era. This period of time, however, represents an important stage in the conceptualization of rights and intellectual disability.

During this time, we see multiple, competing narratives of rights and what came to be called "mental retardation" at play, including the modification of older narratives that emphasized the danger that people with mental retardation posed to the citizenry and the emergence of new narratives that stressed the positive characteristics of this population and their potential contributions to society. Among the new narratives, professionals documented the productive capabilities of people with mental retardation and justified their access to rights and services as a means to develop these capabilities. Parents, the focus of Chapter 6, also worked to create a positive image of their children but one that was less dependent on the idea of productivity. Both professionals and parents increasingly drew on the language of rights to convey the state's moral obligation to people with mental retardation and to demand a variety of services for them, including education, treatment, and work opportunities. While using a language of rights, the formal passage of "rights" was not their top priority; rather, it was a conceptual tool to expand services. They drew on the idea of rights if it led to services and sacrificed it if it did not. Thus, this era was foundational in the development of more positive conceptions of people with mental retardation and an expansion of their human and social rights, but the paternalistic approach to care, services, and rights largely remained unchanged.

Overview of Services and Rights:
Changes and Continuities

From the 1940s to the mid-1960s, the field of education perhaps underwent the greatest transformation among services and rights for people with retardation. In the early twentieth century, the vast majority of children with mental retardation were excluded from any kind of educational program, and the special education that did exist was usually tied to institutional placement. During the 1940s and 1950s, the field of special education experienced a renewed surge of interest, funding, and legislative support, leading to a dramatic increase in the number of special-education classes offered and the number of students enrolled in these classes (Winzer 1993). Between 1948 and 1953 alone, enrollment in special schools and classes increased by 47 percent; the number of school districts providing special education increased by 83 percent; and the number of special-education teachers increased by 48 percent. From 1948 to 1966, the general school population rose by 70 percent, but the special-education population rose by 500 percent. Of course, children with mental retardation were not the only group contributing to the growth of special education, but their numbers in the classroom increased dramatically. Many states passed new laws and expanded existing ones to encourage, mandate, or fund special education, so that "by 1946 there were well over a hundred laws in the United States dealing with the education of exceptional children" (Winzer 1993, 375). Despite these positive changes, by 1966, 50 percent of children labeled retarded still received no education; 50 percent of local school systems still offered no special-education programs; and the dominant model for special-education programs still advocated education in segregated settings for only the highest-functioning retarded children, or those deemed "educable" (Mackie 1969; Trent 1994).

Along with improvements in education, the number of people served by vocational training and employment services increased considerably between 1940 and 1960. When the federal government established vocational rehabilitation programs in 1920, legislators did not include people with mental retardation among those who could be served. However, the Barden-LaFollette Amendments (PL 78-113), passed in 1943, established people with mental retardation as eligible for rehabilitation services and widened the scope of activities considered rehabilitation. In the 1950s, under the direction of Mary Switzer, the Office of Vocational Rehabilitation (OVR) further expanded services to people with disabilities in general and particularly to people with mental retardation.[1] From 1954 through 1961, federal funds for vocational rehabilitation overall increased threefold, while "the estimated funds for vocational rehabilitation of the mentally retarded increased 15-fold" (President's Panel on Mental Retardation 1962). The surge of funding supported many different projects but especially encouraged the development of "sheltered workshops," a model of employment that theoretically offered a protective setting in which individuals with mental retardation could learn and engage in productive paid work at their own pace with the guidance of knowledgeable professional staff (Dyb-wad 1964). As with education, these advances only scratched the surface of existing needs. The 1962 President's Panel on Mental Retardation estimated that approximately seventy-five thousand retarded youths left school each year with the potential for self-support, but only three thousand or four thousand received work-related services.

In addition to community-based educational and vocational programs, the number of institutions for people with mental retardation continued to grow. In his history of intellectual disability, James Trent (1994, 250) documented that "between 1950 and 1970, state authorities built, refurbished, and added to more public facilities than in any other period of American history." Between 1946 and 1967, the number of residents in institutions for people with men-tal retardation rose from 116,828 to 193,188, an increase of 65 percent, nearly twice the increase of the general population. While the federal government funded the construction of institutional facilities, it offered little money for maintenance and programming. As a result, conditions within institutions con-tinued to deteriorate, and criticism mounted.

In this time period, the government also expanded income-support pro-grams for people with disabilities, including people with mental retardation. While Social Security "survivor benefits" (income support offered to the minor children of a covered worker who died) typically ended when the offspring turned eighteen, an amendment passed in 1956 extended these benefits to peo-ple with developmental disabilities throughout their adulthood. By the 1960s, about two-thirds of adult recipients of child survivor benefits had a diagnosis of mental retardation (Shorter 2000).

While the provision of services improved, individuals with mental retar-dation saw little change in their access to "adult" political and civil rights. To note some improvements, the number of sterilization procedures performed decreased; approximately twenty-three thousand operations were performed in the 1930s, approximately sixteen thousand in the 1940s, and ten thousand in the 1950s (Robitscher 1973). Yet according to Philip Reilly's history of steril-ization (Reilly 1991, 129), "As recently as the mid-1960s, long after most steril-ization programs were thought to have ended, a few states were still sterilizing several hundred retarded people each year." Moreover, as of 1961, twenty-six states still had laws permitting compulsory sterilization (although no new laws of this type were passed after 1937).[2] While the number of sterilization pro-cedures declined, no movement had yet emerged to promote the provision of sexual education, rights to privacy, or parenting support. Rather, most profes-sionals still considered procreation by people with mental retardation to be a threat to society.

During this period, marriage restrictions also became less popular; no states passed new laws restricting marriage for this population, and vigorous attempts to enforce restrictions waned. However, laws restricting marriage for people with mental retardation mostly remained on the books without legal challenge. Similarly, there was little activity concerning the rights of people with mental retardation to vote and contract. On the contrary, parents and professionals undertook the creation of new laws that made the establishment of guardianship easier. Thus, at the same time that activists worked to expand access to services and establish these services as "rights," they also left some rights restrictions in place and pursued channels by which to restrict other rights.

How are we to explain the changes and continuities in the understandings of and access to services and rights? In particular, how are we to explain the emphasis on securing social services and even social rights while overlooking or restricting traditional adult civil rights? To answer these questions, this chapter examines divisions among the professionals charged with the care of people with mental retardation as they tried to maintain jurisdiction over mental disability while also seeking new ways to confront the criticisms they faced. Chapter 6 then examines the critical role of the parents' movement as well as new federal initiatives in determining access to rights for people with mental retardation.

The Persistence of Restrictions

Prior to World War II, many critics faulted eugenics as a pseudo-science, yet they often had difficulty countering eugenicists' strong rhetorical position and popular appeal. For many legislators and citizens, the possibility of preventing poverty, crime, and disease (or even the illusion of doing so) outweighed the scientific facts or religious sentiments against eugenics. The abuses of Nazi Germany, though, provided a powerful illustration of the dangers eugenics posed to a democratic society (Larson 1995).[3] Critics of a proposed sterilization law in Alabama, for instance, asserted that "the principle underlying it . . . is the principle actuating Hitlerism in Germany, with its blood purges, its shooting fests, and its deliberately planned famines."[4] Although eugenic thought and policies continued in the United State well after World War II, the Nazi eugenic-based policies allowed critics to equate compulsory measures with absolutist regimes and to spread alarm regarding the "slippery slope" of restricting the liberty of citizens. Meanwhile, the advances in academic disciplines, particularly genetic science, continued to reveal the simplistic, biased, and often incorrect assumptions and methods guiding eugenics.

Despite its weakening hold, the eugenic framework continued to play a powerful role throughout the 1940s and 1950s. Some professionals remained committed to pursuing an explicitly eugenic agenda, including the expanded use of institutionalization and sterilization to prevent "feeblemindedness." (Committed eugenicists were slow to adopt the new terminology of retardation.) One of the most prominent eugenicists of the 1940s and 1950s was Charles Gamble, a wealthy Massachusetts physician, philanthropist, and heir to the Gamble soap fortune. Throughout his career, Gamble published at least twenty articles extolling the benefits of eugenic sterilization; traveled through the Midwest and South lecturing on eugenics; helped to establish sterilization clinics in Michigan, Indiana, Iowa, Nebraska, Kansas, Missouri, and Florida; collaborated with the national eugenicist organization Birthright; and helped found North Carolina's active eugenic society, the League for Human Betterment (Reilly 1991).

In keeping with the traditional tenets of eugenics, Gamble justified the use of sterilization and institutionalization by emphasizing the "large hereditary element" in causing mental disease and mental deficiency (Gamble 1945). Although he primarily justified sterilization based on the likely inheritance of mental deficiency from generation to generation, Gamble updated his eugenics argument by recognizing a multiplicity of additional causes of mental deficiency. In turn, he used these additional causes to advocate for the sterilization of a broader population, including individuals who might transmit "deficiency" in the socialization process rather than through biological inheritance. According to Gamble (1952, 125), mentally defective individuals lacked the skills and values necessary for good parenting, and therefore, whether they were genetically inferior or not, they should be sterilized as an "obvious protection to children who might be reared by a feebleminded parent."

Some superintendents also continued, at least at times, to frame their political discourse in terms of eugenics. For example, W. I. Prichard (1949), superintendent of Virginia's Petersburg State Colony, argued in 1949 that the state should expand Virginia's sterilization law to cover individuals residing in the community (not only people residing in institutions) because they posed the greatest eugenic threat to society. Similarly, in his efforts to establish a eugenic sterilization law in Alabama, in 1946 William Partlow, superintendent of Alabama's institution for people with mental retardation, warned that "in practically all instances the children of feeble-minded parents grow up with the same or lower mental level as their parents, and likewise become local or public burdens" (cited in Larson 1995, 151). Like Gamble, Partlow promoted the use of sterilization not only to guard against the hereditary transmission of deficiency but also to protect against the negative influence of "irresponsible mothers." As late as 1945, the president of the American Association on Mental Deficiency, E. Arthur Whitney, promoted the "fact" that children with mental retardation typically came "from mentally inferior stock" (Whitney 1945, 99) and, as late as 1959, he recommended the establishment of traditional eugenic control measures such as "a central listing of mental defectives" and the prevention of marriage for "hereditary types" (Whitney 1959, 391).

A few key eugenics societies also continued to spread the message of eugenics, although in its updated form. In 1946, the American Eugenics Society (AES) elected Frederick Osborne as its president. Osborne steered the organization away from the class and race bias associated with eugenics and instead strove to re-establish it as a forum for advancing the scientific study of population. He criticized compulsory sterilization programs and instead espoused voluntary and educational methods to improve the quality of the population, including genetic research, population planning, public education, family planning, and marriage and family counseling. In 1954, under his leadership the AES launched a new journal, *Eugenics Quarterly*, and in 1968 he published *The Future of Human Heredity*, in which he argued for the relevance of heredity to society's social problems. By emphasizing high-quality science and voluntary educational programs, Osborne became known as "the respectable face of eugenic research" ("Background Note" 2002).

During this time, scientists made several breakthroughs regarding the biological causes of retardation that further legitimated the use of appropriate scientific methods to study the genetic and biological roots of mental deficiency. Most dramatic among these was the discovery that a missing enzyme could lead to retardation, a condition called phenylketonuria, or PKU. This condition could be easily diagnosed in infants through a urine-screening test and treated through diet, preventing thousands of cases of mental retardation. In 1959, a French physician named Jérôme Lejeune discovered a chromosome abnormality behind what had been referred to as "Mongoloidism," later referred to as Down Syndrome and Trisomy-21, providing a biological explanation for one of the most stigmatized forms of retardation.

Although these scientists examined the role of heredity and genetics in mental disability, their point of view differed in some ways from what was known as eugenics. Whereas eugenicists tended to broadly ascribe heredity as *the* cause of retardation given *any* evidence of intergenerational disability and to prescribe compulsory programs of social control to prevent disability, genetic scientists acknowledged the complexity of heredity and genetics, disassociated mental retardation from simple ideas of poor lineage or "bad blood," and sought to identify specific physical characteristics that could possibly be altered to cure or prevent retardation. Thus, these genetic breakthroughs potentially lessened the stigma of retardation, whereas eugenics had fostered fear and hopelessness. However, the newly emerging branches of genetic science still presented retardation as a defect to be prevented rather than an acceptable form of human variation and assumed that scientific knowledge should be used to prevent mental retardation through the selection of an appropriate mate, wise choices regarding procreation, and pre- and post-natal testing and care.

A new national organization called Birthright assumed the AES's former position as advocate for the restriction of people with mental retardation, particularly for compulsory sterilization. Marian Olden, former director of the Sterilization League of New Jersey, initially established Birthright as a vehicle to promote the passage of national legislation in support of compulsory sterilization (Olden 1974). From the beginning, though, Birthright experienced tensions between Olden's eugenics agenda and its other members' public-health orientation. This disharmony even affected the choice of the organization's name. Olden had wanted to call it the Sterilization League of America to highlight its role in establishing a national eugenic sterilization law; other members, though, preferred "Birthright" to capture a broader sense of ensuring quality of life for America's children and established the motto, "There should be no child in America that has not the complete Birthright of a sound mind in a sound body, and that has not been born under proper conditions."

Both the group's name and its motto implied a broader mission than desired by Olden. However, her role as director of publications ensured that she could promote eugenics anyway. For example, in 1947 Olden created "a pamphlet for beginners" titled, *The ABC of Human Conservation*, in which she positioned photographs of two beautiful "feebleminded" women next to the following warning: "Girls like these, who come from defective stock yet who are trained sufficiently to pass for normal by those with superficial judgment, are the greatest menace to the race when returned to the community without the protection of sterilization. . . . Once feeblemindedness is introduced into the germplasm it can never be eliminated. It may remain hidden indefinitely" (Olden 1947, 6–10). Birthright printed and distributed at least four thousand copies of this pamphlet at exhibitions throughout the nation.

Continued Restrictions
without the Rationale of Eugenics

As the eugenics ideology fell out of favor, restrictive practices remained in place, increasingly stressing the "sociological advantages" of these policies, including environmental, economic, familial and personal benefits (Ladd-Taylor 2004). This trend was particularly clear for sterilization programs as they expanded beyond the institution walls to select candidates from the community, usually targeting poor women with children who received government assistance. Rather than limit sterilization to individuals with inheritable defects, programs increasingly included "those who are physically unable to support, socially inadequate to support themselves or others, and those who are constantly bearing children out of wedlock due to an uncontrolled sex urge, putting burdens on their community" (Vischi 1951, 369). Programs in Georgia, North Carolina, and South Carolina, for example, regularly admitted women referred by county welfare agencies to institutions for the sole purpose of sterilization (Castles 2002; Larson 1995). According to Edward Larson (1995, 160), "Throughout the Deep South, and elsewhere, a quiet practice of sterilizing women on welfare spread."

Superintendents continued to use sterilization as a tool to help manage their institutions, as well. Sterilization helped them keep their population at a manageable size by enabling the parole of inmates without fear that they would procreate. Furthermore, according to many superintendents, sterilization encouraged successful adaptation in the community by removing the potential stress of parenthood. Making this point, Lewis Tune (1951, 382), superintendent of a Kansas training school, noted that "since the mind of those less fortunate never develops beyond that of a child, there is no possibility of curing this condition. Such people, however, can often make satisfactory adjustments to their surroundings, and earn a living by some simple form of work, and can even have a happy marriage life with the same kind of partner, provided the mental and economic strain of parenthood is removed."

As James Trent (1993) noted, sterilization continued to be used in institutions even when parole was unlikely. Through the 1930s and 1940s, the number of patients paroled declined, while the number of sterilization procedures performed increased. Superintendents sterilized high-functioning patients to ensure that they would have a pool of free labor without the worry that their workers would become pregnant. They also sterilized patients as a form of behavioral modification (Tune 1951). Therefore, although the legitimacy of eugenics diminished after the 1940s, sterilization remained relatively popular because it served multiple purposes. The superintendents, psychologists, and social workers who ran sterilization programs did not have an ideological commitment to eugenics; rather, they saw sterilization as a utilitarian problem solver (Carey 1998; Castles 2004; Trent 1993).

Other restrictive practices, such as institutionalization, also continued to thrive. During this time period, the institutionalized population grew, the age of inmates at the time of their first admission went down, and residents stayed on average for a longer time. The medical community, particularly general practitioners and family doctors, overwhelmingly supported institutionalization for school-age children and adults with mental retardation. Rather than basing their support on rationales of heredity, though, physicians more often presented institutionalization as a way to preserve the "normal" family while also meeting the best interests of the disabled child (Castles 2004).

According to most medical professionals, children with disabilities wreaked havoc on the family and placed a particular strain on the mother. Professionals believed that, given the competitive nature of American society, a mother could "not feel free to love her child unconditionally unless he measure[d] up to the age norm of his contemporaries," which would then create in her a tremendous sense of "disappointment and shame" (Greenberg 1950, 5; Stone 1948, 369). Particularly in families with multiple children, the mother's "emotional bank" was drained by the need to provide time-consuming care for her disabled child while also trying to meet her other family obligations (Greenberg 1950; Olshansky 1962). Fathers would suffer, too. The need to devote unusual amounts of time and energy to child care would hinder his career mobility and income growth (Schonnell and Watts 1956). In addition, his relationship with his wife would suffer as she became a nurse and his home became a hospital. Parents would grow isolated from their peers and hostile toward each other (Mandelbaum and Wheeler 1960). John Thurston (1960, 351), professor of psychology, concluded that parents of children with severe handicaps "were highly sensitive, suspicious, anxious, and unhappy individuals, the opposite of what might be desired," and therefore they could not provide a happy environment for their disabled child, themselves, or their other children if the child with a disability remained at home.

Professionals also warned that the presence of a child with retardation in the home posed a great threat to his or her siblings (Frank 1952). With an "abnormal" sibling at home, "normal" children would struggle to gain the acceptance of their peers and to cope with their own feelings of shame and rejection toward their sibling. In addition, the financial expenses incurred by the disabled child would deprive siblings of their "fair share" of family financial resources. Edgar A. Doll (1953), one of the most prominent researchers in the area of mental retardation, even worried that home care of retarded children might lessen the pool of potential marriage partners for siblings, particularly sisters, and suggested institutional placement "at least for the period of marriageability" for the other children.

Professionals also presented institutionalization as in the best interests of the person with a disability, especially compared with a home life marked by rejection, over-protection, and shame. According to medical professionals, in his own home the disabled child would be perceived of as "obnoxious and repulsive in the eyes of his parents," which would destroy the "child's sense of security" and his "self-esteem" (Schumacher 1946, 53). In an institution, by contrast, he would have a community of peers and experience protection from unfair competition and undue pressures, allowing him to feel "important." Dr. Benjamin Spock, American's leading child-care adviser, and his colleague Marion Lerrigo (Spock and Lerrigo 1965, 109) wrote, "The retarded child is happy in a school where he associates with other children of his own level, provided the atmosphere is generally warm. There his companions can enjoy the things he enjoys. He has a chance to do things in which he can succeed. He has a chance to be important. He is not always left out of things because the brighter children take the limelight." Thus, children with disabilities could achieve the greatest progress, if progress was even deemed a possibility, among other children with disabilities and away from their families and communities.

A study of general practitioners (Olshansky et al. 1963) found that about two-fifths favored immediate institutionalization on diagnosis of retardation and almost 50 percent favored it for children diagnosed as "mongoloid." Surveys of parents from the time similarly show that about half of the parents with retarded children reported that they had been "instructed by their physicians to immediately institutionalize their child, with the proportion much higher when the child was diagnosed with Down Syndrome" (Castles 2004, 363).

Exclusion from public school was also rampant and by no means justified by eugenics alone. Educators typically divided mental retardation into three categories: educable (individuals with IQ scores between 50 and 75), trainable (individuals with IQ scores between 25 and 49), and custodial (individuals with IQ scores between 0 and 24). Embedded within these categories was the professional assumption that only those with IQ scores in the highest range could benefit from academic training. Most school administrators insisted that "trainable" and "custodial" children could not and should not be served by the public school. They developed additional criteria to further limit the admission of children with intellectual disabilities, such as requirements that the children be ambulatory, toilet-trained, non-convulsive, able to sit and able to pay attention for periods of time, and able to act appropriately in their behavioral patterns. Therefore, even many children in the "educable" range were denied access to public education. For school administrators, these criteria served as a tool to manage enrollments and resources and ensure the efficiency of public education, with little to do with eugenics.

Macro–Social Changes and the Quest for New Answers

On one hand, institutional populations were growing and restrictions were enduring, despite the criticism of eugenics. On the other hand, change was brewing. Not only did eugenics come under fire; so, too, did the institution, the backbone of the professional system of care and control. In 1946, Albert Q. Masiel wrote an article for *Life* magazine exposing the wretched conditions in institutions for people with mental illness. The same year, Channing B. Richardson published an article describing the sad experiences of mentally retarded patients in institutions, who had "nothing to look back on and less to hope for" (Richardson 1946, 110–111).[5] In his exposé *The Shame of the States* (1948), Albert Deutsch used photography to vividly depict the terrible conditions in American institutions. The Kennedy family even contributed to the escalating criticism. In an article for the *Saturday Evening Post* in 1962, Eunice Kennedy Shriver remembered her visits to several low-quality state institutions: "There was an overpowering smell of urine from clothes and from the floors. I remember the retarded patients with nothing to do, standing, staring, grotesque-like misshapen statues. I recall other institutions where several thousand adults and children were housed in bleak, overcrowded wards of 100 or more, living out their lives on a dead-end street, unloved, unwanted, some of them strapped in chairs like criminals" (Shriver 1962, 72). Even more harshly, Robert Kennedy compared conditions at Willowbrook, an institution for people with mental retardation in New York, to a "snake pit." In 1966, another photographic exposé, *Christmas in Purgatory*, caught the attention of the nation with its shocking images of neglect and abuse (Blatt and Kaplan 1966). And in 1972, Geraldo Rivera brought America's institutional neglect directly into American households with a television documentary about New York State's Letchworth Village, which inspired outrage and pity as American audiences watched naked and poorly clad inmates surrounded by feces and bare walls with nothing to occupy their time but to rock back and forth.

While journalists and public figures initiated pop-culture exposés, scholars and professionals challenged the theoretical rationales for institutionalization. Rather than helping people with disabilities, scholars argued, the very structure of the institution, and the medical model that justified it, actually created and sustained deviance. Drawing on sociological and anthropological studies, researchers argued that society played a role in *creating* deviance, including mental illness and mental retardation; in the act of defining the cultural standards of acceptability, society simultaneously defined what was to be considered "deviant" and "undesirable" (Masland et al. 1958). People associated with these deviant traits were then labeled and stigmatized, producing or exacerbating the very behavior defined as deviant. Applying this to mental retardation, Seymour Sarason argued, "The child with an I.Q. of 68 or 69 is automatically labeled mentally defective and then takes on *in the thinking of the clinician* all the characteristics that have been associated with that label" (Sarason 1958 [1949], 1). In his famous work *The Myth of Mental Illness*, Thomas Szasz (1974) wrote that mental illness was nothing more than a label used to identify and repress socially unacceptable behaviors and that psychiatrists did little more than wield power, sanctioned by the state, to enforce "normality."

If psychiatry unjustly enforced cultural norms, then the institution served as the physical site in which America housed its unwanted, unacceptable, and socially deviant. Ervin Goffman (1961) compared medical institutions to prisons, religious cults, and other "total institutions" and explained their negative impact on inmates. According to Goffman, total institutions imposed on inmates "social death" by cutting them off from normal social roles and relationships and created many of the pathological behaviors they claimed to treat by denying inmates individuality and self-determination. They necessarily failed to create "normal" rehabilitated individuals, as nothing in the institutional regimen replicated the experiences of "normal" citizens. Moreover, because institutions placed total power in the hands of authority figures, inmates were inevitably abused and neglected. Institutions could not be improved with more funding, better administration, or higher expectations, as they were fundamentally flawed in their purpose and structure.

At the same time that institutionalization was being challenged, support burgeoned for community inclusion, civil and human rights, and equality for people with disabilities. In his rhetoric concerning both the New Deal and World War II, President Franklin Delano Roosevelt stressed the importance of human rights and social security as the essential foundations of democracy. His New Deal program consisted of a set of government initiatives to create jobs, provide immediate relief of poverty, assist farmers, fund compensation for unemployment, and create Social Security, all designed to boost the economy and protect citizens from the economic effects of the Depression. In defending the New Deal, Roosevelt (1935) claimed that the federal government's primary objective must be the "security of men, women, and children of the Nation" and that this responsibility could no longer be left solely in the hands of families and local communities. In her speech "Social Responsibility for Individual Welfare," Eleanor Roosevelt (1955) explained the importance of providing economic security to *all* Americans: "We believe that together we should strive to give every individual a chance for a decent and secure existence; and in evolving our social patterns we are trying to give both hope for better things in the future and security from want as far as possible in the present." According to the Roosevelts, social programs should enhance the well-being and security of the entire national community rather than simply providing charity to the needy. New Deal legislation dramatically increased funding for the provision of social services, thereby fueling both the growth of the service professions and the number of people receiving services. It also increased citizens' sense of entitlement and sparked the efforts of citizens' voluntary associations to secure services for their own constituency (Abel 1996; Segal 1970).

With the onset of World War II, the Roosevelts continued to stress that entitlements to social well-being were necessary to ensure democracy, freedom, and national security. In his now famous Address to Congress in 1941, President Roosevelt argued that "freedom means the supremacy of human rights everywhere," and he laid out the "Four Freedoms" that he considered to constitute a moral order:

> The first is freedom of speech—everywhere in the world. The second is freedom of every person to worship God in his own way—everywhere in the world. The third is freedom from want—which, translated into world terms, means economic understandings which will secure to every nation a healthy peacetime life for its inhabitants—everywhere in the world. The fourth is freedom from fear—which, translated into world terms, means a world-wide reduction of armaments to such a point and in such a thorough fashion that no nation will be in a position to commit an act of physical aggression against any neighbor—anywhere in the world. (Roosevelt 1941)

With his four freedoms, Roosevelt moved beyond guarantees of personal autonomy and freedom from government intrusion, the typical liberal notion of rights exemplified in the Bill of Rights, to advocate a federal role in ensuring the well-being and security of American citizens.

As chair of the United Nations Commission on Human Rights, the body that issued the 1948 Universal Declaration of Human Rights, Eleanor Roosevelt took an active role in articulating and institutionalizing the "inherent rights belonging to every human being," which included, among others, a right to nationality; to freedom of thought; to freedom to worship; to participation in the government of one's country; to employment and compensation commensurate with one's abilities and skills; to join a union; to the preservation of health; to social security against the consequences of unemployment, old age, and disability; and to education (Roosevelt 1948). Many of these human rights required the provision of social support and services from the government.[6]

As discussion of human rights grew, so did recognition of the valiant efforts of many members of minority populations in the war, and inequality became more widely acknowledged as an injustice. Many men of minority backgrounds served nobly in the armed forces. On the home front, women left their duties in the home and took on manufacturing jobs to support the war effort. People with mental retardation served their nation as soldiers and laborers, and professionals documented their success in wartime positions to show that these individuals could succeed when opportunities were available (Doll 1944; McKeon 1946; Weaver 1946).[7] Hence, a range of marginalized groups contributed to America's victory over fascism, and this experience raised their expectations of equality—or, at least, of better treatment—in postwar America.[8]

When the war ended, however, most groups did not receive the respect they sought. African American veterans found that they still faced a segregated society in which they were denied equal education, housing, and employment. Even the Veterans Administration insulted African American veterans by denying them the rights conferred by the GI Bill, such as assistance in purchasing a home, getting an education, and obtaining civil work (Jefferson 2003). Women were told to leave their jobs and again be content as housewives. Individuals labeled retarded lost their jobs and were expected to return to dependence and even institutions (Gelb 2004). Not surprisingly, during the 1940s and 1950s these groups expressed dissatisfaction with their social position, increasingly framed their discontent as a problem of social oppression, and sought solutions rooted in civil and human rights.[9]

Concurrently, disability began to receive unprecedented national attention. Wars typically spark advancements in disability policy because the government initiates programs to assist disabled veterans.[10] World War II produced an unprecedented number of returning disabled veterans who needed to be integrated into American life, leading to dramatic changes in disability policy and programs. Professional fields such as physical and occupational therapy grew; new assistive technologies for people with disabilities emerged; and a surge in scientific research generated hope for the amelioration or cure of certain diseases and disabilities (Levy 1951). Federal efforts to assist disabled veterans expanded, coming to include a broad range of people with disabilities regardless of whether they held veteran status. For example, despite an initial focus on veterans, vocational rehabilitation services grew to include a broader set of people with disabilities. Similarly, although Harry Truman established the President's Committee on Employment of the Handicapped in 1949 to promote the employment of disabled veterans, the committee dealt more broadly with the issue of employment and disability. President Roosevelt's experiences with polio also drew national attention to disability. Although Roosevelt hid the severity of his own disability, he and his wife helped to establish the National Foundation for Infantile Paralysis and its fundraising program, the March of Dimes, to raise awareness and fund research to prevent polio (Gallagher 1999).

As the level of activism promoting access to welfare services as a civil right increased, new organizations dedicated to various disability groups popped up throughout the nation. Some of these, such as the League for the Physically Handicapped and the Paralyzed Veterans of America, were led by individuals with disabilities; others, such as United Cerebral Palsy (UCP), the

League for Emotionally Disturbed Children, and the National Association for Retarded Children (NARC), were led by parents; and some, such as the March of Dimes, were led by professionals. These organizations pursued varied goals, but a central theme for all of them was the provision of services for individuals with disabilities in the community.

As parents and people with disabilities demanded a shift away from institutionalization, and as institutional services faced criticism and under-funding, some professionals shifted their own orientations toward the provision of community care. The field of psychiatry, which held significant sway in policy concerning mental retardation, had long expressed an interest in the role of the environment and community in producing and ameliorating mental illness. In the 1920s and 1930s, psychiatrists involved in the mental-hygiene and child-guidance movements called attention to the need to treat individuals within the community and to alter social conditions to improve mental health. In the 1940s, the community health clinic emerged as a model of service delivery, offering patients treatment without the stigma and dislocation of institutionalization. This model became even more feasible in the mid-1950s with the introduction of psychiatric drugs that stabilized behavior and encouraged the continuation of everyday activities. Yet few psychiatrists considered people with mental retardation able to benefit from these new community-based models. In his first major work, *Psychological Problems in Mental Deficiency*, the pioneer Seymour Sarason (1958 [1949]) explored the social and environmental causes of mental retardation and considered the negative impact of the current systems of treatment and education on this population. He criticized community-based psychologists for ignoring this population, relying on IQ tests without serious evaluation of adaptive behavior, creating treatment plans based on diagnostic stereotypes, and devising systems of care and education that harmed the patients. Moreover, he vehemently argued that this disability, like others, needed to be understood and confronted in its real-world context.

As psychiatrists and psychologists re-evaluated their role in the community, so, too, did special educators. In the early twentieth century, the field of special education lacked professional coherence, prestige, and standardized training requirements.[11] Community-based special educators typically saw their role as working with children deemed "educable" while removing children with mental retardation from the public classroom and channeling them into institutional care. Through the 1940s, though, special education expanded and solidified its professional base. The Council for Exceptional Children (CEC),[12] the first professional organization for special educators, increased its membership, became a department of the National Education Association, launched its first official publication, and worked to develop the mission, knowledge base, techniques, and training requirements for special education.[13] As the field of special education developed, educators constructed a positive role for themselves focused on encouraging child development for all children and sought to expand the number of children that they served. Parents of children with disabilities were a key ally, and together they helped to pass legislation to fund the training of special-education teachers, the 1958 Act to Encourage Expansion of Teaching in the Education of Mentally Retarded Children through Grants to Institutions of Higher Learning and to State Educational Agencies (PL 85-926).

The growth of vocational rehabilitation after World War II also promoted an expansion of the number of professionals concerned with disability working in the community, including physical therapists, occupational therapists, speech therapists, recreational therapists, and social workers (Albrecht 1992). While these professions tended to focus on physical disability, they also provided a new professional framework that stressed the importance of serving people with disabilities within their communities and creatively helping people with disabilities overcome the challenges of daily life to attain self-sufficiency and personal fulfillment.

Rethinking Mental Retardation

After years of promoting segregation, some professionals sought to develop services in the community, as well as in institutions, for individuals with mental retardation, but how could funding for these new services be justified? While some professionals continued to rely on the "threat" of the feebleminded, others harked back to the ideas of nineteenth-century advocates such as Howe and Seguin who believed that people with mental retardation could be educated and become productive citizens.

The new optimism among professionals can be readily seen in the article "Exoneration of the Feebleminded" (Kanner 1942). Leo Kanner, a child psychiatrist who wrote extensively about mental retardation and later became renowned for his work on autism, criticized the way in which society treated people with mental retardation. According to Kanner, individuals with mental retardation experienced a "double handicap": They were limited by their own biological differences and, perhaps even more so, by society's negative attitude toward these differences. Because the public assumed the inferiority of those with mental retardation and mistreated them, it exacerbated and even *caused* their dependence and deviance. People labeled retarded appeared to be "misfits" in schools that had placed inappropriately high or low expectations on them and in a society that failed to help them become useful.

Kanner questioned why society held such contempt for people with mental retardation. In direct contrast to eugenicists, who assumed that the feebleminded posed a grave danger to society, he wrote that the greatest threats to humanity had always emerged from the more intelligent segments of society:

> Let us try to recall one single instance in the history of mankind when a feebleminded individual or group of individuals was responsible for the retardation or persecution of humanness and science. They who caused Galileo to be jailed were not feebleminded. They who instituted

the Inquisition were not feebleminded. The great manmade catastro-
phes resulting in wholesale slaughter and destruction were not started
by idiots, imbeciles, morons, and borderliners. (1942, 20)

Rather than causing society's downfall, the feebleminded held great potential to contribute to society, a potential that was too often wasted.

Sewage disposal, ditch digging, potato peeling, scrubbing of floors and
other such occupations are as indispensable and essential to our way of
living as science, literature, and art. . . . But this is not the whole story.
The fortunate fact that people, regardless of IQ, are available for these
performances frees the time and energies of others for tasks which
involve planning and creative activities. (Kanner 1942, 20)

Without services, the potential of those labeled feebleminded was left
untapped. With services, however, they could mature into functioning citizens.
In a twist of civic republicanism (a philosophy that suggests people *become*
citizens through civic participation), Kanner's writings suggest that, because
citizenship is rooted in civic participation, all people deserve the opportunity
to participate in society and thereby become citizens, even individuals who
require support and services to do so.

Documenting the Productive Citizen

Ideas like Kanner's proliferate throughout professional writings of the time.
Most notably, a flurry of articles published in academic and popular magazines
documented the potential of people with mental retardation to be "productive" and "upright" citizens. Professionals claimed that as many as 75–80 percent of students in special education could mature into self-supporting adults,
and most others could contribute to their own support and self-care. A study by
Allen Bobroff (1956) documented the "satisfying and desirable social patterns"
of adults who had been in special education: It showed that 67 percent had
married, 64 percent had voted, 82 percent had no arrest record, and 72 percent
of the men had served in the military. Studies of the parolees of institutions
also showed significant levels of success. For example, one study (Whitney
1955) indicated a 60 percent "record of successful adjustment," based primarily on economic self-support. According to Evelyn Ayrault (1964, 71), a child-
rearing expert, even people with severe disabilities could be "trained to be quite
manageable, be as well behaved as any other child, and be taken with the family to visit or shop."

Not surprisingly, given the era, the criteria for success were gendered.
For men, the primary measure of success was paid employment, whereas for
women, success was measured by domestic achievement. In their study of
female parolees, Ainsworth and her colleagues (1945) measured social adjust-

ment by such characteristics as marrying a self-supporting man, owning a home, maintaining a clean and orderly home, demonstrating good parenting skills, and having friendly relations. Describing a successful female parolee, Ainsworth stated, "Eleanor is an excellent housekeeper and a devoted mother. She is gracious and friendly. Today, unlike [in] 1933, we would not consider sterilization for a person of this type" (Ainsworth et al. 1945, 284). According to Ainsworth, despite an IQ of 60, Eleanor fulfilled her responsibilities as a member of society and therefore would be allowed to exercise rights, including the rights to live in the community, marry, and procreate.

Whereas eugenicists typically made sharp distinctions between the "feeble-minded" and "normal" citizens, professionals increasingly blurred these lines, showing that people with mental retardation were similar to everyone else and even superior in some ways. For example, throughout World War II superintendents and other professionals made frequent positive comparisons of "normal" and "mentally retarded" men to promote the acceptance of mentally retarded parolees in the military and military-related industries (Butler 1945; Coakley 1945; Dunn 1946). F. O. Butler (1945, 299–300), superintendent of California's Sonoma State School, praised the work of mentally retarded men in military-related industries, which he evaluated as "on a comparable basis with normal individuals who usually get most of the praise." And Rebecca McKeon (1946, 51), writing in *Mental Hygiene*, documented that many mentally retarded men "made more satisfactory adjustments with less turnover of job than did many of the more intelligent workers, who felt that the type of work was beneath them."

When people with mental retardation failed to thrive, as they commonly did, the blame increasingly fell on society. According to Seymour Sarason and Thomas Gladwin (1958), society defined a set of people as intellectually inferior and then treated them that way. Schools played a particularly problematic role in labeling, becoming for some individuals the first and only context in which they were defined and treated as retarded. Once testing and academic skills were no longer the sole measure of success, they were able to find a meaningful place in society. Moreover, mental retardation appeared to be far more common among segments of the population who were deprived of cultural and economic opportunities, including the poor, uneducated, and racial and ethnic minorities. Without opportunities to learn valued information and skills, these children were rendered "almost totally unfit for meeting the intellectual problems of our culture" (Sarason and Gladwin 1958, 393). Not only did society play a role in creating retardation; it also heaped stigma and rejection on those so labeled. Paralleling Kanner's idea of the double handicap, professionals argued that the failure and incompetence of people with mental retardation "may, in many instances, be more the consequences of our prescribed social treatment, expectations, and management of those individuals and families" (Kelman 1958, 37). This failure was by no means genetic or inevitable.

While society could harm individuals with mental retardation, it could also transform them into "an asset" through the provision of appropriate services.

Special education could prepare thousands of mentally retarded children "to be responsible, contributing citizens and in no sense a burden to family or community" (Robb 1952, 55). Work training and opportunities could enable "the retarded person to become economically independent, or partially so, and at the same time socially acceptable in his environment" (McKesson 1956, 313). Professionals proclaimed that retarded individuals were "entitled to a chance," and to ignore this potential was to doom them to a fate of dependence and incompetence, an act that was immoral as well as socially and fiscally unwise (Hudson 1955; Nolan 1955; Roselle 1955). Thus, Samuel Kirk and G. Orville Johnson (1951, iv) determined that "it is less costly to provide a special education program that will enable these persons to care for themselves either partially or totally than it is to support them on public relief or in institutions."

Similar ideas justified the expansion of services within institutions, as well. Residents of institutions needed education and work training to prepare them for parole and to "bridge the gap between institutional living and independent citizenship in the community" (Schwartz 1959, 575). Even residents with no chance of parole had a right to services because they, too, had a right to participate in the community within their institution. According to the educator Margaret Hudson (1955, 586), "It does not matter whether the child is ultimately destined to live in a colony or at large in society; he still needs the kind of education that will make him a dependable, self-respecting citizen." Similarly, according to Blaine Nolan (1955, 34), director of education and training at the Winfield State Training School in Kansas, "An institution is a small city; it is a cooperative enterprise. It puts a premium upon a high type of citizenship. Each person depends upon the other. Civic participation is not a remote ideal but an actual necessity."[14]

Dividing the Population

Because professionals often justified the provision of services and inclusion within the community based on the potential success of people with mental retardation, they did not typically advocate rights and services for all people with mental retardation. People with mental retardation were now more likely to be perceived as productive, morally upright, and competent, but those who were deemed unproductive, deviant, unstable, or incompetent were to remain subjected to rights restrictions and to be excluded from services and full participation in society.

Examples of the differential treatment of people with mental retardation are numerous. While some special educators advocated education for all children, most supported education (typically a segregated education) only for "high-functioning" children. In his 1958 presidential address to the American Association on Mental Deficiency (AAMD, formerly the American Association for the Study of the Feeble-Minded), Chris DeProspo (1958), chair of the Department of Special Education at Southern Connecticut State University, argued against the provision of a public education for children with significant disabilities, stating, "If experience shows that most of these children will need constant supervision, then academics become unimportant, but arts and crafts may help them enjoy a life of conformity whether it be at home or in a residential environment." He then suggested that only a "realistic curriculum" could be justified "to the citizens who must pick up the expense tab for such activities," and that children with significant disabilities would be best off if placed "under kindly institutional tutelage." Kirk and Johnson, the authors of *Educating the Mentally Retarded Child* (1951), similarly supported the notion that education should be provided only to those who showed the possibility of becoming self-sufficient. Following this line of professional thought, in 1958 the Illinois Supreme Court found that the state was not required to provide education for those with mental handicaps because a common school education was predicated on the child's capacity to learn (*Department of Public Welfare v. Haas* 1958; Hoffman 1959). According to the court, the state is not required to educate those who showed no potential to learn or be productive citizens.[15]

Competence was also used to differentiate who should receive rights. In the case of the right to vote, for example, usually only those considered "educable" were considered "capable of accepting one of the most important responsibilities of citizenship" (Kokaska 1966, 125). The right to vote for people with more severe disabilities was not even discussed among professionals; it was simply assumed away.

Morality and social adaptation also served to differentiate who among those labeled retarded should gain access to rights and who should not. For example, after describing Eleanor's successful adaptation and advocating her right to parenthood, Ainsworth provided descriptions of other women for whom compulsory sterilization would be appropriate. One such woman, Sally, grew up in an unstable home, and her father spent much of his life in prison. As an adult, she had a child out of wedlock, and then she married a man who was a poor worker, a frequent drinker, and abusive. They lived primarily on public assistance. Although Sally and Eleanor shared an IQ score of 60, the circumstances of their lives were very different, as were their success at economic self-sufficiency and their ability to conform to the norms of society. In Ainsworth's estimation, Sally was unworthy to bear children, due not solely to her low IQ but also to its combination with her life circumstances and poor choices.

Institutionalization also depended heavily on an assessment of one's moral behavior. Delinquents and individuals with behavioral problems often received high priority, while those who could socially adapt to mainstream society received low priority. To help parents make the decision whether to institutionalize their children, the child-care expert Stella Slaughter (1960) offered some examples of children who might remain at home, including a boy who was a "docile, happy appearing lad who got along well." However, children with "quarrelsome attitudes," who were prone to delinquency, or who came from dysfunctional families were best placed in institutions.

Transforming the Criteria

Professionals used the criteria of productivity, competence, and morality to differentiate, but some also sought to reshape and expand these criteria to broaden the potential population of those deemed worthy to participate in services and in the community. As discussed, professionals relied heavily on notions of potential economic productivity to justify the provision of services and inclusion in the community; however, they also began to expand the notion of productivity from the conduct of paid work to any form of social, mental, and emotional development. Special educators in particular sought to change the idea of productivity from the likelihood of future self-support to the potential for personal growth (Caine 1954). According to Eli Bower (1954, 36), a consultant to the California State Department of Education, admission to programs in special education typically relied on "three unwritten assumptions," each of which heavily weighted the likelihood of economic productivity in adulthood: "(1) that despite the handicap, the child was educable, i.e., could profit by some modified academic program, (2) that the child had possibilities of one day being economically productive, and (3) that the child had good possibilities of being socially competent and independent of adult supervision." A broader definition would offer education for all children who showed potential for personal and social growth. Hence, the 1954 "Creed for Exceptional Children," developed by the U.S. Office of Education, declared, "We believe that the nation as a whole, every state and county, every city and hamlet, and every citizen, has an obligation to help in bringing to fruition in this generation the idea of a full and useful life for every exceptional child in accordance with his capacity." Each child could be useful and lead a meaningful life, but the ways in which and extent to which they could do so would vary. While not as appealing to policymakers, this new concept of productivity changed the justification for rights from the economic bottom line to matters related to human development and quality of life.

Professionals also began to reshape notions of competence. Eugenicists often described the feebleminded as necessarily incompetent and attempted to render them legally incompetent based on a medical diagnosis of feeblemindedness. Now, though, professionals began again to disassociate the label of mental retardation from incompetence, arguing that a host of factors such as personality, emotional stability, financial stability, and mental health—not just level of intelligence—played a role in creating competence. For example, in her influential studies of parenting, Phyllis Mickelson (1947, 1949) found little relationship between level of intelligence and the ability to parent. While mothers with IQ scores between 30 and 49 tended to provide less satisfactory care than other mothers, there was almost no difference between those with IQ scores between 50 and 59 and those between 60 and 69, and mothers with IQ scores between 70 and 75 were rated as giving the least satisfactory care of all. Rather than IQ score, other factors seemed more important in determining success as a parent, including "the number of pregnancies, the number of children in the home, the adequacy of income, the satisfactoriness of the marital relationship, and the mental health of the parents, especially that of the mother." For Mickelson, IQ score was only one among many possible factors in determining whether one should be subject to sterilization or not.

Twenty years later, Herbert Lazerow, a professor of law at the University of California, San Diego, reiterated Mickelson's findings when he discussed the essential prerequisites for marriage. Lazerow (1967, 451) argued that the capacity to raise children was essential for marriage, but this capacity was not determined solely by IQ:

> Some people with mental disorders are capable of raising children. Retarded people, in particular, may raise their children without inflicting upon them many of the anxieties that children of "normal" people manifest. What general classes of incompetents are unable to raise children effectively? A person who requires frequent hospitalization would, by his continued absence from home, be unable to effectively raise a child. A person suffering from delusions or hallucinations might be dangerous to the child. A person unable to perform the usual business chores of his sex would be unable to serve as a proper role-image for a child or provide him with support.

The disassociation of retardation and incompetence was certainly controversial among professionals. For researchers such as Edgar A. Doll (1948) and Joseph Jastak (1949), a diagnosis of retardation required both a low IQ score and social maladjustment. For them, "true" retardation by definition was permanent and could never be associated with social success. In direct disagreement, scholars such as Sarason (1958 [1949]) deconstructed the concept of mental retardation and treated it as arbitrary. According to Sarason, because childhood diagnoses of mental retardation relied on *predictions* of future productivity and independence, they could never be certain. Moreover, research had shown that people with low intelligence had the ability to learn, and that this ability varied greatly even for people with the same IQ. Permanent maladaptation, therefore, was never certain.

Conclusion

Although professionals in the early twentieth century were never completely united in their definitions and interpretations of feeblemindedness, a dominant agenda based loosely on the eugenics framework advocating the social control and rights restrictions of people with mental retardation emerged. In the midcentury, this policy increasingly came under fire, and significant divisions among professionals arose. Some attempted to shore up the system of social control, advocating measures such as increased funding for institutions and the expansion of sterilization programs, while others sought a new direction for the treatment of disability, largely focused on the provision of services in the community and based on the potential of disabled individuals to successfully adapt and contribute to society.

Among those advocating for services and access to rights, professionals altered their view of people with mental retardation to stress their potential productivity, competence, and social adaptation. Moreover, they created more expansive definitions of productivity, competence, and adaptation that could better include a range of people with mental retardation. In doing so, they attempted to counter the arguments of eugenicists and portray individuals labeled mentally retarded as good citizens. They did not, however, typically question the criteria themselves. Therefore, advocates tended to split the population, granting access to services and rights to those who fit the criteria and excluding those who did not fit.

As different as eugenicists and professionals seeking to offer community-based services might have been, they both reflect the orientation of professionals, assuring the continued importance of professionals in addressing the "problem" of mental retardation. Whether controlling the problem of the feebleminded through registration, segregation, sterilization, and the broad denial of rights or the problem of underachievement through offering services in the community, professional intervention would save the nation from undue economic and social burdens. In both approaches, professionals used a cost–benefit analysis to show the economic and social worth of their services. To prove their success, they tended to offer their services to the most productive, competent, and moral while relegating others to the system of institutionalization that abandoned the task of treatment and instead offered custodial housing. Professionals also strove to ensure their autonomy and prestige, retaining their role as gatekeeper to rights and services. Not only would they deliver services and assist in inclusion; they would also serve as gatekeepers, determining who should and who should not be included. Educators wanted to determine eligibility for education; superintendents wanted to determine eligibility for institutional admission and parole. Even though they spoke at times of "rights," rarely did they imagine that people with disabilities should have rights that could shape the behavior of professionals or render meaningless professional judgment regarding who should and should not receive services and rights.

6

The Rise of the Parents' Movement
and the Special Child

As professionals began to rethink mental retardation, parents also created new visions and provided the passion and drive necessary to
achieve social change. Parents desperately wanted to see a better life
for their children and themselves, and when they made demands for change,
they did so with vigilance and moral righteousness. Like professionals, parents sought to create a more positive image of their children and their families
and to establish a wider set of services that relied on a more positive approach.
However, whereas professionals tended to justify the provision of services by
documenting increased productivity and adjustment among people with retardation, parents refused to tie their demands for services to potential productivity, economic savings, or likely success. Of course, they wanted their children
to be successful, but they knew that economic cost–benefit analyses would
not necessarily show a "profit" for society's investment; nor they did want their
children judged solely for their ability to earn money. Rather, they argued that,
like a parent, the state had an obligation to care and provide for its needy and
dependent citizens, not for the economic return but because a great nation
cares for its members. Thus, parents created a need-based narrative depicting
their offspring as "eternal children" and a human-rights narrative stressing the
obligation of the state to provide for its members, regardless of their abilities.

Early Growth of Parent Organizations

Some of the first parent groups to advocate for individuals with mental retardation sprang up among parents of institutionalized children. In 1936, parents
of children in the State Custodial School of Washington formed the Children's
Benevolence League, and in 1939, parents of children at New York State's

Letchworth Village organized the Welfare League for Retarded Children.[1] According to Margaret Richards (1953, 57), who helped to form the Illinois Dixon State Hospital Parents' Association, she and parents like her wanted "to bring something of ourselves to Dixon and promote the welfare of the patients there by giving our time, interest, and money. . . . We were a group of parents who did not want to cease being parents because we no longer had our children in our homes."

Parents who were members of these organizations tended to see themselves as allies of the institution in which their children resided; both parents and the institution were dedicated to the care of children, and together they could best ensure that the needs of the children were met. Parents in these organizations visited the residents, organized social events for them, donated money toward purchases such as movie projectors and play equipment, and participated in public-awareness and political campaigns to help meet institutional needs and improve conditions. Given that many physicians recommended a complete break between parents and their disabled child after the child was placed in an institution, and that institutions tended to have rules discouraging strong family bonds, the effort by some parents to become part of the "institutional family" was groundbreaking for its time. The alliance between parents and institutions was tentative, as parents also watched over and at times critiqued the institution; however, even in these situations, parents' groups usually tried to maintain amicable relations. For example, when parents in the Children's Benevolence League expressed great concerns about declining conditions at the State Custodial School, they worked with institutional authorities to lobby the state legislature for funds to build an additional institution, making a cooperative effort to reduce overcrowding and improve conditions throughout the system.

Institution-specific parent organizations did not meet the needs of all parents of children with mental retardation. Some parents wanted to institutionalize a child but could not secure a placement (Abel 1996; Shallit 1956). Joan Werner, a parent activist, recounted her family's experience, which was like that of so many other families: "The doctor said we should place him in an institution. . . . But when we checked there were no facilities available to him. There was only limited space—and a waiting list" (Schwartzenberg 2005). Although about half of parents received advice to institutionalize their disabled children, institutions served only about 10 percent of individuals diagnosed as retarded, leaving most parents to care for their children at home. Large institutions such as the Pennhurst State Hospital in Pennsylvania had waiting lists of more than one thousand individuals, despite the fact that conditions there provoked widespread criticism ("A Shame of Pennsylvania" 1968).

Many parents resisted placing their child away from home. The onslaught of negative media coverage regarding institutions (briefly described in Chapter 5) increased parents' fear and guilt about sending their child to an institution. In addition, many parents simply wanted to keep their children at home. In a study of parents in 1956, many expressed sentiments such as, "This is our child. We don't want to give him away. We want to find out how to help him" (Gordon and Ullman 1956, 160). For parents who kept their child at home, communities offered almost no services or support. Families faced "a very real rejection and non-acceptance by the community" (Weingold and Hormuth 1953, 119); they often lost their friends, were shunned by strangers, and had "no place to go," as their children were routinely excluded from public schools, nursery schools, daycare centers, and other community services. As such, a family with a retarded child became "a social island" (Gramm 1951; Schwartz-enberg 2005).

In addition to the stigma and social isolation, many families lacked the skills needed to address their child's needs effectively. Parents were given little information about their child's diagnosis and prognosis, and even less about techniques for education and discipline. Despite the lack of information, professionals and communities held parents responsible for the supervision and care of their disabled child if the child remained at home. In her self-help book, *The Mentally Retarded Child and His Parent* (1960), Stella Slaughter informed parents that they were responsible for obtaining "a complete knowledge" of their child's disabilities and abilities, providing education to their child, and planning for their child's future. "Failures of school and community," according to Slaughter, "double parental responsibility. The parent must not fail his child. He must to the best of his ability fill the gaps left unclosed by outside help, and join hands with any person or groups who can help him to awaken the public consciousness of the needs of his child and others like him" (Slaughter 1960, 138). Of course, Slaughter neglected to provide practical advice about how parents could take on such responsibility without support from the community (Shriver 1964).

In the period between 1940 and 1960, parents expressed particular frustration with the lack of support and guidance provided by professionals involved with the care of their children. Interviews with parents in the 1950s found that only 25 percent believed they had received satisfactory advice from medical professionals (Waskowitz 1959). Among their comments were statements such as, "I feel the doctors brushed me off"; "We did not find anyone who sat down and told us what the problem was"; and "They all spoke of institutional care as though it was the only thing we could do. They acted as though we had no choice." One parent activist boldly wrote in an article for the *American Journal of Mental Deficiency* that one of the biggest problems faced by parents was "inept, inaccurate, and ill-timed professional advice" (Murray 1959, 1082).

It may not be surprising that parents with disabled children residing in the community eventually turned to other parents for the support that they did not receive from professionals (Castles 2004; Dybwad 1990; Jones 2004; Segal 1970). In 1946, a New Jersey housewife named Laura Blossfeld wrote to the editor of a local newspaper suggesting the formation of a local parents' group. Similarly, a mother in New York City helped to organize the local Association for the Help of Retarded Children (AHRC) when she placed an announcement in a newspaper asking, "Surely there must be other children like him, other parents like myself. Where are you? Let's band together and do something for our children!" (Goode 1998).

By 1950, there were at least 88 local parent groups in 19 states, with a total of approximately 19,300 members. According to the historian Katherine Castles (2004), 77 of these groups were organized between 1946 and 1950. Close ties to professionals in the field led to recognition of the parents' movement by the American Association on Mental Deficiency (AAMD). In 1947, organizers of the annual AAMD conference invited Alan Sampson from the Washington State Association to speak, and thereafter AAMD conferences included some level of parent participation. Parents from across the nation learned about each other's efforts and established a steering committee to guide the foundation of a national organization. In 1950, at a conference in Minnesota, representatives of 23 parent groups established the National Association of Parents and Friends of Mentally Retarded Children, shortened in 1952 to the National Association for Retarded Children (NARC).

Parents' organizations emerged in this period for many reasons. Parents had long faced stigma, isolation, and a lack of services; however, before the medicalization of mental retardation and the corresponding growth of institutions, they had not expected professionals or the state to assist them in caring for their children. After years of professional advice extolling the importance of treatment and education, they felt that their children needed these services and were disappointed and angered by the barriers to receiving them. Parents also felt frustrated that the state's primary effort to help their children through institutions failed to help and tore families apart. Parents felt that the same money (or more) could be used to provide education, treatment, and productive work opportunities—all of the programs that institutions promised but usually failed to provide.

World War II heightened parents' sense of entitlement. One parent activist noted, "Many of us had been in the service, and we came home, and we just weren't ready to take some of the pat answers we used to get before" (quoted in Blair 1981, 149). Phrased even more bluntly, another explained that war veterans and their wives were "not going to take shit from anybody," especially regarding their families and children (quoted in Goode 1998, 39). This sense of entitlement was further encouraged by the focus on human rights and freedom that developed during the war, as well as by the growth of the welfare state and the growing availability of services for returning veterans and people with physical disabilities. Activism across America became widespread, and parents joined the fray. As early as 1951 in Chicago alone, Joseph Levy identified eleven parents' groups for children with the following conditions: mental retardation, cerebral palsy, deafness and hearing impairments, blindness, rheumatic heart disease, and orthopedic handicaps.

The increase in activism was also rooted in America's economic resurgence. After World War II, family income more than doubled (Mattaei 1982), and feelings of economic prosperity and security among middle-class Americans made them generous. Special education, which had been pushed financially to a back burner during the Depression, thrived during the 1940s and 1950s. Money to build institutions similarly plummeted in the 1930s but increased in the 1940s and 1950s. Financial security calmed some of the fears so intimately associated with eugenics.[2] America had become the land of prosperity and freedom, and families with mentally retarded members wanted to share in the success.

They also wanted to participate in the midcentury celebration of the family. As the war ended and the economy boomed, Americans focused on strengthening the family and returning to traditional sex roles and values. Americans married in greater numbers than ever before, and the birthrate shot up to a historic high in the 1950s after experiencing a historic low in the 1930s. The focus on family brought with it criticism of those who deviated from traditional family norms and values.[3] Ironically, concurrent with the national fixation on the ideal family with distinct gender roles, women were economically and politically more powerful than ever before. The number of women in paid employment continued to rise, as did their high-school and college graduation rates. With the economic boom, middle-class women had the time and resources to devote to political change, and in keeping with the tradition of Progressive female activists, they considered the well-being of the family to be one of their principal causes (Castles 2004; Jones 2004).

Coming Out of the Closet: The Rise of Parents' Stories

In the midst of parents' initial efforts at organization building, several groundbreaking memoirs brought national attention to the families of people with mental retardation. Considering their tremendous impact on the public awareness of mental retardation, I give three of these memoirs in-depth attention. In 1950, Pearl Buck, the only woman ever to be awarded both the Pulitzer Prize and the Nobel Prize, published the story of her daughter, Carol. Carol was born in 1920 in China, where Buck and her family lived. At the time of her birth, Carol showed no signs of disability. As she moved through her toddler years, though, her development seemed slower than typical, and her condition seemed to worsen as time progressed. Buck brought Carol to America to seek advice from the top experts in the field. They had little information to offer other than the vague explanation that "somewhere along the way, before birth or after, growth stopped" (Buck 1992 [1950], 42). They did at least confirm for Buck that Carol's condition was permanent and unlikely to improve.

Buck and Carol spent the next four years in China; then they returned to America. Because Carol had no opportunity to attend school, lagged far behind peers of her age developmentally, and already experienced rejection from them, Buck decided that her daughter's happiness could best be secured through placement in an American institution. (Institutions were not available at the time in China). Of this decision, she wrote, "I realized then that I must find another world for my child, one where she would not be despised and rejected, one where she could find her own level and have friends and affection, understanding and appreciation. I decided that day to find the right institution" (Buck 1992 [1950], 57).

Buck's work represents a significant departure from the contemporary understanding of mental retardation. It was rare for a person of her stature to admit publicly and offer the details of raising a mentally disabled offspring, and by doing so she called into question the notion propagated by the eugenics movement that disability invariably indicated tainted lineage. Of this stereotype, Buck said simply, "The old stigma of 'something in the family' is all too often unjust" (Buck 1992 [1950], 27).[4]

She also offered an alternative to the image fostered by eugenicists of the "mental defective" as criminal, perverse, and dangerous. Instead, Buck presented her daughter as "forever a child," and therefore forever innocent and joyful. Buck wrote, "As I watched her at play, myself so sorrowful, it came to me that this child would pass through life as the angels live in Heaven. The difficulties of existence would never be hers. She would not know that she was different from other children. The joys and irresponsibilities of childhood would be hers forever. My task was only to guarantee her safety, food and shelter— and kindness" (Buck 1992 [1950], 48). Later she reinforced this positive vision of eternal childhood, stating that "there is none more innocent than these children who never grow up." Carol was not someone to condemn and imprison; rather, she was a child who needed love, kindness, and the opportunity to play and develop her limited skills for her own enjoyment.

Although Buck decided to institutionalize Carol, she did not condone all institutional practices. She found the search for an appropriate place for her daughter painstaking and saw many places that she felt dehumanized their patients. In one institution, which she referred to as "an abode of horror," she described the patients as "herded together like dogs. . . . [T]here was not one thing of beauty anywhere, nothing for the children to look at, no reason for them to lift their heads or put out their hands" (Buck 1992 [1950], 69). Buck decided to place Carol at the Training School at Vineland, New Jersey, because there she perceived a warmth and commitment to the children's happiness. The staff appeared friendly and treated the residents as important human beings with individual needs. By comparing the various institutions she visited, Buck critiqued the common conditions found within institutions without discarding the potential for high-quality, lifelong care for individuals who needed it.

Buck placed Carol at the Training School when she was nine years old, and she continued to visit regularly. She stressed to parents that they should keep children at home through the toddler years, if possible, and maintain a relationship with them after institutional placement because she felt the parent– child relationship was vital to the well-being of both the parents and the child.

She advised, "Remember, too, that the child has his right to life, whatever that life may be, and he has the right to happiness, which you must find for him. Be proud of your child, accept him as he is and do not heed the words and stares of those who know no better. This child has a meaning for you and for all children" (Buck 1992 [1950], 85). *The Child Who Never Grew* first appeared in an issue of *Ladies Home Journal* in the 1950s and was subsequently published as a book, with excerpts appearing in *Reader's Digest* and *Time Magazine*. With its publication, "the floodgates burst open" (Jablow 1992, 3). Parents inundated Buck with letters and wrote their own stories for publication.

Not long after *The Child Who Never Grew* was published, another parent's memoir, *My Son's Story* by John Frank (1952), attracted national attention. Unlike Buck, who was a famous author, Frank and his wife, Lorraine, represented middle-class America; he worked as a law professor, and she cared for their home. They were young, well-educated, on solid ground financially but not wealthy, and excited to start a family. Like Carol, their first child, Petey, showed no indications of disability at birth, but in his toddler years he seemed slower and smaller than other children his age. When he began to fall unconscious (later identified as seizures), the Franks sought expert advice. The diagnosis shocked them. The doctors told them that a large part of Petey's brain was "dead." When they asked what this condition meant for his future, one physician responded, "It means he has no future. He will continue to have convulsions. He will never develop fully" (Frank 1952, 57). Confirming the diagnosis and prognosis, another doctor told them that the condition was not hereditary and suggested that they "have five more children. You cannot save this one, but a few more will save the parents" (Frank 1952, 79).

As Frank began to share the news of his son's disability with family and close friends, two of his respected colleagues urged him to consider institutionalization. Frank consulted Petey's physician, who advised, "Once it is clear that a child is hopelessly subnormal, there isn't any question about the wisdom of institutionalizing the child. Your wife won't want to, but her life is as much at stake as any other" (Frank 1952, 92). Frank decided to follow this advice and offered several reasons for his decision: He believed that keeping Petey at home would "ruin Lorraine's life" by turning her into a full-time nurse; damage his own life and career; impede the happiness and development of their future children, who would be trapped in a "constant sickroom atmosphere;" and deny Petey the best medical attention. With the doctor's assistance, Frank convinced his wife to place their son in an institution.

With the decision made, the Franks were confronted with the lack of services available for infants with retardation and could not find an affordable institution that would accept their son. Finally, after much searching, they identified a suitable situation, and at nineteen months of age, Petey arrived at St. Rita's. John was impressed by the patience and dedication of the staff, as well as by his son's smooth adjustment. Like Buck, the Franks remained active in Petey's life, receiving regular updates on his progress and visiting three or four times a year. At the conclusion of his story, Frank emphasized his family's good fortune. Unlike many families in the same situation, he and his wife received support from their friends and family, found what they considered to be thoughtful and accurate medical advice, earned an income sufficient to afford a respectable private institution, stayed involved in Petey's life, and had another child whom they could cherish.

Frank's and Buck's accounts share many themes. They both dismissed the eugenic emphasis on heredity, presented their children as wonderful human beings who deserved love and care, and emphasized the importance of preserving the family unit even given institutionalization. They both expressed concern with the conditions in many institutions, yet also supported the appropriateness of institutionalization when high-quality care was available. Unlike Buck, Frank placed Petey while he was an infant, representing a growing trend toward earlier commitment. Frank also more openly acknowledged the financial hardship associated with having a disabled child, even for a middle-class professional, and called greater attention to the barriers to obtaining high-quality care faced by average families.

The most popular parent memoir was still to come. In 1953, Revell Press released Dale Evans Rogers's book *Angel Unaware*, and its sales soared. In the first year following its release, only two other books sold more copies: *The Revised Standard Version of the Bible* and *The Power of Positive Thinking* (Trent 1994). The American entertainment icons Dale Evans Rogers and her husband, Roy Rogers, had starred together in twenty-seven films and a television show that lasted from 1950 to 1957; released approximately four hundred recordings; and conducted worldwide tours. Known as the "Queen of the West," Rogers represented the American values of faith and family. When she told the public that the only child she and Roy had together was severely retarded, Americans overwhelmingly responded with sympathy and devotion.

Rogers wrote the story of her daughter, Robin, who was born with Down Syndrome and lived only two years, from her child's perspective as an angel in heaven recounting to God her brief experiences on earth. Simply by placing Robin in heaven, Rogers demanded that the reader picture her as God's "Little Angel"—innocent, pure, and beautiful rather than as a defective or deviant. Rogers described the positive impact Robin had on their lives: "I believe with all my heart that God sent her on a two year mission to our household, to strengthen us spiritually and to draw us closer together in the knowledge and love and fellowship of God" (Rogers 1953, 7). As God's servant, Robin helped Rogers to see His goodness in all creatures, especially the smallest and the weakest. According to Rogers, the positive effects of her daughter's life reverberated throughout the world. She remembered a doctor who, after working with Robin, decided to go to theological school to better equip himself to help disabled children and their families. She imagined Robin saying, "We really helped him, didn't [w]e? Being with me will make him a better doctor with every patient he has from now on. It's good he didn't want to 'machine-gun' me, like that other doctor!" (Rogers 1953, 60–61).

In Robin, Rogers created the idealized eternal child. Whereas Buck acknowledged the sorrow and burden associated with parenting a disabled child, Rogers portrayed her daughter as the embodiment of innocence and wisdom in an otherwise ignorant and cruel world. Building a Christian interpretation of disability, Rogers presented people with disabilities, like all other people, as a blessing from God, and proposed that acceptance, love, and faith would allow God's blessing to shine and enhance the world.[5]

The Parents' Movement and the Special Child

These memoirs inspired parents, legitimated their feelings, and exposed them to new conceptions of mental retardation. Following in the same path, the parents' movement launched an assault against the common stereotypes of "mental defectives." Echoing Leo Kanner's ideas of the double handicap, a parent claimed that "the greatest handicap that mentally deficient children have is not their low mentality, but the public's lack of understanding" (Richards 1953, 56). In developing new positive images of people with mental retardation, parents compared their children to other children. Like any other child, their children were gentle, lovable, innocent, and pure, with "a child's happy faculty of living in a world where play is a reality" ("Not Like Other Children" 1943, 34). Like other children, their children needed love, patience, guidance, and protection. And like other children, their children had skills and deficits, both of which needed to be acknowledged. One parent argued that for too long society had "thought of these 'forgotten children' in terms of what they cannot do, rather than in terms of what they may be able to do with help and sympathetic understanding" (quoted in Gramm 1951, 154).

Parents proudly showcased their children's many achievements. One father described the many "credits" his son could claim: "Though there are plenty of things Eddie can't do, there are items on the credit side. For one thing, he rides a three-wheeler. It took him a year to learn. So what! He can't play with other kids. But that brings him closer to us" (Piccola 1955, 50). In *"One of Those": Progress of a Mongoloid Child*, Sophia Grant (1957, 52) described how, despite the fact that professionals had suggested that her "mongoloid" son would never learn, she taught him to play the piano, read and write, and roller skate. With each of these hard-won accomplishments, "the very joy of living burst forth" from her son. Like other children, children with mental retardation could learn and progress if given love, acceptance, education, and opportunity.

As Rogers did, parents also claimed that children with mental retardation could teach other individuals something about themselves and the world. A parent involved with the parents' movement wrote, "We learn so much from our children, retarded children are wonderful teachers if we are not too proud

to learn from them. . . . We learn so much in patience, in humility, in gratitude for other blessings we had accepted before as a matter of course" (Murray
1959). These children had value, regardless of what they could and could not
do, because they were human and because they taught others about the value
of human life.

As parents compared their children to other children, they also compared
them to children with physical disabilities.[6] Organizations advocating for individuals with physical disabilities had made enormous strides toward improving
public awareness and increasing public support. By linking mental and physical disability, parents of children with retardation hoped to share in this success. Mental disability often provoked more fear and mistrust among the public
than physical disability. Hence, Steven Spencer (1952, 26) wrote for the *Saturday Evening Post*, "The crippling of an arm or leg is a tangible defect that most
people understand and accept. But crippling of the brain is a strange, dark
affliction, clouded with misinformation, superstition and unwarranted feelings
of guilt and shame, and too often pushed into the back corner of the public's
consciousness—and conscience." Yet parents claimed that mental and physical disabilities were in fact very similar; retardation was simply a disability of
the brain. As part of its public-awareness campaign, NARC published an ad
depicting a little boy with no visible disabilities, with copy that read, "This is
a picture of a 'crippled' child. No you see no braces on his legs, no supporting
crutch." Rather, "It is his little brain that is crippled." Similarly, a parent speaking at a meeting of the Association for the Help of Retarded Children (AHRC)[7]
asked rhetorically, "You would not deny schooling and playmates to a crippled
child—should they be denied to my child because it is his *brain* rather than his
limbs that is crippled?" (quoted in Gramm 1951) Regardless of whether the disability was visible or invisible, children with disabilities deserved access to services and inclusion.

Parents also acknowledged that their children were not completely like
other children. In "A Bill of Rights for the Retarded," Richard Hungerford (1959
[1952], 937) walked the difficult line between recognizing similarities and differences, demanding both equality and unique services and rights. According to Hungerford, children with mental retardation had "in general all the
needs of other children," yet they were "exceptional, not because they differ
from us all in having these needs, but because they have additional or exceptional needs over and above the needs common to the majority." They needed
more, not less, of the same basic things that other children needed: more hours
of education, more services from professionals, more guidance and protection,
more love, and more attention.

What their children did *not* need was negativity, particularly professional
labels that reduced them to idiots, morons, and imbeciles. Parents rebelled
against the "nomenclature of despair," arguing that negative labels dehumanized their children (Goode 1998). According to Gunnar Dybwad (1962, 8–9),
executive director of NARC, by using the terms such as "crib case" to describe

non-ambulatory individuals with severe disabilities, "We label the person rather than the services or facility he needs as we first see him. Once and for all he is a 'crib case.'" Rather, professionals and parents needed terminology to describe the services needed, recognizing that the need for particular services could change over time. They encouraged the transition to the terminology of "mental retardation," with the subcategories of mild, severe, and profound retardation, which at the time seemed less laden with pessimism. Most important, parents argued that behind all labels, services, and treatment "there must be, we think, a belief in the limitless value and a certain equality of every human being regardless of his or her degree of intelligence" ("Equal Right to Training" 1962, 9).

THE CHILD AND THE FAMILY
While parents struggled to improve the image of their children in society, they did not position their children as *individuals*. Rather, the child existed within a *family*, and the entire family unit needed to be acknowledged, respected, and preserved. According to the AHRC leaders Joseph Weingold and Rudolf Hormuth (1953, 118), professionals needed to understand that "no child stands alone; that a child is part of a family and a community; that what happens to the family affects the child and certainly the child affects the family."

Families with mentally retarded members desperately wanted to be seen as normal and good families, fitting the domestic ideal of the 1950s. Therefore, parents stressed their strong family ties, their devotion to each other, and the integral role of the disabled child within the family (Piccola 1955). Describing their love for their child, one couple wrote for *Parents* magazine, "It's as if we love him so devotedly and so specially, and because we know we will not always have him with us [due to their intent to place him in an institution when he reached school age] that we are somehow closer to our baby and he to us than is normally the case" ("Not Like Other Children" 1943, 99). Rather than feeling disgust or rejection, these parents loved their children as parents would love any child, maybe even more so. Indeed, because some parents believed that their disabled child remained childlike throughout his or her lifetime, they felt that they "faced far fewer problems than do most parents of modern teenagers" (Hunt 1967, 30).

To establish themselves as "good" families, parents followed in the footsteps of Buck, Frank, and Rogers and repeatedly sought to dispel the stereotype of tainted lineage. In the first editorial of the NARC newsletter *Children Limited*, Eugene Gramm (1952, 1) told parents, "We know that they [people with mental retardation] are with us everywhere and have always been with us. We know that they come to us regardless of race, creed, religion, social station or level of parental intelligence." When the Kennedy family publicly announced that they had a family member with retardation, they, too, explicitly attacked these stereotypes. Eunice Kennedy Shriver (1962, 72) wrote, "Mental retardation can happen in any family. It *has* happened in the families of the poor and the rich, of governors, senators, Nobel prizewinners, doctors, lawyers, writers, men of genius, presidents of corporations—the president of the United States." Parents could not hope for a clearer absolution of genetic "blame."

Parents recognized that they needed training and services for their children and for themselves to maintain a well-functioning family. Children needed opportunities such as education and job placement, while parents needed to be taught how to raise and educate their children. Only through the provision of a comprehensive set of community-based services could they "obviate the need for institutions" and "enable [children with disabilities] to become acceptable members of their families and neighborhoods" (Education Committee of the National Association for Retarded Children 1954, 357). Services would protect the family unit and ensure that each family member could thrive as an important part of the community.

As Katherine Castles (2004) found, the commitment to family preservation had a double edge, leading to demands not only for community services but also for institutionalization. Families who kept disabled members at home faced tremendous difficulties meeting social expectations, and some felt that the norms of family life of the 1950s could be attained only by placing the disabled child in an institution. One parent explained that, if their daughter had been kept at home, "we should have to curtail normal family activities. . . . [W]e would have to devote the major part of our time to her, leaving her little brother to develop as best he could." Care of their daughter would deprive the other child, "the child who had all the potentialities," of the time, attention, and financial resources necessary for his development ("We Committed Our Child" 1945, 20). From this perspective, the presence of the disabled child at home would destroy the ability of the family to function normally. Another parent explained that, when she and her husband institutionalized their daughter, "It seemed we were being forced to make a choice for either the normal or the subnormal child. There wasn't much choice, stated that way, so we had this relative fill out the necessary papers for her application for admittance to the State School for the Retarded" (Stout 1959, 10).

Some parents who placed their children in institutions did not believe that they were abrogating their parental responsibilities in pursuit of normality. Instead, they saw institutional placement as the means to fulfill their parental responsibilities. As Buck and Frank had shown, some parents went to great lengths to find and afford placements, sought out the best advice, and decided to institutionalize as a way to secure their child's well-being and happiness. Even after institutional placement, they still considered themselves good parents and maintained their parental role through visits, letters, gifts, love, and consideration. One parent, Dorothy Murray (1956, 81), explained that her decision to place her son in an institution was the "most merciful, most kind, and would cause the least suffering to the child itself regardless of what it might cost the parents in mental anguish and sorrow" (see also "School for a Different Child" 1941).

Regardless of whether parents placed a child in institutional care or kept him or her at home, parents' organizations played an important role in helping families feel good about themselves. Parents shared stories and advice, formed play groups and classes with their children, worked toward social change together, and enjoyed family recreation together. One parent remembered, "With our boy we had had no one to talk to. We had no idea of anyone with a similar problem—that was one of the main things that got us together, was just to be able to talk to somebody who understood and shared your problem" (quoted in Blair 1981, 150). Dorothy Murray (1956, 85) described her first meeting with other parents as a "blessed relief to sit down and talk with someone who really understood." For some parents, parents' organizations became "quasi-families" (Levy 1951). In his study of the AHRC, Alfred Katz (1961) found that the organization served many functions for families—providing desperately needed services, a source of information and support, a means for achieving social and political change, a feeling of belonging, and an affirmation of a positive family identity—and that some parents became fiercely committed to the group and correspondingly "militant" about its cause.

Respect for the family was a founding principle of the parents' movement. A strong family strengthened both its individual members and the nation as a whole. According to Pearl Buck and her co-author Gweneth Zarfoss (1965, 149), "The family is the unit of the community, the community is the unit of the nation, and the nation is the unit in the world of human society. It is not too much to say that what one family does with and for its retarded child in time may change the world."

CONNECTING THE CHILD, FAMILY, AND COMMUNITY

Compared with professionals, parents were less likely to base access to services and rights on the potential productivity of their children. Of course, they valorized every achievement of their children, but they also wanted to ensure that every child, regardless of his or her productivity or level of adjustment, received services. Therefore, they developed a needs-based philosophy in which the state and community had an obligation to care for its needy.

As the Roosevelts and other progressive Democrats claimed that the state had a social responsibility to prevent human suffering, so, too, did early parent rhetoric stress the state's obligation to its needy members. Parents argued, for example, that "we should give the most to those who need the most" (Weingold 1954, 480). Alton Lund (1959, 1071), vice president of NARC, asked, "Is it not ironic that a nation which boasts the atomic bomb, the highest standard of living known to man, the marvels of television, radio, advanced education, marvelous hospitals, and also a nation which has always shown the greatest sympathy for the plight of people in foreign nations, has failed to make adequate provision for its retarded children?" According to parent activists, the nation could achieve greatness by taking care of its needy citizens, whereas weakness and treachery flowed from the denial of assistance to even the smallest portion of society.

Portraying people with mental retardation as children worked particularly well in pursuing this needs-based philosophy. No one expected children to earn their keep; rather, they deserved care and protection simply because they were children. By transforming all people with mental retardation into "eternal children," parents attempted to extend the claim to care to the entire lifetime of their retarded offspring. Moreover, the needs of children in general had been, to some degree at least, recognized as *rights*. According to the United Nations, White House Conferences, and some American laws, children had rights to safety and the provision of their basic needs. If parents did not meet these fundamental needs, the state was obligated to step in and provide for the child.[8] In their family-centered vision of rights, parents (not professionals) held the first line of authority over their children. They believed that the state should make family preservation a national priority, and at the parents' request or following their deaths the state should step in as a substitute parent, with both authority over and an *obligation* to care for, support, and protect its dependents throughout their lifetime. Thus, parents and the state would join together to protect their children while also respecting and protecting parents' authority. As explained by Richard Hungerford in the "Bill of Rights for the Retarded," "The state must be to [retarded children] a humane advocate as long as they may live, and this must be a covenant both with the retarded and with their parents" (Hungerford 1959 [1952], 938).

In his address to the newly formed National Association of Parents and Friends of Mentally Retarded Children in 1950, Minnesota's Governor Luther Youngdahl summarized the newly developing parents' rhetoric on rights:

> The retarded child has the right to social assistance in a world in which he cannot possibly compete on equal footing. He has the right to special education and to special institutions for the retarded child who cannot be taken care of at home. He has the right to be provided with the most modern training in an institution that is possible, in an institution marked not only by the pleasantness of its brick and mortar and lawns and play areas and educational services and child speciality and medical services, but by an atmosphere and by a group of people in attendance who will not only give that child patient understanding but to love and be affectionate to that child as other children get at home. He has a right to these things and his parents have a right to know that he has these rights. For they too are entitled to peace of mind about what is happening to a retarded child separated from them.[9]

This quote highlights parents' desire to provide retarded "children" with the rights to love, protection, and services in a way that modeled family relationships. Youngdahl even mentioned parents' "right" to peace of mind, to know that their retarded children would be provided for throughout their lives. In this framework, rights did not establish autonomous contractual relationships as typical of most civil rights; rather, they created a set of formal relationships that supported or substituted for the familial pattern of relationships, with the disabled member situated as the dependent in need and the parent and state situated as the caring provider.

The narrow focus on children, however, had obvious limitations and did not go without criticism. Rosemary Dybwad (1990), secretary of NARC's international-relations committee, argued against the notion of eternal childhood and its use to claim services and rights for people with mental retardation and instead promoted a recognition of basic human rights. According to Dybwad, the belief in eternal childhood denied people with mental retardation their fundamental rights to mature and to participate in society as adults. Human rights, however, "grow out of human existence itself" and were not limited by age or mental condition. Dybwad wrote, "Let me start out with a simple yet most fundamental point: out of human experience has come the recognition that human life can be equated with growth and development. There is no standing still; there may be processes of deterioration leading to death, but growth and development is *the* basic fact of human life, and the most basic human right derived from this is the *right* to grow and develop, the right to move from childhood to adolescence, from adolescence to adulthood" (Dybwad 1990, 142). For Dybwad, all people deserved the rights to grow and to participate meaningfully in their families and communities.

The philosophy of human rights also recognized rights specific to particular human conditions. The UN General Assembly declared in 1959 that "the child who is physically, mentally or socially handicapped shall be given the special treatment, education, and care, required by his particular condition" (United Nations 1959). According to Dybwad, the declaration was significant because "it asserted the right to assistance for all handicapped children without qualification, simply as a consequence of their existence as human beings" (Dybwad 1990, 130–131). The declaration also addressed the right of a child to grow up with his or her parents, and for Dybwad this right further implied "a right for assistance to the family" so that the child and family could develop to their fullest potential. In addition, she told parents that they also had rights, including the rights to be informed and to participate in decision making regarding their children's treatment and services.

In 1968, The International League of Societies for the Mentally Handicapped issued a supplement to the United Nations Universal Declaration of Human Rights that specifically addressed the basic human rights of individuals with retardation. In addition to those accorded to other citizens, it supported the following rights: to the opportunity to develop to one's fullest capacity regardless of cost; to economic security, a decent standard of living, and a safe place to work; to an appropriate and free public education; to appropriate and safe treatment by trained professionals; to just treatment within the criminal-justice system respecting the degree of responsibility; and to the implementation of legal safeguards in cases in which the rights and privileges of citizenship must be limited. "Above all," according to the Declaration of Human Rights, "the mentally retarded person has a right to respect" (International League of Societies for the Mentally Handicapped 1968).

The narrative of human rights recognized human needs without reducing people with disabilities to children or to needy dependents. It recognized the rights of both children and adults. And most fundamentally, it recognized the humanity of people with retardation. However, it also had limitations. The idea of human rights carried little weight in the American legal system, which did not formally recognize rights such as the rights to work, to health care, or to housing for its citizens, making it difficult to transform human-rights rhetoric into actual legislation and funding.

The Parent Agenda

What specifically did parents want for their children and themselves? According to the early NARC leader Eugene Gramm (1952, 1), all of the efforts of NARC had a single goal: "to give every retarded individual the opportunity which is the birthright of every American—the opportunity to develop to his or her fullest capacity."[10] Parents attempted to establish a guarantee of "a complete program for each retarded child wherever he may be" (Lund 1959, 1074) so that all retarded children would have opportunities to thrive as members of their families and communities. This included the following:

- The establishment of community clinics to provide parents with well-informed diagnoses and prognoses in a sensitive and helpful manner (Weingold 1954).
- The guarantee of "regular periodic reexamination and re-evaluation of mental, psychological and social aptitudes," as well as regular periodic physical, medical, and dental examinations, to ensure access for people with mental retardation to the complete range of appropriate medical care throughout each person's lifetime (Bostock 1959, 511).
- The guarantee of state-funded, community-based education and training for *all* children appropriate to their individual needs beginning in early life (including nursery school), lasting longer than for other children, and provided by professionals trained in special education.
- The establishment of community-based parent-education programs to instruct "mothers how to teach basic living habits and simple tasks and amusements to these youngsters," to promote a healthy, well-functioning family and the retention of disabled family members in their own home (Spencer 1952, 27).

- The establishment of vocational training, sheltered workshops, and selective placements in competitive employment that provided adults with a sense of self-respect and responsibility, opportunities for social interaction, and the ability to contribute to their own self-support, regardless of their actual likelihood of attaining self-sufficiency ("National Association for Retarded Children" 1959).
- The integration of retarded children, adults, and their families in all community organizations and services, including worship, recreational programs, social programs, community clinics, and so on, so that individuals with disabilities and their families would no longer face social isolation.
- The establishment of day care, short-term residential programs, and respite programs "where children can be placed for limited periods when the parents are unable to take care of them" (Shallit 1956, 44).
- The establishment of guardianship legislation to ensure the long-term protection of people with mental retardation residing in the community.
- Increased public support for research examining the causes of retardation, techniques for prevention and rehabilitation, and best practices in the provision of programs.
- Increased availability and quality of residential centers, "providing a multiplicity of facilities including diagnosis, education, training, rehabilitation, medical care and treatment and other therapies, together with research units, through the services of a staff comprised of administrators, physicians, psychologists, educators, nurses, social workers, physical, occupational and speech therapists and counselors," focused on ensuring the well-being and development of its residents and their return to community, if feasible (Robbins 1957, 673).
- The standardization of training requirements and provision of funding and high-quality programs to train personnel in relevant fields to enable them to offer appropriate and respectful services.

This list of services and programs actually did not differ dramatically from some of the plans of action developed by professionals in the AAMD throughout the 1940s and 1950s. However, parents believed that these services should be motivated by the best interests and "the happiness of our children" rather than by organizational efficiency or cost–benefit analyses (Robbins 1957, 673). They suggested a "whole-person, total-living-experience approach," which recognized that different people had different needs and that these needs changed throughout an individual's lifespan (Bostock 1959). For parents, all services needed to assume that individuals with mental retardation could and would learn if provided lifelong opportunities. Services made available to other children needed to be made available to *all children*. In addition, because exceptional children had exceptional needs, exceptional children needed to receive *more* than what other children received. From the parents' perspective, policies and programs also had to recognize individuals with mental retardation as an integral part of their families and communities and to serve them within this context, when feasible. Professionals had to offer parents respect, recognize their expertise in their children's welfare, provide them with support in developing any additional expertise that they needed, and include them as important members of decision-making processes.

Most simply, parents wanted professionals and the community to respect and care for their children. When programs failed to value their children as human beings, they quickly transformed into vehicles for rejection and exclusion; such educational programs hid children with disabilities in the most remote classroom of a building and then ignored them; diagnostic services turned into perfunctory advice to institutionalize, and institutions turned into snake pits. Parents wanted to ensure that services actually served the best interests of their children.

Of these goals, parents spent the greatest time and energy on educational and residential services. For early parent activists, the need for educational services was often *the* driving motivation for organizing.[11] Like some educators of the time, but in contrast with the majority of them, parents argued that "every child, even the severely retarded, has some capacity for learning" (Spencer 1952, 110). Their children were not ineducable; rather, the education system had failed to recognize the potential of thousands of children and to discover how they learned. Given that all children could learn, no child should ever "be allowed to vegetate or regress" (Bostock 1959, 512). Hence, in the 1954 "Educational Bill of Rights," NARC demanded, "For every child a fair chance." In addition, education had to provide a curriculum and use techniques appropriate to encourage progress according to the capacities of each individual child. "Our idea was that we must have a broader view of education, not only what we usually envision as hard academics," a parent activist explained. "Education is the whole child, and what we can do to enhance that child's potential—whatever that might be—is education" (quoted in Schwartzenberg 2005, 68). Ultimately, education had to respect the dignity and worth of every child; "There must be no special education that is not both special and education; the manner of teaching must be one of kindness and personal respect, but the curriculum must be one that remembers the tomorrows as well as the todays; there must be no reliance on osmosis, no finger painting on the sands of time" (Hungerford 1959 [1952], 938).

Parents also strove to transform the institution. Institutionalization had always been a controversial topic among parents, and tension existed between those who chose to institutionalize their children and those who chose to keep their children at home. Indeed, institutionalization is one of the rare topics that provoked open in-fighting among parents in NARC newsletters. For example, in a letter to the editor of *Children Limited*, a parent opposed to institutionalization asked, "But where are the parents of these children? Aren't too many parents asking the state to do what they themselves will not do—that is, accept the retarded as human beings?" (Harper 1968, 4). At the same time, pro-institution parents defended themselves. Barbara Scuitto (1974, 8), the mother of an institutionalized nineteen-year-old woman, asked, "Why do you continually hammer at normalization for those that require above normal care? . . . Institutions are *not bad*. Everyone everywhere is developing new attitudes toward the retarded, those working in state hospitals being the first and most advanced. State care is *good care*. It is permanent, uninterrupted, *rested*, and loving care."

In light of the division among parents, through the 1950s and 1960s NARC generally took a middle-of-the-road approach, advocating the expansion, improvement, and transformation of institutional care in addition to the expansion of systems of community care. In his Presidential Address to NARC in 1959, Gunnar Dybwad noted that, although some people believed that "institutions are on their way out," he thought that "we certainly will not only continue to need, but in my opinion will undoubtedly increase the use of, facilities for residential group care of the mentally retarded" (cited in Dybwad 1964, 83).

While institutions were still necessary, according to Dybwad, the way in which they functioned had to be transformed to best meet the needs of their residents. Dybwad asked his audience to "strike the words 'custodial care'" from their vocabulary (Dybwad 1964, 84). Rather than providing custodial warehousing, institutions should serve those who specifically needed residential support, including individuals with severe medical conditions who required around-the-clock, permanent medical and nursing care; young children and teens who would benefit from a short-term, intensive residential educational program; teens at risk of delinquency whose behavior had become difficult to manage at home; and older adults who no longer had family or who wished for "a more sheltered environment with others like themselves."

Following the framework developed by the parents' movement regarding service provision in general, Dybwad stressed that residential centers should treat their charges with respect and as individuals. Like other critics of institutions, he believed that the "power structure" that used mass housing, feeding, and recreation for the sake of efficiency created a tremendous barrier to the institution's primary goals of education and rehabilitation, "so that it is often sheer mockery to speak of development of the person's fullest potential" (Dybwad 1964). Dybwad suggested that, rather than immense dormitories, institutions should instead use cottages with far fewer patients in each to provide a more homelike atmosphere. In all of their programs, institutions needed to foster individual growth, dignity, and respect so that patients would come to "know freedom, laughter, and a sense of giving." Patients needed to learn self-help, academic, and vocational skills, and more broadly they needed to "be given opportunities to grow as a person," including learning to "identify themselves as individuals," to take responsibility, to make decisions, to exercise judgment, and to show respect for others. They needed to feel safe and comfortable in their environment. They needed to be loved and accepted by the members of the institution and to be encouraged to belong to a family unit outside the institution. They needed to have opportunities to build the skills necessary to return to the community and to actually return when appropriate, regardless of institutional interests. To pursue these changes, parents believed that both they and the state needed to exercise greater control over the power structure of the institution. According to parents, in the institution "there must be no corners hidden" (Bostock 1959; Hungerford 1959 [1952]; "Residential Care Position Issued" 1969).

Strategies and Successes

The early parents' movement relied on several key strategies to accomplish its goals. Chapters of the Association for Retarded Children (ARC) built their membership rapidly and spread their message by using advertisements, public postings, public-awareness campaigns, and word of mouth. A survey taken in 1950 recorded about 19,300 parents organized in local efforts in several states; by 1960, NARC alone estimated that it had 62,000 members, and by 1964 its membership had reached 100,000 (Segal 1970). As an organization with a middle-class and upper-middle-class base, its members were typically well educated and had many political and professional resources at their disposal. In addition, they recognized that their status as parents (particularly as middle-class "blameless" parents) of children with disabilities gave their case a moral righteousness useful in political lobbying.

Parents sought out political allies with personal ties to individuals with mental retardation. For example, Arthur Trudeau, the father of a son with Down Syndrome and a leader among parents with disabled children in Rhode Island, introduced his close friend, Rhode Island Congressman John E. Fogarty, to the concerns of the parents' movement. Fogarty emerged as "an avid champion of retarded citizens' needs and rights throughout his long career in Congress" (Blair 1981, 152). Similarly, in New York, Jerry Weingold, director of the AHRC, sought out and built a strong political alliance with State Senator Bill Conklin, who had a son with Down Syndrome. Parents also used letter-writing, phone-calling, and "open house" campaigns to educate politicians about their needs and expectations. The researcher Robert Segal (1970, 98–99) noted, "The primary theme related to these strategies is the attempt to achieve some type of interaction with those persons who are in the position to influence the decision-making process. Once the contact is attained, either 'rational persuasion' (educational material or legislative suggestions) or emotional appeal (the fact of having a retarded child who needs help) is used."

In addition to politicians, parents cultivated ties with key professional groups, including the AAMD, and with celebrities. The AAMD publicly supported and collaborated with NARC at least occasionally (Levy 1951). For example, Elizabeth Boggs, a parent and activist in New Jersey, served on the AAMD Nomenclature Committee and played a key role in pushing professionals to alter their terminology and substitute "mental retardation" for "mental deficiency."[12] Boggs later became the only parent to sit on the President's Panel on Mental Retardation. Parents also became savvy in their use of the media and brought many celebrities to their aid, including Pearl Buck, Judy Garland, Tony Orlando, Barbra Streisand, and even Steven Spielberg's famous character E.T. Conventional grassroots fundraising techniques such as bake sales, dinner galas, and raffle sales allowed parent activists to raise additional money locally and to keep a high profile in their local communities.

As they fought for broad changes in the way in which society viewed and treated their children, parents successfully effected change in their own backyards. They established and operated services that included special-education classes, nursery classes, day care, play-therapy groups, parent-education classes, vocational training, and sheltered workshops. In 1955, just five years after NARC was formed, it reported that local chapters were operating 1,015 activities and projects throughout the nation. NARC encouraged parents to create demonstration projects, with the intent that these services would eventually be taken over by the appropriate agencies. (For example, a successful special-education class run by parents might serve as a model for the local school district.) NARC even provided initial funding for research (Masland et al. 1958) rather than waiting for federal research money to come its way.

By the 1960s, NARC could claim many legislative successes, including the 1956 Social Security amendment that extended survivor benefits for people with mental retardation beyond age eighteen; the 1958 Act to Encourage Expansion of Teaching in the Education of Mentally Retarded Children; the Immigration and Nationality Act of 1965, which lifted the ban on people with mental retardation as potential permanent immigrants; the Manpower Development and Training Act, which funded training both for people with mental retardation for employment and for the aides who worked with them; the 1963 Maternal and Child Health and Mental Retardation Planning Amendments to the Social Security Act of 1935 (PL 88-156), which created programs to prevent mental retardation and plan mental retardation services; and the 1963 Mental Retardation Facilities and Community Mental Health Centers Construction Act (PL 88-164), which, among other things, provided funding to build community-based treatment centers ("NARC" 1969; Segal 1970).

Limitations

Despite all of their successes, parents' organizations faced and created many of their own limitations in the early years. Their focus on eternal childhood reinforced dependence among people with disabilities rather than establishing them as autonomous adult citizens. Parents' views about the family also had their shortfalls. Parents' organizations purposefully depicted their members as part of average, white, middle-class America and did not consistently welcome or represent families that did not conform to these ideals. Despite higher rates of retardation among poor and minority populations, NARC had little to say about poverty, race, ethnicity, single motherhood, or urban renewal. It usually failed to attract or to represent well poor, minority, and uneducated families who could not easily pay membership dues, throw gala parties, or initiate their own demonstration projects (Castles 2004; Segal 1970).

While parents' organizations developed and used their ties to professionals and politicians well, they also experienced tensions in their relationships with the individuals whose help they sought. Parents were suspicious of professionals, especially mental-health professionals, who for so long had ignored and mistreated them. Professionals similarly felt "suspicion and hostility" toward parents who made "apparently impossible demands" on them and tried to run programs best left, they believed, in professional hands.[13] Parents also had difficulty convincing politicians to take up their cause. While children's rights and human rights were symbolically important in this era, they carried little real weight in courts or Congress. Over and over again, professionals and politicians told parents that they had to "sell" their position to the public by explaining what the public would get in return for providing services. Yet parents could not guarantee that that the public would see a return from educating the most severely disabled children or providing them with sheltered workshops.

Parents created many successful programs, but in doing so they often became entrenched within the service-delivery system and resistant to change themselves. Although NARC recommended that parents use a model of "demonstration projects," parents often enjoyed controlling the services and felt they could best provide them. While often very beneficial, these services were typically segregated and specifically for people with mental retardation. When times changed and advocates began to push for programs that stressed inclusion, integration, and individualization, many ARC chapters had institutional interests in preserving their segregated programs, resisting further change rather than advocating for it.

Finally, in a number of situations parents were divided among themselves. Parents who kept their children with disabilities at home feuded with parents who institutionalized their children. Parents of children with mild disabilities had different priorities and strategies from parents of children with severe disabilities. Some parents of children with Down Syndrome established a separate group to deal with issues they felt were specific to this population.[14] Parents' organizations often failed to recognize that some children had multiple disabilities and pushed parents into disability-specific groups that fought against each other for funding and political support.

It is difficult to say how much of the change that occurred during this era resulted directly from the parents' movement. Other changes in society occurred at the same time, including the transition from the Eisenhower administration to the Kennedy administration and the shift in professional paradigms. Certainly, though, parents pushed mental retardation into the local and national consciousness and applied great pressure on the government, professionals, and society to ensure the brightest possible future for their children.

The Role of the Federal Government and the Kennedy Family in the Changing Conceptions of Retardation

Although they kept a distance from the parents' movement, the Kennedy family helped to move the politics of mental retardation to the national level and to formalize the shifting professional and parental paradigms into actual legislation.

Prior to the Kennedy administration, the federal government had sponsored a handful of small and disconnected initiatives related to mental retardation, usually at the behest of politicians directly interested in disability or mental retardation. The Kennedy family sought instead to create a cohesive national agenda to address the issue. Joseph P. Kennedy Sr. and his wife, Rose, had nine children, including a daughter, Rosemary, who was diagnosed as mildly retarded. Her condition worsened through her adolescence and early adulthood, and her behavior became increasingly difficult to manage at home. Joseph Kennedy "settled on one last desperate measure before sending her away: lobotomy," an operation that cuts or destroys the connections to and from the prefrontal cortex, an area of the brain associated with complex cognitive processes such as decision making and planning (Shorter 2000, 32). An unorthodox operation for the treatment of mental retardation, it worsened Rosemary's condition significantly. In the early 1940s, the Kennedy family placed Rosemary in a private institution. Because of her condition, they became acutely aware of the stigma associated with mental retardation and the paucity of available services.

The Kennedys committed themselves to the "MR cause" and sought to create what the historian Edward Shorter (2000) referred to as a "dynastic identification so that when the public thought 'MR,' they would think 'Kennedy.'" At first, they relied on their personal resources, using the Joseph P. Kennedy Jr. Foundation to channel money into services for people with mental retardation, including schools and hospitals for disabled and retarded children. Later, the foundation funded university-based research into the causes of mental retardation.

In 1961, John F. Kennedy became president, and prodded by his sister Eunice, he made mental retardation a priority of his administration. In his first year in office, Kennedy supported the creation of the National Institute for Child Health and Human Development, which, among its other responsibilities, would conduct research into the causes and prevention of mental retardation. He also formed the President's Panel on Mental Retardation, which he charged with developing "a comprehensive and coordinated attack on the problem of mental retardation" (President's Panel on Mental Retardation 1962, 201). Eunice; her husband, Sargent Shriver; and Mike Feldman, a member of the White House Special Counsel's Office, took the lead in organizing the panel, which included basic scientists, behavioral scientists, educators, one parent (Elizabeth Boggs), and a Catholic monsignor who directed a clinic and school for the retarded (Shorter 2000).

Within a year, the panel had produced its report, "A Proposed Program for National Action to Combat Mental Retardation," for the president. The report began by examining the negative effects of mental retardation on society, including the loss of "several billion dollars of economic output because of the underachievement, underproduction, and/or the complete incapacity of the mentally retarded" and the "untold human anguish and loss of happiness and wellbeing" on the part of the retarded and their families (President's Panel on Mental Retardation 1962, 2). Unlike parents' groups, which worked tirelessly to create a positive image of their children, the panel determined that it would be more likely to obtain federal funding if it depicted retardation as a pressing problem or even as a threat to the nation. Thus, the report used vivid, negative language relying on the metaphor of war. America was staging an "attack" on mental retardation, entering "battle," and defending itself against "blight." The panel presented the prevention of mental retardation as the nation's top priority. To pursue this goal, it recommended funding basic scientific research into the varied causes of mental retardation, addressing the "inadequate medical services available to large segments of our population during pregnancy and childhood," and improving the opportunities for America's youth, especially those within economically and culturally deprived families.

Despite this relatively negative portrayal of retardation, the panel argued that many of the negative consequences of mental retardation were rooted in the lack of services, opportunities, and rights for individuals with mental retardation. To improve the life chances of individuals with retardation and to minimize the burden that they imposed, it recommended the development and provision of comprehensive services, including education, vocational opportunities, clinical and social services, day care, recreation, and residential services. These services would be "community-centered" and organized to "meet different types of need" so that no person would experience more segregation or social control than necessary. According to the panel, society held a responsibility "(1) to permit and actually foster the development of their maximum capacity and thus bring them as close to the main stream of independence and 'normalcy' as possible; and (2) to provide some accommodations or adjustment in our society for those disabilities which cannot be overcome" (President's Panel on Mental Retardation 1962, 13). Hence, on one hand, the panel urged the nation to prevent the blight of mental retardation, and on the other, it suggested that individuals with mental retardation should be treated with respect.

To justify these services and accommodations, the panel looked to the potential economic productivity of mentally retarded citizens, directly connecting wage labor with the exercise of rights. However, it also recognized society's responsibility for all of its members, regardless of their productivity. The report stated:

> Every human being has potential for useful activity. Many individuals, ostensibly severely handicapped physically or mentally, possess considerable work potential. . . . Obviously it is a great economic gain when a handicapped individual is rehabilitated from a role of idleness and dependency to the status of full-fledged wage-earner and citizen.
>
> There are many other handicapped individuals in whom the potential for useful work is more limited. In some instances the potential may be so limited that it is insignificant from the standpoint of economic gain. However, it is never insignificant from the standpoint of concern for the welfare and dignity of the individual. The true goal of education and rehabilitation of the handicapped is to help every individual to make the most of his potential for participation in all the affairs of society, including work, no matter how great or small his potential may be. (President's Panel on Mental Retardation 1962, 100)

In addition to describing the services that were needed, the report contained a section outlining the rights of citizens with mental retardation. Boldly, the panel stated, "Like other citizens, the mentally retarded must be assumed to have full human and legal rights and privileges. The mere fact of retardation should never be considered in and of itself sufficient to remove their rights" (President's Panel on Mental Retardation 1962, 150). Simultaneously, though, society had to recognize the difficulties faced by the retarded in exercising rights and offer protections when and as needed. The panel recommended "a new legal, as well as social, concept of the retarded, including protection of their civil rights; life guardianship provisions when needed; an enlightened attitude on the part of the law and the courts; and clarification of the theory of responsibility in criminal acts" (President's Panel on Mental Retardation 1962, 14–15). To ensure that guardianship protected rather than simply controlled people with mental retardation, the panel suggested that guardianship law differentiate between guardianship of the person and of the person's property, allow for limited guardianship in certain judicially determined situations, use comprehensive clinical evaluations to determine when guardianship should be in effect, and establish periodic reviews to assess the need for guardianship or the need for continued institutional care for individuals committed to institutions.

The report brought together many of the emerging ideas of this era, including the recognition of the humanity, potential abilities, needs, and rights of individuals with mental retardation; their integral role in their families and communities; and society's responsibility toward them as citizens. It also reflected many of the tensions of this era. It juxtaposed a negative portrayal with a positive one. In some situations, it connected the exercise of rights to economic productivity, yet it also established people with mental retardation as citizens regardless of their abilities. It called for equal treatment before the law yet also recommended group-specific protections, services, and support. It supported the values of community integration, equality, and respect yet also supported institutionalization. The panel did little to reconcile these tensions, borrowing from both the emerging civil-rights framework and older views of retardation as a threat to society.

The panel itself had no authority to implement its recommendations. President Kennedy hired Stafford Warren to transform its recommendations into actual legislation, and he packaged several of its recommendations into two bills (Shorter 2000). Signed into law in 1963, the Maternal and Child Health and Mental Retardation Planning Amendments to the Social Security Act of 1935 (PL 88-156) authorized $265 million to be spent over five years to increase funding for maternal and child health services aimed at preventing mental retardation, including a health program targeting pregnant women at high risk for having retarded children. It also provided funding for efforts to assist states in developing coordinated and comprehensive services for people with retardation.

Signed into law one week later, the Mental Retardation Facilities and Community Mental Health Centers Construction Act of 1963 (PL 88-164) provided $329 million over a five-year period to create eighteen university-affiliated centers for the diagnosis and treatment of mental retardation, to construct community centers for mental retardation and mental-health centers, and to train special-education teachers. It also provided funding for the establishment of the U.S. Office of Education's Division of Handicapped Children and Youth. While these laws had many positive effects, the Construction Act in particular fueled the construction of institutions without offering support for maintenance or programming, causing institutions to continue to decline in quality.

The assassination of President Kennedy in 1963 abruptly curtailed the federal-level attention given to mental retardation. In 1967, John Fogarty died, another blow to advocates for people with mental retardation. The Johnson administration did not totally ignore mental retardation. As a nod to the Kennedy family, Lyndon Johnson created the President's Committee on Mental Retardation, but it lacked any power to legislate or obtain funding to turn its recommendations into policy. Vice President Hubert Humphrey had a granddaughter with Down Syndrome, and he continued to support the active role of government in retardation policy. The Johnson administration focused its efforts on behalf of people with retardation on special education, supporting the passage of the Elementary and Secondary Education Act (PL 89-10), which provided grants to states for special education; PL 89-105, which provided funds for research and demonstration projects in special education; and PL 89-750, which established the Bureau of Education of the Handicapped and provided funds for special-education programs. Johnson also created a program to employ people with retardation in jobs with the federal government.

The Kennedy family continued to be active in the politics of mental retardation. Ted Kennedy took over the family foundation and continued to provide funds to initiatives related to mental retardation, including a massive campaign created by the Ad Council and NARC to raise public awareness. Eunice Shriver created one of the best-known programs for people with mental retardation, the Special Olympics, which envisioned people with mental retardation as able to grow, compete, have fun, and represent their communities through sports (Shorter 2000). Representative of its era, though, the Special Olympics established participation in sports as a segregated charity event, a model that provided opportunities to athletes with disabilities but did not push for integrated recreational programs. In only a few short years as president, John Kennedy had put mental retardation on the federal map, pushed for the development of coordinated state and national plans to address mental retardation, and passed significant legislation. However, these results did not come close to reaching the goals laid out by parents. The Kennedy administration would serve only as the beginning of national change.

Conclusion: Paternalism and Citizenship

From the 1940s through the 1960s, multiple conflicting narratives of disability and citizenship existed side by side; people with mental retardation were depicted as eugenic threats and as productive citizens, special children, and humans with human rights. While these narratives reflected very different concepts of mental retardation, each tended to support a paternalistic system in which social services were more important than individual rights.

The American legal system in part forced activists to choose between services and rights. Unlike other industrialized nations, America never developed strong welfare programs or social rights to services. In America, public social services were typically reserved for the deserving poor. Education was the one social program guaranteed as a right, and even that had been denied to disabled children. In the absence of the force of law, or even an accepted ideology recognizing social rights, activists used various arguments to justify the provision of services and rights to people with disabilities. Each narrative connected loosely with traditional ideas of American citizenship but also was subject to fundamental limitations and failed to overcome American resistance to the establishment of social rights.

Whereas liberalism posits competence and autonomy as the basic requirements for rights, professionals emphasized the importance of productivity, essentially relying on a cost–benefit analysis to suggest that the provision of services would be less costly than a policy of neglect or institutionalization. Professionals, and sometimes parents, tried to use the notion of productivity to their advantage, documenting the abilities of this population and showing its potential for self-care and social contribution. Yet relying on productivity left the "unproductive" without access to services and allowed plenty of room for debate regarding the level of productivity required to access services. Even if 75–80 percent of people with mental retardation could be self-supporting, society in the 1950s did not support this degree of inclusion, and capable people therefore remained dependent. Thus, basing services and rights on productivity was particularly precarious in the case of people with mental retardation, as they were provided few opportunities to contribute and had difficulty contributing in expected ways. In addition, their contributions frequently were not valued by society. As an alternative, parents devised the narrative of the eternal child. This narrative offered parents a better opportunity to extend services to all children with mental retardation, yet it confined all people with mental retardation to the narrow role of the "dependent" and made it difficult for them to exercise "adult" civil rights. Activists such as Rosemary Dybwad rejected the notion of the eternal child in favor of an appeal to human rights. However, this, too, fell short as the American legal system lacked a mechanism to transform the rhetoric of human rights into actual legislation

In addition to determining the rationale on which they would base their appeal for services, activists had to decide on the degree to which they would emphasize the similarities and differences between people with mental retardation and other citizens. Newer narratives tended to recognize greater similarities than the older ones, yet professionals and parents alike tended to advocate for group-specific services and rights for the retarded. Because the United States lacked a strong precedent for social rights, activists were forced to portray people with retardation as "needy" and "incompetent." In other words, at the same time that new narratives were presenting positive conceptions of mental retardation, professionals and parents were justifying group-specific services on the grounds that people with mental retardation ultimately could not compete on an equal footing with other citizens. At times, professional and parents' groups even fought against the inclusion of other groups in legislation and programs to maximize the benefit for people with retardation.

The emphasis on services and group differentiation fit well with America's traditional paternalistic attitude toward those seen as deserving and in need. Although activists frequently employed a rights rhetoric, few parents and professionals believed that individuals with mental retardation were capable or worthy of autonomously exercising of rights or of making significant life choices. Indeed, they typically fought against rights that limited their own authority. Professionals typically supported "rights" that expanded services for their clients but resisted rights that would limit their professional discretion. Similarly, parents supported "rights" that expanded their children's opportunities, yet they wanted to retain for themselves the right to determine which of these options their children would take, failing to recognize that their own wishes and the best interests of their children might conflict. Activists used a rhetoric of rights to express a moral imperative but did not sacrifice their authority over the lives of people with retardation.

The most expansive services provided in this era—education and institutional placement—fit well with and encouraged the expansion of paternalism by casting their recipients in the role of dependents. They encouraged people with mental retardation to contribute to society as best they could, even if the contribution was simply some level of self-care within the confines of the institution. But they also allowed social control to be exercised over those who did not meet the expectations of society. At the same time, activists were far less likely to advocate for traditional "adult" civil rights for the retarded, such as voting, contracting, and marrying, and often positioned themselves as gatekeepers for these rights.

Parents and professionals were caught in a tangle of dilemmas. They were advocating for social rights in a country that did not tend to recognize them; they were fighting for rights to services for their children yet wanted control over them; they wanted to recognize the abilities of their children and their status as equal citizens, yet they also wanted to secure group-specific care and protection for their children. Given the barriers they faced, the progress made was remarkable and led the way toward even greater change.

7

Creating the Mentally Retarded Citizen

Prior to the late 1960s, professionals and parents frequently drew on a rhetoric of rights to convey a symbolic and moral message about the importance of including people with retardation in the community and increasing funding for services for them. This rhetoric usually portrayed people with mental retardation as eternal children, needy dependents, or incompetents who could potentially become competent, but rarely as autonomous individuals capable of exercising rights. Parents, professionals, and policymakers, as opposed to people with disabilities, continued to determine the policies and services for people with retardation. Significant changes were on the horizon, though. Propelled by the successes and failures of activists in the 1950s and 1960s and the successes of other groups in obtaining civil rights, activists and professionals revamped the image of mental retardation yet again, this time as Americans with all of the rights that other citizens enjoy. Unlike in the 1950s and 1960s, this new image was incorporated into the law.

The greatest gains in the 1970s were made in the area of social rights, including the provision of education, treatment, and community services. Following several court cases mandating the provision of education to children with disabilities, Congress passed the 1975 Education for All Handicapped Children Act (later renamed the Individuals with Disabilities Education Act [IDEA, P.L. 94–142]), granting children with disabilities the right to a free and appropriate education in the least restrictive environment and the right to due process in educational placement. Dramatic changes also took place as deinstitutionalization, the movement of people out of large hospitals and training schools, became national policy. As access to education and community services expanded, so, too, did the potential for people with mental retardation to form their own organizations. "Self-advocacy" organizations started forming throughout the nation, in which people with mental retardation spoke out about their experiences, supported each other as they faced the challenges of living in the community, and fought to increase their access to rights.

Macro–Social Changes and the Quest for New Answers

In the 1950s and 1960s, professionals, parents, and the federal government each played a role in building a new, positive image of people with mental retardation. People with mental retardation were recognized as *people*; they were children just like other children, adults with special needs capable of contributing to society, and neighbors who belonged in the community like any other person. Professionals and parents produced tangible evidence that people with mental retardation could thrive in the community, created many successful community-based programs, and secured some local, state, and even federal funding for these programs. The future seemed bright.

But in the late 1960s, people were still waiting for that bright future to materialize. The existence of community-based services depended heavily on local and state-level politics, leading to dramatic variation in the extent and types of services available. Many projects were funded primarily through grass-roots efforts such as bake sales and gala events, making their long-term sustainability dubious. The institutionalized population continued to grow through most of the 1960s, often with little or no improvement in living conditions. By 1979, after more than two decades of reform efforts and a decade after the publication of *Christmas in Purgatory* (Blatt and Kaplan 1966), Burton Blatt and his colleagues revisited the institutions he had previously exposed. The situation had not improved significantly:

> The buildings were the same. They were less crowded, less dirty, less foul-smelling, but the same. In Building 8, more people were wearing clothing, but not in a way that makes a difference. No inmate yet has clothes of his own. . . . For most of the inmates there are still no activities: no recreation, no education, no deviation from the routine of purposelessness. After ten years of promises, the people caught in this institution continue to be reduced to the same collection of headbangers, shit-kickers, vomiters, droolers, sore-pickers, screechers, assaulters, sleepers, weepers; and, armed with their authoritative rings of keys is the same collection of a few attendants sitting or standing around, watching, chatting, drowsing. (Blatt et al. 1979, 43–44)

They found some improvements but concluded, "What we have to say about institutions for the mentally retarded is mostly bad news. They are dreary places where people are cast out of society and secluded. They are places where it is common to spend childhood under a table and where adulthood—predictably—is pretty much the same" (Blatt et al. 1979, 114). Blatt portrayed the administrators as a dying species who had lost their pride, prestige, and purpose, unable to save their sinking ships or themselves.

After two decades of raising funds, spreading awareness, creating demonstration projects, and building friendly relationships with politicians, the parents' movement was ready to try new tactics to achieve its goals. Parents turned to the courts to fight for their children's rights. This decision must be understood within the context of the civil-rights movements raging through the 1950s, 1960s, and 1970s. As the sociologist Richard Scotch (1984, 24) noted, "The social movement that defined the concept of civil rights in the United States since World War II has been the movement for equality for black Americans." African Americans framed their activism in terms of the pursuit of equality and equal access to all spheres of American life. In *Brown v. Board of Education*, a turning point for America's legal understanding of equality, the U.S. Supreme Court rejected the notion that segregated programs could be equal and instead mandated the racial integration of educational programs. With that precedent in hand, African Americans proceeded to challenge the entire system of Jim Crow and institutionalized segregation.

Through the 1960s, African American civil-rights activists broke away from the constraints of legitimate channels of protest and turned to mass demonstrations and civil disobedience to disrupt the operation of oppressive institutions (Morris 1986). After years of struggle, they achieved several tremendous victories. Congress passed the 1964 Civil Rights Act mandating that "no person in the United States, on the grounds of race, color, or national origin, shall be excluded from participation in, be denied the benefits of, or be subjected to discrimination under any program or activity receiving federal financial assistance." In addition, Congress passed the Voting Rights Act of 1965, which guaranteed access to the franchise, and the Civil Rights Act of 1968, which forbids discrimination in housing.

Both the tactics and the legislative achievements of the Civil Rights Movement served as models for other social movements pursuing equality. Peace activists, feminists, Chicano activists, Hippies, student radicals, and others created a culture of protest that challenged the moral hegemony of the 1950s, exposed oppression and corruption, and imagined new paths to individual happiness and social justice. Feminists were particularly successful in building on the success of the African American Civil Rights Movement. For example, in the final negotiations over the Civil Rights Act of 1964, politicians also made discrimination on the basis of gender illegal. They then drew on the language of the Civil Rights Act for Title IX of the 1972 Education Amendments to forbid sex-based discrimination in educational programs that receive federal funding.

The Civil Rights Movement and broader culture of protest inspired people with disabilities (Fleischer and Zames 2001; Scotch 1984; Switzer 2003). Earlier activism among people with disabilities mostly had been limited to disability-specific organizations that strove to raise funds, establish services, and secure rights for their specific group. In the 1970s, people with many types of disabilities joined together to fight for the civil rights of all people with disabilities (Stroman 2003). Ed Roberts, one of the founders of the Independent Living Movement, was among the early activists to envision a movement composed of people with various types of disabilities. As a student at the University of California, Berkeley, he initiated the Disabled Student Program, an organization designed to meet the needs of wheelchair users on campus, and the Rolling Quads, a political group that worked to create a barrier-free environment on campus. In 1972, the Rolling Quads established the Center for Independent Living (CIL), in which people with disabilities offered advocacy, resources, training, and peer-counseling services to other disabled individuals to promote independent living. The CIL offered an alternative approach to the delivery of services based on the principles of consumer sovereignty, self-reliance, and the need to ensure the political and economic rights of people with disabilities, in contrast with the traditional medical model that assumed the pathology of people with disabilities and allowed medical professionals to dictate their best interests. By the late 1980s, more than three hundred CILs were operating across the nation (Independent Living Research Utilization 1986).

Meanwhile, efforts to ensure the rights of individuals with disabilities were also emerging in other parts of the country. In New York City, Judy Heumann founded Disabled in Action, which quickly received notice as one of the first disability-rights groups to use street demonstrations as a primary tactic. In some ways, the government encouraged cross-disability activism as it created policies and laws that grouped people with disabilities together. For example, the President's Committee on Employment of the Handicapped brought activists with various disabilities together to work on employment issues, some of whom then branched off to form their own organization, the American Coalition of Citizens with Disabilities. The passage of the 1973 Vocational Rehabilitation Act had a particularly dramatic effect on the growing Disability Rights Movement. While drafting it, congressional staff members expressed concern that the money spent on rehabilitation would be wasted because employers refused to hire people with disabilities. To deal with this concern, they drew on the language of Title VI of the 1964 Civil Rights Act to create Section 504, which forbids employment discrimination based on handicap by any program that receives federal funding.[1] Although it was little debated at the time, Section 504 became a focal point for disability activism when the U.S. Department of Health, Education, and Welfare (HEW) stalled in developing the regulations necessary for its implementation, culminating in demonstrations by disability activists at HEW's offices in Washington, D.C., and around the nation in 1977 (Scotch 1984). Ironically, then, federal initiatives helped to bring activists with disabilities together and legitimized a civil-rights framework, while the government's reluctance to actually enforce federal policies provided a cause around which activists could rally.

Although the Disability Rights Movement included activists with a variety of disabilities, parents of individuals with mental retardation and professionals who worked in the field of mental retardation did not typically position themselves as an integral part of this movement. The Disability Rights Movement proclaimed that all people with disabilities, regardless of the severity of their disability, could and should exercise control over their lives. However, many parents and professionals questioned the feasibility of self-determination for people with mental retardation and still sought to make decisions for them and to control their services (Jones and Ulicny 1986). Nor did activists with physical disabilities necessarily welcome the entrance of parents and people with intellectual and mental disabilities into their movement. Because they rested their claim to rights in part on their cognitive capacity to make self-determined decisions, the presence of intellectual disability was seen as potentially hindering the achievement of their goals. Moreover, the inclusion of parents seemed to undermine the presentation of people with disabilities as autonomous decision makers. Thus, the movements related to mental retardation and physical disabilities intertwined during the 1970s and 1980s but did not unite as one.

Nor did parents and professionals concerned with mental retardation completely take on the protest tactics used by the African American Civil Rights Movement or the emerging Disability Rights Movement. Despite the common use of demonstrations and civil disobedience in other civil-rights movements, parents and professionals had little interest in marching through the streets or even in breaking down the moral mandates of the 1950s for family and order. Indeed, parents typically did *not* want to bring negative attention to themselves or their children by presenting themselves as troublemakers, radicals, or communists or by "parading" their disabled children through the streets (Segal 1970). Rather, they wanted their families and children to be encouraged to participate in American society as "normal" families and children.

Although parents did not closely ally with or model themselves after other civil-rights movements, they did come to realize the power of cross-disability coalitions. In the 1960s, the mental retardation lobby had become one of the country's most powerful disability constituencies. Yet, in 1969 NARC decided to abandon its sole focus on retardation and expand its reach to people with "developmental disabilities," thereby incorporating several other disability constituencies under a single umbrella.[2] NARC, in cooperation with other organizations, including United Cerebral Palsy, worked to create a definition of developmental disability that united groups that had often allied together politically, such as those focused on retardation, cerebral palsy, and epilepsy, yet excluded individuals with mental illness and physical disabilities. Formalizing this new political category, the Developmental Disabilities Act of 1970 (a reauthorization of the 1963 act) defined developmental disability "to include mental retardation, cerebral palsy, epilepsy, and other neurological conditions closely related to mental retardation which originate prior to age 18 and constitute a substantial handicap."[3] Although "developmental disabilities" encompassed many groups, mental retardation remained the dominant one, so much so that the terms became somewhat interchangeable in popular usage.

Parents and professionals also came to realize the power of the courts. By using the judicial system, they could tap into the successes of civil-rights movements while using a more respectable and palatable political tool than public demonstrations. As is discussed in greater detail later in this chapter, mental retardation organizations adopted a civil-rights framework that had proven effective in identifying and fighting against social injustice for other groups. NARC even altered its name in 1973, from the National Association for Retarded Children to the National Association for Retarded Citizens, to recognize its constituency as including children and adults and to stress the new identification of people with mental retardation as citizens.

As well-established groups such as NARC and the AAMD continued their activities in the politics of mental retardation, new organizations also formed, many of which were focused on civil rights. As society increasingly recognized people with mental retardation as citizens, people with mental retardation themselves increasingly saw themselves as worthy of respect and rights and began to create self-advocacy organizations. Alongside the AAMD, professional organizations focused more directly on advocacy emerged.[4] The Center for Human Policy at Syracuse University was founded in 1971 "in response to widespread abuse of and discrimination against people with disabilities in society" (Center on Human Policy n.d.). Created by Burton Blatt, its principal goals were to examine policy, conduct research, and provide advocacy to secure the rights of people with disabilities. In 1975, professionals, parents, people with disabilities, and others formed the American Association for the Education of the Severely and Profoundly Handicapped (which later became the Association for the Severely Handicapped, and then known simply by its acronym, TASH). Recounting TASH's history, Lou Brown, a past president of the organization, explained that "in the late 1960s and early 1970s it was abundantly clear to a few parents and professionals that no other organization was addressing the ideological, research, financial, and programmatic rights and needs of people with severe disabilities; the most vulnerable, segregated, abused, neglected, and denied people in our society" (Brown 1991). The government also created many organizations through mental retardation policy. The Kennedy administration established a network of "university-affiliated programs" to conduct research and demonstration programs to promote best practices in serving people with mental retardation, some of which grew to emphasize inclusion, the provision of services in the community, and civil rights. Through the 1970s, federal law also created state-level Developmental Disability Councils to plan and coordinate the delivery of services and Protection and Advocacy agencies to ensure access to rights for people with developmental disabilities.

The civil-rights framework was further encouraged by the growth of public-interest law, a field dedicated to ensuring that all citizens have full access to the legal system and to their rights as guaranteed by American law. A small number of lawyers, including Charles Halpern, Thomas Gilhoon, David Ferleger, and Stanley Herr, began to specialize in the legal rights of people with mental retardation (Halpern 1979). The success of early court cases sparked further growth in this field. Public-interest legal centers focused on disability were established, including the National Center for Law and the Handicapped, the Public Interest Law Center of Philadelphia, and the Institute for Public Interest Representation. In addition, national organizations formed sub-units dedicated to legal advocacy for this population, including the American Bar Association's Subcommittee on Law and the Mentally Retarded, NARC's National Legal Advocacy Committee, and the National Council on the Rights of the Mentally Impaired, founded by the American Civil Liberties Union Foundation and the Center for Law and Policy (Roos 1976). Bringing together this new legal expertise, the President's Committee on Mental Retardation sponsored the compilation *The Mentally Retarded Citizen and the Law* (President's Committee on Mental Retardation 1976b), a landmark statement of the civil-rights approach to mental retardation. These legal professionals played a key role in transforming professional and parental rhetoric about rights into a legal framework that could be used in the courts to challenge the status quo.

The Civil-Rights Framework and Mental Retardation/Developmental Disability

Advocates for people with mental retardation did not simply apply the ideas used by the African American Civil Rights Movement and by feminists to people with mental retardation. African American and feminist activists tended to argue that the differences related to race and gender were irrelevant to the exercise of rights, whereas parents saw disability as directly related to rights. Because disability may affect the rate at which one works, the physical and programmatic accommodations required, the training necessary for personnel, and so forth, the same opportunity would rarely be equal opportunity for people with mental retardation. Nor did advocates for people with mental retardation believe that they could simply apply the ideas of independent living and self-determination from the emerging Disability Rights Movement. They believed that they needed to establish rights in a way that acknowledged the potential impact of intellectual limitations. Thus, activists modified the framework of civil rights to achieve rights for people with mental retardation, basing civil rights on four key principles: the developmental approach, normalization, equal citizenship, and disability-specific rights.

The Developmental Approach

In the 1950s, parents had proclaimed that children with mental retardation were just like all other children. This idea gained professional credence and coherence in the 1960s when it was introduced as the "developmental approach" by the psychologist Edward Zigler. Arguing against the well-accepted idea that the intellectual development of children with retardation is inherently different from that of children without retardation, Zigler (1969) proposed that children with mental retardation proceed through the usual sequences of development but at a slower pace. He argued that, like that of other children, the development of children with mental retardation is multifaceted, including cognitive, psychological, physical, social, and emotional aspects; that they have developmental needs related to each of these facets; and that their development is affected by factors similar to those that affect children without disabilities, such as exposure to positive and negative reinforcement and the availability of opportunities to learn. Organizations such as NARC, the President's Committee on Mental Retardation, and the International League of Societies for Persons with Mental Handicap (formerly the International League of Societies for the Mentally Handicapped) quickly incorporated the developmental approach as a guiding principle and used it to justify the provision of services to all children, regardless of the severity of their disability. As expressed by NARC, "Retarded children and adults are capable of learning and development. Each individual has potential for progress, no matter how severely handicapped he or she might be" (Patterson 1980).

Normalization

While the developmental approach provided the foundation that all people with mental retardation could learn, the principle of normalization provided a philosophy to guide the delivery of services and encourage learning. First developed in Scandinavian countries by Neils Erik Bank-Mikkelsen, Bengt Nirje, and Karl Grunewald, the normalization principle was formally introduced to Americans when the President's Committee on Mental Retardation invited Nirje, then head of the Swedish Parents Association for Retarded Children, to tour the United States and write a chapter for its publication *Changing Patterns in Residential Services for the Mentally Retarded*. In his chapter, Nirje (1969, 181) explained that normalization entailed "making available to the mentally retarded patterns and conditions of everyday life, which are as close as possible to the norms and patterns of the mainstream of society." Nirje elaborated that people with retardation should have the opportunity to experience the normal rhythms of the day, such as typical times for waking up, going to bed, and eating meals (as opposed to unusual schedules dictated by the interests of staffs); a normal daily and weekly routine that includes varied settings and typical leisure events; the normal rhythm of the year, including vacations and the celebration of holidays; and normal developmental experiences such going to school, developing intimate relationships, working, and retiring. Overall, the normalization principle suggested that individuals with mental retardation would best develop into well-adjusted members of society if they were given the same opportunities and experiences as other citizens.

Wolf Wolfensberger, who became aware of the normalization principle while also participating in *Changing Patterns*, further developed it in *The Principle of Normalization in Human Services* (1972). In this work, Wolfensberger laid out five key components of normalization intended to guide the service-delivery system: (1) integration—the dispersal and integration of services throughout a community, encouraging disabled and non-disabled members of the community to interact together in typical activities; (2) smallness—the tailoring of services to individuals or to a small number of clients, thereby promoting integration, individualization, and the humane treatment of clients; (3) "separation of the domiciliary function"—the separation of residence and the provision of services so that individuals received services in the community where other people received services; (4) specialization—the development of a range of services to meet the varied needs of individuals while providing only as much structure and supervision as necessary; and (5) continuity—the provision of "a continuum of living facilities" that offered the appropriate level of supervision, a level that would be expected to change through one's lifetime.

In legal terms the principle of normalization, and particularly the components of integration and continuity, became expressed as the "least restrictive environment," a concept mandating that services be offered in a setting that provided the greatest liberty possible and imposed the least supervision and social control possible, given the client's needs. Rooted in the right to liberty, the state could not impose greater restrictions on its citizens than necessary. Practically, this concept came to mean that the state ensured the provision of a continuum of services, ranging from the most to the least restrictive, so that all people could be served in the least restrictive settings according to their needs (Taylor 1988).

Equal Citizenship

Disability-rights advocates did not view the opportunity to live and mature as a typical member of society as simply a rhetorical ideal; they presented it as a right encompassed within the principle of equal opportunity or equal citizenship. According to Professor Karst (1977, 6), "The principle of equal citizenship presumptively insists that the organized society treat each individual as a person, one who is worthy of respect, one who 'belongs'. Stated negatively, the principle presumptively forbids the organized society to treat an individual either as a member of an inferior or dependent caste or as a non-participant." Equality was guaranteed primarily through two constitutional provisions: the right to equal protection and the right to due process. The Fourteenth Amendment of the U.S. Constitution provided that "no state shall . . . deny to any person within its jurisdiction the equal protection of the laws," thereby ensuring all citizens equality before the law.

Disability-rights activists used this principle and these constitutional protections to argue that individuals with mental retardation, as equal citizens, had the same rights as other citizens, and the mere diagnosis of mental retardation could not disqualify them from exercising these rights. According to the attorney Patricia Wald (1976, 4), "There appears to be little legal justification for laws now on the books which deny persons with mental disabilities an entire set of rights on one omnibus finding of 'incompetency' or 'mental retardation.' . . . Only an individual's capacity to do specific things can be judged. . . . Each person's capacities must be judged individually before he can be denied rights of citizenship or humanity." Stressing this principle, the President's Committee on Mental Retardation's publication *Mental Retardation: Century of Decision* began its discussion of "Full Citizenship and Legal Rights" with the premise that "retarded people have the same rights, legal and constitutional, as every other United States citizen, including the rights to due process and protection of the laws" (President's Committee on Mental Retardation 1976a, 58).

In addition to equal protection, the constitutional guarantee of due process protected citizens' liberty and provided a series of safeguards for situations in which their liberty might be curtailed. These safeguards included, for example, notifying individuals of any decision that might restrict their rights; providing individuals with the opportunity to have a hearing and to be present and represented at it; and ensuring the regular review of restrictions.

Legal experts also stressed the importance of the right to privacy, seen as a component of the right to liberty. Wald (1976, 5) explained, "There is a fundamental right to be left alone, a right to be allowed to succeed or fail, a right to ignore gratuitous advice, a right not to tell every problem to the social worker, a right not to answer the door. These components of the right to privacy belong to, and are valued by, all people and must not be taken away from mentally retarded individuals without a particularized showing that they cannot cope by themselves without disastrous consequences." Similarly, Robert Perske, a journalist and freelance author who wrote extensively on issues related to mental retardation, urged families and professionals to appreciate the "Dignity of Risk." According to Perske (1972, 24), "Overprotection endangers the retarded person's dignity and tends to keep him from experiencing the normal taking of risks in life which is necessary for normal human growth and development." He continued, "The world in which we live is not always safe, secure, and predictable. . . . This is the *real* world. We must work to develop every human resource within us in order to prepare for these days. To deny any retarded person his fair share of risk experiences is to further cripple him for healthy living" (Perske 1972, 26).

Group-Specific Rights

As advocates in the 1950s had recognized, providing the same rights and opportunities that other citizens had would not necessarily meet the needs of people with disabilities. Thus, the United Nations Declaration on the Rights of Mentally Retarded Persons followed its initial statement regarding equal rights with a list of group-specific rights, including the right to proper medical care; to appropriate education, training, and rehabilitation; and to protection from exploitation, abuse, and degrading treatment. Similarly, the Developmental Disabilities Assistance and Bill of Rights Act of 1975 suggested that people with developmental disabilities had unique rights to "appropriate treatment, services, and habilitation for such disabilities . . . designed to maximize the developmental potential of the person and . . . provided in the setting that is least restrictive of the person's personal liberty" (Developmental Disabilities Assistance and Bill of Rights Act 1975, 17).

These principles gained considerable acceptance among activists involved in mental retardation policy, including parents, professionals, and legal experts. More important, they were integrated into the law. An examination of several early civil-rights court cases shows how and why this framework achieved some legal legitimacy.

Early Court Cases in Education

Parents helped to usher in the civil-rights era for mental retardation in 1971 when they sued the Commonwealth of Pennsylvania in *Pennsylvania Association for Retarded Children (PARC) v. the Commonwealth of Pennsylvania*. For decades, parents had been concerned about the conditions within Pennsylvania's institutions. To improve the quality of care, they had volunteered time and money to these institutions, documented the numerous problems in the institutions, lobbied their representatives for reforms, and used the media to expose problems of institutional neglect and provoke public outrage. However, as a PARC historian noted, "Persuasive tactics seemed of no avail" (Pennsylvania Association for Retarded Citizens ca. 1977). Gunnar Dybwad, a former executive director of NARC, recalled offering the following advice to the leaders of PARC: "Our government has three parts, the legislative, the executive, and the judicial, and you've never used the judicial part. It is time to go to the courts" (Pelka 2004, 27).

To prepare for court, PARC hired Thomas Gilhoon, a parent of a disabled child and a lawyer associated with the Public Interest Law Center of Philadelphia, to study the feasibility of legal action.[5] It also passed "A Bill of Rights for Pennsylvania's Retarded Citizens" (1969) affirming that "every retarded person, no matter how handicapped he is, is first of all in possession of human, legal and social rights. As much as possible retarded persons, whether institutionalized or not, should be treated like other ordinary persons of their age are treated in the community." In this simple statement, PARC combined the principles of the developmental approach, normalization, and equal citizenship to present its vision of citizenship for people with mental retardation.

Although PARC proposed to sue Pennhurst for denying its patients the right to treatment, Gilhoon instead suggested they pursue the right to education. The right to education was already a well-recognized right for children without disabilities and therefore would need only to be extended to children with disabilities. At the same time, little precedent supported the right to treatment for any population. Moreover, Gilhoon argued, ensuring access to education would improve the care of institutionalized school-age patients and opportunities for disabled youth in the community, thereby decreasing the need for institutions.

At the time, Pennsylvania had "permissive legislation" that allowed, but did not require, schools to provide special education. Several laws gave school administrators the power to exclude children who were defined as uneducable or not ready for education from public schools.[6] PARC estimated that up to one hundred thousand children with disabilities were excluded from Pennsylvania's public-education system.

Twelve children and their next of kin became the plaintiffs in a class-action suit representing all Pennsylvania children excluded from public education on the basis of disability. Among the plaintiffs, Emery Thomas had been refused admission to kindergarten. School administrators told Emery's mother, "We don't feel he is ready," and postponed his admission until age eight. School administrators also turned Glenn Lowry away from kindergarten because he had an IQ of 56 and, according to a psychologist, had not yet attained the mental age of five. His parents were simply told he was "not yet ready for school, perhaps he'll be ready at eight." According to PARC, these actions denied children their right to a public education and violated the legal standards for equal protection and due process (*PARC v. Commonwealth* 1971, complaint filed by PARC).

With expert testimony from Burton Blatt, Gunnar Dybwad, and many others, the PARC team laid out the developmental approach and convinced the court that all children could benefit from education and training and therefore that the denial of such education constituted discrimination. The court's decision explicitly affirmed the developmental approach and mandated that the commonwealth provide a free public education to all children with disabilities, just as it guaranteed an education to all other children in Pennsylvania. Moreover, it obligated the commonwealth to ensure that "every mentally retarded child is placed in a program of education and training appropriate to his learning capacities" (*PARC v. Commonwealth* 1971, 1266), thereby requiring the provision of individualized services to meet the diverse needs of children with mental retardation. Endorsing the principle of the least restrictive alternative, the court specified that "placement in a regular public school class is preferable to placement in a special public school class and placement in a special public school class is preferable to placement in any other type of program of education and training" (*PARC v. Commonwealth* 1971, 1260). Affirming the right to due process, the court also required school administrators to notify parents about decisions regarding educational placement, to provide the opportunity for a hearing related to the placement, and to conduct two-year reevaluations of the appropriateness of each student's placement. This decision opened the doors to thousands of children who had been denied a public education.

Mills v. Board of Education of District of Columbia (1972) came on the heels of the PARC case and further supported the right to education for children with disabilities. This case was filed on behalf of seven children who had been denied a public education. The Board of Education defended its actions, claiming that it had legitimate reasons to exclude these children. According to the board, the right to education promised only a minimum level of education, not an education ideally designed to meet the unique needs of individual children. However, because of their disabilities, these children could not benefit from a typical minimal education. Furthermore, providing a beneficial education for these children would impose a grave financial hardship on the district and threaten the success of its entire educational system. Thus, according to the Board of Education, it had not engaged in arbitrary discrimination but had acted in accordance with the best interests of the school district and within the guidelines of the law.

Disagreeing with the board, District Judge Joseph C. Waddy supported the right to education for all children and the right to individualized instruction for disabled children, deciding that "the Board of Education has an obligation to provide whatever specialized instruction that will benefit the child" (*Mills v. Board of Education* 1972, 874). According to the court, the failure to provide education or due process "cannot be excused by the claim that there are insufficient funds. . . . If sufficient funds are not available to finance all of the services and programs that are needed and desirable in the system[,] then the available funds must be expended equitably in such a manner that no child is entirely excluded from a publicly supported education consistent with his needs and ability to benefit therefrom" (*Mills v. Board of Education* 1972, 867). Like the PARC case, the Mills case supported a definition of equality that recognized different needs and prioritized the inclusion of all citizens rather than channeling resources toward only the most productive. The court also supported the right to due process, finding that parents had the right to be informed of decisions regarding educational placement and provided an opportunity for a hearing to contest these decisions.

Legal battles occurred throughout the nation, many of which supported the right to education for disabled children.[7] Due to the trends in the courts and state legislatures, Congress passed the Individuals with Disabilities Education Act, which was originally titled the Education for All Handicapped Children Act, an incredible milestone in the fight for rights for children with disabilities. IDEA became a model for civil-rights legislation for people with disabilities. Built on the developmental approach, it asserted that all children, even those with the most severe disabilities, could learn and therefore had a right to an education. Supporting equal rights, IDEA required public schools that received federal funds for special education to provide children with disabilities a free and appropriate education. Moreover, it mandated that schools offer a range of educational services to meet the diverse needs of students, to develop individualized education plans for every exceptional student, and to provide culturally fair testing, thereby individualizing education to the meet the needs of disabled children. The law supported the principles of the least restrictive environment and due process, requiring notification of educational placement, opportunities for hearings and review, notification of the rights it provided, and confidentiality in educational placement. IDEA also recognized parents as experts regarding the best interests of their children and required that they be given opportunities to participate in planning their children's education.

While IDEA applied only to schools that accepted federal money for the provision of special education, Section 504 of the 1973 Rehabilitation Act prohibited discrimination on the basis of disability by programs or activities that received *any* federal financial assistance. Applied to education, it mandated that all schools receiving federal funds provide disabled students with free and appropriate educational services to the same extent that they served the needs of students without disabilities. To compare these laws briefly, IDEA provided funding for special education and mandated the provision of a wide range of services and individualization, but schools could more easily opt out of it. Section 504 did not provide funding for special education and required the provision of fewer services and accommodations, but it had greater reach. In conjunction, these laws established the right to education for children with disabilities as the law of the land and indicated a clear preference for inclusion and accommodations designed to meet the needs of the individual child. By 1984, more than 90 percent of disabled children were receiving an education in integrated schools (Winzer 1993).

Early Court Cases, the Right to Treatment, and Deinstitutionalization

As PARC's attorney Thomas Gilhoon had predicted, the right to treatment proved far more controversial than the right to education. The first major case regarding the right to treatment, *Wyatt v. Stickney*, opened in 1970. In the midst of a budget crisis and state cutbacks, employees of Alabama's state mental hospital were afraid that they would lose their jobs and that the quality of care for patients would decline as staff positions were cut. Establishing a right to treatment seemed to offer a way to improve institutional conditions for patients while simultaneously preserving jobs for those providing the care.[8] Mrs. W. C. Rawlins Jr., who was both an employee at Bryce Hospital and the aunt and guardian of a patient residing there named Ricky Wyatt, filed a class-action suit on behalf of her nephew and other patients at Bryce against Alabama's Commissioner of Mental Health, charging that the substandard conditions at the hospital violated its patients' constitutional right to treatment. Although the case originally pertained only to patients of Alabama's institutions for the mentally ill, the plaintiffs later petitioned the court to include residents of the Partlow State School and Hospital for people with mental retardation.

Federal Judge Frank Johnson, a "larger-than-life figure" in Alabama politics, was clearly moved by the atrocious conditions in the state's institutions and made a strong statement in support of the right to treatment (Stickney 2001). Relying on a precedent from a 1960 case regarding mental illness, Johnson argued that the only constitutional justification for civil commitment of the retarded or mentally ill was habilitation; without habilitation, a hospital was transformed "into a penitentiary where one could be held indefinitely for no convicted offense."[9] Therefore, once committed, a person possessed "an inviolable constitutional right to habilitation" (*Wyatt v. Stickney* 1972, 390). According to Johnson, Alabama's public state institutions not only failed to provide habilitation but they also failed to protect the very basic health and safety of their residents. The district court ruled in the plaintiff's favor and established minimal constitutional standards for habilitation, including the right "to a habilitation program which will maximize his human abilities" (*Wyatt v. Stickney* 1972, 396).

As it is in the early education cases, the civil-rights framework is readily apparent in this decision. For example, supporting the developmental approach and normalization, the court stated, "The institution shall recognize that each resident, regardless of ability or status, is entitled to develop and realize his fullest potential. The institution shall implement the principle of normalization so that each resident may live as normally as possible" (*Wyatt v. Stickney* 1972, 396). Supporting the least restrictive alternative, the court recommended admission to an institution only when appropriate community services were unavailable; the institution was determined to be the least restrictive environment; and the potential patient was severely or profoundly retarded.

Although *Wyatt v. Stickney* (1972) offered a dramatic affirmation of the right to treatment, during the following year a judge in New York explicitly disagreed with the decision and found no constitutional right to treatment for residents at Willowbrook State School (*New York State Association for Retarded Children, Inc., v. Rockefeller* 1973). Nor did he offer support for normalization, equal rights, or the individualization of treatment. Rather, he accorded institutional residents only the same basic rights as prisoners. According to the U.S. district court, all wards of the state had the right to protection from harm while under state care, which included the rights to protection from assault, mistreatment, and neglect; to freedom from the routine use of physical restraints unless necessary to prevent injuring to the resident or others; and to conditions meeting the standards of human decency, including adequate heat, necessary elements for basic hygiene (such as working toilets), basic medical care, and the opportunity for exercise and outdoor recreation. Sadly, given the dilapidated conditions at Willowbrook, even this narrow interpretation of patients' rights represented an important advancement. To ensure these basic rights, Willowbrook's administrators were required to improve living conditions and hire additional personnel, including ward attendants, physical therapists, physicians, and recreation staff (Rothman and Rothman 1984).

In 1974, Pennsylvania began its historic battle for the right to treatment. Twenty-one-year-old Terri Halderman, a resident of the Pennhurst State School and Hospital who had suffered numerous injuries while living there, and her mother, Winifred Halderman, stepped forward to become the lead plaintiffs, joined by seven other residents and the Parents and Family Association of Pennhurst. Represented by the attorney David Ferleger, director of the Mental Patient Civil Liberties Project, they charged Pennhurst with violating patients' rights and sought the improvement of conditions and services at the institution. After the case began, Congress passed the Developmental Disabilities Assistance and Bill of Rights Act (referred to as the DD Act) of 1975, which affirmed that individuals with developmental disabilities had the right to receive individualized treatment in the least restrictive environment. At this point, the U.S. Department of Justice and PARC joined the lawsuit, transforming the case into a class-action suit representing all patients at Pennhurst. The new legal team introduced the position that all Pennhurst residents had a federal and constitutional right to treatment in the least restrictive environment. Institutionalization was therefore an unconstitutional infringement of rights, they argued, because similar services could be received in the community in less restrictive circumstances (Ferleger 1978).

After hearing testimony regarding the abuse and neglect at Pennhurst, such as the frequent use of restraints, seclusion, and overmedication, the U.S. district court concluded, "The physical environment at Pennhurst is hazardous to the residents, both physically and psychologically. . . . The environment at Pennhurst is not only not conducive to learning new skills, it is so poor that is contributes to losing skills already learned" (*Halderman v. Pennhurst State School and Hospital* 1977, 1308). Supporting the developmental approach and normalization, Judge Raymond J. Broderick came to the dramatic conclusion that "the environment at Pennhurst is not conducive to normalization. It does not reflect society. It is separate and isolated from society" (*Halderman v. Pennhurst State School and Hospital* 1977, 1311). He continued, "There is no question that Pennhurst, as an institution for the retarded, should be regarded as a monumental example of unconstitutionality with respect to the habilitation of the retarded" (*Halderman v. Pennhurst State School and Hospital* 1977, 1320). Judge Broderick became the first judge to mandate that all residents be moved into community placements, in effect ordering the closure of Pennhurst.

Broderick's historic decision was not universally applauded, and forces began to line up to prevent the closing of Pennhurst. The parents who filed the case had sought to improve conditions there, and some were dismayed when Judge Broderick ordered its closure. A group of about forty parents protested the closure in various ways, including participating in hearings, organizing community demonstrations, and seeking political support to prevent the closure. About thirty parents, including the lead plaintiff, Winifred Halderman, asked to be removed from the case and to dismiss their attorneys. Although they had used a civil-rights framework in making their case, these parents did not believe that their children would be best served in the community. Rather, they wanted their children to have the right to high-quality services within institutions (Cass 1979; Contos 1979b; "Group Pickets Court Hearings for Pennhurst" 1979; Lichtenwalner 1979). The Reverend L. David Schlosser, a parent leader at Pennhurst, told a local newspaper, "One of the options ought to be an institution, not necessarily Pennhurst. We ought to have a range of options or alternatives" (Rebenkoff 1979).

While many residents rejoiced at the opportunity to leave Pennhurst, some resisted. Theodore Thomas, a resident of Pennhurst for twenty-five years, made headlines when he refused to move to a facility in the community (Franklin 1979; "Pennhurst Is Home" 1979). Harry Wolf, a Pennhurst resident for fifty-four years, told a local newspaper that, despite being beaten up, locked up, and herded about, he had seen improvements at Pennhurst over the years, considered it home, and did not want to leave ("Reflections of a Life at Pennhurst" 1979). Even Terri Halderman argued that it would be best for Pennhurst to remain open: "I just wanted them to do away with the old fire traps. I don't want to see Pennhurst people put in ghettos" ("Pennhurst Closing Leader Now Expressing Doubts" 1979).

Pennhurst's superintendent, George Kopchick, criticized the court's decision, suggesting that it showed a "complete lack of concern for the individual client" and put "the cart before the horse" by moving people into the community before the patients or the community members were adequately prepared (Jones 1979; "Shocking Decision" 1979). Pennhurst employees and the union representing them protested, as well, concerned both for their jobs and for the well-being of their patients. Employees of institutions had believed that the right to treatment would help secure their jobs and better treatment for patients, not lead to the closure of the facilities in which they worked (Contos 1979b; Dougherty 1979; Maneely 1979a). They had been trained in a model of care that accepted the incompetence of people with disabilities and, given the conditions at Pennhurst, they rarely saw patients show self-care skills. Therefore, it may not be surprising that many of the employees believed that their patients could not survive in the outside world. Finally, many people residing in the neighborhoods surrounding Pennhurst feared that the release of thousands of people with disabilities would have a negative impact on their communities and spoke out against the court order (Maneely 1979b; "Residents Oppose Closing of Pennhurst" 1979).

Ultimately, the case came before the U.S. Supreme Court (*Pennhurst State School and Hospital v. Halderman* 1981). The court did not find that federal law, specifically the DD Act, conferred the right to treatment. It stated that "We are persuaded that [Section] 6010, when read in the context of other more specific provisions of the Act, does no more than express a congressional preference for certain kinds of treatment" (*Pennhurst v. Halderman* 1981, 19). It then sent the case back to a state court to determine whether Broderick's decision was supported by state law. The state Appellate Court upheld Broderick's decision. In 1984, after ten years of litigation, the parties involved signed the final settlement agreement and proceeded with plans to close Pennhurst State School and Hospital.

The Supreme Court again considered the right to treatment when the guardian of Nicholas Romeo filed suit against Pennhurst. Romeo, a man with severe mental retardation and a history of self-abusive behavior, experienced frequent physical restraint while at Pennhurst (*Youngberg v. Romeo* 1982). In addition, he was injured on "at least sixty-three occasions," at times by himself and other times by staff and residents. Romeo's lawyers argued that the failure by Pennhurst administrators to provide treatment placed Romeo in jeopardy of harming himself and led to the frequent use of restraints, thereby denying him his fundamental rights to safety and freedom from restraint (rights accorded even to prisoners).

In this case, the Supreme Court found a constitutional right to treatment conditional on Romeo's status as a ward of the state without likelihood of release and based on the connection between his specific disabilities, his fundamental rights as a ward of the state, and the potential success of the treatment. The court conceded that "the respondent's liberty interests require the State to provide minimally adequate training or reasonable training to ensure safety and freedom from undue restraint" (*Youngberg v. Romeo* 1982, 319). While the court recognized a right to treatment to protect patients' rights to safety and freedom from physical restraints, the narrow reach of the Supreme Court decision did not question institutionalization itself, demand the least restrictive environment, or broadly extend the right to treatment to all people in institutions or to all people in the community.

Thus, after many court cases, two of which went to the Supreme Court, a federal or constitutional right to treatment had been only minimally established. People residing within institutions had basic rights to ensure their safety, but the right to treatment was supported only as needed to protect their fundamental rights. People residing in the community in essence had no right to treatment and could face years on a waiting list for services or be told that the services they needed did not exist. If in jeopardy of institutionalization, people with mental retardation could demand services in a less restrictive environment. For those who were not in jeopardy of institutionalization, they had little legal standing to demand much of anything.

These cases regarding the right to treatment became part of the much broader political movement toward deinstitutionalization, the transition of people out of institutions and into community-based settings (Bradley 1978; Rothman and Rothman 1984). In 1971, President Richard Nixon reversed national policy supporting institutions and announced his commitment to "enable one-third of the more than 200,000 retarded persons in public institutions to return to useful lives in the community."[10] The number of institutional residents had already begun to decline, and by 1977 institutional populations had decreased to 149,892 residents.

The factors leading to deinstitutionalization were complex. Parents and professionals had exposed problems in institutions that seemed irreparable, and they increasingly presented institutions as structurally inhumane, necessarily leading to dehumanization, isolation, and the loss of skills among residents. Simultaneously, they were putting greater faith in, documenting the successes of, and clamoring for more community-based services. The majority of research comparing outcomes of community services with institutional outcomes lent credence to the belief that community services produced greater gains in adaptive skills, greater choice, improved integration, and more contacts with family members and community members (Kim et al. 2001; Larson and Lakin 1989). Court successes like the Wyatt and Pennhurst decisions then provided legal backing for these preferences. Case after case mandated the improvement of institutional conditions and the elimination of unnecessary institutionalization.

Whereas in the past parent and professional organizations had taken a middle-of-the-road approach and advocated both for the improvement of institutional conditions and the provision of services in the community, they became increasingly strident in their position that institutions should close and residence in the community should be supported. In 1979, the Center on Human Policy at Syracuse University developed a statement titled, "The Community Imperative: A Refutation of All Arguments in Support of Institutionalizing Anybody because of Mental Retardation." According to the statement, citizens' moral and constitutional rights included the right to community living, and this right could not be abrogated merely due to disability. Many organizations, such as the President's Committee on Mental Retardation, NARC, the Council for Exceptional Children, United Cerebral Palsy, and various legal centers endorsed this statement. In the same year, a Nebraska self-advocacy organization held a press conference to express its position that all institutions should be closed and that people with disabilities had a right to live in and be served in the communities of their choice. Institutions were not a service "option"; they were a violation of one's human and civil rights (Williams and Shultz 1982).

To better meet the demands for community-based care, the federal government developed several funding sources. The Mental Retardation Amendments of 1967 (P.L. 90–170) authorized federal funds to help meet the costs of initiating services in community mental retardation facilities, and the DD Act of 1970 (P.L. 91–517) further encouraged states to plan and implement a comprehensive program of services for people with developmental disabilities. The 1981 Omnibus Budget Reconciliation Act created the Home and Community Based Medicaid Waiver Program, a key funding source that allowed reimbursement through Medicaid to pay for non-institutional services for individuals at risk of institutional placement or for individuals who had received institutional care and needed help to return to the community.

As options for community-based care grew, so, too, did the costs associated with institutional care. The declining number of the institutionalized required the fixed costs of institutional care to be spread across a smaller set of people. Furthermore, the proportion of patients requiring intensive and specialized care increased, including the elderly and those with severe forms of retardation, behavioral concerns, and multiple disabling conditions.[11] Administrators faced a new emphasis on standards and accreditation, which also increased costs.

Just as the needs of their patients and expectations regarding the quality of care were increasing, administrators lost access to the unpaid labor that had been provided by patients with mild disabilities, who were now more likely to be moved to the community or never to be admitted to an institution. In 1973, *Souder v. Brennan* prohibited the use of unpaid inmate labor. Given the rising costs per patient in institutions, politicians began to believe that community-based services offered a more cost-effective option than institutions.[12]

Deinstitutionalization of people with mental illness also had a significant impact on deinstitutionalization for people with mental retardation. The successful use of psychoactive drugs to treat psychiatric patients formerly considered incurable and the concomitant rise of community psychiatry encouraged the trend toward community-based treatment (Dowdall 1994). While no miracle drugs altered the prognosis of people with mental retardation, the same ideals of community placement and treatment were applied to them.

Deinstitutionalization was controversial. Advocates hoped that the provision of services in the community would improve the quality of life of people with mental retardation, while critics worried that deinstitutionalization was merely a cost-cutting device that would actually lead to the denial of treatment and support for people with mental retardation—and to their abandonment in the community.

Section 504 and the 1975 DD Act

While court cases advanced the right to education and treatment for individuals with disabilities, other dramatic accomplishments came through the legislative process. One of these, Section 504 of the 1973 Vocational Rehabilitation Act, was actually passed with little input from advocates for people with mental retardation or other disability activists. Section 504 made it illegal for recipients of federal funds to engage in employment discrimination against otherwise qualified individuals with disabilities. It stated that "no otherwise qualified disabled individual in the United States . . . shall, solely by reason of a disability, be excluded from the participation in, be denied the benefits of, or be subjected to discrimination under any program or activity receiving federal financial assistance." Hailed as the "first major civil rights legislation for disabled people," this legislation affirmed that people with disabilities held the same broad set of civil rights as other citizens and defined the denial of such rights as discrimination (Scotch 1984, 3). It recognized the role of discrimination and prejudice in causing low employment rates for people with disabilities and conceptualized full social participation by people with disabilities as both a goal and a right. Moreover, it contained no hint that, in prohibiting discrimination, it was offering people with disabilities charity or that they were inferior or incompetent compared with other citizens. As citizens, they deserved equal access, if qualified.

As noted in the discussion of deinstitutionalization, the DD Act was reauthorized in 1975 as the Developmental Disabilities Assistance and Bill of Rights Act. Most notably, the reauthorized bill included funding to build a system of Protection and Advocacy agencies charged with ensuring the safety and well-being of individuals with developmental disabilities, protecting them from abuse and neglect, and guarding their human and civil rights. It also put forth a "Bill of Rights" for this population, which stated that "individuals with developmental disabilities have a right to appropriate treatment, services, and habilitation for such disabilities . . . designed to maximize the potential of the individual and should be provided in the setting that is least restrictive of the individual's personal liberty." Although these "rights" were reduced to "preferences" by the Supreme Court in *Pennhurst v. Halderman*, the DD Act at least rhetorically affirmed the nation's commitment to the development of people with disabilities, their rights as afforded to other citizens, and their rights to reside in and receive services as appropriate given their needs and in the least restrictive environment.

The Seeds of the Self-Advocacy Movement

People with developmental disabilities took note of the increased importance given to them and their rights and began organizing, as well. Like the parents' movement, the self-advocacy movement began as local groups formed in different states, largely disconnected from each other. The concomitant rise of various self-advocacy groups across the nation was in part spurred by deinstitutionalization. For the first time, large numbers of people with developmental disabilities were dislocated from institutions and related support systems and placed in the community. Not surprisingly, they sought each other out, looking for old friends, something to do, and advice and support regarding life in the community. They were also responding to the controversies regarding deinstitutionalization in their local communities. As communities debated the fate of institutions, former residents saw that they could influence these debates by sharing their experiences (usually negative) with institutionalization and supporting the provision of community-based services.

As with the parents' movement, the growth of the self-advocacy movement in America occurred as part of a larger international phenomenon in which people with mental retardation around the world, particularly in Sweden (the birthplace of the principle of normalization), Britain, and Canada, were organizing. In 1973, three staff members and two residents of Oregon's Fairview Hospital and Training Center attended a conference for people with mental retardation held in British Columbia. They returned resolved to establish a similar organization in Oregon, yet they wanted it to be run *by*, not just *for*, people with mental retardation. Self-advocate Valerie Schaaf explained, "We wanted to let those in authority know that we are just like them and would like to be treated in the same way. How would you like it if someone did all your talking for you? We wanted to speak for ourselves and show the world and our communities that we can do many things for ourselves" (Schaaf with Bersani 1996, 171).

With this goal in mind, eight residents and former residents of Fairview met on January 8, 1974, at a group home in Salem, Oregon, and decided to hold their own conference that year. They selected the theme "We Have Something to Offer" and requested suggestions for a name for their organization. According to J. Edwards, "All at once out of the back of the room someone suggested that the name ought to reflect what they were all about. Their name should say who they were and what they wanted. 'We are people first,' someone said in a loud voice. 'PEOPLE FIRST!' As the vote was taken and the decision was made to call the organization 'People First', a real step was taken in giving a sense of identity to the group."[13] Five hundred sixty people attended the conference.

Meanwhile, in Nebraska a former resident of an institution, Ray Loomis, had what he referred to as a "brainstorm." Because of his own difficulties making the transition to community living, he thought there should be a group of people with disabilities that provided support to individuals as they left institutions and established their lives in the community. Although neither Loomis nor the organizations with which he worked had heard of the term "self-advocacy," Loomis "knew instinctively that the group must be self-directing" (Williams and Shultz 1982, 19). He called his group Project Two.

Early in its history, Project Two became a political force as well as a support system, encouraging former institutional residents to share their experiences with the public and to work to close Nebraska's institutions. In 1977, the agency that coordinated Nebraska's services for people with mental retardation held a public forum as part of its planning process, and Project Two members attended and shared information about their needs and concerns. When a parent spoke up to support the continued funding and provision of services through institutions, Project Two members described their painful experiences as residents of institutions in contrast with their positive experiences in the community. According to Paul Williams and Bonnie Shultz (1982, 23), "It was the first time that mentally handicapped people in Nebraska had spoken out for themselves and against institutionalization of people with handicaps. It may have also been the first time that county officials, businessmen and others really listened to what mentally handicapped people had to say. Speaking out for themselves had become a reality." At the end of the 1970s, Project Two was the only organization in Nebraska that explicitly demanded the closure of all institutions and the right for every citizen to live and receive services in the community.

In Pennsylvania, the process of closing Pennhurst had a direct impact on self-advocacy as former residents of the institution came together within the community to share their experiences and support each other in community living. Speaking for Ourselves became one of the most influential self-advocacy groups in the nation. Its former president, Roland Johnson (1999, 67), explained that its purpose was to "get people out of institutions. Make sure that people can get their rights. Stand up for the client; stand up for people's rights. Make sure that they get all that they can to better the system. And make sure [abuse] does not take place in other places—[community living arrangements] and group homes—because I been a victim to [sic] abuses in places."

Although diverse, early self-advocacy groups typically shared several key goals, the most basic was the goal of self-advocacy itself. Project Two defined self-advocacy as "people speaking for themselves" (Williams and Shultz 1982, 24). In 1978, a Project Two resolution explained the philosophy behind self-advocacy:

1. We believe that we are people first, and our handicaps are second. We wish people would recognize this and not give us a tag like "handicapped" or "retarded."
2. We believe that we have to fight for our own rights, and unless we do we won't get them.
3. We believe that people shouldn't just stay at home and feel sorry for themselves and ask for pity; there's a beautiful world out there, and we want to be part of it.
4. We believe that we should work to destroy the physical and mental restrictions on *everybody*, not just on ourselves.
5. We believe that it is important to get people out on their own.
6. We believe that it is wrong for the public to run us down and treat us badly.
7. We believe that we can win this fight, if we work together. (Williams and Shultz 1982, 223–224)

Central to self-advocacy was the notion of human respect, summed up in the term "People First." Johnson (1999, 70) explained, "Our members do not like the name 'mental retardation.' I think they're scared of that name. Because that means they're dummies; they're stupid persons; something like that" (Johnson 1999, 70). Labels prevented the recognition of the humanity and abilities of each person. According to a self-advocate from New Zealand (Martin with Corrigan 1996, 64), "Everybody in this room today has abilities. I want you to remember that is true as well for us who are self-advocates. We have a lot to offer. Let's get rid of labels. Our disabilities are only a small part of our lives. We are people too and we want to join you and not watch the world pass us by."

Because they commonly experienced devaluation within the services and training programs they were offered, people with disabilities needed to overcome their past oppression to discover their voice. People with disabilities existed in a "retarding environment" created by policies and service systems that impaired their opportunities to develop and succeed in mainstream society. In its scathing report of services for people with mental retardation in California, People First of California (1984) explained that the channeling of funding to professional agencies, rather than directly to individuals with disabilities, offered agencies no incentive to support their consumers in actually achieving integration and independence. The limits the Supplemental Security Income program imposed on earnings and savings punished and prevented financially responsible behavior; the lack of public transportation imposed isolation on individuals who typically do not drive; the legal system and the policies of service agencies prevented the development of intimate relationships, marriage, and parenthood; and the perpetuation of the institutional system kept individuals imprisoned on the basis of their retardation, while other groups with disabilities of similar severity successfully received services in the community.

Learning of their rights and developing independent living skills were not sufficient for fulfillment, however. As people gained independence, they faced the daunting question, "My god, now what do I do with my life?" (People First of California 1984, 49). Self-advocacy enabled them to imagine the possibilities for their future and make those possibilities a reality. As summarized by Williams and Shultz (1982, 94), "Far from wanting protection from the hurly-burly of everyday life, for example, mentally handicapped people have made clear that they want to be an integral part of community life, with all the problems and worries that it brings." This was not easy. For example, a woman with developmental disabilities sadly said, "I just can't make myself take the bus because it hurts so much when nobody will sit down beside me" (People First of California 1984, 50). Thus, self-advocacy organizations offered not only a political venue but also a crucial social support system. According to some of its members, People First of California "produced a sense of belonging and participating in a group that comes close to the idealized family that some never experienced" (People First of California 1984, 113). For Ginny Sellman, president of People First of Washington, People First "lets us get out more, and make friends, so we don't get lonely. We learn alot [sic] from our organization. We get over being shy, we learn to make speeches and to speak out more" (Furman 1996, 194). People First also gave its members opportunities to help others. Cast in the role of dependent for their entire lives, self-advocates embraced the chance to help other people. According to Roland Johnson (1999, 57), "Speaking for Ourselves had opened my eyes to be a better person and to try to help other people. . . . I just try to help people and give back into the community. It just came naturally."

The self-advocacy movement grew through the 1980s. In 1980, more than one thousand people attended the People First International Conference held in Portland, Oregon, and by 1986 at least twenty states had People First chapters. Other organizations and the government began to take notice of the movement. Gunnar and Rosemary Dybwad, leaders in the parents' movement, praised the self-advocacy movement, and several ARC chapters took a direct role in supporting the movement by training self-advocates and offering resources to self-advocacy organizations.[14] Yet, many ARC chapters ignored the movement and chose not to offer their consumers input into their services and policies. Other organizations also sent mixed messages about their support of self-advocates. For example, the International League of Societies for Persons with Mental Handicap began to include self-advocates in its conferences and eventually in the management of the organization, but that inclusion had to be encouraged by Rosemary Dybwad and self-advocates and entailed a long struggle (Spudich 1996).

Conclusion

The civil-rights successes in the courts and the rise of the self-advocacy movement seemed to indicate that, in some ways, people with mental retardation had attained the standing of equal citizens—or, at least, they were on their way. Yet there were signs of problems on the horizon. In developing the civil-rights framework, parents and professionals did not assert the position of people with mental retardation as autonomous citizens. Rather, they couched their rights in concepts such as normalization and the least restrictive environment, which still allowed some degree of professional control and segregation. The civil-rights framework, for parents, had been largely a means to an end, a tool to improve the services offered to their offspring, not an ideological stand on the equality of people with mental retardation. Therefore, advocates were not necessarily prepared for the fact that the courts' acceptance of the framework might lead to deinstitutionalization and an insistence on inclusion. They did not, despite their rhetoric, necessarily perceive people with mental retardation as full-fledged citizens. Parents spent a great deal of energy striving to gain the rights to education and treatment for their offspring; they spent far less time advocating for traditional "adult" rights such as the rights to privacy and to marry, and they pursued easier access to guardianship. They were also cautious of the self-advocacy movement, as self-advocates began to develop a more strident view of equal rights, to demand self-determination, and to situate themselves as the rightful representatives of people with mental retardation.

Legal support for the rights of people with mental retardation was also mixed. Courts had largely supported the right to education for children with disabilities (a well-established right for American children), yet they showed weaker support for the right to treatment and for civil rights that guarantee autonomy in one's action such as the freedom to marry and to bear and raise children. Congress passed the DD Act to ensure the equal and unique rights of people with developmental disabilities, but the Supreme Court reduced this to a symbolic nod that encouraged, but did not mandate, equal rights and inclusion. As the next chapter shows, advocates found that they had to engage in battle after battle to exercise and retain the rights they thought they had already established.

8

The Difficult Road of the 1980s

Advocates with developmental disabilities and their allies achieved considerable success in establishing formal rights during the 1970s, but they found it difficult to actually use and to maintain these rights. As civil-rights activists across marginalized groups fought to maintain and expand their rights, other constituencies fought to preserve the traditional bases of liberalism and to reduce spending on particular populations, including people with disabilities.

The Social Model versus Reaganomics

As various populations fought for equality, the meaning and utility of rights increasingly came into question. The Civil Rights Movement at first emphasized color-blind policies, which fit well within the liberal framework guiding the American legal system; African Americans were not asking for "special" or "preferential" treatment, just the same treatment as other citizens. They soon realized, however, that the same treatment did not ensure equality for people in unequal social positions. Hence, a White House report found that "private and public institutions alike too often seemed impervious to the winds of change, remaining all-white or all-male long after court decisions or statutes formally ended discrimination" (White House Staff 1995).

Through the 1960s and 1970s, a series of presidential executive orders and court decisions moved beyond color-blind policies and supported the use of group-conscious strategies to open the doors of workplaces and educational institutions.[1] For example, in 1969 President Nixon and Secretary of Labor George Shultz implemented the "Revised Philadelphia Plan," which required unions in the construction trade whose members were working on federal projects to establish "goals and timetables" to increase the number of African American employees. Of the plan, Nixon (1978, 437) noted, "A good job is as basic and important a civil right as a good education. . . . I felt that the plan Shultz devised, which would require such [affirmative] action by law, was both necessary and right." Some African American activists at first expressed skepticism regarding affirmative-action policies, fearful that such programs would delay the creation of a color-blind society, promote divisions among the working class, and provoke a backlash against them, but through the 1970s race-conscious policies became a key strategy to promote racial equality (Golland 2003).

Feminists had a long history of embracing differential standards for citizenship. In the early twentieth century, "progressive feminists" explicitly based their political agenda on the particular roles and virtues of women (Skocpol 1992). They supported policies such as maternal benefit programs to support poor widows with children and protective labor legislation for women and children. By 1970, their interest in protective legislation for women had faded, but feminists continued to argue that men and women—who were seen as difference due to biology, social expectations, or both—at times required different treatment to achieve equal outcomes. In particular, because women experienced pregnancy and bore greater responsibility for caretaking, they needed policies such as maternity leave, affordable day care, and flexible work schedules to achieve economic success.

As group-specific policies gained legitimacy, scholars from disadvantaged groups built a body of literature criticizing liberalism and creating new ideas of social justice and equality. Liberalism demanded equal treatment for similarly situated groups, yet scholars noted that individuals were not all similarly situated. What did it mean to be similarly situated? Based on whom? In liberalism, the white, able-bodied male became the unquestioned norm against which all other citizens were judged, and natural conditions such as pregnancy and disability became "problems" to be overcome by the individual. If individuals could not succeed under the same conditions provided to white able-bodied men, their failure was rooted within their own deficiencies. Thus, unless individuals could uphold the standards of the norm, the provision of rights proved ineffective.

Scholars began to envision new frameworks of citizenship and rights to achieve social justice. The social model developed by disability activists saw disability not as a biological limitation rooted in the individual but, rather, as a social disadvantage resulting from an *interaction* between an individual's biological traits and the larger social context (Linton 1998; Oliver 1990). For example, people who processed information more slowly would not necessarily be "disabled" in settings that did not require them to process complex information or that provided support for them to do so. By calling attention to the role of environmental barriers, including physical, cultural, and social barriers, the social model also emphasized the importance of removing these barriers to improve the opportunities and quality of life for people with disabilities.

A linchpin to emerging feminist models of rights became the concept of relationality. According to the feminist scholar Christine Koggel (1998), a relational approach asks what individuals who are embedded in interdependent relationships need to develop and thrive. Relational models assume that the attempt to exercise rights is mediated by the expectations and power dynamics embedded in one's relationships. Because women, for example, typically exist in familial relationships that assume their responsibility for caregiving and in employment settings that deny the importance of those responsibilities, it is difficult for them to exercise their right to pursue employment and to benefit as much as men from their employment. For women to achieve employment success, social programs would need to support women (as well as men) in the fulfillment of their roles as both employee and caregiver. The notion of relationality does not rest in categorical or ascriptive assumptions; women do not require different or "special" treatment because they are women. Rather, because they tend to hold particular roles in society and face particular relational expectations, they will tend to need programs that support them in fulfilling these roles. Some women will not. Some men who hold caregiving responsibilities will. Social justice demands the recognition that one's relational context affects one's access to rights and the alteration of the social context to encourage equal access and outcomes among individuals who hold unequal positions in various social contexts.

As activists created visions of a just society that relied on recognizing difference and creating differential support and rights for people based on these differences, other constituencies had different ideas of what constituted a just society. Ronald Reagan served as president of the United States from 1981 to 1989, and his political agenda of hyper-individualism and laissez-faire economics dominated politics through the 1980s. In his inaugural address in 1981, he declared, "In this present crisis, government is not the solution to our problem; government is the problem" (Reagan 1981). What the nation needed was not expensive social programs that created debt and dependence or group-conscious policies that he believed impeded meritocracy and encouraged racism. Rather, power needed to be restored to the states and to individuals to promote their freedom and responsibility.

Reagan launched a campaign against affirmative-action programs. During his presidency, the U.S. Department of Justice abandoned its policy of vigorous enforcement of federal equal-opportunity laws, and the courts became increasingly hostile to affirmative action. This hostility culminated in the 1989 case *City of Richmond v. Croson*, in which the U.S. Supreme Court declared a city program giving preference to minority-owned business in the awarding of municipal contracts to be a violation of equal protection and therefore unconstitutional. Reagan also opposed many initiatives of the feminist movement, including the equal-rights amendment and the right to reproductive choice that included abortion. Disability rights also became a primary target. During the 1980s, the Reagan administration openly criticized federal disability programs and disability-rights legislation as too expensive and unfair, creating special opportunities for people with disabilities that did not exist for other citizens.

Reagan's politics represented and inspired a sentiment among many Americans against government interference and social support programs. Instead, they looked to a leader who would support individualism; the use of volunteerism and Christian charity to help the "needy" rather than government programs; and fiscal conservatism in which individuals paid fewer taxes and relied less on the government. In 1984, Reagan decisively won his bid for reelection, winning forty-nine of fifty states, and he is remembered today as one of America's most popular presidents.

Division among parents and professionals also impeded progress toward attaining rights. Whereas early court victories had inspired some unity among advocates for people with mental retardation, many parents and professionals balked at the ideal of full inclusion and equal civil rights and instead preferred to maintain some level of segregation and restriction to preserve their own control over the services provided and the lives of people with mental retardation.

The Battle for Rights

The Battle over the Right to Education

Despite the clear mandates of early court cases, the Individuals with Disabilities Education Act (IDEA), and Section 504, parents quickly learned that establishing the right to education represented only the *beginning* of their battle to secure an appropriate education for their children. For example, the decision in *PARC v. Commonwealth of Pennsylvania* (1971) clearly indicated a preference for education provided within the least restrictive setting, but politicians in Pennsylvania still attempted to build separate educational facilities for children with disabilities on the grounds of state institutions and hospitals. PARC had to battle with the Department of Welfare, the Department of Education, and the governor of Pennsylvania to ensure that education would be provided in community settings (PARC ca. 1977).

Nor were the problems resolved with the passage of Section 504 and IDEA. On signing IDEA into law, President Gerald Ford openly criticized it as too expensive and expansive, arguing, "Unfortunately, this bill promises more than the Federal Government can deliver. . . . Despite my strong support for full educational opportunities for our handicapped children, the funding levels proposed in this bill will simply not be possible if Federal expenditures are to be brought under control and a balanced budget achieved over the next few years" (Ford 1975). IDEA committed the federal government to increasing its responsibility for the cost of special education incrementally so that by 1981 federal dollars would pay 40 percent of the excess cost of special education; however, actual appropriations never reached that level. According to an evaluation conducted in 1989 by the National Council on Disability (NCD), funding remained lower than promised throughout the 1980s, reaching only 9 percent in 1989. As part of a broader attack on disability-rights legislation, President Reagan sought to "resolve" the funding disparity by repealing IDEA altogether. When unsuccessful in these efforts, he suggested cutting IDEA's budget and modifying the legislation to reduce required services and parental participation and to offer states and local school districts greater flexibility regarding the provision of special-education services and the removal of children from the classroom (Anderson 1982). Parents and disability-rights organizations found that constant vigilance was required simply to maintain the integrity of the law.

Because of the minimal financial support, school districts perceived the provision of an appropriate education for disabled children to be an economic burden. According to a survey of classroom teachers, 38 percent reported that their school had students with disabilities who either had not been identified as such or were not receiving services.[2] An advocate for families with disabled children quoted in the NCD's evaluation explained, "The states are 'evaluating' children to deny them service" (National Council on Disability 1986). The burden to secure services for children with disabilities fell largely on parents. However, according to a 1989 survey by Louis Harris and Associates, 61 percent of parents knew little or nothing regarding their rights under Section 504 and IDEA, and less than 1 percent of parents of children with disabilities had requested due-process hearings. The same survey found that 56 percent of parents of children with disabilities reported that they had to work hard to obtain educational services for their children (Louis Harris and Associates 1989).

Nor was there agreement even among professionals regarding the best implementation of IDEA. They were particularly conflicted about whether the "least restrictive alternative" actually encouraged the most "appropriate education." While some experts strongly favored integrated settings, others believed that some degree of segregation in education could be "appropriate" and beneficial. Disability organizations were also divided on this subject. Although major organizations for children with mental retardation favored integration, organizations for deaf children believed that segregated settings better supported education in sign language and deaf culture, and organizations serving autistic children typically wanted to retain options for the provision of education in intensive one-on-one and small-group settings (Martin et al. 1996).

Although the majority of students with mental retardation were being educated in integrated schools by the late 1980s, the majority (56 percent) were still being educated primarily in separate classes (National Council on Disability 1989). In fact, the implementation of Section 504 and IDEA seemed to perpetuate separate educational systems. According to Lisa Walker (1987, 108), "P.L. 94-142 may have served to reinforce a hybrid structure, one with elaborate protections to assure the rights of disabled students, but carried out by a separate delivery system of special education services, which remains in many instances outside the normal scope of school business."

The Long Road to Deinstitutionalization

While some states, often sparked by court cases, proceeded relatively quickly with deinstitutionalization, others, such as Arkansas, Louisiana, Mississippi, North Carolina, and Virginia, continued to channel support primarily into their public institutional system (Braddock 2002; Lakin et al. 2003). The process of deinstitutionalization also posed considerable problems. In the early 1970s, when deinstitutionalization began, relatively few services were offered in the community. Therefore, many people who left institutions experienced "trans-institutionalization," or the movement from one large institution to another large facility, such as a mental hospital, a nursing home, or an Intermediate Care Facility (ICF), which all tended to run according to the medical model and offered patients/clients little control over their life decisions.[3] Legislation enacted during the late 1960s and early 1970s further encouraged the growth of these options. In 1977, the average ICF housed 186 residents, a figure much smaller than that for most public institutions but still much larger than a typical home (Prouty et al. 2003, viii).

Furthermore, early in the history of deinstitutionalization the release of patients from institutions into the community was often poorly planned.[4] Howard Cobb (1998, 42–43), a self-advocate in West Virginia, described his struggle to survive once he had entered the community:

> The first time I was out, I went to Morgantown and stayed with my sister. The second time I was out was for one day visiting my mom. The third time I stayed out for three days trying to find a place where people would accept me as a person. That didn't work out. When I would leave the hospital, there was pretty much no support set up for me. I would be given $100 or so from my trust account and go to the Greyhound station and catch a bus somewhere. . . . Eventually things would end up falling apart, and I would go back to the hospital.

Even when community services were available, they varied tremendously in their commitment to the principles of normalization and integration. In their study of the deinstitutionalization of Willowbrook State School in New York, David and Sheila Rothman (1984) found three typical models of care within group homes. Some followed a family model in which the service setting was designed to replicate a home, and the staff was supposed to act like caring parents. Others followed an educational-therapeutic model in which the service setting became a classroom, and the staff interacted as teachers and counselors. Still others replicated institutional models in which the service setting was impersonal and rigid, and staff interacted as authority figures. The emerging structure of funding and accountability encouraged group homes to move toward the classroom and institutional models, both of which cast the residents as dependent and incompetent.

President Reagan, who had once referred to California's institutions as "the biggest hotel chain in the state," primarily saw deinstitutionalization as a way to reduce government expenditures rather than as a means to ensure rights (cited in Trent 1994, 256). As deinstitutionalization proceeded, the Reagan administration cut funding for social services and for Section 8 programs that helped low-income individuals pay for housing, making it difficult for people with disabilities to find affordable housing and receive support in the community. Based on these concerns, the goals and outcomes of deinstitutionalization were called into question, and divisions over deinstitutionalization magnified, particularly among parents (Prouty et al. 2003; Scheerenberger 1976). The Association for Retarded Citizens (ARC [formerly the National Association for Retarded Citizens and, even earlier, the National Association for Retarded Children]), the largest parents' organization for people with mental retardation, took a more strident position in favor of deinstitutionalization and the channeling of funds into community-based services. Other parent groups formed to defend institutional options, as they saw community-based services as dangerous, under-funded, and unstable (Frohboese and Sales 1980; Larson and Lakin 1991).[5]

Two significant national-level parents' organizations developed to defend the delivery of services in institutional settings. In 1979, Frances Sloan, a parent of a child with mental retardation and cerebral palsy, founded the Congress of Advocates, and in 1983, Marty Pratt, a parent of an institutionalized child, formed Voice of the Retarded (VOR). These groups strongly opposed the interpretation of civil rights offered by mainstream mental retardation organizations. In contrast to the developmental approach, these organizations argued that people with severe and profound retardation had "permanent conditions" that made the significant improvement of their skills unlikely and necessitated the provision of highly specialized services best offered in institutions. In light of their children's needs for care and protection from exploitation, they considered the assumption that the community offered "normalization" or liberty to be misguided, at best, and dangerous, at worst. In an amicus brief, members of the Congress of Advocates argued, "The reality of mental retardation is inconsistent with a presumption in favor of deinstitutionalization. It cannot be assumed that for a particular retarded individual, a [community living arrangement] will be 'less restrictive' or 'more normalizing' than an institution; for many retarded people, only an institution can produce adequate services and programs."[6] Residence in the community, according to these groups, placed too much pressure on people with severe disabilities and posed an unacceptable level of risk to them, as well. Active treatment and the pressure to meet certain developmental standards were not "normal"; on the contrary, "to require a human being to participate involuntarily in a futile daily training regimen extending over months, even years, may constitute cruel and inhumane treatment" ("Motion for Modification" 1978).

According to these organizations, rather than being forced to conform to some standard of "normality," individuals should have "a right to be retarded," encompassing a subset of rights that includes the right to reside in a safe space that encourages one's growth and activity without provoking fear or undue stress and "the right to be free from being pushed and programmed and 'trained' in such a manner which causes the retarded persons to have extreme frustration from overprogramming."[7] Because they believed that institutions provided a high-quality staff, a community of peers, and protection from the dangers of the community, they argued that institutions potentially offered a more normalizing environment in which people with mental retardation were free to be themselves.

These organizations did not necessarily seek to limit community-based services. Rather, they framed their argument in terms of maintaining institutions as part of the "continuum of choice," a carefully chosen phrase that drew on liberal notion of freedom of choice to defend segregated options.[8] Explaining his decision to join VOR, the activist Sam Golden noted that his severely disabled daughter was living an active and happy life with the support of the staff at the institution in which she resided: "With her limitations, she would not have a good life in a small group home—the limited staff could not care for her or involve her in the kinds of activities she now engages in" (Golden 2006). Similarly, the VOR activist Fanny Janazzo explained that "the severely and profoundly retarded need four sheltered walls that house them; and to destroy the concept of training schools is to destroy the retarded themselves" (Janazzo 2006).

These parents also worried about the loss of their own rights to determine the best interests of their children. A host of court decisions called into question and limited parents' rights in relation to their children, and these parents wanted to retain what they believed to be their "constitutionally protected right" to pursue the service options they believed to be in the best interests of their children (including their adult children). Although they had fewer members and were less well known than the ARC, these groups exerted influence on legislation, including the DD Act and court cases.[9]

In addition to parents, the National Association of Superintendents of Public Residential Facilities for the Mentally Retarded (1974) advocated "selective deinstitutionalization," which offered institutions as a "responsive residential environment" for those who were not prepared for community living. Unions that represented employees of state institutions defended the care the institutions provided and stressed the need to continue the provision of care by well-paid, trained staff. Moreover, community members frequently expressed concerns about deinstitutionalization. Rather than creating a national-level organization, residents of particular communities tended to use local community resources to exert influence regarding their own situations. Typical tactics included persuading property owners not to sell to agencies establishing group homes, as well as using building permits, zoning regulations, and fire-clearance ordinances to block the establishment of residential services (Graham and Hogan 1990; Mamula and Newman 1973; Rothman and Rothman 1984). A town in California, for example, required any agency establishing a group home to obtain a permit and hold a public hearing, while other buyers faced no such restrictions. In 1970, the California State Legislature attempted to remove local barriers to the establishment of group homes, yet even with explicit legislative measures in place, many communities continued to find ways to control the number and placement of group homes and services (Mamula and Newman 1973).

The issue of the right of people with mental retardation to live in the community versus the right of residents to control the composition of their neighborhoods came before the U.S. Supreme Court in the Texas case *City of Cleburne v. Cleburne Living Center* (1985). As addressed in Chapter 1, the Supreme Court was hesitant to affirm the rights of people with disabilities to reside in the communities of their choice. Although the court supported the right of the group home in question to be established, it did not question the requirement of a special-use permit to establish a group home or the application of different standards in housing for mentally retarded citizens. Thus, it did little to establish a broad right to community residence for all people with mental retardation.

The level of resistance from various constituencies slowed the rate of deinstitutionalization; however, political momentum in general was in its favor. Even without a clearly established "right," community-based services seemed to offer superior consumer outcomes, greater liberty, and better cost-efficiency and therefore to be the more practical and ethical choice for politicians. Thus, even during the recession of the 1980s, when the right to education for children with disabilities came under attack and mental-health budgets were cut, deinstitutionalization proceeded. Of course, politicians' sense of practicality did not, by any means, ensure rapid closures or the establishment of appropriate services in the community, but it did at least offer a rationale for continuing the process of deinstitutionalization in the absence of a clear national-level law or court decision requiring it.

Work and Income

The passage of Section 504 promised to open employment opportunities to people with disabilities, yet it had a limited impact on the employment of people with mental retardation, as they were rarely seen as "otherwise qualified" for employment. Ironically, the same act channeled money into sheltered workshops, maintaining them as the dominant model of employment for this population. Ideally, sheltered workshops provided appropriate work training and employment opportunities for those who were unable, temporarily or permanently, to work in the competitive labor market. However, they also isolated people with disabilities, paid little, and maintained for them a separate system of employment with few opportunities to learn the skills needed for competitive work placements.

Recognizing the lack of employment opportunities and the high risk of poverty for people with disabilities, the federal government established income-maintenance programs for them. Title XVI of the 1972 Social Security Act established the Supplemental Security Income (SSI) program, which offered direct cash payments and Medicaid coverage for the elderly, blind, and people with significant disabilities who were deemed poor. People with disabilities also became eligible for Social Security Disability (SSDI) payments if they had participated in the workforce for the necessary length of time.[10] SSI and SSDI helped the elderly and people with disabilities avoid homelessness and hunger but also forced people to define themselves as "totally disabled" to receive economic support and created disincentives and barriers for their employment (Hahn 1983, 1987). Thus, assistance came at the cost of legitimating the exclusion of people with disabilities from the workforce by defining them as totally unable to work rather than by analyzing and overcoming the social and economic barriers to employment.

Negative Liberties and the Franchise

Despite the passage of Section 504 and the DD Act, surprisingly little attention was given to advancing access to negative liberties (rights in which the state primarily offers individuals autonomy in their actions) such as the rights to vote, to enter into contracts, to marry, and to bear and keep one's children. Looking at the right to vote, throughout the 1970s and 1980s several states explicitly stated that the receipt of services for people with developmental disabilities did not disqualify one from voting; however, in the 1980s forty states still had laws prohibiting "certain classes of mentally disabled persons from exercising their franchise," usually based on blanket labels of disability (e.g., retardation, feeblemindedness, idiocy, mental illness) or adjudication rather than an assessment of the individual's political knowledge and skills (Mason 1986). Nor were these laws simply out-of-date remnants of the past. In 1979, when the Oklahoma legislature updated its statute related to voting rights, it decided to replace the term "idiot" with "mentally retarded" rather than remove the prohibition.

Some legal experts criticized these statutes. According to the attorney Steven Metcalf (1989), voting restrictions based on labels of mental disability and incompetence suffered from both over-inclusivity and under-inclusivity. The statutes were over-inclusive because many people with mental retardation were competent to vote yet faced restrictions. They were under-inclusive because many different types of people lacked political knowledge and faced difficulties in learning, gaining access to, and processing complex political information, yet only people with mental disabilities were denied the right to vote. Furthermore, no accepted legal standards existed to determine competence to vote, making it impossible to restrict voting based on an assessment of skill.[11] Due to the problems in developing skill assessments and in enforcing restrictions in a fair manner, a lawyer writing for the *Yale Law Journal* concluded that "states should discard all devices that single out mentally disabled citizens for exclusion from political participation" ("Editorial Note" 1979).

In addition to formal laws, other barriers existed to meaningful participation in the political system for people with mental retardation. Studies found that only a minority of adults diagnosed as mildly retarded adults who had received special education were registered to vote and the majority lacked basic knowledge of the American political system (Gozali 1971; Kokaska 1972; Olley and Fremouw 1974; Olley and Ramey 1976). Few formal programs existed to promote voting, and parents and staff commonly assumed away this right, failed to educate individuals about the voting process, or failed to provide assistance for the actual practice of voting.

Contracting and Guardianship

The increasing presence of people with mental retardation in the community encouraged greater attention to guardianship. In the past, guardianship had most commonly been established during the process of institutionalization. Now that people with mental retardation were remaining in the community, parents wanted to ensure that they received, and continued to receive, the necessary support and protection. As parents' interest in establishing guardianship increased though, the civil-rights framework called into question the liberal use of guardianship. Experts criticized guardianship laws as upholding an "all or nothing" process that imposed unnecessary restrictions on people with mental retardation, failed to recognize and meet individuals' unique needs, failed to encourage the attainment and recognition of skills and maturity over time, supported institutional commitment, prioritized financial matters above broader conceptualizations of the individual's well-being, and proved "cumbersome and expensive" for families (Hodgson 1972).

The American Association on Mental Retardation (AAMR) and the ARC created position statements regarding guardianship in which they emphasized the use of guardianship to support rather than to restrict the rights of people with developmental disabilities. Serving in this way, guardians would "act on behalf of the ward in securing his or her personal civil rights" and "allow the ward to make as many decisions as possible and participate as meaningfully as possible in other decisions affecting his or her life ("Guardianship for Mentally Retarded Persons" 1974). According to these organizations, people with mental retardation had the group-specific right to support systems, including guardianship. Tying this to the principle of normalization, the attorney Amie Bruggeman (1980, 326) explained, "The principle of 'normalization' . . . cannot work without the awareness of those around [the mentally retarded individual] that he not only has the basic human right to such a life within his capabilities, but also that with proper support systems he can be a functioning asset to society."

Drawing on the principle of least restrictive alternatives, experts suggested ways to provide guardianship to maximize assistance while imposing as few restrictions as possible given the person's needs. This goal could be achieved through the establishment of forms of limited guardianship based on the assessment of various competencies rather than the traditional all-or-nothing approach. To further ensure liberty, experts stressed the need to provide due-process protections, such as the right to be present and represented at one's own guardianship hearing and the periodic review of competencies that recognized the individual as "a changing, developing person."

States took very different actions to support and protect people with mental retardation in the process of guardianship. Many states modified their guardianship laws to distinguish between guardianship of the person and guardianship of his or her property or based guardianship on an assessment of an individual's "legal disabilities." In addition, states developed a series of mechanisms to provide support without adjudicating someone incompetent, including special-needs trusts, which allowed for money management; systems of "protectorship," which relied on agencies charged with the care of people with mental retardation to provide support and services to a person in exercising his or her rights; Protection and Advocacy agencies, which were charged with the specific task of protecting the legal rights of people with disabilities; and funding for a network of community-based organizations that provided legal advocacy.

As an example of both the progress and the barriers to enacting changes in guardianship laws, in 1978 North Carolina enacted a law providing for partial guardianship based on an assessment of an individual's "legal disabilities." Examining the impact of this law more than a year after its passage, Gary Mesibov and his colleagues (1980) found that fewer than ten people had been placed under partial guardianship, while the vast majority of those under guardianship remained under the traditional system. The reasons he cited included the fact that citizens and legal officials were poorly informed about the law; that they did not understand the concept of partial guardianship; that they feared its effects; that they preferred the "protections" of full guardianship; and that they had no responsibility to review already established guardianships or to initiate petitions to alter an individual's guardianship status.

Mesibov's study revealed two other significant concerns. First, it found a mismatch between the type of assistance desired by people with mental retardation and the type provided by guardians. People with mental retardation most commonly reported that they desired help in developing their relationships, learning about marriage, and finding a place of residence. Yet guardians focused on financial management. Second, group-home staffs, other professionals, and the individuals themselves were often confused about and unaware of an individual's guardianship status. Physicians, for example, typically assumed that the parent's wishes represented the best interests of the disabled adult and asked for a parent's signature prior to medical procedures, regardless of the individual's guardianship status. Thus, some people who had not been adjudicated still faced restrictions. At the same time, individuals with guardians often failed to receive meaningful support. Actual guardianship status frequently was irrelevant, replaced instead with varying levels of informal control and guidance.

Marriage and Sexuality

While antidiscrimination statutes presumably guaranteed individuals the right to marry regardless of their disability, Richard G. Mason (1986) found that in the 1980s, forty states still restricted marriage based on mental disability. A few legal experts criticized these statutes as outdated in their eugenic assumptions and devaluation of the skills of this population, as vague due to the reliance on outdated terminology, as ineffective in preventing relationships and procreation, and as discriminatory (Jacobs 1976–1977); however, only a few states removed these laws, and others seemed hesitant to do so. In 1984, the West Virginia legislature took the time to modify its marriage statute. It chose to delete the reference to "feebleminded persons[s]" but retained restrictions for "idiots," "imbeciles," and "insane persons"; failed to define these terms; and failed to explain the reasons for maintaining these restrictions.

Studies found that people with mental retardation, like other citizens, placed a high value on relationships and marriage. Robert Edgarton's sociological study of people with retardation residing in the community found that marriage served as a support system and as a symbol of normality (Edgarton 1993 [1967]). Experts increasingly recognized the benefits of marriage for this population, and popular acceptance seemed on the rise, as well. In 1978, Robert Meyers published *Like Normal People*, a true story of the marriage of two people with mental retardation. He wrote, "A generation ago, this marriage probably would not have taken place. . . . They would have been warehoused, probably involuntarily sterilized, drugged for easy institutional care, and given little more to do than wait for sleep" (Meyers 1978, 4). Yet in the 1970s, they had been encouraged to make the transition from institutional environments into their own apartments, to work, and to build relationships.

Despite the success stories, legal and informal restrictions kept marriage out of reach for many people with retardation. As documented by Mesibov and his colleagues (1980) and Sol Gordon (1971), people with mental retardation were given little information and support in developing relationships. Parents tended to view the sexuality of their disabled children negatively, as a problem to be managed rather than as a healthy component of one's life. Group-home policies also reflected negative attitudes toward the sexuality of their clients. Lous Heshusius (1982) found that group homes tended to be segregated by gender, entailed strict supervision, prohibited physical contact beyond light kissing, provided little privacy, and offered little or no sex education. Most residential services excluded married couples, and because services were often provided only within residential facilities, those who married were in effect ineligible for assistance (Koller et al. 1988).

An article by Barbara Raymond in the popular magazine *McCall's* (Raymond 1976) described the barriers to marriage and procreation for one woman with developmental disabilities. At age twenty-six, Patty, a woman with Down Syndrome who lived in a group home, fell in love with a man who worked at her sheltered workshop. He had a learning disability, owned his own home, and supported himself. When they became engaged, Patty's group-home "mother" forbade the marriage, although she had no legal justification. During the next several years, the group home's staff established goal after goal for Patty to meet before she would be "allowed" to marry. Patty became pregnant and was advised to abort and to avoid marriage or she would not be allowed to remain in the group home. Patty's future mother-in-law offered to help care for the child, and Patty decided to move out of the group home and have the baby; however, only a few days after the baby's birth, the Department of Social Services removed the child. Whereas other parents would be considered fit parents until contrary evidence arose, Patty was forced to *prove* to the Department of Social Services that she was a fit parent before the child was returned. To do so, she was required to take parenting classes and to have supervised visits with her son. In 1984, Patty and the Department of Social Services went to court to determine whether Patty was "potentially neglectful." After months of separation from her son, the case was dismissed due to lack of evidence of neglect. Although this is only one woman's story, Patty's experiences highlight the potential informal and formal restrictions faced by people with mental retardation, despite their progress in attaining civil rights. As in Patty's case, the techniques of active learning and individualized goals, while often important educational tools, could be used informally to prevent people with developmental disabilities from exercising their rights without due process or adjudication, and access to services more generally could be made conditional on their compliance.

Also suggested by Patty's story, the right to procreation for people with mental retardation remained highly controversial. By the 1980s, two standards had generally been accepted. First, legal experts recognized that individuals with mental retardation who were deemed competent to consent should not be subjected to compulsory sterilization merely because of mental retardation. Most states repealed their compulsory sterilization laws, although eleven retained them through this period (Elkins and Andersen 1992).[12] Second, for individuals deemed able to consent, legal experts recognized their right to choose voluntary sterilizations as a means of birth control (Vitello 1978; Wald 1976). Although well accepted, these standards were not met by all states.[13]

The greatest controversy, however, involved individuals deemed unable to consent.[14] Some states offered no legal avenue for the sterilization of this population, suggesting that sterilization without consent necessarily constituted abuse.[15] Other states, though, argued that such strict rules denied people with significant disabilities their right of access to the full range of contraceptive options available to other citizens. Hence, the protection of one right (bodily integrity) led to the denial of another (choice in reproductive decision making). Without a consenting individual, who would prioritize these rights? Some states allowed substitute consent, granting guardians the power to consent, while others required the courts to review each case, at times with little guiding legislation (Dodge 1978).[16]

Ironically, at the same time that states increased their efforts to protect the rights to bodily integrity and procreation, courts also upheld laws that terminated the parental rights of adults with mental disabilities who were proved unable to "discharge parental responsibilities" (Mason 1986). These laws were usually upheld because they required some evidence that the parent was unfit and thus were not based on disability alone. However, the standard of evidence was much lower than that needed to terminate the parental rights of a person without a disability. Termination of parental rights for a person without a disability typically would require proof of child abuse or neglect; however, such evidence was not needed to terminate the rights of disabled parents under these laws.

For example, when Donna Pauletich Cobb's parenting rights were removed in 1984, a court in Lawrence County, Pennsylvania, presented her level of mental retardation and her IQ among the reasons for determining that she could not develop sufficient parenting skills. The court stated, "Considering the full scale intelligence quotient of 58, which placed her in the mild range of retardation, . . . it is highly unlikely that Donna Pauletich Cobb will ever gain the necessary skills to properly mother a child."[17] The court also found that she had been unable to profit from county programs to assist in family reunification. Disagreeing with the court's decision, the Developmental Disabilities Law Project (1985) argued that mental retardation in itself should never serve as the basis for the termination of parenting rights. Moreover, it found the county's attempts to offer services inadequate. Cobb had been provided with only classroom-based instruction removed from her home and from actual interaction with her child, and her disabilities made it difficult for her to benefit from this form of education. The brief argued that, prior to terminating such fundamental rights, the agencies charged with providing parenting training and reunification services must design services to meet the "reasonable, individual needs of each such person" (Developmental Disabilities Law Project 1985, 10).

Right to Life-Sustaining Medical Treatment

Even the right to life for disabled infants has provoked controversy. Historically, doctors made difficult decisions about whether to treat disabled infants, but only on rare occasions did these decisions emerge as part of public discourse (Pernick 1996). In 1982, though, an Indiana case caught the attention of the Reagan administration. Immediately after birth of the child in question, physicians informed the parents that the infant had Down Syndrome and a detached esophagus. A relatively routine medical procedure was needed to treat the esophagus and intestinal blockage or the child would not survive; of course, no medical treatment was possible to reverse the Down Syndrome. The parents decided not to allow the treatment because they felt that Down Syndrome would significantly detract from their child's quality of life. President Ronald Reagan, a pro-life advocate, stepped in to protect "the sanctity of life" and used Section 504 to charge the hospital with medical discrimination against people with disabilities (an ironic act given his prior efforts to limit the scope of Section 504).

Although the infant died, the Reagan administration developed the "Baby Doe Guidelines" to ensure the future protection of disabled infants. These guidelines prohibited medical discrimination (defined as the denial of "medically beneficial treatment" on the basis of a present or anticipated physical or mental impairment), mandated the reporting of suspected discrimination, and provided for the investigation of alleged cases. The American Medical Association, the American Hospital Association, and the American Academy of Pediatrics quickly opposed these rules, which they believed allowed the government to usurp decisions best left to the family and to physicians.

Before the final rules even came into effect, another controversial case led to a challenge against them. In 1983, "Baby Jane Doe" was born with multiple severe disabilities, including spina bifida, hydrocephaly, microcephaly, and other conditions. Although surgery to drain excess fluid from her brain would have prolonged "the child's life past the age of one or two," the parents decided against the surgery (Huefner 1986). The U.S. Department of Justice, in accordance with the guidelines, requested the relevant medical records to investigate the hospital for medical discrimination under Section 504. When the hospital refused to provide the records, the Department of Justice brought suit against it. The case eventually went to the U.S. Supreme Court, and the federal government lost at every stage. The court found no evidence of medical discrimination; according to the court, the hospital's decision to withhold treatment was based on the lack of parental consent not on the presence of a disability, and discrimination by parents was outside the purview of Section 504. The opinion noted that "nothing in the statute authorizes the Secretary to dispense with the law's focus on discrimination and instead employ federal resources to save the lives of handicapped newborns, without regard to whether they are victims of discrimination by recipients of federal funds or not" (quoted in Huefner 1986, 187).

Using a different approach, President Reagan then asked Congress to amend child-abuse laws to prohibit medical neglect and discrimination. Passed in 1985, PL 98-457 required child protective agencies to report and investigate instances of medical neglect against disabled infants. Whereas discrimination by parents was outside of the scope of Section 504, child-abuse laws could regulate and even overturn parental decisions if they were found to constitute medical neglect and therefore a form of child abuse or neglect. These legislative changes helped to protect children with disabilities; however, life-and-death decisions regarding infants with severe disabilities continued to be made privately between medical professionals and family members (Anspach 1993).

Alliances and Divisions at the Close of the 1980s

By the late 1980s, mental retardation policy was being influenced by a complex array of parents, self-advocates, disability-rights activists, academics representing a range of fields, lawyers, and service-delivery professionals. The self-advocacy movement had gained recognition, particularly on the local level, and was poised to establish a national organization of its own. The ARC had become one of the largest disability organizations in the nation, with twelve hundred chapters; a successful Action Alert Network that monitored political activity and generated thousands of communications with politicians when needed; and a strong record of influencing legislation and the courts. As the parents' movement grew in political influence, so did the broader disability-rights movement. By the late 1980s, independent living centers had been established across the country and had been accepted as a legitimate model of service provision by the federal government. Disabled in Action and ADAPT were well-known cross-disability grassroots organizations that engaged in demonstrations and protests.[18] The Disability Rights Education and Defense Fund, established in 1980, worked to develop ties with broader civil-rights movements and situate disability rights within the larger organizational and political fight for civil rights.

Increasingly, parents and self-advocates and activists in the Disability Rights Movement recognized an intersection of interests. Institutionalization and access to community services affected people with developmental disabilities, mental illness, significant physical disabilities, and the elderly. Access to a public education affected all children with disabilities. Access to adequate and accessible public transportation was crucial for all those whose disabilities, whether physical or cognitive, made it unlikely they would drive.

Working at least somewhat collaboratively, they achieved several remarkable successes, such as the passage of IDEA, the deinstitutionalization of thousands of individuals with disabilities, and the creation of a vast system of community services and new funding streams to support them. Other successes of the Disability Rights Movement included the passage of the regulations for Section 504, the Civil Rights Act of Institutionalized Persons Act of 1980, the Voting Accessibility for the Elderly and Handicapped Act of 1984, the Handicapped Children's Protection Act of 1986, the Air Carriers Act of 1986, the Civil Rights Remedies Equalization Act of 1986, the Civil Rights Restoration Act of 1987, the Hearing Aid Compatibility Act of 1988, the Telecommunications Accessibility Enhancement Act of 1988, and the Fair Housing Amendments Act of 1988. As recorded by the NCD (1997, 33–34), "Washington likes winners. Through the 1980s, the disability community recorded an impressive string of judicial and legislative victories that helped build the disability movement's credibility in Washington."

However, alliances were tenuous, at best. Divisions among parents sharpened through the 1970s and 1980s as some vehemently lined up to support community integration, while others defended segregated options. Even within the ARC, such divisions intensified. Some ARC chapters concentrated on advocacy and civil rights, while others transformed themselves into large-scale community-based service providers and became entrenched in a system of professionalized, segregated (albeit "community-based") group homes, sheltered workshops, "special" schools, and recreational programs. As progressive centers of thought such as the Center on Human Policy fought for self-determination and full inclusion for people with developmental disabilities, they often found themselves in conflict with parents rather than allied with them. Self-advocates also found themselves at times in conflict with the parents' movement. Hank Bersani Jr. (1996, 264) explained that "many parents and parent organizations have been reluctant to give up any of their power and influence to self-advocates. Nationally, there is still a parent organization called The Voice of the Retarded. If a group exists to be *The* Voice for a group (unfortunately still called 'The Retarded'), then why would they support self-advocates?"

Alliances with the Disability Rights Movement were also delicate. In the 1960s, the ARC had built strong alliances with organizations representing other developmental disabilities such as United Cerebral Palsy. In 1975, Paul Marchand took a lead role in connecting the ARC to other disability-rights organizations with the creation of the Consortium for Citizens with Developmental Disabilities, an organization headquartered in Washington, D.C., and created to advocate political reforms to achieve full integration in society. This organization later became the Consortium for Citizens with Disabilities, representing approximately one hundred organizations across the disability spectrum. Although powerful allies, neither the ARC nor self-advocates seemed fully integrated into the Disability Rights Movement through the 1970s and 1980s. Disability-rights activists still tended to be suspicious of parents' movements and hesitant to accept people with cognitive and mental disabilities as fellow activists. Meanwhile, many parents remained cautious of the ideal of self-determination and the protest tactics used by the Disability Rights Movement. Thus, the various organizations and movements often pursued similar interests and at times worked closely together but remained distinct.

Civil Rights and Mental Retardation
at the Close of the 1980s

The legal victories of the 1970s and 1980s significantly altered American views of citizenship and people with mental retardation. Most notably, legislation began to recognize the notion of different and equal and the responsibility of the community to support all of its members in reaching their potential. People with mental retardation were both equal to and different from other citizens; they had the same set of rights as other citizens, as well as additional rights to support their development and integration. "Positive" rights (rights that require action on the part of the government or other citizens) were determined to be essential for the achievement of equality in real-world settings. However, as seen throughout this chapter, the commitment to equal rights and additional positive rights was weak at best. The nation fell short of guaranteeing necessary social rights, such as the rights to treatment, to live in the community with support, and the guarantee of support for the exercise of one's negative liberties in the community. Nor did states systematically remove old legislation barring people with disabilities from exercising basic rights accorded to other citizens.

Presenting a more subtle yet serious problem, the framework offered by advocates, built on the principles of the developmental approach, normalization, equal citizenship, and group-specific rights, was itself fraught with tensions. The principle of normalization and its related concept of the least restrictive environment stressed the pursuit of equality and liberty, but it also legitimated professional supervision and control. Individuals without disabilities do not typically live in settings dominated by professionals; however, normalization assumed that professionals would play a key role in determining and creating "normal" experiences, such as consumers' goals, activities, living situations, and relationships, and in providing the training believed to be necessary for people with mental retardation to engage in these "normal" experiences.

Similarly, the principle of the least restrictive environment supported the creation of a continuum of services to meet varied needs and thereby assumed that some people with mental retardation required segregation (Taylor 1988). Professionals retained the power to determine the "appropriate placement" for a person, and therefore restrictions on liberty could still occur outside legal processes. Moreover, in practice the continuum approach often required people with mental retardation to experience more restrictive services initially and "earn" their way into less restrictive environments. For example, individuals commonly began their work experience in sheltered workshops and moved to competitive job placements only after proving their skills. Similarly, individuals in group homes often had to achieve success at a variety of professionally established goals to prove their ability to live independently, marry, and parent.

As the National Council on Disability suggested in its criticism of IDEA, normalization and the least restrictive environment legitimated the rise of complex professionalized systems that remained largely separate from those serving the rest of the community and treated people with mental retardation as fundamentally different from other individuals. To serve their own bureaucratic interests, these professional systems tended to create policies geared toward efficiency and accountability rather than to meet the needs of those they served. Integration then became partly an illusion. This is not to say that thousands of people were not better served in the community than in institutions; however, measured by the ideal of integration, the move into the community too often represented a move into professionalized settings that dictated individuals' access to interpersonal relationships, determined their schedules, and limited their choices and privacy, with little focus on achieving meaningful integration with neighbors and community members.

A tension also existed between the principles of equality and group-specific rights. On one hand, claims for equality rested on the understanding of people with mental retardation as the *same* as other citizens, yet advocates stressed the existence of unique needs among this population for protection, assistance, and support. Therefore, for example, the fight for equal education actually became a fight for group-specific accommodated education. Advocates *could* have made the argument that *every child* needed an individualized education with specific accommodations, thereby envisioning individualized education as a universal right rather than a group-specific one. In doing so, they would have maintained the notion that people with mental retardation were similar to other citizens in that all citizens have particular needs that must be assessed and addressed. This, in turn, would have allied them with movements to improve education for children from minority and economically disadvantaged backgrounds, for children who speak English as a second language, for gifted children, and so on. But advocates for people with mental retardation did not choose to take on that larger battle. Rather, they created group-specific rights that ideologically positioned this population as fundamentally different from, and therefore perhaps inferior to, other citizens.

Because people with mental retardation were positioned as different, claims for group-specific rights could be used to invalidate claims to equal rights. For example, in *City of Cleburne, Texas, v. Cleburne Living Center* (1985), the U.S. Supreme Court addressed the issue of whether mental retardation should be established as a "quasi-suspect classification," a status that is intended to protect groups from discrimination by mandating heightened scrutiny of laws identifying those specific populations. The court argued that people with mental retardation did not constitute such a class. In the court's opinion, Justice Byron R. White argued that, while gender required a heightened standard for review because there typically was "no sensible ground for differential treatment," individuals with mental retardation "have a reduced ability to cope with and function in the everyday world . . . , and the States' interest in dealing with and providing for them is a legitimate one." The court continued, "Such legislation thus singling out the retarded for special treatment reflects the real and undeniable differences between the retarded and others. That a civilized and decent society expects and approves such legislation indicates that governmental consideration of those differences in the vast majority of situations is not only legitimate but desirable" (*City of Cleburne, Texas, v. Cleburne Living Center* 1985, 3254–3256). Thus, individuals with mental retardation were not the same as those without, and differential treatment was expected.

Given that differential treatment was allowed and expected, the protections offered through civil-rights legislation seemed dubious. Although people with mental retardation were supposed to be protected from discrimination in employment, for example, they were rarely seen as "otherwise qualified," and they continued to work primarily within sheltered workshops, with their pay often supplemented by government benefits to make ends meet. Many children remained in segregated classrooms, which were often poorly funded, inadequately staffed, and stigmatized within the school. Making the picture even murkier, equal-rights legislation sat side by side with older laws prohibiting the vote, voiding marriage, and terminating parenting rights.

Not only were these principles in tension; they were also open to interpretation. Some advocates stressed the "right" to live in the community, while others stressed the "right" to choose one's services, potentially including segregated options. Some stressed the right to an integrated education, while others stressed the right to an appropriate education that potentially included segregated options. Some stressed the right to be treated like a "typical" citizen, while others stressed the right to "be mentally retarded." Some stressed the right to bodily integrity and protection from sterilization, while others stressed the right to sterilization as part of reproductive choice. Without a strong voice from individuals with mental retardation themselves, the purpose for civil rights was easily confused, various rights were difficult to prioritize, and a rhetoric of rights became a tool employed by multiple constituencies to promote their own preferences, often in direct conflict with other constituencies that were also supposedly promoting rights for this population.

Fundamentally, the movement to gain rights for people with mental retardation still suffered from the absence of strong leaders with mental retardation to provide guidance. Some still assumed that, due to their disability, people with mental retardation simply could not evaluate and communicate their own self-interests. Others made a more subtle argument that also potentially discounted the voice of people with retardation, suggesting that because people with mental retardation tended to experience sheltered lives with little exposure to typical or varied experiences, they had limited ability to make meaningful choices. Hence, when several Pennhurst residents expressed an interest in remaining at the institution despite the order to move everyone to community placements, advocates of deinstitutionalization pointed out that those residents had no other experience to compare with institutionalization, and they were therefore poorly informed of alternative possibilities. While limited experience certainly limits one's ability to make choices, a quandary presents itself: In the absence of a range of typical experiences and opportunities, could indi-

viduals with mental retardation exercise self-determination? If exposure to varied life experiences was a requirement for choice, were people with intellectual
disabilities being held to a higher standard in making choices than other citizens? If they did not want exposure to varied experiences, could they be forced
to gain such experiences in the name of informed choice? Could the movement in effect force inclusion, integration, and rights on those individuals who
preferred segregation, care, and protection and still focus the movement on
"self-determination"?

Other barriers to achieving rights hampered progress, and advocates realized that significant dedication was required to sustain and implement rights.
Funding levels for services for people with developmental disabilities were consistently low. The lack of available services and trained personnel meant that
many people were denied services and placed on waiting lists. In a Catch-22,
though, the growth of the service system also in some ways became a barrier.
David Braddock's research indicates that from 1962 to 1984, federal funds for
programs related to developmental disabilities grew from $118 million to $7.4
million (Braddock 2002). The proliferation of services supported the meaningful participation of people with mental retardation in mainstream society
in many ways, yet the rise of the service industry also subjected consumers to
constant monitoring and evaluation, segregation, rights restrictions, and control over their daily lives. Moreover, developmental disability had become big
business (Albrecht 1992). Who would control that money? Agencies fought to
retain control over funding streams as advocates for the rights of people with
mental retardation increasingly called for consumer control. Thus, the same
service system that offered support also became an impediment to securing
self-determination and inclusion.

Resistance came from diverse sources and even from people and organizations that saw themselves as advocates. Professionals fought to retain their
autonomy to dictate best practices within their fields, parents fought to determine the best interests of their children, and communities resisted the development of community-based residences. One's relational network (e.g., one's
family, friends, and place of residence such as in an institution or community)
still greatly influenced one's access to rights. Some families encouraged their
children to participate in as many aspects of community life as possible and
fought to secure their rights. Other families denied their children the opportunities to date, to make self-determined choices, and to privacy; lacked knowledge of the rights they and their children might have; or believed segregation
and protection better served their children's interests. Professionalized settings
also varied greatly in their orientation and commitment to rights and opportunities for their consumers. Given the scarcity of opportunities for residential
and independent living and their need for services, individuals with retardation
often could not simply leave the living situation, even if they were unhappy.
Moreover, exercise of a specific right may not be considered important enough
to sacrifice an otherwise comfortable living situation. States varied tremen-

dously in their commitment to the provision of services in the community and in their respect for and support of the exercise of rights by people with mental retardation.

In conclusion, opportunities greatly expanded during this period, and the narrative of the mentally retarded citizen became the dominant rhetoric in policy circles. Access to rights, support, and self-determination, though, remained quite limited, in part hindered by the very narrative of civil rights and the system of support created to encourage access.

9

Reimagining Retardation, Transforming Community

After the challenges of the 1980s, the 1990s kicked off with two significant events: the passage of the Americans with Disabilities Act (ADA) and the formation of the first national self-advocacy group, Self-Advocates Becoming Empowered (SABE). Each of these events encouraged the other: Activism by many groups led to the passage of the ADA, while the fervor around the ADA inspired activism and further cemented group identities and goals. For the sake of conceptual clarity, I discuss these two events separately, beginning with the rise of SABE and changes in the conceptualization of mental retardation and then moving on to the ADA and its impact for people with intellectual disabilities.

Reimagining Retardation, Removing Labels

In 1990, self-advocates met in Estes Park, Colorado, for the First North American People First Conference. At that meeting, a steering committee was formed to plan for the establishment of a national organization to unify the state and local chapters and exert political influence at the national level. The steering committee drafted a statement of belief that read, "We believe people with disabilities should be treated as equals. That means that people should be given the same decisions, choices, rights, responsibilities, chance to speak up to empower themselves, and to make new friendships and old friendships. Just like everyone else. They should also be able to learn from their mistakes. Like everyone else" (Shoultz and Ward 1996, 222). A year later, more than eight hundred self-advocates attended the second North American People First Conference and voted to establish an organization based on the recommendations of the steering committee. Later that year they selected a name: Self-Advocates Becoming Empowered.

Members of SABE positioned it as an organization within the Disability Rights Movement, not as a charity to help people with disabilities or as an off-shoot of a professional or parent organization. They took care to ensure that people with disabilities, not professionals, would provide its leadership. Any person with a disability could join as a voting member of the organization, whereas people without disabilities could join only as non-voting members. They also restricted the role of "advisers," who provided support but could not engage in substantive decision making. In solidarity with the Disability Rights Movement, they framed their movement in terms of self-determination and drew on disability-rights slogans such as "Free Our People" and "Nothing about Us without Us." Through their alliance with disability organization such as ADAPT, SABE members learned an array of techniques for activism, including demonstrations, the education of policymakers, collaboration with state agencies, and the development of programs to assist individual residents to leave institutional settings if they so desired. They also collected stories from the people who had resided in institutions and began to build a history and a set of heroes from their own perspective.[1] In SABE's early history, it established a particularly strong relationship with Justin Dart, an iconic figure of the Disability Rights Movement who is best known for his role in the passage of the ADA. Dart helped establish ties between SABE and other national organizations such as ADAPT, the President's Committee on Employment of People with Disabilities, and the National Council on Disability.

Whereas parents and professionals in the 1970s had taken a cautious stand on the autonomy of people with mental retardation, SABE stridently supported self-determination. According to SABE, all people with disabilities could exercise control over their lives, including people with developmental disabilities. No person, they argued, should have to sacrifice his or her rights for the receipt of services. All individuals should choose where to live, how to live, with whom to build relationships, and so on. Some might need support to make these choices; however, they did not need professionals who claimed to be experts determining the details of their lives. *They* were the experts in disability, and they should shape their own lives, influence the policies that affected them, and determine which services they needed. The self-advocate Liz Obermayer explained,

> I live in America, the land that gives me the right to make choices and speak my mind. But I have a disability. . . . Nobody allows me to make choices. People tell me all the time what to wear, what to eat, what job to have and who are my friends. Is that fair? I say no! But I have a disability. . . . [P]eople don't listen to me anyway. . . . [W]hy should I give my opinions? I fight so hard for someone to listen . . . just want someone to listen . . . and give a damm about what I want. If people with disabilities can live with everyone else, than why can't I make choices like anyone else . . . if that's my right as a citizen of the U.S.A. (Obermeyer 2004; ellipses in the original)

SABE's emphasis on choice and self-determination stood in stark contrast with the institutional and agency-run group-home models of service delivery. Institutions and even most group homes were run by administrators who continued to make rules based on bureaucratic efficiency and legal liability rather than on the wishes of their residents. For example, many group homes still compelled residents to attend programs, work, or school during the day so they could reduce staffing. Similarly, many did not allow residents to have privacy with members of the opposite sex. Thus, to receive services, people with disabilities had to accept a host of restrictions on their lives.

Support of deinstitutionalization became one of SABE's first and most pressing political tasks. It defined an institution as "any facility or program where people don't have control of their lives," a much broader definition than typically used (Self-Advocates Becoming Empowered 1999). In contrast with many other organizations in the field of developmental disabilities, SABE demanded the closure of traditional group homes, sheltered workshops, day facilities, and any other segregated group services, in addition to large-scale residential facilities, in favor of individualized support controlled by the person with a disability. In alliance with ADAPT and other disability organizations, SABE demanded that the government and professional agencies "Free Our People," comparing institutions to prisons and their residents to prisoners (Nelis and Ward 1995–1996). A former resident of an institution in Oklahoma argued, "Everybody has rights, just because we are different or look different does not make us have to be in institutions. We are people just like you and anyone else, so start treating us like other people, not animals" (Nelis and Ward 1995–1996, 12). Activists and self-advocates emphasized the abuse people had experienced in institutions and compared this with the better quality of life they experienced in the community. For example, a self-advocate named Leon remembered that in the institution in which he had lived, "They used to pound me and beat me up." As a member of the community, he explained, "I have a good life now. Make my own coffee. . . . I live by myself now, and I have my own apartment." He continued, "When I was in the institution, I was shy. I like where I am now. I like myself. I am better off now" (Hayden 1997).

Tackling the service system ultimately meant tackling the structure of government benefits. Disability activists had argued for decades that the Medicaid funding structure contained an "institutional bias" toward reimbursing services provided in institutional settings (including nursing homes and Intermediate Care Facilities for the Mentally Retarded (ICR-MFs) rather than services provided in the home and the community. Twice as many people received their services in community-based setting as institutional settings, yet only about one-quarter of Medicaid's budget for long-term care was spent on community-based services. Therefore, many individuals with disabilities were forced to reside in an institutional setting to receive services, to live in the community without services, or to pay out of pocket for their services. Moreover, by directing funding to agencies rather than individuals, the funding structure encouraged agency control over the lives of people with disabilities and limited consumer choice and empowerment.

Self-advocates and other disability-rights activists imagined a system in which services were disaggregated and could be purchased without an expectation regarding one's residence or other aspects of one's life. The Disability Rights Movement espoused the use of "personal assistants," people hired by people with disabilities to support them in their daily tasks. Self-advocates believed that this model of service provision could also work for them. Because individuals with disabilities hired and directed their personal assistants, they held power in this relationship to direct and individualize the services provided. Moving from agency control to consumer control, though, required that government funds "follow the person" to give individuals the power to use their disability benefits to purchase services as they felt appropriate.

SABE also worked on other major initiatives, including reforms of the criminal-justice system. People with developmental disabilities were disproportionately likely to be victims of crime, yet they were unlikely to report their experiences to the authorities for several reasons. Most commonly, those who decided not to report feared the possible consequences (especially if the perpetrator was a caregiver), had difficulties articulating their experiences, or were unaware that they had been a victim of a criminal act. Those who did report often found that legal officials discounted them as incompetent and unreliable and that the agencies' staff members treated their experiences as administrative problems rather than as crimes requiring legal intervention (Lumley and Miltenberger 1997; McCabe et al. 1994; Sobsey 1994; Stromsness 1993).

People with developmental disabilities suspected of crimes experienced similar problems. On arrest, some people with developmental disabilities did not understand their Miranda rights and waived them, seemingly "voluntarily"; sought to please authority figures and avoid stressful questioning, leading them to offer false confessions; and hid their disability rather than requesting accommodation. In addition, they often had difficulty assisting their counsel, if they became confused, forgot timelines, or struggled to communicate their thoughts. Defendants with developmental disabilities also had difficulty impressing jurors, as they at times failed to follow the expected rules of "impression management." Defendants, for example, might appear bored or sleepy during their trials, leading jurors to conclude that they were indifferent or hostile. Due to these issues, people with developmental disabilities faced higher rates of arrest and conviction as well as longer sentences than people without disabilities who committed similar crimes. National organizations, including SABE, took on this issue, demanding accommodation in the criminal-justice system for people with disabilities.

In addition to deinstitutionalization and reform in the criminal-justice system, SABE worked on a broad array of policy areas, such as health insurance and the education of health professionals, accessible transportation, SSI and Medicaid regulations, the ADA, and the ADA Restoration Act. It demanded a place at the political table when policies that would affect people with disabilities were at issue. By end of the twentieth century, SABE had grown into a respected organization within the Disability Rights Movement and in the field of developmental disabilities. Indeed, as the only national organization predominantly of people with developmental disabilities, SABE found it held a position of symbolic power, and its participation and approval was increasingly sought, especially among those claiming to fight for the rights and inclusion of people with developmental disabilities. For example, in 2003 eleven major organizations, including the Center on Human Policy, TASH, The Arc,[2] and SABE, joined forces to create the Alliance for Full Participation (AFP), an organization designed to promote the full participation of people with developmental disabilities in communities of their choice. Members of SABE withdrew their support from the AFP, however, because they felt that professionals were excluding them by using jargon, moving discussions along too quickly, and creating goals and objectives without them. In a statement to the AFP, SABE made clear its agenda for full participation and its dissatisfaction with the way in which the alliance was run:

The Founding groups are looking for priorities for the future

Our answer is:

JUST DO IT!!!

Many have listened, some have taken action and we thank you.
But we have talked enough and waited too long!!!

We have told you what is important to us
Get rid of the infamous and hurtful "r" word, do not label us

We will not put up with
the "r" word continuing as part of an organization's name
even as initials
If you are working with me and for me then do not disrespect me

We have been prepared enough
ASK the people who are living in institutions
Would you trade places

Close institutions

Get us real jobs
Close sheltered workshops

Give US the money to live OUR lives
Money follows the person means it is OURS not programs

We have the right to make our own decisions
with or without the support from others
WE CAN RUN OUR LIVES

> Support our movement,
> IT IS OURS
> You receive millions of dollars in our name
> We want to control this money
> As we are the EXPERTS
>
> You must change, we have changed, we are taking the power
> Walk the Walk, Respect Us or We will go on without you!
>
> (SABE ca. 2005)

The AFP wrote an apology, and SABE rejoined its efforts. For the other organizations to proceed in the fight for full inclusion without this national self-advocacy group would have been embarrassing and ineffective.

SABE also did not hesitate to take on parents' groups, especially Voice of the Retarded (VOR), which continued to support the provision of state funding for institutions as part of the "continuum of choice." SABE found VOR's name and mission to be offensive: "This organization doesn't speak for us. They do not agree with what we want—the freedom to live in the community, authority to make decisions for ourselves and to spend money the way that we want, the support we need to be successful, and the responsibility to give back to our communities, help others learn to speak-up for themselves so they will become self-determined individuals" (SABE 2000). While less adversarial, perhaps, SABE's condemnation of the provision of group services such as group homes and sheltered workshops also placed it in conflict with The Arc and with many service providers that administered these services.

Thus, as SABE joined the national political fray, it quickly grew into a respected organization that consistently and stridently demanded social change. At the heart of its mission was a belief in the rights of all people to make choices, exercise control over their lives, receive support in exercising their rights, and, ultimately, be treated as respected members of the community. As such, it positioned people with developmental disabilities within the liberal requirements for the exercise of rights, arguing that all people with support could make self-determined choices and pursue their own happiness.

Individuals with developmental disabilities who were not formally affiliated with the self-advocacy movement also burst into the public limelight. Chris Burke, an actor with Down Syndrome, made history when executives at the ABC television network decided to cast him in the lead role in a show about a teenager with Down Syndrome and his family. From 1989 to 1993, *Life Goes On* portrayed the challenges and joys experienced by the Thatcher family as Burke's character, "Corky," received an education in an integrated school, pursued a job, dated, and eventually married. As an actor, author of a best-selling autobiography, musician, and spokesperson for the National Down Syndrome Society, Burke stressed, "We need to be out there in the community. We need to have our voices heard. When I have a job, I do my job and I like to work.

Everyone should have that chance. I say to people 'Give them a chance! Make their dreams come true!'" (Burke and McDaniel 1991, 255).

In 1994, Jason Kingsley and Mitchell Levitz published *Count Us In*, a book of their conversations about living with Down Syndrome, school, work, relationships, religion, and many other topics. Like Burke, Kingsley and Levitz emphasized their pride in themselves and their accomplishments and their desire to participate fully in mainstream society. They joked that, rather than Down Syndrome, the term should be "Up Syndrome" to emphasize the abilities and sense of self-worth of individuals with Down Syndrome. Describing life as a "learning adventure" that required participating, taking risks, and making choices, they explained that they wanted to participate in the adventure along with everyone else.

Controversies over Terminology

The new image of the self-determined citizen with intellectual disabilities was very positive, stressing group pride and demanding self-determination. In this context, the label "mental retardation"—once seen as an improvement over terms such as "feebleminded," "idiot," and "moron"—now seemed pejorative. The definition of "mental retardation" relied on a "deficit model" that defined the condition as a permanent, individual-based limitation. The social model of disability promoted by the Disability Rights Movement, however, called the deficit model into question. According to the social model, disability resulted from the interaction between an individual and his or her environment and thus was fluid and contextual. This model emphasized the importance of removing environmental and social barriers to improve the opportunities and quality of life for people with disabilities rather than "fixing" individuals with disabilities. "Retardation" was seen as representing the old deficit model, and as such it seemed inappropriate and even offensive. Self-advocates resented this label, referring to it as the "r" word, and demanded that organizations serving them stop using it. Many professionals and parents also voiced concerns that the term was "tarnished" and that its use hindered their activities, offended the people they served, and made their organizations appear outdated.[3]

While many people agreed that the term "retardation" had outlasted its usefulness, there was little agreement about how to proceed. Self-advocates resisted any professional label that placed a "diagnosis" on them. SABE tended to use the phrase "person with a disability," an identification that could be self-defined, was associated with disability pride, and placed them alongside other activists in the Disability Rights Movement. However, the legislative successes achieved in the 1970s and 1980s, such as IDEA and expanded access to income support, were largely predicated on specific professional diagnoses, and some parents and professionals feared that a significant change in terminology or definition might have a negative impact on people who received services or funding.

The term "developmental disabilities" had become popular since its legislative inception in 1970, but its meaning was broad and ambiguous. Initially created to join together particular childhood disabilities affecting development, such as mental retardation and cerebral palsy, the federal government redefined it in the 1978 reauthorization of the DD Act to include any severe, lifelong disability that originated from birth through age twenty-one, including, for example, blindness, paralysis, and schizophrenia. This new definition was much broader than its predecessor and created confusion as some people continued to use the term to refer to a narrow set of disabilities, whereas others began to use it more broadly as intended by the 1978 DD Act.

Because the definition of developmental disability had come to include such diverse disabilities, other terms emerged that identified a narrower set of disabilities related to cognitive functioning, including "cognitive disabilities," "intellectual disabilities," and "learning disabilities." Cognitive disabilities were typically seen as those that involved limitations in mental and intellectual function, such as retardation, autism, traumatic brain injury, and Alzheimer's disease (not including mental illness), but the term carried no specific requirement regarding age of onset. "Intellectual disability" was typically used to refer to a population similar to those diagnosed as "mentally retarded" and referred to limitations rooted in sub-average intellectual and adaptive functioning occurring early in life. "Learning disabilities" included disabilities that affected the brain's ability to receive, process, analyze, or store information. In Europe this term included what Americans referred to as "retardation," but in America it was typically reserved for disabilities such as dyslexia, which affect specific learning activities without necessarily limiting one's overall level of intelligence.

Leading organizations in the field developed different strategies to replace the term "mental retardation." As noted earlier, in 1992 the Association for Retarded Citizens (ARC) decided to drop the acronym and become simply The Arc, redefining itself as an organization of and for people with developmental and intellectual disabilities. Similarly, in 1995 the Association for Persons with Severe Handicaps voted to use its acronym, TASH, without referring to its full name, because that name "didn't reflect current values and directions" (TASH n.d.). It described its mission as the inclusion of all people in all aspects of society, regardless of disability. In organizing SABE, self-advocates purposefully avoided reference to any specific types of disability and instead framed their mission as including all people with disabilities. Whereas The Arc, TASH, and SABE attempted to pursue their missions to some degree without reference to a specific disability, other organizations replaced the term "mental retardation" with the term "intellectual disability." In 2003, President George W. Bush signed an executive order renaming the President's Committee on Mental Retardation the President's Committee for People with Intellectual Disabilities. And in 2007, the American Association on Mental Retardation (AAMR) changed its name to the American Association on Intellectual and Developmental Disability (AAIDD).

The AAIDD and the Difficulties of Social Change

The tensions between the old deficit model, the new social model, and various terms and definitions are perhaps most vividly apparent in the AAIDD's response to the ongoing changes in the field. The AAIDD, first formed in 1876, is the oldest professional organization focusing on intellectual disability, and its long history and professional membership made change both difficult and crucial to its continued role as a leader in the field.

Between 1908 and 2008, the AAIDD updated its definitions related to intellectual disability ten times (Smith 2000). Throughout these definitions, three criteria for the diagnosis of intellectual disability remained relatively consistent. A diagnosis required evidence of limitations in intelligence and limitations in social adaptation, both of which had to be manifested early in life. The various changes in definition mostly involved shifts in the diagnostic importance or measurement of intellectual and adaptive limitations and in the requirements regarding age of onset (Luckasson et al. 2002; Schalock and Luckasson 2004; Schalock et al. 2002). For example, in 1973, the AAIDD (then named the AAMR), changed the definition of "subaverage intelligence" from one standard deviation below the mean (an IQ score of 85 or below) to two or more standard deviations below the mean (an IQ score of 70 or below), thereby reducing the number of people potentially defined as retarded from 16 percent of the population to about 2 percent. Although this was a dramatic shift, the three-prong definition remained intact.

In 1992, as other organizations were moving away from the term "mental retardation," the AAMR decided to retain it and create a new definition in an attempt to recognize the growing dominance of the social model. In its new definition, "mental retardation" was characterized by "substantial limitations in present functioning" in the areas of intellectual functioning and adaptive skills. While the definition retained the traditional focus on the onset of limitations in intellectual and adaptive functioning prior to age twenty-one, the phrase "present functioning" was inserted to recognize the role of social factors in shaping disability and the potential fluidity of this diagnosis.

In 2002, the AAMR made additional changes to further address the social model. It elaborated on the factors that influenced an individual's ability to function, including social factors such as participation in and access to meaningful roles and typical activities. It also allowed for more flexibility in assessing the boundaries between "normal" and "subnormal" IQ scores by offering a range of scores (between 70 and 75) rather than one set number. Seen as a bold move by some, the AAMR rejected its previous classification system, which categorized people with mental retardation as profoundly, severely, moderately, or mildly retarded. According to this organization, this schema incorrectly assumed that the severity of one's condition was permanent and that it could be used to determine which services an individual needed. In its place, the AAMR created a classification system based on the pattern and intensity of support needed by the individual, recognizing that these needs could change over a person's life course. The new system, it claimed, avoided reducing an individual to a fixed state defined by his or her limitations and proposed to use the labeling process not to stigmatize, but to identify needs and implement positive individualized support to "promote the development, education, interests, and personal well-being of a person" (Schalock and Luckasson 2004, 142).

In 2007, the membership of the AAMR voted to adopt the term "intellectual disability" and renamed the organization the AAIDD. According to the AAIDD, unlike "mental retardation," which presumed a medical model, "intellectual disability" reflected the social model. It presumed that disability is in part shaped by the environment; that it is possible to have a positive "disability identity" and a sense of disability pride; and that support should be individualized and respectful of the recipient's needs and interests (Schalock et al. 2007). Thus, the new terminology was more consistent with the trends in the field and the terminology used by other disability organizations.

Interestingly, as the AAIDD touted its acceptance of the social model and leadership in the field, others criticized it as slow and conservative. On one hand, it had adopted new terminology and measurements that reflected the social model; however, it continued to assert the importance of distinguishing intellectual disability from other disabilities through professionally assessed diagnosis and subcategories and used "intellectual disability" to refer to the same population previously labeled "mentally retarded." Consistency was necessary, according to the AAIDD, to ensure the continuation of services for people receiving them; however, self-advocates criticized the AAIDD's decision as creating yet another stigmatizing label. From the other end of the spectrum, some scientists and professionals argued that the changes in terminology and classification were political in nature and without medical and scientific merit.

The AAIDD was by no means alone in confronting the dilemma of disability-related terminology. Access to the services and benefits offered by disability legislation, such as laws concerning special education, vocational rehabilitation, and income supports, required specific medical diagnosis. To recognize disability as contextual and transitory potentially imperiled access to these services. Moreover, to rely on terminology that was broad in its scope, like "people with disabilities," or to abandon labels made advocacy to address specific needs difficult. Thus, the social model, which was so useful for exposing disadvantages rooted in the social environment and advocating for social change, also threatened the classification systems on which disability and mental retardation policy had been established. Organizations such as the AAIDD walked a fine line and juggled many interests as they attempted to preserve the victories won, maintain a respected role for professionals as experts in the delivery of services, recognize the social model, and collaborate with self-advocates who increasingly demanded the rights to self-definition and control of the services offered to them.

Redesigning "Services" into "Individualized Support"

In the shift toward self-determination and a social-ecological model, some organizations, including TASH and the Center on Human Policy, joined self-advocates in criticizing prepackaged group services controlled by professionals and supporting the individualization of support and self-determination for those receiving support services (O'Brien 1993; O'Brien and O'Brien 2006; Taylor et al. 1987). John O'Brien (1995, 3), a leading advocate for community inclusion, argued that individualized services should do the following:

- Assist people with developmental disabilities to develop their individual abilities and personal interests.
- Discover and respond to individual choices.
- Support important personal relationships and encourage positive participation in community life.
- Deal effectively with people's vulnerabilities.
- Promote personal and organizational learning which leads to continual improvement of service provider ability to make these four essential contributions.

Person-centered planning (PCP) was designed to serve as a starting point for the provision of individualized support by assisting people with disabilities in defining, planning for, and pursuing their desired futures, including housing arrangements, employment, relationships, and leisure activities. At the outset of the process, the person with a disability typically selects a team of people to provide support. While professionals may serve as important members of these teams, PCP prioritizes the identification and development of informal, community-based relationships that will provide support to people with disabilities as they move toward greater participation in the community. Hence, the process of PCP should enhance an individual's capacity to articulate his or her interests, set goals, and make choices; an individual's social capital—or, in other words, his or her access to relationships that provide various forms of support toward the pursuit of his or her goals; and an individual's access to the resources and services provided in the community for people with disabilities and for all members of the community (Mount 1992; O'Brien and O'Brien 2006). In this framework, "support" that is chosen and directed by individuals with disabilities takes the place of "services" that are designed and controlled by professionals.

Transforming the Community

The effective provision of individualized support would require a massive overhaul of the service-delivery system, funding streams, and, ultimately, the community. People with disabilities would need access to a pool of personal assistants and services disentangled from large-scale, prepackaged options;

accessible community options, including affordable housing, accommodated employment, and accessible public transportation; members of the community to serve as natural supports; professionals willing to provide support rather than supervision; and, state funding structures that offered people with disabilities, instead of agencies, control of their Medicaid dollars. Ironically, perhaps, self-determination cannot be achieved through individual decision making or actions; rather, it requires the redistribution of power across relationships and the transformation of community so that people have feasible options and the power to pursue them.

Activists began to articulate a new ideal of community. In the era of eugenics, policy and law assumed that "the community" included "normal," "productive" citizens and that people who deviated from the norm could and should be segregated for the common good. In the 1950s, parents and professionals sought to retain people with disabilities in "the community" but placed few expectations on communities to value or support people with disabilities. At the end of the twentieth century, activists began to imagine a community that included, valued, and supported all of its members, including its members with disabilities.

According to John McKnight (1995), whereas professional systems were necessarily artificial, segregated, and restrictive, the community could offer natural and creative social support to its members. His proposed "community vision" argued that embedded within each community are the associations, relationships, and other resources necessary to creatively incorporate diverse people. Rather than develop artificial segregated options, we should strive to develop strong natural relationships embedded within communities to encourage inclusion while also strengthening the capacity of communities to include all of their members. In advocating for the inclusion of *all* people with disabilities in the community, a consortium of major organizations described the community in the following way:

> It is not an idealized place, like Lake Wobegon, where all are perfect. Communities have strengths and weaknesses, highs and lows. But community is the place where you make friends, have the choice of things to do or not do, where you share your joys and sorrows, where your parents brought you when you were born, where your grandparents live out their lives, it is where people care about each other or stay distant, again their choice. . . . Community is where all people belong, disability or not, in need of a lot of supports, or some or none. Community is possibility and opportunity and hope for the future. It is not a program, or services or an alternative. It is the only choice. ("What Is the Community?" 2004)

As this quote suggests, community is not simply a place; it is a network of relationships embedded with roles, rules, and institutional patterns that shape how power is distributed. Building community therefore entails building meaningful relationships, enabling people to participate in social roles of value to them, providing them with valued resources, and appreciating the contributions they make. Building community is not principally about building individual capacity, although this might be part of an overall strategy. It relies on "social capital," a concept that refers to the use of relationships and social networks as resources to achieve one's goals. According to Al Condelucci, executive director of United Cerebral Palsy of the Pittsburgh district, "It is through our social capital that people get closer to the most basic quality of life indicators: healthfulness, happiness, and longevity. . . . Quite simply, the more relationships in your life, the happier you are, the healthier you are, and the longer you live" (quoted in Lavigne 2004).[4]

Proponents of the "community vision" imagine a world of freely given, natural support. While they often rely on a language of rights, the community vision goes beyond establishing formal claims that demand access. It attempts to envision and create a world that values its members so that formal claims to rights are largely unnecessary. Some people believe this vision to be unrealistic, due to the inconsistency of natural support and the potential for abuse and exploitation in unmonitored environments. In response, advocates for the community vision argue that segregation and administrative regulations impose unnecessary restrictions, often fail to protect, and impose their own harm. In contrast, increasing the visibility and the value of people with disabilities in the community, incorporating them into mainstream organizations and associations, and building networks of natural relationships will offer people with disabilities maximal support and protection. According to Julie Pratt (1998, 8), "No matter where you live, the more people who know and care about you, the safer you are. We found that caring relationships are central to safety and to people's satisfaction with their lives."

Integrating the Social Model into Legislation

As these changes took place, the Americans with Disabilities Act of 1990, believed to be "one of the most formative pieces of American social policy legislation in the 20th century," established a significant new understanding of rights based on the social model of disability (National Council on Disability 1997, xi). The fight for its passage inspired tremendous levels of activism, and once passed, it influenced much of the disability activism and policy thereafter.

Passage of the ADA

Several histories have already documented the passage of the ADA (Fleischer and Zames 2001; National Council on Disability 1997; Switzer 2003). I begin this section with a brief review of the historical roots of the ADA, focusing on the role of organizations and activists representing people with developmental disabilities.

The National Council on the Handicapped, which was renamed the National Council on Disability (NCD) in 1988, is an independent federal agency charged with making recommendations to the president and Congress regarding policies and legislation to improve the quality of life for Americans with disabilities. The NCD first recommended the establishment of a comprehensive federal rights law to prohibit discrimination on the basis of disability and to require the provision of equal opportunity to people with disabilities in its report "Toward Independence: An Assessment of Federal Laws and Programs Affecting Persons with Disabilities—with Legislative Recommendations" (1986). According to the NCD, federal programs for people with disabilities over-emphasized income support and under-emphasized equal opportunity, independence, and self-sufficiency. To rectify this imbalance, it argued that legislation had to address the removal of barriers and disincentives that prevented people with disabilities from achieving independence. Although some civil-rights laws, such as Section 504 and IDEA, already prohibited discrimination based on disability in particular settings by particular people, they did not provide the broad protection offered to some other minority groups in the Civil Rights Act of 1964.[5]

From the outset, the processes of crafting, publicizing, and passing the ADA involved a tremendous number of groups representing a wide range of disabilities, including many in the field of developmental disabilities. For example, the Consortium for Citizens with Developmental Disabilities (renamed the Consortium for Citizens with Disabilities in 1989), led by Paul Marchand of The ARC, played a key role in formulating early drafts of the ADA and later in organizing efforts to publicize and pass it. Once the disability community was ready to mobilize support for the legislation, he and Liz Savage of the Epilepsy Foundation of America led lobbying efforts in Washington, D.C., with support from many organizations related to developmental disabilities, such as United Cerebral Palsy, the National Association of Developmental Disabilities Councils, the National Association of Protection and Advocacy Systems, The ARC, and local self-advocacy organizations, as well as, of course, from organizations representing other types of disabilities and from cross-disability organizations. The point here is not to over-emphasize the role of organizations in the field of developmental disabilities but, rather, to show that they were involved in early efforts to draft and support the ADA.

After the ADA was introduced to Congress, Representative Major R. Owens (D-N.Y.) established the Congressional Task Force on the Rights and Empowerment of Americans with Disabilities, co-chaired by Justin Dart Jr. and Elizabeth Boggs, and charged it with making recommendations to Congress regarding the bill. Elizabeth Boggs had been a leader in the parents' movement since its formation and was the first parent of a child with a developmental disability to serve on the President's Panel for Mental Retardation. Justin Dart, who became disabled as a teenager due to polio, came from a wealthy and politically influential family. After committing himself to disability activism, he served as the chair of the Texas Governor's Committee for Persons with Disabilities, a presidential appointee to the National Council on the Handicapped, and the head of the Rehabilitation Services Administration. In addition to Boggs, several other members of the task force represented the field of developmental disabilities, including Marchand, Savage, and Connie Martinez, a self-advocate from People First of California. People with developmental disabilities also participated in the grassroots mobilization efforts. As Justin Dart traveled across the nation to conduct public forums at which he collected testimony to document the need for the ADA, he took care to include many people with developmental disabilities. They vividly described the discrimination they experienced, such as undesired institutionalization and exclusion from programs and services in the community. Self-advocates from around the nation also joined in campaigns to raise awareness and show their support for the ADA.

The collaborations formed in advocating for the passage of the ADA certainly were not the first between organizations for people with developmental disabilities and organizations representing other types of disabilities. However, the process of passing the ADA seemed to transform these collaborations. Self-advocates grew as activists and became better integrated into the Disability Rights Movement, and other organizations such as The Arc and TASH, whose memberships also had professionals and parents, gained increasing respect by activists with disabilities as significant potential allies. On July 26, 1990, President George Bush signed it into law, declaring, "With today's signing of the landmark Americans with Disabilities Act, every man, woman and child with a disability can now pass through once-closed doors into a bright new era of equality, independence, and freedom" (Bush 1990).

The Key Components of the ADA

The ADA defines a "person with a disability" as someone who (1) has a physical or mental impairment that substantially limits at least three major life activities; (2) has a record of such an impairment; or (3) is regarded as having such an impairment. Title I of the act requires employers with at least fifteen employees to provide equal opportunities to qualified individuals with disabilities. Title II requires state and local governments to provide equal opportunities in all programs, services, and activities (e.g., public education, public transportation) to individuals with disabilities. Title III requires all privately operated sites open to the public, such as stores, theaters, and hotels, to comply with standards of nondiscrimination and equal opportunity, including meeting architectural standards and providing reasonable accommodations. Finally, Title IV addresses access to telephone and television services.

The ADA was built on the foundations of the Civil Rights Act of 1964 and prior disability-related civil-rights laws, particularly Section 504; however, it stepped beyond these precedents to offer a remarkable new paradigm regarding disability, rights, and citizenship. Its definition of disability rejected the medical model based on individualized impairment and instead embraced the social model (Ball 2005; Dugan 1993; Francis and Silvers 2000). The act recognized that the performance of many significant life activities—such as working, learning, communicating, and reproducing—depended not only on individual abilities but also on environmental factors, including the attitudes of others and the accessibility of physical structures. Moreover, by including individuals with a record of impairment as well as those who were regarded as having an impairment, the ADA acknowledged that public stigma associated with disability could lead to discrimination, even in the absence of an actual impairment. For example, a person with an "ungraded" high-school diploma (an indication of receiving special education) might experience discrimination based on the presumption of disability, regardless of his or her actual abilities.

Drawing on the traditional view of discrimination embedded in the Civil Rights Act, the ADA prohibited the denial of services, goods, or employment on the basis of disability. In addition, it recognized that disability-blind protection would not necessarily ensure equal opportunity. Without the provision of a ramp, for example, a person who uses a wheelchair cannot make use of his or her "equal opportunity" to interview for a job or participate in a public program. With this in mind, the ADA mandated the provision of "reasonable accommodations" to ensure "equal opportunity" for people with disabilities. Reasonable accommodations might include the provision of physical modifications such as a ramp; technology such as screen readers or smoke detectors that flash a light as well as sound an alarm; and programmatic accommodations such as the delivery of information in a different format or the alteration of a typical work or break schedule. The ADA also protected the rights of employers and the providers of goods and services by exempting them from the provision of accommodations that imposed "undue hardship" based on the cost or impact of the modification to their organizations. As with the definition of disability, the understanding of discrimination and equal opportunity presented by the ADA situated citizens with disabilities within networks of relationships that shaped their access to rights and opportunities and suggested that all members of society held mutual obligations toward one another. For people with disabilities to gain access to the opportunities enjoyed by other citizens, all members of society—including employers, hotel owners, school administrators, and the managers of public recreation services, for example—had to take responsibility for the provision of reasonable accommodations.

Supporters of the ADA claimed that the law mandated "differential equality," not "preferential treatment" or "affirmative action." Differential equality made available to people with disabilities, in the form of reasonable accommodations, the same opportunities given to other citizens. It did not require employers or providers of goods and services to seek out or increase the number of people with disabilities hired or provided with services; nor did it require employers and providers to hire or serve anyone who failed to meet the essential requirements of the job or program, given reasonable accommodations. Thus, supporters framed the provision of reasonable accommodations as within the liberal ideal of equal opportunity; at the same time, they challenged the traditional view that equality required the provision of the same thing to all people.

Although the ADA was considered revolutionary, some wondered whether it would have a significant impact on the lives of people with intellectual disabilities. The potential definitely existed. The ADA promised inclusion in several ways: It prevented private and public entities from denying services to people based on their disability; specified that public and private services could not exclude people with disabilities from one service by providing an alternative, segregated option; and required that services and activities for people with disabilities be administered in the most integrated setting appropriate to their level of need. Moreover, the concept of reasonable accommodations held great promise. As ramps and handrails might open opportunities for people with physical disabilities, other types of accommodations might open opportunities for people with intellectual disabilities. The simplification of written information, the provision of information in a visual or audio format, or the redesign of complex tasks into smaller steps, as just a few examples, might better enable them to obtain and retain employment or participate in public programs.

Despite the potential of the ADA, activists quickly felt frustrated by the disregard of intellectual disabilities in the efforts to ensure compliance with the law. In "The Battle Half Won," Rick Berkobien (1992–1993, 3) of The Arc argued, "Educating our nation to comply with the ADA is a challenge that affects all people with disabilities, but gaining recognition and accommodations for individuals with cognitive disabilities involves additional challenges." Businesses typically held a narrow understanding of accessibility, focusing on alterations to the physical environment to achieve accessibility for people with physical disabilities. The government reinforced this narrow view, providing information on the ADA that focused primarily on physical disabilities. It even failed to make its own information easily accessible to people with intellectual disabilities (Jones 1992–1993).

The Integration Mandate and Deinstitutionalization

In 1995, the first major court battle involving intellectual disability and the ADA began (*Olmstead, Commissioner, Georgia Department of Human Resources et al. v. L. C.* 1999). In 1992, Louis Curtis, a woman diagnosed with mental retardation and schizophrenia, was voluntarily committed to Georgia Regional Hospital for psychiatric treatment. A year later, her medical team agreed that her condition had stabilized and that her needs could be met by services provided in the community. Two years after this assessment, she remained in an institution due to a lack of available community-based services. Susan Jamieson, an attorney with the Atlanta Aid Society, filed suit for Curtis, claiming that the state's failure to place her in community services, given the medical determination that such placement was appropriate, violated Title II of the ADA, which prohibited discrimination by public services on the basis of disability. In 1996, a patient named Elaine Wilson stated an identical claim and joined the suit. Wilson had been diagnosed with retardation and a personality disorder and was voluntarily committed in 1995. By 1996, her medical team stated that she could be treated within the community, but she also remained institutionalized due to lack of available services.

The state defended itself against these charges. First, the state's legal team argued that these women did not face discrimination *on the basis of their disability*. The slow pace for community placement was caused by limited funding for the provision of community services, not their disability. Moreover, it argued that no "discrimination" had occurred. A finding of discrimination on the basis of disability required evidence that people without disabilities had received preferential access to services over people with disabilities, yet people without disabilities did not need community-based services, and therefore the defendants concluded that the charge of discrimination was nonsensical.

The U.S. Supreme Court, however, rejected both of these arguments. In the court's opinion, Justice Ruth Bader Ginsberg wrote, "Unjustified isolation, we hold, is properly regarded as discrimination based on disability" (*Olmstead v. L.C.* 1999, 597). According to the court, unnecessary institutionalization perpetuated stereotypes that people with disabilities could not participate in social life and actually limited their opportunities to do so. The court noted that it departed from the traditional view of discrimination, which, as the state had argued, required evidence that a similarly situated group had received better treatment. On this matter, Ginsburg stated, "We are satisfied that Congress had a more comprehensive view of the concept of discrimination advanced in the ADA" (*Olmstead v. L.C.* 1999, 598). The state was expected to offer treatment in the most integrated setting feasible given the individual's needs and preferences. If medical experts deemed community-based services to be appropriate and the patient desired such services, then the denial of such services constituted discrimination.[6]

The requirement for community integration was not boundless, however. The *Olmstead* decision did not require the closure of institutions. It accepted the argument, advanced by organizations including the American Psychiatric Association and the VOR, that some people were temporarily or permanently unable to benefit from community services, or they preferred institutional services, and therefore institutions constituted a necessary service option. In support of the continued role of institutions, Justice Ginsburg quoted a brief filed by the VOR, which argued, "Each disabled person is entitled to treatment in the most integrated setting possible for that person—recognizing that, on a case-by-case basis, that setting may be an institution." The *Olmstead* decision also allowed states to take into account their resources and to consider the needs of others with mental disabilities in determining the speed of transfers.

All states had to take notice of the *Olmstead* decision or face their own litigation. The Supreme Court suggested that states could comply with its decision by creating "comprehensive, effectively working plans" to reduce unnecessary institutionalization and by making reasonable progress toward the provision of services in the community to individuals on their waiting lists. Most states began planning. By 2006, thirty states had published Olmstead plans, and fourteen had developed alternative strategies of compliance; however, eight states had no clear Olmstead compliance plan or any clear alternative strategies. Even the states with compliance plans, though, faced extensive barriers to implementing them, including the "financial constraints on Medicaid, the lack of affordable and accessible housing, labor shortage of home care workers and political pressure of institutional care facilities" (Kitchener et al. 2006, 3).

To assist states in the process of deinstitutionalization, President Bush announced the New Freedom Initiative, which lent support to the dramatic restructuring of Medicaid funding. This initiative "encouraged" systems change by funding grants to implement Money Follows the Person (MFP), a system of flexible financing of long-term services and support in which the funds move with the individual to pay for the most appropriate and preferred setting. According to its enthusiasts, MFP would give individuals with disabilities choice and control over the location and content of their services, thereby giving people the option to leave institutional settings, increasing freedom of movement and choice for people with disabilities, encouraging competition among services, improving quality among services, and promoting community integration. While these grants encouraged change, they had no "teeth" to demand it, and by 2007 seventeen states had not even applied for grants to implement MFP (American Association of People with Disabilities 2007).[7]

Disability-rights organizations desired federal legislation that would require MFP and similar policies throughout the nation to support people with disabilities in community living. A coalition of disability organizations united to pass the Medicaid Community-Based Attendant Services and Supports Act (MiCASSA). Introduced in 1999 and again in 2003, MiCASSA would institute MFP and require states to allow individuals eligible for nursing-home and ICF-MR care through Medicaid to choose to receive community-based attendant services. Congress has not yet passed this law or a similar one.

Given the long-standing struggle for deinstitutionalization and the lack of federal legislation requiring it, activists used the *Olmstead* decision as an opportunity to file lawsuits and complaints to bring their states into compliance. A report by the Kaiser Commission on Medicaid and the Uninsured (2004) estimated that by May 2004, 627 *Olmstead*-related complaints had been filed with the Office of Civil Rights, and 59 *Olmstead* lawsuits had been initiated (Kitchener et al. 2006). *Olmstead* case records so far indicate mixed levels of willingness by the courts to press states to deinstitutionalize faster than they prefer. As the *Olmstead* decision had suggested, a plan of action and indications of progress typically serve as sufficient indicators of progress to satisfy the courts.

Hence, the ADA provided the legal footing to challenge the continued practice of institutionalization and the system of Medicaid funding that supported it; however, it did not reject the practice of institutionalization for people with intellectual disabilities altogether. Unnecessary institutionalization continues to be a significant problem throughout the nation, leaving tens of thousands of people in segregated settings when they would prefer to receive services in the community (Lakin et al. 2004).[8] Eight states have closed all of their large public institutions, but other states continue to channel a significant proportion of their funding for long-term care into institutions (Braddock 2002).[9] Furthermore, as people move into the community, they continue to face significant barriers to inclusion and the receipt of appropriate individualized services. In 2003, the NCD concluded that, "ultimately, only comprehensive amendments to Title XIX of the Social Security Act, similar to the amendments proposed in MiCASSA will overcome the institutional bias within the Medicaid program. . . . Our nation will be much more prosperous when it makes real the right of people with disabilities to live in the most integrated setting" (National Council on Disability 2003).

The ADA and Employment

The barriers to achieving the promises of the ADA are by no means simply practical or financial. They are also philosophical. Supporters of the ADA presented the legislation as an equal-opportunity law, yet because only people with disabilities would receive accommodations, the courts have interpreted the ADA as providing "special" rights to individuals on the basis of their disability. Whereas discrimination cases involving race and gender discrimination tend to focus on whether or not discrimination occurred, ADA cases tend to focus on whether or not the claimant is "disabled" as defined by the ADA. Thus, in trying to gain access to the guarantees of equal opportunity, people with disabilities are forced to emphasize their biological limitations and their differences from other, "able" citizens, reinforcing the very stereotypes that the ADA is meant to challenge.

The subversion of the ADA's goals has been particularly clear in cases concerning employment. Through a series of decisions, the Supreme Court imposed a strict standard for disability so that many people who identified as disabled were made ineligible to gain access to the rights established through the ADA. People with mild disabilities or for whom medical treatment ameliorates the impact of the disability (e.g., people with epilepsy for whom medication reduces the likelihood of seizures) were disqualified on the basis that their disabilities were not substantial enough; other people with disabilities were denied rights because their condition did not limit "major life functions," such as walking, breathing, or learning (Consortium for Citizens with Disabilities 2007b; Grossman 1992).

In *Charles Irvin Littleton Jr. v. Wal-Mart Stores, Inc.* (2007), the courts continued in this pattern and denied a man diagnosed with mental retardation the rights accorded by the ADA because he did not meet the standards of disability established in previous case law. Charles Littleton was diagnosed with mental retardation as a child, graduated from high school with a special-education certificate, received disability income benefits from the federal government, and received a variety of services based on his diagnosis, including job coaching services. At twenty-nine, he applied for a job at Wal-Mart as a "cart pusher." Littleton requested that Wal-Mart allow his vocational counselor to accompany him in the interview and assist him with understanding and responding to the questions. According to Littleton, the store manager initially agreed but at the time of the interview did not allow the counselor to attend the interview. Wal-Mart decided not to hire Littleton because, according to the store's customer service manager and assistant manager, he displayed poor interpersonal skills and little enthusiasm about the job. Littleton sued, claiming that Wal-Mart had not provided him with reasonable accommodations in the hiring process and therefore had denied him equal opportunity.

The Alabama court never addressed Littleton's right to accommodations in the hiring process; rather, they found him to be insufficiently disabled to qualify for protection under the ADA (thereby making the question of accommodations moot). According to the court, Littleton failed to present evidence "that his retardation substantially limits one or more of his major life activities. Littleton, Agee [the vocational counselor], and Littleton's mother all swear that he is able to perform all types of jobs. He is able to read, to comprehend, and to communicate."[10] In 2007, an Alabama court affirmed this decision, again finding that Littleton failed to prove that his mental retardation created substantial limitations in his abilities to read, comprehend, work, or learn.

In part, this decision can be viewed as a victory, as the legal system actually recognized people diagnosed with mental retardation as able to participate in social life. Littleton had achieved a measure of success in his life and overcame many potential limitations. Instead of a victory, though, this recognition was used against Littleton to deny him an accommodation that might have increased his likelihood of obtaining employment and gaining independence. This ruling is particularly ironic when situated next to the decision in the *Cleburne* case. In that case, the U.S. Supreme Court declined to grant people with mental retardation the status of suspect class, which would have required heightened scrutiny for all laws that treat citizens with retardation differently from other citizens. The Supreme Court stated that individuals with mental retardation are essentially different from other citizens, and therefore differential treatment is often justified. Yet in the *Littleton* case, the Alabama court suggested that people diagnosed as retarded are not necessarily "disabled" and are not necessarily entitled to the rights provided through the ADA. Thus, courts seem to move among different understandings of disability as suits their decisions. No matter which view is espoused, the particular portrayal of disability often seems to be used to deny rather than support the rights claimed by people with intellectual disabilities.

Littleton requested that the U.S. Supreme Court hear his case. In the petition, the attorney David Ferleger (who also argued the *Pennhurst* case) was forced to come dangerously close to the essentialism that activists have fought against for decades to "prove" his client's inabilities and thereby claim the rights offered by the ADA. He argued, "People with mental retardation, by the nature of the impairment, have difficulty interacting with others, thinking and communicating. Mental retardation obviously limits many such major life activities, the Court has repeatedly observed" (Ferleger 2007, 15). Thus, although the ADA was established as an equal-opportunity law, Littleton had to engage in the demeaning process (for him and all people with mental retardation) of documenting the significance of his limitations in order to secure these rights, reinforcing in the public's mind once again that all people with mental retardation have significant limitations that are internal to them based on their disability. Of course, Ferleger also criticized the courts for undermining the intent of the ADA by setting "an insurmountable standard for an ADA plaintiff on whether an impairment limits a major life activity" (Ferleger 2007, 4).

In 2001, the NCD issued a report condemning the decisions by the judiciary involving the ADA. It stated, "The result of the Court's harsh and restrictive approach to defining disability places difficult, technical, and sometimes insurmountable evidentiary burdens on people who have experienced discrimination. The focus of many time-consuming and expensive legal battles is on the characteristics of the person subjected to discrimination on the basis of disability, rather than on the alleged discriminatory treatment meted out by the accused party" (National Council on Disability 2001, 43). In addition, it drafted a bill called the ADA Restoration Act, which "refocuses the ADA on prohibiting discrimination on the basis of disability rather than drawing sharp, technical distinctions among people based on how inherently debilitating their conditions are or not." Passed in July 2007, the new law is meant to restore the intent of the ADA and allow people to be judged "on the basis of their *abilities*, not their actual or perceived *disabilities*" (Consortium for Citizens with Disabilities 2007a). Thus, the ADA represents a dramatic new vision of rights, yet its potential so far has been limited by decisions that treat it as offering "special" rights rather than equal opportunity and by the courts' hesitance to impose change on corporations and states and demand inclusion and equal opportunity.

Achieving Inclusion in Education

Inclusion in education also remained elusive. As the ADA and the *Olmstead* decision had encouraged community placement without rejecting institutionalization, Section 504 and IDEA required communities to provide students with disabilities a free education in the least restrictive setting appropriate to meet their unique needs but did not necessarily mandate inclusion. According to Dorothy K. Lipsky and Alan Gartner (2004, 50), inclusion entails

> the provision to all students, including those with severe handicaps, equitable opportunities to receive effective educational services, with the needed supplementary aids and support services, in age-appropriate classes in their neighborhood schools, in order to prepare students for contributing lives as full members of society.

A tremendous amount of research supports the benefits of inclusive education for children with intellectual disabilities.[11] In a meta-review of thirty-six studies that compared inclusive and segregated settings, S. Freeman and M. Alkin (2000) found that inclusive settings led to better academic and social outcomes for students with disabilities. The magnitude of research and the level of agreement led Christopher Kliewer, a scholar in the field of special education, to conclude that "the empirical debates over inclusion of students with developmental disabilities are over and this should have been recognized a decade ago."[12] While the academic debate might have been over, the political one clearly was not. According to The Arc, in 1993 only 7.1 percent of students with mental retardation had placements in a "regular class." The Arc also found tremendous variation among states, with Vermont providing 75 percent of its students with intellectual disabilities placement in a regular classroom, and New Jersey, Illinois, and Iowa providing fewer than 1 percent placement in a regular classroom.[13] The traditional separation of "regular" and "special" education left most teachers unprepared to teach children in inclusive settings. Faced with untrained teachers and hostile school districts, some parents preferred to shield their children from the stigma, embarrassment, and failure they feared would come with inclusion.

A number of court cases recently considered issues of inclusion and reveal a pattern in which courts weigh the costs and benefits of inclusion (for the child with a disability, other children in the district, and the school system) rather than show clear support for it. In support of inclusion, the U.S. Court of Appeals for the Eleventh Circuit in *Greer v. Rome City School District* (1991) argued, "Before the school district may conclude that a handicapped child should be educated outside of the regular classroom, it must consider whether supplemental aids and services would permit satisfactory education in the regular classroom." It also concluded that cost alone cannot serve as a basis for the denying supplemental aids and services, although the cost must not be unreasonable. In *Oberti v. Board of Education of the Borough of Clementon School District* (1993), the U.S. Court of Appeals for the Third Circuit also ruled in favor of a more inclusive setting for the child in question. In making its decision, the court examined (1) whether the district made "reasonable efforts" to educate the child in a regular classroom, including the provision of accommodations and a range of supplemental aids and services; (2) the benefits to the child of education in a regular classroom with supplemental aids and services compared with the benefits of education in a special-education classroom; and (3) the effects, positive and negative, of inclusion on other children in the regular classroom.

Using similar standards as developed in the *Oberti* case, though, two recent cases decided against inclusion. In *Poolaw v. Parker Unified School District* (1995), a U.S. Court of Appeals found that the district had adequately explored the benefits of inclusion for the child in question and that they were minimal. In spite of the parents' wishes, the court found that only residential placement would appropriately meet the child's needs. Similarly, in *School District of Wisconsin Dells v. Z. S.* (2002), a U.S. Court of Appeals decided against including a boy with autism and significant behavioral issues in a regular classroom. Referring to his violent and disruptive behavior, the court decided that he was unable to function well in an integrated environment and would receive only minimal, if any, benefits from it. At the same time, the court held that the other children would be disrupted and potentially harmed in the pursuit of their education.

For disability-rights activists, the right to an inclusive education is about far more than the quality of knowledge received. The public education system represents a mini-society, a training ground in diversity, civic responsibility, and social interaction. If inclusion cannot be achieved in a facilitated environment that purports to value human development in all of its diverse forms, can such a goal be achieved among adults who are accustomed to the established hierarchies and entrenched in their own belief systems?

Matters of Life and Death: The Death Penalty and Prenatal Screening

Since the 1990s, issues of life and death for people with intellectual disabilities have also been raised. On one hand, they received protection from the death penalty. On the other hand, prenatal screening targeting Down Syndrome has led to abortion rates as high as 90 percent among women who receive positive test results, terminating lives well before rights can be claimed.

The Death Penalty

Early in its history, America established laws to protect "idiots," typically defined as people who had no understanding or self-awareness, from harsh punishment. Whereas the concept of "idiots" assumed a severe level of disability, contemporary definitions of intellectual disability include a far greater range of people, many of whom can understand the moral implications of their actions yet still face disadvantages in their interactions with the criminal-justice system. Given their varied abilities yet persistent disadvantages, controversies arose concerning the degree to which the courts should show them leniency. The death penalty was of particular concern, as a disproportionate number of people with intellectual disabilities sat on death row. The harshest punishment in the nation was supposed to be reserved for the gravest crimes and the most heinous criminals, but instead its use seemed to be influenced by the resources and abilities or disabilities of the defendant. In a system that failed to provide accommodations to people with intellectual disabilities, the imposition of the death penalty seemed biased and potentially cruel.

The U.S. Supreme Court heard two cases regarding the death penalty and intellectual disability. In 1986, Johnny Paul Penry was sentenced to death for the rape, assault, and murder of a woman. Twenty-two years old at the time of the crime, Penry had been diagnosed with mental retardation and organic brain damage as a child. IQ tests performed throughout his youth yielded scores of 50 to 63, indicating mild to moderate mental retardation. Despite his history of cognitive disability, a Texas jury found that he knew the difference between right and wrong, possessed the potential to obey the law, and therefore did not suffer from legal insanity. Furthermore, they found that he had committed his crime "deliberately," that the crime was unprovoked, and that he posed a future threat to society. Based on these findings, they sentenced him to death.

Penry's legal team appealed, and the case went to the Supreme Court (*Penry v. Lynaugh* 1989). They argued that the jury had received insufficient instructions and could not adequately consider Penry's disabilities as a mitigating factor. More broadly, they claimed that people with mental retardation existed as a coherent category of people who shared significant impairments that diminished their responsibility for criminal actions, and therefore a sentence of the death penalty constituted cruel and unusual punishment. The nature of mental retardation, they argued, diminished one's ability to process information, reason, control impulses, learn from mistakes, and conduct long-term planning and therefore diminished one's moral culpability. Drawing on the concept of "mental age," they suggested that executing someone with a mental age of a child would be like executing a child, which the court had previously established as cruel and unusual punishment.

The U.S. Supreme Court decided that the jury must be able to consider mitigating factors such as mental retardation in sentencing and that Penry's trial had imposed improper limitations on the jury's ability to do so. However, it failed to conclude that a diagnosis of mental retardation necessarily transformed the death penalty into cruel and unusual punishment. In justifying this decision, the Supreme Court drew on progressive thinking in the field of mental retardation (as the court did in *Littleton v. Wal-Mart*). In the opinion, Justice Sandra Day O'Connor argued that people with this diagnosis varied greatly and possessed many of the skills needed to live, work, and function in their communities. "In light of the diverse capacities and life experiences of mentally retarded persons," she stated, "it cannot be said on record before us today that all mentally retarded people, by definition, can never act with the level of culpability associated with the death penalty" (*Penry v. Lynaugh* 1989, 338–339). Moreover, she argued that the concept of mental age had been acknowledged as problematic by leading mental-health professionals; a person with a mental age of five did not necessarily act like a five year old and should not be treated as such. The court did, though, leave room for future reconsideration. Because the boundaries of cruel and unusual punishment were determined by "evolving standards of decency that mark the progress of a maturing society," national consensus regarding the imposition of the death penalty on people with mental retardation could change over time.

Thirteen years later, the Supreme Court again considered this issue (*Atkins v. Virginia* 2002). In 1996, Daryl Atkins and William Jones abducted, robbed, then shot (eight times) and killed a twenty-one-year-old airman from Langley Air Force Base in Virginia. Atkins's defense team presented him as a man with mental retardation, indicating that he had an IQ of 59. (The prosecution contested this diagnosis.) Jones presumably had an IQ in the normal range, as this was not presented as an issue for him. Although both men admitted to the abduction and robbery, they pleaded not guilty to the murder charge and accused each other of pulling the trigger. The jury found Atkins's testimony less convincing than that given by Jones, decided that he had committed the murder, and sentenced him to death.

Atkins's legal team requested that the Supreme Court consider the case, as they believed that a national consensus had emerged against the execution of people with mental retardation. When the *Penry* case was decided, people with mental retardation were protected from the death penalty in only two states and in federal cases.[14] By 1996, sixteen additional states had passed legislation protecting this population; numerous organizations, including the American Bar Association, had issued policy statements denouncing the execution of people with mental retardation; and public-opinion polls showed increasing support for such protections. As Penry's defense team had, Atkins's defense argued that, as a category, people with retardation possessed diminished abilities relevant to thinking through a crime and its consequences and that these limitations lessened their moral culpability.

This time the court accepted the argument. Justice John Paul Stevens, who delivered the court's opinion, noted the "consistency of the direction of change" toward protecting people with mental retardation. Moreover, the Supreme Court found that people with mental retardation, as a category, had diminished culpability for their crimes. Stevens argued:

Mentally retarded persons frequently know the difference between right and wrong and are competent to stand trial. Because of their impairments, however, by definition they have diminished capacities to understand and process information, to communicate, to abstract from mistakes and learn from experience, to engage in logical reasoning, to control impulses, and to understand the reactions of others. . . . Their

deficiencies do not warrant an exemption from criminal sanctions, but
do diminish their personal culpability. (*Atkins v. Virginia* 2002, 318)

Many groups were thrilled with this decision because it protected this
vulnerable group of people from receiving the harshest penalty from a biased
criminal system that often failed to protect citizens with disabilities; however,
it placed people diagnosed with mental retardation in a precarious position.
Once again, to confront the disadvantages posed by a social system, advocates
had been forced to rely on categorical thinking that defined people with retardation as a cohesive group and emphasized their limitations. Interestingly, in
their joint position statement, the AAIDD and The Arc (2002) supported the
prohibition because of the failures of the criminal-justice system in dealing
with a vulnerable population but said nothing about the categorical limitations
of this population. In contrast, the Supreme Court opinion said little about the
failures of the criminal-justice system (a discussion that would open the door
to prohibiting the death sentence for groups made vulnerable by poverty, language skills, racial discrimination, and other factors) and instead relied on an
argument asserting the biological and seemingly fixed differences between people with and without mental retardation.[15]

The Growth of Prenatal Genetic Screening and Selective Abortion

While the *Atkins* decision protected people with intellectual disabilities from
the imposition of the death penalty, the rise of prenatal genetic screening and
the use of selective abortion threatened the existence of people with Down
Syndrome before they could even claim rights.

In the 1980s and 1990s, an array of prenatal diagnostic tests became
widely available to pregnant women. Although these tests identify an assortment of genetic disorders, Michael Bérubé (1996, 71) points out that they "fixate on Down Syndrome—as if *that* were the one card in Fate's arsenal about
which every prospective parent must learn as soon as possible." Non-invasive
blood tests that can be performed in the first trimester include the maternal
serum alpha-fetoprotein (AFP) blood test; the triple and quad blood tests that
examine AFP, as well as additional substances in the blood, to assess a fetus's
risk level for particular disabilities; sonograms that measure "nuchal translu-
cency," or, in other words, the amount of fluid at the back of the fetus's neck to
assess the probability of Down Syndrome; and ultrasounds that provide sugges-
tive evidence because this condition is often associated with particular physical features. Amniocentesis and chorionic villus sampling (CVS) offer more
conclusive results but require invasive techniques to allow examination of the
amniotic fluid and the placental tissue, respectively.

In 2007, the American College of Obstetricians and Gynecologists (ACOG)
recommended the use of a range of first-trimester prenatal genetic testing for

Down Syndrome for all pregnant women, regardless of age. According to its recommendations, the information gathered from such tests would provide women with greater choice in their reproductive decision making than later testing allowed. The ACOG's recommendation specifically targeted Down Syndrome, listing no other disability that required such proactive detection.

The problems associated with prenatal screening are numerous. On a technical basis, most of these tests are inconclusive, providing only a risk-level, and the AFP in particular yields a high rate of false positives. Although the disabilities detected by the AFP screening occur in one to two live births per thousand, fifty to one hundred women who undergo screening receive a positive result. These women then experience tremendous anxiety, and many choose to have more invasive procedures, which carry the risk of infection and miscarriage. Hence, although genetic counselors suggest that these tests will provide "reassurance" to women about their pregnancies and provide them with value-neutral information, they in effect foster fear of disability and construct particular disabilities as especially dreadful (Rapp 1988).

According to Annette Patterson and Martha Satz (2002), genetic counseling, despite its best intentions, cannot be value-free. Because it is rooted in the medical model, it assumes that the traits to be identified are "defects" and offers potential parents information about these defects with the implied goal of preventing them. By targeting Down Syndrome, physicians and genetic counselors reify and exacerbate the notion that this trait (more so than other traits that cannot be genetically assessed at that stage) is particularly terrible. According to the disability-rights activist and bioethicist Adrienne Asch, this attitude, and the selective abortion that it inspires, is a form of discrimination: "As with discrimination more generally, with prenatal diagnosis, a single trait stands in for the whole, the trait obliterates the whole. With both discrimination and prenatal diagnosis, nobody finds out about the rest. The tests send the message that there's no need to find out about the rest" (Asch 2000, quoted in Parens and Asch 2003, 42).

In explaining the diagnostic tests, counselors tend to inform women of the negative consequences of particular conditions, as well as of the risks and benefits of the tests. They typically do not provide positive information regarding a disability until an "abnormality" is found, and then they *might* present a more balanced view (Patterson and Satz 2002). A recent study of women who underwent genetic counseling (Roberts et al. 2002) found that 91 percent of them reported that they had received useful information about prenatal disorders. Only 13 percent, however, reported that they had received information about future quality-of-life considerations for children with disabilities, and only 17 percent reported that they had received a balanced view of giving birth to a child with a disability, with both the positives and negatives explained. Of the women who received positive test results for Down Syndrome, only 9 percent were encouraged to talk with a parent of a child with a disability or a person with Down Syndrome. According to the ACOG (2007), 85–90 percent of pregnancies with fetuses that show indications of Down Syndrome are terminated. Thus, genetic prenatal screening, while trying to distance itself from eugenics, serves to define who is worthy to live, and fetuses with indications of Down Syndrome in particular do not seem to make the grade.

Unlike the compulsory nature of eugenic measures legislated in the early twentieth century, genetic testing is not required by law; nor are women required to undergo abortion if they have a "disabled" fetus. Genetic testing and information is provided—in rhetoric, at least—to enhance women's freedom of choice. As Bérubé (1996, 75) states, though, "Although technologies do not, in and of themselves, impel conclusions, technologies are also inevitably part and product of larger social apparatuses whose sole purpose it is to impel conclusions." The technology itself impels society to consider which traits should be identified, and the identification then alters the experience of pregnancy, the perception of the fetus, and the decision to carry the pregnancy to term or terminate it. Parents who carry a "disabled fetus" to term may face blame for perpetuating disability and wasting resources, while parents who abort it may be criticized as unethical. Despite the controversy surrounding prenatal genetic testing, consideration of these ethical dilemmas is silenced by its routinization. Physicians present screening not as a controversial ethical choice in and of itself but, rather, as a routine part of caring for the fetus (Patterson and Satz 2002). Thus, most women do not *choose* to receive prenatal genetic testing so much as they simply follow their physician's recommendations.

Most disability activists believe that women should have the right to privacy in reproductive decision making, including the right to abortion. Thus, they do not typically seek to deny prospective parents access to either prenatal testing or abortion. They do, however, raise concerns about the implications of practices that encourage selective abortion based on disability. With abortion rates as high as 90 percent, Down Syndrome may be nearly eradicated— a cause for celebration among some, and cause for alarm among those who see disability as a valuable form of human diversity. Disability-rights activists also worry about the impact of genetic testing and selective abortion on people who are currently alive with that trait. People with Down Syndrome, and the public more broadly, may receive a message that individuals with this trait are not worthwhile human beings. Can society truly respect and support people with intellectual disabilities as equal citizens as it simultaneously encourages women to identify and abort fetuses with this condition?

Disability activists strive to encourage prospective parents to make *informed* decisions about testing and selective abortion. The Down Syndrome Congress suggests that genetic counseling should provide prospective parents with information that dispels common misconceptions about disability; presents the perspectives of people with disabilities and their families; increases knowledge of the services, resources, and legal protections available for people with disabilities; and raises awareness of special needs adoption (Patterson and Satz 2002). Erik Parens and Adrienne Asch (2003) also recommend that balanced information be provided at several junctures throughout counseling, including at the initial session when testing is discussed, and that counselors should present the tests as a choice to be made, encouraging parents to examine their value system and consider how they might use the results, rather than as a routine part of care.

Conclusion

As with every era, the successes also lead to contradictions and tensions. This is true of this era, as well. Self-advocates demanded a voice in politics, and the ADA and other laws offered exciting new visions for achieving equality. Despite these indications of progress, many problems in achieving basic rights and inclusion in the community remained. The final chapter presents the ongoing tensions in citizenship, rights, and intellectual disabilities, including the limitations of the self-advocacy movement, of rights movements more generally, and of achieving the "community vision."

10

Conclusion

Citizenship establishes membership in a national community, confers respect and rights on its members, and enables their participation in society's institutions. As such, it is not simply a legal status, but rather a dynamic practice in which individuals interactively claim rights in negotiation with other citizens in the pursuit of their interests. The benefits of citizenship and rights, though, have not been available to all people. The history of intellectual disability reveals the deepest quandaries of American citizenship: Who should be able to claim and exercise rights and who should not? What are society's obligations to people who need support? Should we strive to include all people as valued members of society, and if so, how might we achieve this lofty goal? What are the key values that should guide the creation of community?

The "problem" of intellectual disability when we consider the issue of rights is not simply rooted in an individual's low intelligence. This is not to say that the presence of an intellectual disability may not pose certain challenges as one attempts to perform particular aspects of citizenship. It is to say, though, that if citizenship is a mechanism by which to confer membership, respect, and participation in valued roles and responsibilities, then all people regardless of disability theoretically could be treated as respected members of our national community and encouraged to participate as they are able to do so. Yet we continue to struggle with whether and how to include people considered to have intellectual disabilities in our national community. If the problem is not solely rooted in an individual's lack of abilities, then where is it rooted?

The Challenges of Rights as a
Means to Attain Inclusion

Negotiation of Rights and Devaluation

Rights are human constructions established and negotiated in real-world contexts. We may rhetorically claim that all people have the right to live in the community or to receive an education, yet the claim exists only in rhetoric unless it is recognized and supported by other people and social institutions. Even when a law substantiates a right, the right does not exist as a neat guarantee. An individual must claim the right, and then that claim is negotiated within the contexts of micro-relationships and macro–social institutions, possibly including the legal system, where concerns are expressed, costs are weighed, and conflicts are mediated. Disability law is vague precisely to allow this negotiation to occur. Take, for example, education law. While school administrators and the courts have been relatively consistent in ensuring that all children receive some minimal level of education, they have been far less consistent in ensuring an appropriate, accommodated, or inclusive education. Administrators, family members, and the courts still consider and negotiate the costs and benefits of providing particular forms of education, and they are given plenty of room to do so.

Because people with intellectual disabilities have experienced marginalization in the past, the recognition of their rights now is often met with resistance by those who perceive these new demands as conflicting with long-standing practices. Thus, the right to live in the community is often countered by residents of communities fighting for their right to maintain what they perceive to be the integrity and safety of their neighborhoods; the right to equal and accommodated employment is countered by employers fighting for their right to hire the people of their choice; and the right to an education is countered by parents of non-disabled children fighting for the right of their children to an education structured for their benefit. Rights for people with intellectual disabilities are constantly positioned within a relational cost–benefit analysis in which the merits of granting rights to them are weighed against the potential negative consequences for other citizens and social institutions. In these negotiations, adversarial relationships are often magnified as potential conflicts of interest are resolved through litigation rather than through cooperation and creativity.

The constant negotiation of rights both reflects and reinforces the devaluation of people with intellectual disabilities. The devaluation of people based on intelligence was readily apparent during the eugenics era, and it is still is deeply enmeshed in our culture today. On one hand, we are now more attuned to the importance of respecting and appreciating diversity than ever before. On the other hand, in our world of fast-paced competition, standardized tests, and genetically engineered designer babies, few things remain as highly valued in American society as intelligence. We measure it, rank children by it, and assume that people's successes and failures are shaped by it (as if "it" is some clear concept, despite the fact that science tells us that intelligence is extremely complex, poorly understood, and impossible to accurately and fully empirically assess). We view intelligence as an integral component of achieving other core values such as progress, international dominance, and economic productivity. More broadly, the social norms dictate particular ways to look, act, speak and move, so that a slow gait, flailing of arms, atypical speech patterns, or "mismatched" clothing provokes confusion, anxiety, and fear. For rights to be effective, though, a person must be able to claim them, and other people and social institutions must define that individual as an appropriate rights bearer. The devaluation of people with disabilities makes it easier to assume away their rights and less likely that they will perceive and assert themselves as rights bearers.

Social conditions also reduce the efficacy of rights to create respect and inclusion. The American job market is increasingly bifurcated between jobs that require higher education and pay well and those that require minimal education and pay poorly, offer few benefits, and evoke little sense of creativity, self-expression, or pride. Hence, although the Americans with Disabilities Act (ADA) mandates equal opportunity and the provision of accommodations in employment settings, the jobs available to people with intellectual disabilities often offer low pay, inspire little self-satisfaction, and garner them little respect. Similarly, the Individuals with Disabilities Education Act (IDEA) promises a free and appropriate public education to all children, but the drive toward standardizing curricula, tests, and eventually our children impedes creative approaches to include and support all children. Laws now protect the bodily integrity and life of people with intellectual disabilities, shielding them from compulsory sterilization and the death penalty; however, the medical profession has made routine the identification of birth "defects" including Down Syndrome, labeling a child defective before he or she is even born. Thus, the march toward efficiency, cost-effectiveness, and "progress" often entails the implementation of practices that discourage and devalue difference and limit the efficacy of rights in promoting respect for and participation of all members of society.

The Uneasy Fit with Liberal Political Theory

A key theme of this work has been that the dominant narrative of citizenship, liberal political theory, constrains the discourse and strategies of activists. Liberal political theory assumes that citizens must be independent and rational, and thereby it allows for and even encourages the exclusion of many people who are not seen as meeting these standards. Hence, eugenicists were able to use liberal political thought to promote deeply undemocratic policies and laws by portraying people with intellectual disabilities as profoundly unfit for citizenship. In striving toward a more inclusive society, activists still must contend with the assumptions of liberalism; as a result, many have attempted to redefine relevant concepts such as competence, independence, and equality and, in doing so, reimagine the relationship between intellectual disability and rights.

The prevailing narratives of intellectual disability and rights throughout the twentieth century draw on and play with liberalism. The narrative of the special child, for instance, typically accepts the incompetence of people with intellectual disabilities and their resulting exclusion from "adult" civil rights and uses their status as incompetents to claim the rights to care and protection for them. The civil-rights framework developed in the 1970s similarly accepts the dichotomies embedded within liberalism. It broadens the definitions of competence and autonomy and demands that all people with disabilities be treated as equal citizens; however, it also offers mechanisms such as guardianship and the least restrictive environment for the restriction of rights and the maintenance of control when deemed necessary by parents and professionals. The recent narrative of self-determination portrays all people with disabilities as capable of competent and autonomous decision making given appropriate supports and demands rights on this basis. Each of these narratives reinterprets liberalism and represents a potential way to advance the rights and inclusion of people with intellectual disabilities; however, none resolves the fundamental problems posed by liberalism.

Liberalism establishes false dichotomies by which to judge the worthiness of citizens for the exercise of rights, positioning people as independent or dependent, competent or incompetent, equal to or different from other citizens. It then devalues those people considered to be dependent, incompetent, or different. The dichotomous view of humanity found in liberalism has been a constant source of tension, leading to often unproductive debates concerning whether people with intellectual disabilities are the same as or different from other citizens; whether they have the prerequisite skills to exercise rights or not; whether intellectual disability is fixed or fluid; and whether intellectual disability is rooted in biology or the social context. Either pole in each dichotomy presents problems. Insofar as disability is seen as permanent and biological, people with disabilities may be denied opportunities to develop and participate in society. Insofar as it is seen as fluid and rooted in the social context, individuals may be subjected to continuous monitoring regarding their state of functioning and their access to benefits and services, and even rights may fluctuate with their label.

Because there is no correct answer regarding where to position people with intellectual disabilities given these poles, various constituencies move between them as it is useful to them for various fights. Parent activists, for example, fight for stable systems of guardianship and income benefits for their offspring based on the assumption that intellectual disability is stable and simultaneously fight for service and classification systems that respect the life-course changes of their offspring. The courts also use various portrayals of disability as suit their interests. For example, when the U.S. Supreme Court denied people with intellectual disabilities protection from the death penalty, it described individuals with this label as varied in their skills and limitations, influenced by their social contexts, and essentially similar to other citizens. Yet, when the court later granted this protection, it described these individuals as a distinct category of people with particular, predetermined, and fixed limitations who therefore required differential treatment. Hence, the court justified similar treatment (that is, the same possibility of receiving a sentence of the death penalty) by portraying people with intellectual disabilities as similar to other citizens and justified differential treatment (that is, protecting people with intellectual disabilities from the death penalty) by portraying them as different.

Activists with disabilities also find themselves negotiating these dichotomies. The social model suggests that disability is caused by social and environmental barriers. Thus, all people who face barriers could be considered "disabled" and deemed deserving of accommodations to promote equal access. However, activists with disabilities typically fight for the rights of "people with disabilities," relying to some degree on a biological or essentialist model of disability at the same time that they fight against it. The social model has served people with disabilities well in their struggle for rights, but has also been harnessed by other constituencies in their fights against disability rights. As can be seen in both the Penry and the Littleton cases, the courts used progressive depictions of people with disabilities (e.g., people with disabilities have many abilities; disability is contextual and fluid) to refuse accommodations, protections, and differential means of attaining equal opportunity. The movement between depictions of disability may seem hypocritical, but is actually driven by the false dichotomies embedded in liberalism. There is no "typical" citizen against whom people with intellectual disabilities can be compared; nor is there some "typical" person with an intellectual disability whose characteristics can be assessed.

The Ambiguity of Rights

The debate about rights for people with intellectual disabilities is not simply between those for and those against rights. Rather, it is often between constituencies who have different visions of what rights people should hold. For example, we see debates about whether people with intellectual disabilities should have the right to live in the community or the right to live in a protected environment among "peers"; whether they should have the right to an accommodated education that might allow for segregation or the right to full inclusion; and whether they should have the right to the full range of reproductive choices, including sterilization, or the right to bodily integrity, which may preclude sterilization.

The confusion over rights is heightened for several reasons. Liberalism asserts that individuals should be free to make choices in pursuit of their best interests. If individuals possess such freedom, there is little reason for society to debate which choices they should have or should make. People with intellectual disabilities, though, may be unable to make free and autonomous choices due to their disability or social barriers. If someone else is making the choice, then the potential for controversy increases, and a litany of questions emerges: Should the individual with an intellectual disability control the choice made? If not the person with the disability, who? How will the individual's preferences be known and protected? Are all choices appropriate and positive?

The controversies concerning rights also arise because liberalism traditionally stresses negative liberties and the provision of autonomy, yet disability activists often seek the establishment of "positive" rights that require other individuals and institutions to engage in action, such as the provision of accommodations or services in the community. Furthermore, access to some rights, particularly positive rights such as the provision of education, treatment, and income support, may require the creation of an infrastructure with funding streams and bureaucratic procedures that thereby places power in the hands of professionals and administrators while simultaneously limiting the autonomy and potential choices of the rights bearer. For example, the provision of the right to an education requires an infrastructure, including schools, trained teachers, curriculum, and a variety of policies. To the extent that the infrastructure creates different programs for special education and regular education, the state de facto encourages the delivery of segregated education to children with disabilities and discourages inclusion. The provision of inclusive education requires an overhaul of the total system, which then reduces the availability of segregated options. The state (or agencies) cannot, nor should it necessarily, support all possible choices equally well. As articulated by Steven Taylor (2001), the state should develop systems that support the dignity and inclusion of its citizens and is under no obligation to encourage or fund segregated settings. An individual's perception of any particular set of choices as satisfying one's "right" or denying it then depends on the choice she or he would have made if all were equally available. If the system encourages segregation, someone who prefers segregated educational options may successfully claim and feel satisfied that his or her right to an education has been upheld, whereas someone who prefers an inclusive education may feel that he or she has been denied the right to an education. While more apparent with positive rights, even negative liberties are constrained by the creation of social institutions and relational patterns that encourage and discourage particular behaviors.

The boundaries among rights, privilege, and oppression become all the more complicated by the intersection of oppression and the denial of services and rights to particular populations. Today disability-rights activists typically speak of institutionalization as a form of oppression. Historically, though, many people sought services from institutions, and some populations, such as African Americans, were systematically denied access to this care. Are we to consider African Americans privileged because they were not subjected to institutionalization or oppressed because they were denied access to the minimal treatment, care, and shelter that the state provided? If they were oppressed because they were denied services in institutional settings, were the individuals who received those services privileged? Today, African American children are over-represented in special education. Similarly, does this indicate that African American children are receiving their rights to an appropriate education or being denied it as they are channeled into segregated classrooms with lower expectations and success rates?

Relationality and Intersectionality

Much of the political activism around intellectual disability and rights concerns the structure of relationships and stratification in our nation. In other words, rather than creating autonomous spheres of action, rights are a means to establish and evoke relational power. Not surprisingly, perhaps, the narratives of rights offered at different times and by different constituencies offer very different visions of relational power. Parents in the 1950s tried to assert their own power, alongside that of professionals and a paternalistic state, to ensure the proper lifelong care of their offspring. Even when parents turned to a civil-rights narrative, they did so in a way that created various levels of inclusion and exclusion and gave parents and professionals the power to determine the most appropriate placements. Narratives of self-determination, by contrast, attempt to place people with disabilities in control of their own choices and support systems.

Rights are often understood as a resource ensuring the freedom of individuals to pursue their interests. However, rather than consistently conferring freedom of choice to people with disabilities, the rights granted to them often situate them within environments that impose supervision and demand conformity, a phenomenon that I refer to as controlled integration. Some rights, such as the rights to education and access to equal opportunity in employment, grant people with disabilities access to contribute to their own self-care and to the well-being of society while simultaneously placing them in hierarchical relationships in which their actions are closely monitored and structured. Access to other rights that do not provide similar opportunities for supervision and are perceived as having greater potential negative consequences for others, such as the right to privacy in decision making regarding one's sexuality and reproduction, is often still discouraged for this population.

Other factors such as variations in one's relational setting also affect access to rights. Tremendous variation exists across states in levels of support for rights. Some states have closed all of their large-scale institutional residential facilities, while other states continue to rely on such facilities as their primary form of service delivery. Some states retain old laws excluding people with various labels, such as mentally retarded and feebleminded, from the rights to vote, to marry, and to make contracts, while other states have removed or never established such laws. One's micro-setting also has a significant impact on one's ability to effectively claim and pursue rights. Some people live in settings and among people who strongly support the exercise of their rights, so they may never need to claim rights in an adversarial way. Other people live in settings and among people who deny some or perhaps all of their rights so that the exercise of rights and participation in typical activities is a constant challenge. Unfortunately, the reality for most people with intellectual disabilities is that there are few options regarding living arrangements, service providers, and informal support systems. Given recent research indicating that adults with intellectual disabilities still experience high levels of loneliness and exercise little control in their daily lives, they may see little opportunity to exercise rights and may prefer not to jeopardize their relationships by asserting themselves as rights bearers.

Resources, or "capital," may provide a means to advance one's interest across relationships. These resources might include such things as money, knowledge, social relationships, laws, and support systems. One ironic lesson in this history is that, for people with intellectual disabilities, greater resources do not consistently overcome the barriers to their access to rights. Intersecting marginalized statuses often lead to greater vulnerability, so that, for example, poor people with intellectual disabilities have low rates of employment, and women with intellectual disabilities experience high rates of sexual abuse. However, people who seem to have greater resources or favored statuses do not always have more opportunities to exercise rights. For example, people with intellectual disabilities who inherit significant economic resources are often subjected to guardianship procedures, so that the possession of these resources actually encourages their restriction rather than their empowerment. Similarly, middle- and upper-class families have often used their resources to purchase segregated placements for their disabled family members when poor families could not. Men with intellectual disabilities may tend to earn a higher income than women with intellectual disabilities, but women are more likely to marry. Thus, access to rights is influenced by one's demographic background, but not in a simple or necessarily linear fashion.

Rights for People with Intellectual Disabilities and for All Citizens

In some ways, the experiences of people labeled intellectually disabled are unique. Because intellectual disability is associated with limitations in intelligence, people with this label or associated labels face particular challenges in their fight to gain rights and to participate as valued members of society. Moreover, the experience of medicalization led to unique forms of exclusion, including institutionalization and sterilization, that could be justified in the name of "treatment."

In many other ways, though, this work situates the experiences of people with intellectual disabilities alongside the experiences of other citizens. Most of the lessons learned from this book are relevant to any population. Rights are relational for all citizens, and as such, access to rights varies by one's social environment. As people try to claim rights informally and formally, their claims are at times contested and negotiated within their micro-settings, so that rights fail to offer neat guarantees; rather, they serve as resources to be used in pursuing one's interests. Because rights are relational, people must be supported to exercise them. Others must treat them as rights bearers; there must be a feasible set of choices and real opportunities to engage in their desired course of action; and if formal claims are made, the courts must support their claims. These observations are not specific to people with intellectual disabilities. Citizens are embedded in relational contexts that provide various levels of support for claiming and exercising rights. As such, we are all disadvantaged in our participation and exercise of rights when our relationships and the social institutions with which we interact establish barriers, and we are all advantaged when they support our participation. Issues of accessibility, social barriers, relational power, and interdependence therefore are not simply issues for people with disabilities. They are issues that affect all citizens.

While it may not be remarkable to suggest that the basic issues in the practice of rights are the same for all citizens, so far this has not been largely recognized for people with intellectual disabilities. Scholarship has focused on the idea that they have followed a different path characterized simply by exclusion and medicalization. As such, they seem different from other citizens, and their exclusion continues to be seen as resting in their "condition"—or, at least, in the social construction of that condition. By bringing their experiences into mainstream citizenship theory, however, we find that we may not need "special" rights per se. Instead, we need to discover ways to respect the diversity and needs of all citizens as they all struggle to build fulfilling lives embedded in their communities.

Rights may be considered an end in and of themselves, as they officially recognize a person as a respected member of society. Primarily, however, they are a relational tool to achieve relational goals, including access to valued roles, relationships, and resources. In accomplishing this end, the results so far have been mixed. Most people believe that life for people with intellectual disabilities is far better today than it was in the 1930s; however, people with intellectual disabilities still face low rates of employment, report high levels of loneliness and victimization, and have little control over the most basic decisions in their lives, such as where they will live, with whom they will spend time, and what work they will perform. Thus, we still have much work to do, some of which may still be achieved through the extension and enforcement of rights, and some of which may require additional strategies to enhance the likelihood that people with disabilities will be valued and included in their communities.

Looking to the Future

There are no easy answers to the questions posed in this book. Each answer as implemented creates its own contradictions, and each step forward helps us to imagine an even better world. While I do not propose to have the right answer, I discuss several directions that I find promising.

Self-Advocacy

Self-advocacy is rooted in the heart of liberalism and is a revolutionary concept for people with intellectual disabilities. Democracy demands the provision of real choices to people and the freedom to make these choices. Our choices rest in our assessments and understandings of our options, interests, values, relationships, and identities. The exploration of self and the development of a sense of self-efficacy are important well beyond the realm of formal politics; they are part of developing our humanity. In a dialectical relationship, we enter the political realm with interests but simultaneously become citizens and form interests as we are allowed to participate and to make choices. We earn respect and come to see ourselves with a new respect. Because the personal is political, and vice versa, political participation is not merely about formal actions such as voting. Rather, it includes participation in making a range of everyday choices such as where to live, what kind of work to do, and with whom to spend time.

As liberalism has limitations, so, too, does the self-advocacy movement. First, like many movements, the self-advocacy movement faces the issue of representation. Given the relatively small number of self-advocates compared with the population of people labeled with developmental disabilities, the degree to which self-advocates represent the demographic distribution, political interests, and diverse needs of people with developmental disabilities is unclear. Reaching and recruiting individuals with severe disabilities, limited networks, and limited social opportunities poses a particular challenge for this movement.

Related to the issue of representation, many social movements experience tensions when they attempt to both help people "find their voice" and function as effective agents of political change.[1] Strategies to promote self-awareness and feelings of self-efficacy among members typically recognize and encourage a diversity of opinions; however, the pursuit of a particular social agenda requires activists to adhere to the movement's ideology and agenda. Hence, effective political mobilization may lead to the repression of diverse views. Not enough studies of the self-advocacy movement have been done to know the extent to which this has been a concern, but one wonders the degree to which all voices and walks of life are welcome, given the strident politics of the group. Are people encouraged to find their voice even if they, for example, enjoy their jobs at sheltered workshops, believe in limited government and the reduction of social programs, or adhere to cultural practices that demand strict respect of their parents' wishes?

SABE and local chapters have become relatively influential in disability politics and have successfully demanded a place at the political table when policies regarding developmental disability are being addressed. However, they face many challenges as they strive to influence policy. Many people still discount the ability of people with developmental disabilities to assess complex policy issues rationally. As individuals acquire skills in activism, they may experience questions regarding their legitimacy, as people ask whether they are "really" developmentally disabled and represent this population. SABE also is positioned within a political field with many other active and powerful social-movement organizations, such as The Arc, TASH, and the American Association on Intellectual and Developmental Disability (AAIDD), who also claim to serve and represent people with developmental disabilities. While these groups often act as SABE's allies, they also represent potential sources of conflict. The AAIDD still adheres to a professional model of diagnosis and assessment, and many chapters of The Arc continue to operate large-scale, segregated facilities and programs. Organizations such as The Arc and the AAIDD have large memberships, long-standing reputations, and significant resources at their disposal with which to influence policy debates, whereas SABE is a relatively young organization with less access to a variety of resources.

Most important, the self-advocacy movement, like the broader Disability Rights Movement, largely accepts the liberal assumption that people should strive to be autonomous and competent to exercise rights. This can certainly be seen as an important strength: By reinterpreting notions of competence and autonomy to allow for the provision of support and guidance, the self-advocacy movement defines many previously excluded people as good citizens and rights bearers. Moreover, it encourages people to see themselves and to act as rights-bearing citizens. However, the assumption that all people are competent and autonomous and can participate in self-determination, even given supports, seems questionable. The rhetoric of this movement seems to assume away the existence of people who cannot determine or express their best interests. To the extent that some people exist who cannot self-advocate, what is their role in society? What are society's obligations to them? Who determines their best interests? The self-advocacy movement seems uncomfortably silent on these questions. Because it accepts the liberal criteria of autonomy and competence, so, too, self-advocacy at times valorizes the individualism inherent in the liberal understanding of rights and emphasizes the pursuit of individual interests over social obligation. Moreover, it often positions self-determination as the defining or essential element for a valuable life and a valuable person.

In a simplistic form, then, self-advocacy may encourage the same individualism that characterizes American politics. Even if it does this, the self-advocacy movement represents a vital step forward in achieving the equal participation of people with intellectual disabilities in politics and their broader communities. To create a world in which all members are respected, included, and supported, though, it is vital that Americans gain a sense of self situated among our relationships and our communities. The social model asks that all citizens consider the impact of their choices on others in creating a community that values the common good over individualism and promotes equal access for all citizens, even at personal cost. Self-advocacy at its best therefore promotes not simply the "self" but also a sense of self as citizens situated within families, networks, national community, and, ultimately, global community, who seek social responsibility, respect, and justice for people in all their diversity.

Building Community Capacity and Social Capital

To move us beyond the limitations of rights (although not discounting the importance of rights), some activists have proposed the "community vision." This notion seeks to embed the individual within a community in a network of meaningful and respectful relationships and thereby de-emphasize the individualism and adversarial stance inherent in the politics of rights. It abandons the liberal criteria for the exercise of rights and instead claims that all people have a right to be in and receive support in the community, regardless of their abilities or disabilities. It seeks to encourage the maximal development of and participation in community by all members of the community. It encourages and supports self-determination, but it does not fixate on the making of self-directed choices as the act that establishes one as a respected member of the community or defines a valuable life. It sees the goal as the creation of inclusive communities, and rights serve as one among many means to this end.

This paradigm shift is revolutionary in its potential but a long way from being realized. The search for community is emerging at a time that, sociologists argue, traditional forms of community may be deteriorating. In his famous book *Bowling Alone*, the sociologist Robert Putnam (2000) writes that Americans are less politically active, belong to fewer voluntary associations, and spend less time with neighbors, friends, and family. A group of complex factors—such as surburbanization; the dominance of cubicle-based work life; the rise of the dual-income family; and the growth of technology, including computers, television, and videos—have all contributed to the decline of American civic community. Meanwhile, large-scale bureaucracies and the rise of technology have made the interactions that we do have increasingly depersonalized and standardized. These changes may make it more difficult for people to build natural supports and participate meaningfully in community, as Americans in general feel greater isolation and alienation.

Prior to medicalization and the growth of developmental-disability services, communities were highly variable in their support of people with intellectual disabilities. Since medicalization and the growth of service systems, proponents of the community vision charge that society has created segregated programs designed to supervise and control people with disabilities rather than to include them. Embedding people within the community may improve this situation, yet contemporary survey data indicate that people who live in the community continue to experience marginalization there. According to a 2000 poll conducted by the National Organization on Disability and Harris Interactive, people with disabilities were 15 percentage points less likely than people without disabilities to report socializing with friends, relatives, or neighbors at least once a week; 15 percentage points less likely to go to events related to hobbies; 18 percentage points less likely to go to a place of worship at least once a month; and 34 percentage points less likely to report being "very satisfied" with their life in general (National Organization on Disability, 2000). In a survey taken in 1992 of adults with intellectual disabilities residing with their families in the community, researchers found that only 25 percent of participants reported having friends of their own and that loneliness was a pervasive problem (Castle 1996; Krauss et al. 1992). The community may offer superior outcomes compared with segregated settings, but given the failures of "the community" so far, it is clear that these outcomes will not be achieved simply by placing people in the community. American communities must make a commitment to foster the inclusion of all of their members and social justice.

Furthermore, the development of a new paradigm by cutting-edge professionals and activists does not mean that agencies and direct support staff will alter their practices. Agencies typically prefer to deliver services in ways that are cost-effective and stable, minimize liability, and promote the expertise of the administrators and staff. Direct support personnel are often poorly paid and have little access to research in the field. If they are trained at all, they may hear about the importance of civil rights and self-determination, yet their work is structured by intense regulation, paperwork, and demands for efficiency. Thus, it is questionable whether the agencies and staff who provide direct support will in practice support the community vision. Transforming each local community is a daunting task. Without support among the supposed allies of people with disabilities, then transformation becomes all the more difficult and potentially infeasible.

While there are numerous challenges to creating inclusive, supportive communities, the ideal is an important one. Whereas self-determination focuses on transforming the individual into a political agent, the community vision calls attention to the need to transform the entire community for self-determination and social justice to occur. Participation in democracy requires that people have meaningful choices to make. Communities therefore must have the capacity to make relevant choices available. Communities must provide affordable housing, low-skill jobs that pay a living wage, and accessible systems of public transportation. They must have available a labor pool of personal assistants and a range of services disaggregated from each other so that individuals can fashion their own service systems to meet their own needs. Services must be provided in a way that respects human dignity and choice and that imposes as few restrictions as possible. Communities must make available to people with disabilities all of the services and programs available to other citizens, including places to shop, eat, worship, and engage in recreation. Schools should serve as model inclusive communities, continually striving to teach America's children not only about academic skills and individual success but also about how to create socially just communities that respect and involve all citizens, regardless of differences. Teachers, judges, physicians, service providers, and many other members of the community should increase their understanding of disability and diversity more broadly so they can better serve all people.

As communities build their capacity to include people with disabilities, policies must also promote the development of capacities among people with disabilities for participation. These projects go hand in hand. This may include strategies to increase human capital (e.g., knowledge, skills, and personal abilities) by providing education, training, and many opportunities to participate in varied experiences. It also should include strategies to develop one's social capital, the set of relationships that encourage and support one in pursuing one's goals. This may involve one's family members and service professionals, but it may also include people throughout the community, such as a helpful bank teller, a yoga instructor willing to show people different techniques depending on their abilities, a bus driver who assists people taking unfamiliar routes, and a fellow employee who raises awareness about disability issues among other employees and even among management. Although civic community as experienced in the 1950s may be in decline, we may find people all the more willing now to develop interpersonal connections in the little ways that they can. Ultimately, inclusion is truly possible only if communities create the capacity to ensure that all people feel that they belong and are valued as members.

Human Rights

Human-rights philosophies propose that there are a set of rights that all people have simply on the basis of their humanity, typically including the right to life, liberty, freedom of worship, freedom of assembly, health care, education, employment, and a decent income. Some of these human rights are negative liberties that provide the freedom or autonomy to engage in an action such as assembly or worship, and others are positive rights, that require intervention by the state and social institutions (to provide, for example, education and health care). American law typically offers positive rights only to populations who are defined categorically as in need, dependent, or incompetent. Therefore, the positive rights and accommodations granted through laws such as the ADA and IDEA rely on medical diagnosis and legal assessment of the incapacities of people with disabilities. In doing so, even as they try to create equality, these laws exacerbate the differences between people who have and who do not have disabilities and lead to the dichotomous thinking already discussed. American law and policy engages in a constant cost–benefit analysis to assess who is worthy of these positive rights and whether the cost of providing accommodation and support merits the benefits.

As discussed by Martha Nussbaum (2006, 87), philosophies of human rights avoid the pitfalls of liberalism because they are "under no pressure to hypothesize that the parties to the social compact are 'free, equal, and independent.'" They also avoid the pitfalls of civic republicanism because they do not presume that all citizens can be active and involved in the political sphere. Rather, philosophies of human rights seek to support all people, regardless of their abilities and backgrounds, in living lives that are meaningful and respectful of their humanity. They recognize that all people have needs and that these needs vary by person, by context, and over the life course, so that there is no clear division of people in need versus citizens. They also recognize our social obligation to create just and respectful societies rather than espouse pure individualism and meritocracy. Human-rights philosophies allow us to position people with disabilities, including people with significant disabilities, alongside other citizens as equal and valuable members, whereas liberalism and civic republicanism too often fail to do so.

That said, the problems associated with human rights are numerous. The United States has a poor record in recognizing human rights, preferring instead to promote individualism, competition, and a bifurcated legal system based on competence and rationality. Moreover, when we offer positive rights to particular Americans, they tend to be embedded in social institutions that stigmatize, espouse a rhetoric of charity rather than rights, and subvert many of their own goals through policies of fiscal austerity and the restriction of the people served. Given our long history of liberalism and individualism, human rights may be politically infeasible.

It may also be a potentially dangerous option. Currently, we have various sets of rights laws and policies designed for particular populations. In the realm of disability law and policy, laws such as the ADA draw attention to the barriers faced by people as they try to participate in their communities and demands that we remove these barriers to provide equal access. A human-rights approach looks at the needs and barriers faced by all populations. As it would recognize the barriers to participation for people with disabilities, it would also recognize the barriers to participation for women, immigrants, the poor, people of diverse ethnic and racial backgrounds, and others. Consideration of the needs of all people may make it difficult to consider the needs of particular populations and instead lead to some standard set of human rights based on an assumption of a typical American or a typical human. Just as some African Americans feared that the inclusion of many populations within the Civil Rights Act would dilute its power for them, the inclusion of all human needs as worthy of consideration and accommodation may dilute the power of people with disabilities to have their particular needs addressed.

Despite the limitations of this approach, it does offer an alternative to liberalism that explicitly recognizes the accountability of society for the support and development of its members. It recognizes that rights are a means to create respect and access to valued roles and must be understood as relational rather than based on individual-level skills or as creating individual freedoms divorced from social obligations. While each constituency would like to pursue its own interests, a human-rights approach demands a consideration of social justice and brings us into a dialogue about how to meet the diverse needs of all of our members. While perhaps not politically expedient, a human-rights approach philosophically seems more consistent with the community vision and the goal of supporting and respecting all members in an inclusive society.

Conclusion

We continually seek new ways to improve the lives of citizens with disabilities and our communities. Each solution poses its own challenges so that there is no single path to such goals as equal citizenship, inclusion, respect, and social justice. Indeed, the very meaning of these ideas is under constant negotiation. At the dawn of the twenty-first century, Americans are still engaging in numerous debates about intellectual disability and rights, including the merits and costs of inclusion; the best way to include and respect diverse populations; the meaning and coherence of our labels and categories; whether intellectual disability should be seen as a valued form of diversity or a condition best prevented prior to birth; and the role of professionals in providing support to this population. We are still far from resolving these debates. Indeed, these debates lie at the heart of our conceptualization of, and divisions over, what makes for a good citizen and a good society.

To the extent that we seek a society that respects, supports, and includes all of its members, the political and social ideals discussed earlier—self-advocacy, the community vision, and human rights—together point out that promises of individual autonomy will not be sufficient. The passage of laws alone will not empower or create a sense of belonging in the national community. Instead, Americans must build micro- and macrostructures that support its citizenry. Individuals need to have knowledge of the law as it pertains to them; they need to see themselves as empowered; they need to gain experiences in making choices and pursuing their interests. Moreover, citizenship cannot occur on an individual level. The personal and institutional networks in which individuals are embedded must also recognize them as the bearers of rights, provide meaningful choices and opportunities for inclusion and participation, and offer support and accommodations to enable them to live fulfilling lives as part of their communities. The need for an interpersonal and community infrastructure that supports the practices of rights and citizenship is important not only for individuals who are considered to have intellectual disabilities or disabilities more broadly. This is not a matter of "special" rights. The exercise of rights is inherently relational; we all exercise rights within the context of our communities and we all must be supported in doing so.

Notes

CHAPTER 1

1. Scholarship on the role of citizenship in defining community involves two key strands. The first strand discusses distinctions between members and foreigners and includes such works as Brubaker 1992. The second strand discusses contested membership and participation among different categories of Americans and includes such works as Glenn 2004, Lister 1997, Mink 1999, and Minow 1990.

2. For a discussion of the removal of rights in the delivery of services, see O'Brien 1994 and Racino et al. 1993.

3. According to Stephen Jay Gould (1984), school records indicate that Carrie's daughter, Vivian, showed no later indications of feeblemindedness. Vivian was adopted by Carrie's guardian, Alice Dobbs, and died at age eight of enteric colitis. Carrie Buck was paroled after her sterilization and married. When mental-health professionals examined her later in life, they considered her to be neither mentally ill nor retarded. Gould concludes that none of the women representing the three generations was in fact feeble-minded.

4. For a discussion of relationality of rights and the impact of "dependence," see Fraser and Gordon 1992, Minow and Shanley 1997, and Okin 1989.

5. These laws—24 Purd. Stat. Sec. 13-1375; 24 Purd. Stat. Sec. 13-1304; Purd. Stat. Sec. 13-1330; and 24 Purd. Stat. Sec. 13-1326—were used by the Commonwealth of Pennsylvania in its defense.

6. For analyses of the *Cleburne* case, see Miller 1994 and Reininger 1986.

CHAPTER 2

1. Expanding on the idea of social construction, Robert Bogdan and Stephen Taylor (1976, 47) argue, "The meaning of the term mental retardation depends on those who use it to describe the cognitive states of other people. . . . A mentally retarded person

is one who has been labeled as such according to rather arbitrarily created and applied criteria."

2. For a discussion of what Licia Carlson terms "oppositional analysis" and intellectual disability, see Carlson 2005. In this work, she points to several tensions that affect our understanding of intellectual disability, including (1) the perception of qualitative and quantitative differences between people with intellectual disabilities and without, (2) the understanding of intellectual disability as static versus dynamic, and (3) the understanding of intellectual disability as clearly identifiable versus invisible.

3. Not all rights flow from one's citizenship status per se. For example, regardless of one's citizenship status, in the United States one has the right to be free from physical harm inflicted by others. The rights to life and bodily integrity are considered to be human rights enjoyed by all people. By tying rights to citizenship, I suggest not that all rights flow simply from citizenship but, rather, that a political narrative exists that sets forth the rights to be enjoyed by citizens, such as life, liberty, and the pursuit of happiness. Not all citizens actually have access to these rights, however.

4. Although feminist scholars highlight the misapplication of rationality and autonomy based on stereotypes, many leave intact the central role of these criteria in determining citizenship. By doing so, their work assumes the merit of these criteria *if correctly applied*. To whom is it correctly applied? Feminist analysis often assumes people with disabilities to be among the legitimately excluded. Thus, one finds feminist analyses that criticize the unjust application of compulsory sterilization statutes to poor women without questioning the use of these statutes in the case of the "truly feebleminded" or analyses that criticize selective genetic screening, abortion, and euthanasia of girls on the basis of gender but leave unquestioned these practices when a significant disability is present. For further discussion of this topic, see Baynton 2001.

5. In political rhetoric, civic republicanism can often be difficult to differentiate from liberalism. For example, economic dependence poses a problem for both philosophies. For liberalism, economic dependence limits the potential for autonomy, whereas for republicanism economic dependence is symptomatic of moral laziness and a failure to adequately contribute to society. The rationales are different, yet they are frequently conflated, resulting in a mixture of the liberal emphasis on rationality and autonomy with the moralistic messages of contribution and participation.

6. See also Mariner 2003 and Thomas 2004.

7. See also Barnes et al. 2004, Bérubé 2003, and Soysal 2000.

8. It may be that people with disabilities do not need rights to contribute to society. If in the absence of rights employers are willing to hire and school boards are willing to educate, then it is most efficient not to establish rights. As Jerome E. Bickenbach (1993) argues, rights can make policy inefficient from the perspective of policymakers by granting people the power to demand something even if economics or politics dictates another policy direction. Problems emerge, however, when the gatekeepers to mainstream society, such as employers and school boards, refuse to include people with disabilities.

9. For a discussion of naturalization of social concepts, see Somers 1995.

CHAPTER 3

1. In this chapter, I use the term "idiocy" primarily when discussing the concept of intellectual disability in early America. While this terminology is considered offensive today, "idiocy" was the prevalent term of the day in law, medicine, and popular culture.

2. *Laws and Liberties of Massachusetts* 1976, cited in Wickham 2001, 106. Little-page's first committee members did engage in several unethical acts in pursuit of their own best interests, such as selling a piece of Littlepage's land to one of the commit-tee members and neglecting to account for his finances accurately. A new committee, appointed after the death of Littlepage's executor, found the discrepancy and brought suit for damages to be paid to his estate.

3. Edward Jarvis, "Insanity and Idiocy in Massachusetts: Report of the Commis-sion on Lunacy," 1855, cited in Ferguson 1994.

4. Colonial Massachusetts also developed a law called Liberty 14, which extended the right to dispose of property to "any women that is married, any child under age, Ideott or distracted person . . . if it be passed and ratified by the consent of the generall Court" (*Laws and Liberties of Massachusetts* 1976, cited in Wickham 2001, 105). Liberty 14 rec-ognized women, minors, and people with intellectual and mental disabilities as disad-vantaged by their exclusion and attempted to provide a way by which they could exercise rights under supervision or with approval. However, Liberty 14 was never enacted into the *Laws and Liberties* of 1648, in part because it contradicted English law.

5. According to R. C. Scheerenberger (1983), this decision was upheld in several later court cases, including *Hays v. Commonwealth* (1896); *Pettigrew v. Texas* (1882); *State v. Richards* (1873).

6. Therefore, according to Kim Nielsen (2006), the adjudication process created a strong tie between one's financial ability and one's overall citizenship status, prioritizing the ability to manage money and property among the traits required for responsible citi-zenship.

7. Most of the women whom Nielsen discusses faced charges of "excessive old age" rather than idiocy, but economic concerns also tended to dominate adjudication hearings involving idiocy.

8. *Massachusetts Province Laws* 1978, cited in Wickham 2001, 109–110.

9. According to Philip M. Ferguson (1994), by 1850, Massachusetts was running 204 almshouses, and by 1857, New York was reporting almshouses operating in fifty-six of sixty counties.

10. Ferguson (1994) notes that—despite the unpleasant conditions—almshouses were unsuccessful in excluding the able-bodied poor, who actually made up the majority of inmates.

11. For a discussion of race and disability in history, see also Baynton 2001 and Gould 1981.

CHAPTER 4

1. In the historical chapters, I use the term most frequently employed during that era. While "feebleminded" roughly corresponds with intellectual disability, it contains very different assumptions, including a broader defectiveness that frequently led to delin-quency and sexual deviance.

2. Because of this alarm, Congress passed a succession of laws from 1875 to 1924 aimed at preventing "undesirables" from entering the nation; these laws culminated in the 1924 Immigration Restriction Act, which tied immigration to the proportions of nationalities living in the United States in 1890. By using 1890 rather than 1910 or 1920 as a baseline, the act effectively limited the immigration of newer groups such as those from Southern Europe and Eastern Europe.

3. C. Vann Woodward (2001 [1955]) argues that during Reconstruction, considerable mixing of the races occurred, yet with the introduction of Jim Crow laws in the 1890s, segregation reached unprecedented heights.

4. See also Ladd-Taylor 2001.

5. For a discussion of the gendered character of eugenics, see Gordon 1974; Katz and Abel 1984; Kennedy 1970; Paul 1995; Rafter 1992, 2004; Richardson 2003; and Soloway 1995.

6. For a discussion of these works, see Rafter 1988.

7. Goddard created the name "Kallikak" by joining the Greek words for beautiful (*kalos*) and bad (*kakos*). Thus, the two lineages represent people who are beautiful on one side and bad on the other. According to Diane Paul (1995), this work was so well recognized that it went through twelve editions, almost became a Broadway play, and was abundantly referenced. Goddard was one of the most frequently cited authorities on the inheritance of mental defect. For a discussion of the rise and fall of this work, see Zenderland 2004.

8. For additional writings that support the exclusion of feebleminded children from public schools and cite the problems posed by their presence in public schools, see Anderson 1918, Barr 1915, Bliss 1916, Byers 1916, Cast 1923, and Wallin 1916.

9. An interesting example of this is found in the writings of William Louis Poteat, an early-twentieth-century leader of Christian Progressivism in the South. The biographer Randal Hall notes that as Poteat expanded his "imagined and eagerly anticipated community" to include upstanding white women and well-educated black people, he increasingly focused as well on eugenic measures to exclude, control, and prevent the existence of the unfit who drained the resources of society and threatened his imagined community (see Hall 2000).

10. JoAnne Brown (1992) argues that the IQ test provided an important professionalization tool for psychologists, creating parallels between psychology and better-established sciences such as medicine and engineering.

11. The term "feeblemindedness" was sometimes used to describe the overall condition, encompassing all three levels (idiots, imbeciles, and morons) and other times used to describe the highest level of functioning, comparable to the "moron."

12. When the military administered IQ tests to World War I draftees to help determine their training and assignment, the results indicated the average mental age of white and black male recruits to be only thirteen and ten, respectively, and 47 percent of white recruits were identified as potentially feebleminded (Paul 1995).

13. Many histories of developmental disability fail to provide any account of what life was like for people with mental retardation, including those within institutions. Several histories have begun to fill that void, including Bogdan and Taylor 1993, Edgarton 1993 (1967), Noll and Trent 2004, and Trent 1994.

14. For writings that discuss the difficulty of determining feeblemindedness without medical evaluation and the consequent importance of the medical label for restrictions, see Bliss 1916, Doll 1929a, Fernald 1915, Oswald 1930, and Wolfe 1924.

15. Scull argues that institutionalization sorted able-bodied workers from those exempted from the labor market. Similarly, Stone presents the category of disability as functioning to distinguish those who should be exempted from the labor market and receive benefits from those who should be expected to work. My argument extends the sorting function to broader issues of rights and societal participation.

16. While Myerson's committee opposed compulsory sterilization, it did present sterilization of the feebleminded as appropriate at times, although not through compul-

sory programs, as seen in this quote: "There need be no hesitation in recommending sterilization in the case of feeblemindedness, though it need not, of course[,] be urged in the case of those conditions which are definitely of environmental origin. Though we hesitate to stress any purely social necessity for sterilization, it is obvious that in the case of the feebleminded there may be a social as well as a biological situation of importance" (Myerson 1938, 256).

17. According to Christine Rosen (2004), particularly prior to *Casti Connubi*, Catholics varied in their views on eugenics.

18. Ellen Dwyer (2004) refers to the idea of "compassionate investment," the government's preference for making investments most likely to "produce social dividends." Those most likely to be self-supporting would be the most likely to receive education and training, while those with the most severe disabilities would most likely be ignored in the back wards of an institution.

19. North Carolina, one of the wealthier southern states, remained poor compared with northern states; in 1944, the average per capita income in North Carolina was less than two-thirds of the national average, according to Moya Woodside (1950). North Carolina did have some eugenics leaders, however (see, e.g., Randal L. Hall's [2000] work on William Louis Poteat).

20. See also Gamble 1951, 1952 and Human Betterment League 1967.

21. Emily Abel's (1996) study of parents' appeals to the Children's Bureau shows that many parents sought institutional placements but were denied them because of long waiting lists, inability to pay, race, and other factors. Yet her study also shows parents who removed their children from institutions for a variety of reasons—such as distance from home, lack of treatment, and allegations of abuse—and who were distraught that they had no option other than institutionalization, thus indicating the blurred line between their understanding of institutions as a privilege and as a type of oppression.

CHAPTER 5

1. Switzer's sister, Ann Switzer, served as executive director of the ARC of Connecticut and may have inspired Mary's interest in mental retardation.

2. South Carolina and Georgia became the last states to pass sterilization statutes, in 1935 and 1937, respectively. In the 1940s, sterilization bills were proposed in Alabama, New Jersey, Pennsylvania, and Idaho, but each of these initiatives failed.

3. According to Edward J. Larson (1995), Nazi Germany was not used only to showcase the destructive powers of eugenics. Many eugenicists looked admiringly toward German success with eugenics. Larson documents the positive evaluation of Germany and, once abuses became more widely known, the ways in which eugenicists tried to deflect this criticism.

4. Obering 1935, cited in Larson 1995.

5. See Trent 1994 for a discussion of Richardson and wartime conscientious objectors serving their country by working in institutions for people with mental retardation.

6. On Eleanor Roosevelt's role in developing ideas on human rights, see also Glendon 2001 and Pubantz 2005.

7. Pressed to utilize their resources fully, the military discarded hard-and-fast rules about IQ in favor of the determination that personality factors often had a far greater role in successful adaptation in the military. Given the tremendous need for manpower, "the armed services were more interested in making marginal recruits useful than in labeling them." As a result, many young men who had been labeled retarded, and even

those who had been institutionalized, were allowed to join the military or to obtain jobs in the defense industry (see Gelb 2004).

8. Scott Kurashige (2004, 57) notes that, as some groups were being acknowledged and integrated through the war effort, Roosevelt simultaneously ordered the internment of Japanese Americans. Thus, there were "divergent trajectories of different racialized groups."

9. The idea of "framing" suggests that the same experience can be "framed" or understood multiple ways. The frame provides an organizational schema that structures information in a meaningful way. The new expectations for equality encouraged oppressed groups to frame their experiences as instances of legal injustice and violations of the U.S. constitution. Some classic works on framing are Gamson and Modigliani 1989, Snow et al. 1986, and Somers 1995.

10. During the Civil War, Congress established pensions for veterans with war-related injuries. After World War I, Congress passed the first vocational rehabilitation legislation and founded the Veterans Bureau. World War II led to another expansion of vocational rehabilitation, among many other programs.

11. For example, Alexander Graham Bell and Joseph Gordon of Gallaudet College had formed a department of special education in the National Educational Association in 1897. However, by 1918 the department had disappeared, with little debate.

12. It was first named the International Council for the Education of Exceptional Children and later the International Council for Exceptional Children.

13. Formed in 1923, the Council for Exceptional Children claimed only 389 members. Membership rose to 4,134 in 1944; 6,500 in 1950; and 67,000 by 1977 (Winzer 1993).

14. Amy L. Fairchild (2006) discusses the idea of fulfilling one's citizenship as a resident of an institution for people with mental illness and the idea of patients' rights tied to the fulfillment of these citizenship obligations.

15. This case revolved around a boy who was institutionalized at the Lincoln State School and his father, who was charged with owing the institution maintenance fees equaling $60 per month. The father alleged that his salary did not permit such an expense and that the state had failed to provide free common educational and training facilities for children who develop at slower rates, despite a statute authorizing the special education of the educable and trainable mentally retarded. The court discounted this argument, stating, "While this constitutional guarantee [to education] applied to all children in the State, it cannot assure that all children are educable" (*Department of Public Welfare v. Haas* 1958, 213; see also Hoffman 1959). Central to this case was the notion that those with mental handicaps would not develop into productive citizens and that therefore their public education represented an extraordinary burden on society.

CHAPTER 6

1. The Council for Retarded Children in Cayuga County, Ohio, is the first recorded parents' group for mental retardation known. The group, which was not institution-based, was formed in 1932 to protest the exclusion of children from public schools and to provide them with a special-education class.

2. On social policy in the era, Arlene S. Skolnick (1987, 35) states, "Even when poverty was 'discovered' in the early 1960s, the answer to it seemed obvious and easy:

to incorporate the disadvantaged and 'culturally deprived' into the general affluence and well-being." Skolnick continues, "Indeed, for mainstream opinion leaders during the 1950s and early 1960s, prosperity was in the process of solving all social problems."

3. For example, the psychoanalyst Helene Deutsch (1944–1945) preached that women's true fulfillment lay with their husbands and children, not in employment. And in their influential book *Modern Woman: The Lost Sex* (1947), Ferdinand Lundberg and Marynia F. Farnham declared that men and women who reached their thirties unmarried suffered from emotional incompetence and required psychotherapy.

4. Ironically, Carol's disability resulted from PKU, a genetic disorder in which the body is unable to use the essential amino acid phenylalanine.

5. I do not delve into other Christian writings regarding retardation at this time, as the parents' movement did not typically embrace an explicitly Christian perspective, although it was relatively common (see, e.g., Grant 1957 and Stout 1959).

6. Although parents drew comparisons between their own children and children in general, as well as between their own children and children with physical disabilities, they kept a sharp distinction between their own children and children with mental illness, believing that the two types of disabilities had too often been conflated.

7. State and local chapters of NARC typically used the convention of specifying their region and then Association for Retarded Children (ARC [e.g., the Pennsylvania ARC]). New York's largest organization of parents with children with mental retardation, however, went by the name Association for the Help of Retarded Children (AHRC).

8. Like rights for people with disabilities, rights for children have a contentious history (see Lindenmeyer 1997).

9. Luther Youngdahl, "Speech at the First Convention of the National Association of Parents and Friends of Mentally Retarded Children," 1950 (quoted in Dybwad 1963).

10. For a description of NARC's goals, see "Spotlight on Basic Aims and Prime Objectives" 1966.

11. The push for educational services was so dominant within the AHRC that parents with "educable" children who already received education through the public schools split off and formed their own group, the Association for Children with Retarded Mental Development (ACRMD).

12. In 1959 the American Association on Mental Deficiency became the American Association on Mental Retardation.

13. Weingold 1950, cited in Levy 1951, 4–5.

14. Since Down Syndrome is evident at birth, parents believed that specific actions were needed to address parents' post-birth shock and dismay and the particularly high rate of institutionalization of infants and children with this disability.

CHAPTER 7

1. According to Richard K. Scotch (1984), in 1972 Senators Hubert Humphrey and Charles Percy submitted a bill to amend the Civil Rights Act of 1964 to include discrimination on the basis of handicap. However, opposition arose from members of minority communities who wished to protect the Civil Rights Act from being diluted by the inclusion of too many other marginalized populations. The proposed disability language of the Civil Rights Act was instead used in the Vocational Rehabilitation Act.

2. Cross-parent alliances were built before the initiative to establish the concept of "developmental disabilities." The Council for Exceptional Children took the initiative to build bridges across parents' groups in 1964, when William Greer invited parents from various organizations to a meeting to consider how to lobby for handicapped children in general. For a discussion of cross-parent alliances in this time period and the rise of the term "developmental disabilities," see Shorter 2000, 162–167.

3. Promoted by Senator Edward Kennedy, this act provided funds for the planning and construction of service facilities, the creation of state-level Developmental Disability Councils, and the provision of interdisciplinary training in higher education to meet personnel needs.

4. The rise of other organizations is in part related to the declining power of medical professionals in this field. James Trent (1994, 246) states, "Between [the AAMD's] founding in 1876 and 1948, medical superintendents had dominated the editorial decisions of the journal. After 1947, no physicians were ever again the senior editor of [the *American Journal of Mental Deficiency*], and by the 1970s only a few were associated editors. Psychiatrists might still control the administration of the state schools, but they would become hard pressed after the 1960s to influence thinking about mental retardation."

5. For information on the decision to go to court and preparation, see "High Time to Stop Hoping" 1969, "Study Legal Action" 1969, and Wilson 1980.

6. The Pennsylvania laws allowing for the exclusion of children with disabilities included 24 Purd.Stat. Sec. 13-1375, which relieved the State Board of Education from any obligation to children who were certified as "uneducable and untrainable" by a public-school psychologist; 24 Purd. Stat. Sex 13-1304, which justified the indefinite delay of admission for any child with a mental age below five; 24 Purd. State. Sec 13-1330, which excused from education any child determined by a psychologist to be unable to profit from school; and 24 Purd. Stat. Sec. 13-1326, which defined compulsory school age from eight to seventeen and was used to delay admission of disabled children until age eight.

7. These included cases such as *Colorado Association for Retarded Citizens v. State of Colorado* (1972), *Kentucky Association for Retarded Citizens v. Kentucky* (1974), and *Panitch v. State of Wisconsin* (1974).

8. For background on the Wyatt case, see Alabama Department of Mental Health and Mental Retarded (2003a, 2003b). For a film clip and transcript of the case, see the Minnesota Governor's Council on Developmental Disabilities Web site at www.mncdd.org/parallels2/one/video/wyatt.html.

9. In this quote, Judge Johnson is citing *Ragsdale v. Overholser* 1960.

10. In 1974, President Nixon signed Executive Order 11776, further supporting de-institutionalization.

11. According to Lakin et al. 2003, from 1977 to 1996 the percentage of residents older than sixty-three increased from 3.7 percent to 7.7 percent; that of residents with profound retardation increased from 45.6 percent to 65.9 percent; that of residents with behavioral disabilities increased from 25.4 percent to 45.7 percent; and that of residents requiring assistance to walk increased from 23.3 percent to 35.7 percent.

12. The cost of community versus institutional services is a very controversial topic. Although community services tend to cost less than institutional services, much of this difference is due to the lower wage paid to community direct-care workers. For cost comparisons and discussion, see Stancliffe and Lakin 2005.

13. Edwards 1982, cited in Schaaf with Bersani 1996, 171–179.

14. In 1977, the Wisconsin ARC produced *Life, Liberty, and the Pursuit of Happiness: A Self-Advocacy Curriculum* (Hallgren et al. 1977). Organizations in New York, Hawaii, and Nebraska also produced curricula and other materials to train individuals in self-advocacy.

CHAPTER 8

1. See, e.g., *NAACP v. Allen* 1974.

2. L. Harris and Associates, "International Center for the Disabled Survey III: A Report Card on Special Education," New York, 1989, cited in National Council on Disability 1989.

3. In *The Willowbrook Wars*, David Rothman and Sheila Rothman (1984) explain that, in the early years of deinstitutionalization at Willowbrook, 55 percent of the residents went to another state facility for individuals with retardation, 20 percent went to mental hospitals, 16 percent went to boarding homes, and 9 percent went to nursing homes. The network of community group homes simply did not exist at the beginning of deinstitutionalization.

4. Although many people did fall through the cracks, activists promoting deinstitutionalization for people with mental retardation learned important lessons from the experiences of people with mental illness. According to Sharon Landesman and Earl C. Butterfield (1987, 810), deinstitutionalization for people with mental retardation "occurred more gradually and selectively, involved less recidivism (the 'revolving door phenomenon'), and was accompanied by fairly stable (low) rates of new admissions."

5. These studies found that the vast majority of parents with institutionalized children, despite their concerns about quality of care, actually expressed satisfaction with the care that institutions provided, and many feared deinstitutionalization. They worried about the quality and consistency of community-based services, and they worried that the transition to the community—which would involve the loss of their children's home, staff, peer group, and services—might be detrimental. Many parents also expressed concerns about the disruption of long-established patterns of family interaction (or noninteraction) and the possibility of heightened family obligations.

6. M. H. Gottesman, R. M. Weinberg, and J. A. Collins, "Motion for Leave to Brief Amici Curiae of Congress of Advocates for the Retarded, Inc., et al. in the Supreme Court of the United States," October term, 2004, U.S. Supreme Court, Washington, D.C., cited in Landesman and Butterfield 1987, 809–816.

7. Mental Retardation Association of America, Nebraska Chapter, "Response by Mental Retardation of America to Governor's Amended Plan of Implementation," July 1979, cited in Frohboese and Sales 1980.

8. Steven Taylor's article "On Choice" (2001) criticizes the rhetoric of these groups as falsely using the words of democracy to justify what amounts to imposed segregation. He argues that the state has no obligation to support segregation in the name of choice.

9. For a list of VOR's accomplishments, see Voice of the Retarded 2008.

10. Deborah A. Stone (1984) traces the development of disability as a state administrative category, particularly through income-maintenance programs.

11. Because literacy tests historically had been used to deny the franchise to people of color and the poor, the use of testing to assess political competence was fraught with controversy and was potentially illegal under the Voting Rights Act of 1970.

12. Arizona, California, Georgia, Indiana, Iowa, Kansas, Michigan, Montana, Nebraska, New Hampshire, North Dakota, Oregon, South Dakota, West Virginia, and Wisconsin repealed or altered their sterilization laws.

13. See, e.g., Rauh et al. 1989 and Silverstein 1979. Vermont's voluntary sterilization law required consenting adults with developmental disabilities to meet particular eugenic criteria before they were allowed access to sterilization. In Ohio, consenting adults with mental retardation could not obtain voluntary sterilization except for medical reasons.

14. Relevant court cases include *In the Matter of Conservatorship of Valerie N.* 1985, *In the Matter of Hayes* 1980, *In the Matter of Grady* 1981, and *In the Matter of Moe* 1982.

15. In *In the Matter of Conservatorship of Valerie N.* (1985), the California Supreme Court denied the request to sterilize a twenty-nine-year-old woman with severe mental retardation, concluding that the applicable statute did not allow the sterilization of those unable to consent (see Jaegers 1992–1993). In discussing the need for sterilization law in South Dakota, Sandra S. Coleman (1980) argues that a statute should be passed banning all involuntary sterilization, including sterilization for those who cannot consent.

16. *In the Matter of Hayes* (1980) provides the most frequently cited model for decision making in cases without consent: "In the rare case sterilization may indeed be in the best interests of the retarded person . . . the court must exercise care to protect the individual's right of privacy, and thereby not unnecessarily invade that right. Substantial medical evidence must be adduced, and the burden on the proponent of sterilization will be to show by clear, cogent and convincing evidence that such a procedure is in the best interests of the retarded person." The Washington Supreme Court specified several factors that should be taken into account, including the age and educability of the individual, his or her potential as a parent, previous attempts to use less restrictive forms of contraception, ability to consent to sterilization, the extensiveness and views of evaluations, and the viewpoint of the individual.

17. Lawrence County Court, Pennsylvania, order terminating parental rights of Donna Pauletich Cobb, 1985, 8, cited in Developmental Disabilities Law Project 1985.

18. In the 1980s, ADAPT stood for American Disabled for Accessible Public Transit. In the early 1990s, ADAPT focused its attention on issues of attendant care, and the name was changed to stand for American Disabled for Attendant Programs Today. Now the organization goes simply by ADAPT because its mission is broadly construed and relates to numerous issues facing Americans with disabilities.

CHAPTER 9

1. See, e.g., Hayden 1997 and Johnson 1999. For a discussion of the importance for "new social movements" focused on identity building to create their own history and framing, see Gamson 1996, Longmore 2003, and Morris and Mueller 1992.

2. What began as the Association for Retarded Children and then became the Association for Retarded Citizens—both of which used the acronym ARC—eventually dropped the acronym and took the name The Arc.

3. For discussion of the concerns regarding changing the name of the AAMR to remove the term "mental retardation," see American Association on Mental Retardation 2001.

4. Lavigne 2004. For a discussion of social capital and disability, see also Condelucci 2004 and Potts 2005.

5. According to its historical account (National Council on Disability 1997), the NCD had considered including the term "disability" among groups protected by the Civil Rights Act of 1964, but doing so seemed politically infeasible. In 1972, Senator Hubert H. Humphrey had proposed the addition of disability to the Civil Rights Act, but there was little support and there was opposition by African American activists who believed that the addition might lessen the effectiveness of the legislation for already protected classes. Moreover, members of the NCD felt that a unique law for people with disabilities could better tackle the specific issues confronting them.

6. See the opinion by Justice Ruth Bader Ginsburg in *Olmstead, Commissioner, Georgia Department of Human Resources, et al. v. L. C.* 1999. For discussion of the nontraditional use of the concept of discrimination, see the dissenting opinion written by Justice Clarence Thomas.

7. According to the American Association of People with Disabilities, by 2007 seventeen states had not applied for MFP grants, and three states had had their grant proposals rejected. In these twenty states, more than sixty-eight thousand people still lived in institutional settings who reported that they preferred to receive their services in the community.

8. This research found that the rate of deinstitutionalization slowed after the *Olmstead* decision; the population of state hospitals continued to decrease but at a slower rate in the three years after *Olmstead* than in the thirty years prior.

9. In 1991, New Hampshire became the first state to close all of its large institutions, followed by Alaska, Hawaii, Minnesota, New Mexico, Rhode Island, Vermont, West Virginia, and Washington, D.C. For information on trends in institutionalization, see Braddock 2002.

10. In its opinion (*Charles Irvin Littleton, Jr., v. Wal-Mart Stores, Inc.* 2005), the U.S. District Court cited *Toyota Motor v. Williams* (2002) to argue that the presence of an impairment did not necessarily qualify one for ADA protection. Rather, one must show that the impairment "severely restricts [one] from doing activities that are of central importance to most people's daily lives."

11. As noted in Chapter 8, not all members of the disability community seek solely inclusive education. In response to its resolution "For Full Implementation of Promising Practices for All Children with Disabilities," PARC received criticism from the deaf community, including a letter in 1991 from Joseph Angelo, president of the Pennsylvania Society for the Advancement of the Deaf, stating that his society "strongly opposed any policy that promotes one 'right' way of education" and that "would ignore the positive effects of interaction among linguistic peers." Sandy C. Duncan, director of the Pennsylvania Office for the Deaf and Hearing Impaired, similarly wrote, "Does the Arc understand that for many deaf/hard of hearing students the least restrictive environment is many times most restrictive because of communication barriers?" The letters are in PARC's archives, Harrisburg, Pa.

12. Christopher Kliewer, "Declaration of Christopher Kliewer, Ph.D.," submitted by the legal team of Lydia Gaskin in *Lydia Gaskin, et al. v. Commonwealth of Pennsylvania*, Pennsylvania Department of Education, 2005.

13. Ibid.

14. When Congress reinstated the federal death penalty in 1988, it prohibited the execution of people with mental retardation.

15. For a legal discussion of the implications of the *Atkins* decisions for people with intellectual disabilities, see Slobogin 2004.

CHAPTER 10

1. This tension is also found in the feminist movement, which claims to represent and empower women, despite the fact that many women reject the label "feminist" and its associated values, such as equal opportunity, equal pay, and privacy in reproductive decision making.

References

Abel, Emily K. 1996. "Appealing for Children's Health Care: Conflicts between Mothers and Officials in the 1930's." *Social Service Review* (June): 282–284.

Ackerman, Bruce. 1971. *Reconstructing American Law*. Cambridge, Mass.: Harvard University Press.

Addresses and Abstracts of Committee Reports, White House Conference on Child Health and Protection, Called by President Hoover. 1931. New York: Century.

Ainsworth, Mildred H., Elizabeth A. Wagner, and Alfred A. Strauss. 1945. "Children of Our Children." *American Journal of Mental Deficiency* 49 (3): 277–289.

Alabama Department of Mental Health and Mental Retardation. 2003a. "The Legacy of Wyatt." Press release, December 5.

————. 2003b. "Historical Wyatt Case Ends." Press release, December 8.

Albrecht, Gary L. 1992. *The Disability Business: Rehabilitation in America*. Newbury Park, Calif.: Sage Publications.

Allen, Garland E. 2004. "Was Nazi Germany Created in the U.S.?" *EMBO Reports* 5:451–452.

American Association of People with Disabilities. 2007. "States without Money Follows the Person Awards." Information bulletin no. 210. Washington, D.C.: AAPD.

American Association on Mental Deficiency (AAMD). 1974. "Sterilization of Persons Who Are Mentally Retarded: Proposed Official Policy Statement of the American Association on Mental Deficiency." *Mental Retardation* 12 (2): 59–61.

American Association on Mental Retardation (AAMR). 2001. "Minutes from the Open Board of Directors Forum," June 1. Available online at http://aaidd.allenpress.com (accessed May 2007).

American Association on Mental Retardation (AAMR) and The Arc. 2002. "Position Statement: Criminal Justice." Available online at http://www.aaidd.org/policies/pos_criminal_justice.shtml (accessed May 2007).

American College of Obstetricians and Gynecologists (ACOG). 2007. "New Recommendations for Down Syndrome: Screening Should Be Offered to All Pregnant Women."

Press release, January 2. Available online at http://www.acog.org (accessed May 2007).

Anderson, Meta L. 1918. "Instructions of the Feebleminded." *Proceedings of the National Conference of Social Work.* 536–543.

Anderson, Susan Heller. 1982. "The Reagan Effect: Goals on Handicapped Meet Widespread Resistance." *New York Times,* November 14.

Anderson, V. V. 1919. "A State Program for the Custody and Treatment of Defective Delinquents." *Proceedings of the National Conference on Social Work.* 257–259.

Andrews, Jonathan. 1998. "Begging the Question of Idiocy: The Definition and Sociocultural Meaning of Idiocy in Early Modern Britain, Part 1." *History of Psychiatry* 9 (33): 65–95.

Anspach, Renee. 1993. *Deciding Who Lives.* Berkeley: University of California Press.

Atkins v. Virginia. 2002. 536 U.S. 304.

Ayrault, Evelyn West. 1964. *You Can Raise Your Handicapped Child.* New York: G. P. Putnam's Sons.

"Background Note." 2002. Frederick Henry Osborne Papers, American Philosophy Society, Philadelphia. Available online at http://www.amphilsoc.org/library/mole/o/osborn.xml (accessed May 2007).

Baker, B. W. 1939. "Parole and Sterilization." *Training School Bulletin* 35:177–179.

Ball, Carlos A. 2005. "Looking for Theory in All the Right Places: Feminist and Communitarian Elements of Disability Discrimination Law." *Ohio State Law Journal* 66 (1): 105–174.

Barnes, Rebecca, Timothy Auburn, and Susan Lea. 2004. "Citizenship in Practice." *British Journal of Social Psychology* 43:187–206.

Barr, Martin W. 1902. "The Imbecile and Epileptic versus the Tax-Payer and the Community." *Proceedings of the National Conference of Charities and Corrections.* 161–165.

———. 1915. "The Prevention of Mental Defect, the Duty of the Hour." *Proceedings of the National Conference of Charities and Corrections.* 361–367.

Barton, Len. 1993. "The Struggle for Citizenship: The Case of Disabled People." *Disability, Handicap and Society* 8 (3): 235–248.

Baynton, Douglas C. 2001. "Disability and the Justification of Inequality in American History." Pp. 33–57 in *The New Disability History: American Perspectives,* ed. Paul K. Longmore and Lauri Umansky. New York: New York University Press.

Benhabib, Seyla. 1992. *Situating the Self: Gender, Community and Postmodernism in Contemporary Ethics.* New York: Routledge.

Berkobien, Rick. 1992–1993. "The Battle Half Won." *Impact* 5 (4): 3.

Berlin, Isaiah. 1984 (1969). "Two Concepts of Liberty." Pp. 15–36 in *Liberalism and Its Critics,* ed. Michael Sandel. Oxford: Basil Blackwell.

Berry, Charles Scott. 1925. "The Case for the Mentally Retarded." *Proceedings of the National Conference of Social Work.* 440–444.

Berry, Richard J. A., and R. G. Gordon. 1931. *The Mental Defective.* New York: Whittlesey House.

Bersani, Hank, Jr. 1996. "Leadership in Developmental Disabilities: Where We've Been, Where We Are, and Where We're Going." Pp. 258–269 in *New Voices: Self Advocacy by People with Disabilities,* ed. Gunnar Dybwad and Hank Bersani Jr. Cambridge, Mass.: Brookline Books.

Bérubé, Michael. 1996. *Life as We Know It: A Father, a Family and an Exceptional Child.* New York: Vintage.

———. 2003. "Citizenship and Disability." *Dissent* 50 (2): 52–57.

Bickenbach, Jerome E. 1993. *Physical Disability and Social Policy.* Toronto: University of Toronto Press.

"Bill of Rights for Pennsylvania's Retarded Citizens, A." 1969. *Pennsylvania Message* (newsletter) 5 (2): 8.

Black, Edwin R. 2003. *War against the Weak: Eugenics and America's Campaign to Create a Master Race.* New York: Four Walls Eight Windows.

"Black Code" of Louisiana, The. 1724. In *Afro-American Almanac.* Available online at http://www.toptags.com/aama/index.htm (accessed January 2007).

Blair, Barbara. 1981. "The Parents' Council for Retarded Children and Social Change in Rhode Island." *Rhode Island History* 40 (June): 145–159.

Blatt, Burton, and Fred Kaplan. 1966. *Christmas in Purgatory: A Photographic Essay on Mental Retardation.* Boston: Allyn and Bacon.

Blatt, Burton, Adrejs Ozolins, and Joe McNalley. 1979. *The Family Papers: A Return to Purgatory.* New York: Longman.

Bliss, George S. 1916. "The Danger of Classifying Merely Backward Children Who Are Feeble-minded." *Proceedings of the National Conference of Charities and Corrections.* 263–266.

———. 1919. "Mental Defectives and the War." *Proceedings and Addresses of the Forty-Third Annual Session of the American Association for the Study of the Feeble-Minded* 24:11–17.

Bobroff, Allen. 1956. "A Survey of Social and Civic Participation of Adults Formerly in Classes for the Mentally Retarded." *American Journal of Mental Deficiency* 61 (July): 127–133.

Bogdan, Robert, and Stephen Taylor. 1976. "The Judged, Not the Judges: An Insider's View of Mental Retardation." *American Psychologist* 31:47–52.

———. 1993. *The Social Meaning of Mental Retardations.* New York: Teachers College Press.

Boris, Eileen. 1991. "'Reconstructing the Family': Women, Progressive Reform, and the Problem of Social Control." Pp. 73–86 in *Gender, Class, Race and Reform in the Progressive Era*, ed. Noralee Frankel and Nancy S. Dye. Lexington: University Press of Kentucky.

Bostock, Norma L. 1959. "The Parent Outlook." *American Journal of Mental Deficiency* 63 (January): 511–516.

Bower, Eli M. 1954. "The Education of the Mentally Retarded Child in a Democratic Society: A Panel Discussion, Introduction." *American Journal of Mentally Deficiency* 59 (1): 35–37.

Braddock, David, ed. 2002. *Disability at the Dawn of the 21st Century and the State of the States.* Washington, D.C.: American Association on Mental Retardation.

Bradley, Valerie J. 1978. *Deinstitutionalization of Developmentally Disabled Persons: A Conceptual Analysis and Guide.* Baltimore: University Park Press.

Brockley, Janice. 2004. "Raising the Child Who Never Grew." Pp. 130–164 in *Mental Retardation in America*, ed. Steven Noll and James W. Trent Jr. New York: New York University Press.

Brown, JoAnne. 1992. *The Definition of a Profession: The Authority of Metaphor in the History of Intelligence Testing, 1890–1930.* Princeton, N.J.: Princeton University Press.

Brown, Lou. 1991. "Who Are They and What Do They Want? An Essay on TASH." In *Critical Issues of People with Severe Disabilities*, ed. L. H. Meyer, C. A. Peck, and

L. Brown. Baltimore: Brookes Publishing. Available online at www.tash.org/WWA/WWA_history.html (accessed February 2009).

Brubaker, Rogers. 1992. *Citizenship and Nationhood of France and Germany*. Cambridge, Mass.: Harvard University Press.

Bruggeman, Amie. 1980. "Guardianship of Adults with Mental Retardation." *Akron Law Review* 55 (1): 321–339.

Buck, Pearl S. 1992 (1950). *The Child Who Never Grew*, 2d ed. Bethesda, Md.: Woodbine House.

Buck, Pearl S., and Gweneth T. Zarfoss. 1965. *The Gifts They Bring: Our Debt to the Mentally Retarded*. New York: John Day.

Buck v. Bell. 1927. 274 U.S. 200.

Burchell, David. 1995. "The Attributes of Citizenship: Virtue, Manners, and the Activity of Citizenship." *Economy and Society* 24 (4): 540–558.

Burke, Chris, and Jo Beth McDaniel. 1991. *A Special Kind of Hero*. New York: Doubleday.

Bush, George. 1990. "Statement on Signing the Americans with Disabilities Act of 1990," July 26. American Presidency Project. Available online at http://www.presidency.ucsb.edu (accessed May 2007).

Butler, Amos. 1907. "The Burden of Feeble-mindedness." *Proceedings of the National Conference of Charities and Correction*. 1–10.

Butler, F. O. 1945. "Mental Defectives in Military Service and War Time Industries." *American Journal of Mental Deficiency* 50 (2): 296–300.

Byers, Joseph P. 1916. "A State Plan for the Care of the Feeble-minded." *Proceedings of the National Conference of Charities and Corrections*. 223–239.

Caine, Frances A. 1954. "Public Education and the Severely Retarded Child." *American Journal of Mental Deficiency* 63 (1): 37–38.

Campbell, Fiona Kumari. 2005. "Legislating Disability: Narrative Ontologies and the Government of Legal Identities." Pp. 108–130 in *Foucault and the Government of Disability*, ed. Shelley Tremain. Ann Arbor: University of Michigan Press.

Carey, Allison C. 1998. "Gender and Compulsory Sterilization Programs in America: 1907–1950. *Journal of Historical Sociology* 11 (1): 74–105.

———. 2003. "Beyond the Medical Model: A Reconsideration of 'Feeblemindedness' and Eugenic Restrictions." *Disability and Society* 18 (4): 411–430.

Carlson, Licia. 2005. "Docile Bodies, Docile Minds: Foucauldian Reflections on Mental Retardation." Pp. 133–152 in *Foucault and the Government of Disability*, ed. Shelley Tremain. Ann Arbor: University of Michigan Press.

Cass, Julia. 1979. "Don't Move Pennhurst Children, Parents Urge Judge at Hearing." *Philadelphia Inquirer*, June 2.

Cast, C. 1923. "Elimination of the Unfit: A Problem of Waste in Public Education." *School and Society* 18 (447): 84–87.

Castle, Elaine E. 1996. *"We're People First": The Social and Emotional Lives of Individuals with Mental Retardation*. Westport, Conn.: Praeger.

Castles, Katherine. 2002. "Quiet Eugenics: Sterilization in North Carolina's Institutions for the Mentally Retarded, 1945–1965." *Journal of Southern History* 4 (4): 849–878.

———. 2004. "'Nice, Average Americans': Postwar Parents, Groups and the Defense of the Normal Family." Pp. 351–370 in *Mental Retardation in America*, ed. Steven Noll and James W. Trent Jr. New York: New York University Press.

Center on Human Policy. N.d. "History." Available online at http://thechp.syr.edu/chp.htm (accessed September 2007).

Charles Irvin Littleton, Jr. v. Wal-Mart Stores, Inc. 2005. N.D. Ala., April 12.

———. 2007. 231 Fed. Appx. 874, 11th Cir.

City of Cleburne, Texas, v. Cleburne Living Center. 1985. 473 U.S. 432.

Coakley, Frances. 1945. "Study of Feeble-minded Wards Employed in War Industries." *American Journal of Mental Deficiency* 50 (2): 301–306.

Cobb, Howard. 1998. "Civil Unliberties." Pp. 39–46 in *On the Outside: A Look at Two Decades of Deinstitutionalization through the Eyes of People with Developmental Disabilities*, ed. Julie Pratt. Charleston: West Virginia Developmental Disabilities Planning Council.

Coleman, Sandra S. 1980. "Involuntary Sterilization of the Mentally Retarded: Blessing or Burden?" *South Dakota Law Review* 25 (Winter): 55–68.

Commonwealth v. Abner Rogers Jr. 1844. 48 Mass. 500.

Condelucci, Al. 2004. *Advocacy for Change: A Manual for Organizing.* Alexandria, Va.: American Network of Community Options and Resources Foundation.

Conrad, Peter, and Joseph W. Schneider, eds. 1992. *Deviance and Medicalization: From Badness to Sickness.* Philadelphia: Temple University Press.

Consortium for Citizens with Disabilities. 2007a. *Chronology of the ADA Restoration Act.* Washington, D.C.: CCD.

———. 2007b. *The Effect of the Supreme Court's Decisions on Americans with Disabilities.* Washington, D.C.: CCD.

Contos, Mike. 1979a. "AFSCME Fights Back: Pennhurst Union Breaks Ties with Broderick." *Mercury* (Pottstown, Pa.), May 10.

———. 1979b. "Pennhurst Parents Plan to Withdraw. *Mercury* (Pottstown, Pa.), May 23.

Corbett, J. 1997. "Independent, Proud, and Special: Celebrating Our Differences." Pp. 90–98 in *Disability Studies: Past, Present and Future*, ed. L. Barton and M. Oliver. Leeds: Disability Press.

"Creed for Exceptional Children." 1954. U.S. Office of Education Conference on Qualification and Preparation of Teachers of Exceptional Children.

Cynkar, Robert J. 1981. *"Buck v. Bell:* 'Felt Necessities' versus Fundamental Values?" *Columbia Law Review* 81:1418–1461.

Danielson, Florence Harris, and Charles Davenport. 1912. *The Hill Folk: Report on a Rural Community of Hereditary Defectives.* Cold Spring Harbor, N.Y.: Eugenics Record Office.

Das, Veena, and Renu Addlakha. 2001. "Disability and Domestic Citizenship: Voice, Gender, and Making of the Subject." Pp. 511–531 in *Public Culture*, ed. Carol A. Breckenridge and Candace Volger. Durham, N.C.: Duke University Press.

Davenport, Charles B. 1913. *Heredity, in Relation to Eugenics.* New York: Henry Holt.

Davies, Stanley P. 1923. *Social Control of the Feebleminded: A Study of Social Programs and Attitudes in Relation to the Problems of Mental Deficiency.* Utica, N.Y.: State Hospital.

Davis, Angela Y. 1983. *Women, Race, and Class.* New York: Vintage Books.

Davis, Lennard J. 1997. "Constructing Normalcy: The Bell Curve, the Novel, and the Intervention of the Disabled Body in the Nineteenth Century." Pp. 9–28 in *The Disability Studies Reader*, ed. Lennard J. Davis. New York: Routledge.

D'Emilio, John, and Estelle Freedman. 1988. *Intimate Matters: A History of Sexuality in America.* New York: Harper and Row.

Department of Public Welfare v. Haas. 1958. 15 Ill. 2d 204.

DeProspo, Chris J. 1958. "Presidential Address: Crossroads." *American Journal of Mental Deficiency* 63 (1): 3–11.

Deutsch, Albert. 1948. *Shame of the States*. New York: Harcourt Brace.

Deutsch, Helene. 1944–1945. *The Psychology of Women: A Psychoanalytic Interpretation*, vols. 1–2. New York: Greene and Stratton.

Deutsch, Richard L. 1949. *Mentally Ill in America*. 2nd ed. New York: Columbia University Press.

Developmental Disabilities Assistance and Bill of Rights Act. P.L. 94-103. 1975, 89 stat. 502.

Developmental Disabilities Law Project. 1985. "Amicus Brief Filed on Behalf of Pennsylvania Association for Retarded Citizens and Lawrence Court ARC, in the Interests of Carol Ann Pauletich." *In the Matter of Carol Ann Pauletich*, Superior Court 237, Pittsburgh.

Dexter v. Hall. 1872. 82 U.S. 9.

Dix, Dorothea L. 1850. "Memorial of Miss D. L. Dix to the Senate and House of Representatives of the United States." Disability History Museum. Available online at http://www.disabilitymuseum.org (accessed February 2007).

Dodge, Gary. 1978. "Sterilization, Retardation, and Parental Authority." *Brigham Young University Law Review* 1:380–407.

Doll, Edgar A. 1929a. "Community Control of the Feebleminded." *American Association for the Study of the Feeble-Minded* 34:161–175.

———. 1929b. "Feeble-mindedness as a State Problem." *Training School Bulletin* 26:17–27.

———. 1944. "Mental Defectives and the War." *American Journal of Mental Deficiency* 49 (1): 64–67.

———. 1948. "What Is a Moron?" *Journal of Abnormal and Social Psychology* 43 (4): 495–501.

———. 1953. "Counseling Parents of Severely Mentally Retarded Children." *Journal of Clinical Psychology* 9 (2): 114–117.

Dorr, Lisa Lindquist. 1999. "Arm in Arm: Gender, Eugenics, and Virginia's Racial Integrity Acts of the 1920s." *Journal of Women's History* 11 (1): 143–166.

Dougherty, Joseph. 1979. "Pennhurst Workers Have Alternatives: Other State Jobs." *Evening Phoenix* (Phoenixville, Pa.), May 22.

Dowdall, George W. 1994. *The Eclipse of the State Mental Hospital: Policy, Stigma, and Organization*. Albany: State University of New York Press.

Drinkwater, Chris. 2005. "Supported Living and the Production of Individuals." Pp. 229–244 in *Foucault and the Government of Disability*, ed. Shelley Tremain. Ann Arbor: University of Michigan Press.

Dugan, James C. 1993. "The Conflict between 'Disabling' and 'Enabling' Paradigms in Law: Sterilization, the Developmentally Disabled, and the Americans with Disabilities Act of 1990." *Cornell Law Review* 78 (3): 507–542.

Dugdale, Richard L. 1877. *The Jukes: A Study in Crime, Pauperism, Disease, and Heredity*. New York: Putnam.

Dunn, William H. 1946. "The Readjustment of the Mentally Deficient Soldier in the Community." *American Journal of Mental Deficiency* 51 (1): 48–51.

Dwyer, Ellen. 2004. "The State and the Multiply Disadvantaged: The Case of Epilepsy." Pp. 258–280 in *Mental Retardation in America*, ed. Steven Noll and James W. Trent Jr. New York: New York University Press.

Dybwad, Gunnar. 1962. "Old Words, New Challenges." *Children Limited* 11 (5): 8–9.

———. 1963. "Farewell Address." Paper presented at the Annual Convention of the National Association for Retardation Children, Disability History Museum, Washington, D.C. Available online at www.disabilitymuseum.org/lib/docs/2233card.htm (accessed May 2006).

————. 1964. *Challenges in Mental Retardation*. New York: Columbia University Press.

Dybwad, Rosemary F. 1990. *Perspectives on a Parent Movement: The Revolt of Parents of Children with Intellectual Limitations*. Brookline, Mass.: Brookline Books.

Edgarton, Robert B. 1993 (1967). *The Cloak of Competence: Stigma in the Lives of the Mentally Retarded*, 2d ed. Berkeley: University of California Press.

"Editorial Note: Mental Disability and the Right to Vote." 1979. *Yale Law Journal* 88 (8): 1644–1664.

Education Committee of the National Association for Retarded Children. 1954. "Day Classes for Severely of Retarded Children: A Report of the Education Committee of the National Association for Retarded Children." *American Journal of Mental Deficiency* 59 (1): 357–369.

Edwards, J. 1982. *We Are People First*. Portland, Ore.: Ednick. Cited in Schaaf, with Bersani 1996.

Eisenberg, Ed. 1982. *Disabled People as Second Class Citizens*. New York: Springer.

Elkins, E., and H. Frank Andersen. 1992. "Sterilization of Persons with Mental Retardation." *Journal of the Association for Persons with Severe Handicaps* 17 (1): 19–26.

Engle, David M., and Frank W. Munger. 2003. *Rights of Inclusion: Law and Identity in the Life Stories of Americans with Disabilities*. Chicago: University of Chicago Press.

English, Walter M. 1931. "Presidential Address: The Feeble-minded Problem." *American Journal of Psychiatry* 11 (1): 1–8.

"Equal Right to Training." 1962. *Children Limited* 11 (5): 9.

Estabrook, Arthur H., and Charles B. Davenport. 1912. *The Nam Family: A Study in Cacogenics*. Cold Spring Harbor, N.Y.: New York Era Printing.

Fairchild, Amy L. 2006. "Leprosy, Domesticity, and Patient Protest: The Social Context of a Patients' Rights Movement in Mid-Century America." *Journal of Social History* (Summer): 1011–1043.

Farber, Bernard. 1968. *Mental Retardation: Its Social Context and Social Consequences*. Boston: Houghton Mifflin.

Feinstein, Celia S., Robin M. Levine, James A. Lemanowicz, and Colleen A. McLaughlin. 2005. *Independent Monitoring for Quality (IM4Q): A Statewide Summary, 2003–2004*. Philadelphia: Institute on Disabilities, Temple University.

Ferguson, Philip M. 1994. *Abandoned to Their Fate: Social Policy and Practice toward Severely Disabled People in America, 1820–1920*. Philadelphia: Temple University Press.

Ferleger, David. 1978. "The Failure of Institutions for the Retarded: Pennhurst, a 'Monumental Example of Unconstitutionality.'" *Health Law Project Bulletin* 3 (3): 1–11.

————. 2007. "Petition for Writ of Certiorari." *Charles Irvin Littleton Jr. v. Wal-Mart Stores, Inc.*, 11th Cir. May 11.

Fernald, Walter E. 1915. "State Care of the Insane, Feeble-Minded and Epileptic." *Proceedings of the National Conference of Charities and Corrections*. 289–297.

————. 1919. "After-Care Study of the Patients Discharged from Waverly for a Period of Twenty-five Years." *Ungraded* 5:25–31.

Fleischer, Doris Zames, and Frieda Zames. 2001. *The Disability Rights Movement: From Charity to Confrontation*. Philadelphia: Temple University Press.

Ford, Gerald. 1975. "Statement on Signing the Education for All Handicapped Children Act of 1975." American Presidency Project. Available online at http://www.presidency.ucsb.edu/ws/index.ph p?pid=5913 (accessed May 2007).

Forrest, D. W. 1974. *Francis Galton: The Life and Work of a Victorian Genius*. New York: Taplinger.

Foucault, Michel. 1965. *Madness and Civilization*. New York: Vintage Books.

———. 1979. *Discipline and Punish*. New York: Vintage Books.

Francis, Leslie Pickering, and Anita Silvers, eds. 2000. *Americans with Disabilities: Exploring the Implications of Rights for Individuals and Institutions*. New York: Routledge.

"Francis Sloan, Obituary." 1983. *New York Times*, August 5.

Frank, John P. 1952. *My Son's Story*. New York: Alfred A. Knopf.

Frankenberg, Ruth. 1993. *White Women, Race Matters: The Social Construction of Whiteness*. Minneapolis: University of Minnesota Press.

Franklin, Stephen. 1979. "Pennhurst: As Closing Nears, Fears Multiply." *Bulletin* (Philadelphia), June 10.

Fraser, Nancy, and Linda Gordon. 1992. "Contract versus Charity." *Socialist Review* 22 (3): 45–67.

———. 1994. "Genealogy of Dependency: Tracing a Keyword of the U.S. Welfare State." *Signs* 19 (2): 309–336.

Freeman, S., and M. Alkin. 2000. "Academic and Social Attainments of Children with Mental Retardation in General Education and Special Education Settings." *Remedial and Special Education* 21:3–18.

Frohboese, Robinsue, and Bruce Dennis Sales. 1980. "Parental Opposition to Deinstitutionalization: A Challenge in Need of Attention and Resolution." *Law and Human Behavior* 4 (1–2): 1–87.

Funk, Robert. 1987. "Disability Rights: From Caste to Class in the Context of Civil Rights." Pp. 7–30 in *Images of the Disabled, Disabled Images*, ed. Alan Gartner and Tom Joe. New York: Praeger.

Furman, Bob. 1996. "The History of People First of Washington State." Pp. 180–202 in *New Voices: Self-Advocacy by People with Disabilities*, ed. Gunnar Dybwad and Hank Bersani Jr. Cambridge, Mass.: Brookline Books.

Gallagher, Hugh Gregory. 1999. *FDR's Splendid Deception*. Arlington, Va.: Vandamere.

Galton, Francis. 1907. *Inquiries into Human Faculty and Its Development*. New York: Dutton.

———. 1962 (1869). *Hereditary Genius: An Inquiry into Its Laws and Consequences*. Cleveland: Meridian Books.

Galvin, Rose. 2004. "Challenging the Need for Gratitude: Comparisons between Paid and Unpaid Care for Disabled People." *Journal of Sociology* 40 (2): 137–155.

Gamble, Clarence J. 1945. "State Sterilization Programs for the Prophylactic Control of Mental Disease and Mental Deficiency." *American Journal of Psychiatry* 102 (2): 289–293.

———. 1951. "The Prevention of Mental Deficiency by Sterilization." *American Journal of Mental Deficiency* 56 (2): 192–198.

———. 1952. "What Proportion of Mental Deficiency Is Preventable by Sterilization?" *American Journal of Mental Deficiency* 57 (1): 123–126.

Gamson, Joshua. 1996. "The Organizational Shaping of Collective Identity: The Case of Lesbian and Gay Film Festivals in New York." *Sociological Forum* 11 (2): 231–261.

Gamson, William, and André Modigliani. 1989. "Media Discourse and Public Opinion on Nuclear Power: A Constructionist Approach." *American Journal of Sociology* 95 (1): 1–37.

Gelb, Stephen A. 2004. "'Mental Deficients' Fighting Fascism: The Unplanned Normalization of World War II." Pp. 308–321 in *Mental Retardation in America*, ed. Steven Noll and James W. Trent Jr. New York: New York University Press.

Glendon, Mary Ann. 2001. *A World Made New: Eleanor Roosevelt and the Universal Declaration of Human Rights*. New York: Random House.

Glenn, Evelyn Nakano. 2004. *Unequal Freedom: How Race and Gender Shaped American Citizenship and Labor*. Cambridge, Mass.: Harvard University Press.

Goddard, Henry H. 1912. *The Kallikak Family: A Study in the Heredity of Feeblemindedness*. New York: Macmillan.

———. 1914. *Feeble-mindedness, Its Causes and Consequences*. New York: Macmillan.

———. 1917a. "Mental Levels of a Group of Immigrants." *Psychological Bulletin* (February): 68–69.

———. 1917b. "Mental Tests and the Immigrant." *Journal of Delinquency* 2 (September): 243–279.

———. 1932. "Anniversary Address." *Training School Bulletin* 29:1–14.

Goffman, Erving. 1961. *Asylums*. New York: Anchor Books.

Golden, Sam. 2006. "All about Anne Golden." Voice of the Retarded History Project. Available online at http://www.vor.net/Anne%20Golden.html (accessed June 2006).

Golland, David Hamilton. 2003. "Only Nixon Could Go to Philadelphia: The Philadelphia Plan, the AFL-CIO, and the Politics of Race Hiring." Paper presented at the Race and Labor Matters Conference, Graduate Center, City University of New York.

Goode, David. 1998. *And Now Let's Build a Better World: The Story of the Association for the Help of Retarded Children, New York City, 1948–1998*. New York: AHRC.

Goodell, William. 1853. *The American Slave Code in Theory and Practice: Its Distinctive Features Shown by Its Statutes, Judicial Decision, and Illustrative Facts*, pt. 1, chap. 1, paras. 31–32. New York: American and Foreign Anti-Slavery Society. Available online at http://www.dinsdoc.com/goodell-1-1-1.htm (accessed January 2007).

Gordon, Edmund W., and Montague Ullman. 1956. "Reactions of Parents to Problems of Mental Retardation in Children." *American Journal of Metal Deficiency* 61 (1): 158–163.

Gordon, Linda. 1974. *Woman's Body, Woman's Right*. New York: Penguin Books.

Gordon, Sol. 1971. "Missing in Special Education: Sex." *Journal of Special Education* 5:351–354.

Gosney, Ezra, and Paul Popenoe. 1929. *Sterilization for Human Betterment: A Summary of Results of 6,000 Operations in California, 1909–1929*. New York: Macmillan.

Gossett, Thomas F. 1965. *Race: The History of an Idea in America*. New York: Schocken Books.

Gould, Stephen Jay. 1981. *The Mismeasure of Man*. New York: W. W. Norton.

———. 1984. "Carrie Buck's Daughter." *Natural History* 93 (7): 14–18.

Gozali, Joav. 1971. "Citizenship and Voting Behavior of Mildly Retarded Adults: A Pilot Study." *American Journal of Mental Deficiency* 75 (5): 640–641.

Graham, Laurie, and Richard Hogan. 1990. "Social Class and Tactics: Neighborhood Opposition to Group Homes." *Sociological Quarterly* 31 (4): 513–529.

Gramm, Eugene. 1951. "New Hope for a Different Child." *Parents Magazine* 26 (48): 152–156.

———. 1952. "Just One Voice to Speak for All of America's Retarded." *Children Limited* 1 (1): 1.

———. 1962. "An Ad That Made History." *Children Limited* 11 (5): 16–17.

Grant, Madison. 1916. *The Passing of the Great Race*. New York: Charles Scribner's Sons.

Grant, Sophia. 1957. *"One of Those": The Progress of a Mongoloid Child*. New York: Pageant.

Greenberg, Harold A. 1950. "Problems of Parents of Handicapped Children." *Journal of Exceptional Children* 17 (October): 1–6.

Greer v. Greers. 1852. 82 Sup. Ct. VA. 330.

Greer v. Rome City School District. 1991. 950 F.2d 688.

Grossman, Paul David. 1992. "Employment Discrimination Law for the Learning Disabled Community." *Learning Disability Quarterly* 15 (4): 287–329.

"Group Pickets Court Hearings for Pennhurst." 1979. *Daily News* (Lebanon, Pa.), June 1.

"Guardianship for Mentally Retarded Persons: Principal Features of a AAMD Policy Statement." 1974. Presented at the 96th Annual Meeting of the American Association on Mental Deficiency, Toronto, June, C15–16.

Hahn, Harlan. 1983. "Paternalism and Public Policy." *Society* (March–April): 36–46.

———. 1987. "Civil Rights for Disabled Americans: The Foundations of a Political Agenda." Pp. 181–204 in *Images of the Disabled, Disabling Images*, ed. Alan Gartner and Tom Joe. New York: Praeger.

———. 1997. "Advertising the Acceptably Employable Image." Pp. 172–186 in *The Disabled Studies Reader*, ed. Lennard J. Davis. New York: Routledge.

Halderman v. Pennhurst, 1977. 446 F. Supp. 1295.

Hall, Randal L. 2000. *William Louis Poteat: A Leader of the Progressive-Era South*. Lexington: University Press of Kentucky.

Hallgren B., A. Norsman, and D. Bier. 1977. *Life, Liberty and the Pursuit of Happiness: A Self-Advocacy Curriculum*. Middleton: Wisconsin Association for Retarded Citizens.

Halpern, Charles. 1979. "Introduction." *Stanford Law Review* 31 (4): 545–551.

Harper, Emma D. 1968. "Letter to the Editor." *Children Limited* 17 (6): 4.

Hasian, Marouf Arif, Jr. 1996. *The Rhetoric of Eugenics in Anglo-American Thought*. Athens: University of Georgia Press.

Hayden, Mary F. 1997. *Living in the Freedom World: Personal Stories of Living in the Community by People Who Once Lived in Oklahoma's Institutions*. Minneapolis: Research and Training Center on Community Living, Institute on Community Integration, University of Minnesota.

Heshusius, Lous. 1982. "Sexuality, Intimacy, and Persons We Label Mentally Retarded: What They Think—What We Think." *Mental Retardation* 20 (4): 164–168.

"High Time to Stop Hoping . . . Time to Act!" 1969. *Pennsylvania Message* 5 (2): 1, 7.

Hodgson, Robert J. 1972. "Guardianship of Mentally Retarded Persons: Three Approaches to a Long Neglected Problem." *Albany Law Review* 37 (1): 407–441.

Hodson, William. 1919. "What Minnesota Has Done and Should Do for the Feebleminded." *Journal of Criminal Law and Criminology* 10 (2): 208–217.

Hoffman, James M. 1959. "Mental Health Schools and School Districts." *Illinois Bar Journal* (April): 725–728.

Howe, Samuel Gridley. 1958 (1848). *On the Causes of Idiocy [Being the Supplement to a Report by Dr. S. G. Howe and the Other Commissioners Appointed by the Governor of Massachusetts to Inquire into the Condition of the Idiots of the Commonwealth]*, repr. 1958 with 1848 report, ed. Chris Borthwick and Murray K. Simpson. Available online at http://www.personal.dundee.ac.uk/~mksimpso/howe.htm (accessed September 2006).

Hudson, Margaret. 1955. "The Severely Retarded Child: Educable versus Trainable." *American Journal of Mental Deficiency* 59 (2): 583–586.

Huefner, Dixie Snow. 1986. "Severely Handicapped Infants with Life-Threatening Conditions: Federal Intrusions into the Decision Not to Treat." *American Journal of Law and Medicine* 12 (2): 171–205.

Hughes, Bill, Rachel Russell, and Kevin Paterson. 2005. "Nothing to Be Had 'Off the Peg': Consumption, Identity and the Immobilization of Young Disabled People." *Disability and Society* 20 (1): 3–17.

Human Betterment League. 1967. "An Idea Come of Age." In the Collection of the Human Betterment League of North Carolina, Archives of the University of North Carolina, Chapel Hill.

Humphrey, Seth K. 1913. "Parenthood and the Social Conscience." *Forum* 49:457–464.

Hungerford, Richard H. 1959 (1952). "A Bill of Rights for the Retarded." *American Journal of Mental Deficiency* 63 (April): 937–938.

Hunt, Douglas. 1967. "Preface." In Nigel Hunt, *The World of Nigel Hunt: The Diary of a Mongoloid Youth*. New York: Garrett.

Independent Living Research Utilization. 1986. *ILRU Directory of Independent Living Programs*. Houston: Independent Living Research Utilization. Cited in Nosek, Jones, and Zhu 1989.

International League of Societies for the Mentally Handicapped. 1968. *Declaration of General and Special Rights of the Mentally Retarded*. Available online at http://www.mncdd.org/parallels2/posters/images/poster20Txt.pdf (accessed June 2008).

In the Matter of Conservatorship of Valerie N. 1985. 707 P.2d 706. Calif.

In the Matter of Guardianship of Edith Melissa Maria Hayes. 1980. 608 P. 2d 635. Wash.

In the Matter of Lee Ann Grady. 1981. 426 A.2d 467. N.J.

In the Matter of Mary Moe. 1982. 432 N.E.2d 712. Mass.

Jablow, Martha M. 1992. "Introduction." In Pearl S. Buck. *The Child Who Never Grew*, 2nd ed. Bethesda, Md.: Woodbine House.

Jackson, Vanessa. 2001. "Our Own Voice: African American Stories of Oppression, Survival and Recovery in Mental Health Systems." Unpublished ms. Available online at http://dsmc.info/pdf (accessed August 2006).

Jacobs, Lois Guller. 1976–1977. "The Right of the Mentally Disabled to Marry: A Statutory Evaluation." *Journal of Family Law* 15:463–507.

Jaegers, Eric M. 1992–1993. "Modern Judicial Treatment of Procreative Rights of Developmentally Disabled Persons: Equal Rights to Procreation and Sterilization." *University of Louisville Journal of Family Law* 31 (4): 947–979.

Janazzo, Fanny M. 2006. "My Jimmy 'J.'" Voice of the Retarded History Project. Available online at http://www.vor.net/JimmyJ.html (accessed May 2006).

Jastak, Joseph. 1949. "A Rigorous Criterion of Feeblemindedness." *Journal of Abnormal and Social Psychology* 44 (3): 367–378.

Jefferson, Robert F. 2003. "'Enabled Courage': Race, Disability, and Black World War II Veterans in Postwar America." *Historian* 65 (Fall): 1102–1124.

Johnson, Mary. 2003. *Make Them Go Away: Clint Eastwood, Christopher Reeve, and the Case against Disability Rights*. Louisville, Ken.: Avocado.

Johnson, Roland, as told to Karl Williams. 1999. *Lost in a Desert World*. Plymouth Meeting, Pa.: Speaking for Ourselves.

Jones, Betty. 1979. "'Putting the Cart before the Horse': Order to Close Pennhurst by '81 Has Heads Shaking." *Times Herald* (Norristown, Pa.), May 11.

Jones, Kathleen W. 2004. "Education for Children with Mental Retardation: Parent Activism, Public Policy, and Family Ideology in the 1950s." Pp. 351–370 in *Mental*

Retardation in America, ed. Steven Noll and James W. Trent Jr. New York: New York University Press.

Jones, Michael L., and Gary R. Ulicny. 1986. "The Independent Living Perspective: Applications to Services for Adults with Developmental Disabilities." Pp. 227–244 in *The Right to Grow Up*, ed. Jean Ann Summers. Baltimore: Paul H. Brookes.

Jones, Robin A. 1992–1993. "The ADA and Employment: Does It Go Far Enough?" *Impact* 5 (4): 4.

Jost, Dean Timothy. 1980. "Illinois Guardianship for Disabled Legislation of 1978 and 1979: Protecting the Disabled from Their Zealous Protectors." *Chicago-Kent Law Review* 56 (4): 1087–1105.

Joyce, Patrick. 1991. *Visions of the People*. Cambridge: Cambridge University Press.

Kaiser Commission on Medicaid and the Uninsured. 2004. "*Olmstead v. L.C.*: The Interaction of the Americans with Disabilities Act and Medicaid." Policy brief, Henry J. Kaiser Family Foundation, Washington, D.C., June.

Kambon, Afi-Tiombe A. 1993. "Black Diamond." Pp. 10–12 in *Range of Motion: An Anthology of Disability Poetry, Prose and Art*, ed. Cheryl Marie Wade. Albany, Calif.: Squeaky Wheels Press.

Kanner, Leo. 1942. "Exoneration of the Feebleminded." *American Journal of Psychiatry* 99 (1): 17–22.

Kaplan, Oscar J. 1944. "Marriage of Mental Defectives." *American Journal of Mental Deficiency* 48 (4): 379–384.

Karst, Kenneth L. 1977. "The Supreme Court 1976 Term Forward: Equal Citizenship under the Fourteenth Amendment." *Harvard Law Review* 91 (1): 1–71.

Katz, Alfred H. 1961. *Parents of the Handicapped: Self-Organized Parents' and Relatives' Groups for Treatment of Ill and Handicapped Children*. Springfield, Ill.: Charles C. Thomas.

Katz, Janet, and Charles F. Abel. 1984. "The Medicalization of Repression: Eugenics and Crime." *Contemporary Crises* 8 (3): 227–241.

Kelman, Howard R. 1958. "Social Work and Mental Retardation: Challenge or Failure?" *Social Work* 3:37–42.

Kennedy, David M. 1970. *Birth Control in America*. New Haven, Conn.: Yale University Press.

Kenyon, J. Miller. 1914. "Sterilization of the Unfit." *Virginia Law Review* 1 (6): 458–469.

Kevles, Daniel J. 1985. *In the Name of Eugenics: Genetics and the Uses of Human Heredity*. New York: Alfred A. Knopf.

Kim, Shannon, Sheryl A. Larson, and K. Charles Lakin. 2001. "Behavioral Outcomes of Deinstitutionalization for People with Intellectual Disabilities: A Review of U.S. Studies Conducted between 1980 and 1999." *Journal of Intellectual and Developmental Disability* 26 (1): 35–50.

Kingsley, Jason, and Mitchell Levitz. 1994. *Count Us In: Growing Up with Down Syndrome*. San Diego, Calif.: Harcourt Brace.

Kirk, Samuel A. and G. Orville Johnson. 1951. *Educating the Retarded Child*. Cambridge, Mass.: Houghton Mifflin.

Kirkbridge, Franklin, 1912. "The Right to Be Well-Born." *Survey* 28 (18): 1838–1839.

Kitchener, Martin, Micky Willmott, Alice Wong, and Charlene Harrington. 2006. *Home and Community-Based Services: Introduction to Olmstead Lawsuits and Olmstead Plans*. San Francisco: Center for Personal Assistance Services, University of California, San Francisco.

Kite, Elizabeth S. 1913. "The 'Pineys.'" *Survey* 31 (1): 7–13.

Kittay, Eva Feder. 2001. "When Caring Is Justice and Justice Is Caring: Justice and Mental Retardation." Pp. 557–580 in *Public Culture*, ed. Carol A. Breckenridge and Candace Volger. Durham, N.C.: Duke University Press.

Kline, Wendy. 2001. *Building a Better Race: Gender, Sexuality, and Eugenics from the Turn of the Century to the Baby Boom*. Berkeley: University of California Press.

Knight, Committee, & C. v. Watts's Adm'rs et al. 1885. Sup. Ct. W.Va., Wheeling, 26 W. Va. 175.

Koggel, Christine. 1998. *Perspectives on Equality: Constructing a Relational Theory*. Lanham, Md.: Rowman and Littlefield.

Kokaska, Charles J. 1966. "The Mentally Retarded and the Ballot Box." *Digest of the Mentally Retarded* 3 (2): 124–125.

———. 1972. "Voter Participation of the EMR: A Review of the Literature." *Mental Retardation* 10 (5): 6–8.

Koller, H., S. A. Richardson, and M. Katz. 1988. "Marriage in a Young Mentally Retarded Population." *Journal of Mental Deficiency* 32:93–102.

Kostir, Mary S. 1916. *The Family of Sam Sixty*. Mansfield: Press of the Ohio State Reformatory.

Krauss, M. W., M. M. Seltzer, and S. J. Goodman. 1992. "Social Support Networks of Adults with Retardation Who Live at Home." *American Journal on Mental Retardation* 96:432–441.

Kurashige, Scott. 2004. "The Many Faces of Brown: Integration in a Multiracial Society." *Journal of American History* 91 (June): 56–68.

Ladd-Taylor, Molly. 2001. "Eugenics, Sterilization and Modern Marriage in the U.S.A.: The Strange Career of Paul Popenoe." *Gender and History* 13 (2): 298–327.

———. 2004. "The 'Sociological Advantages' of Sterilization: Fiscal Policies and Feebleminded Women in Interwar Minnesota." Pp. 281–307 in *Mental Retardation in America*, ed. Steven Noll and James W. Trent Jr. New York: New York University Press.

Lakin, K. Charles, Sheryl A. Larson, Robert W. Prouty, and Kathryn Coucouvanis. 2003. "Characteristics and Movement of Residents of Large State Facilities." Pp. 31–46 in *Residential Services for Persons with Developmental Disabilities: Status and Trends through 2002*, ed. Robert W. Prouty, Gary Smith, and K. Charles Lakin. Minneapolis: Research and Training Center on Community Living, Institute on Community Integration, University of Minnesota.

Lakin, K. Charlie, Robert Prouty, Barbara Polister, and Kathryn Coucouvanis. 2004. "States' Initial Response to the President's New Freedom Initiative: Slowest Rates of Deinstitutionalization in 30 Years." *Mental Retardation* 42 (3): 241–244.

Landesman, Sharon, and Earl C. Butterfield. 1987. "Normalization and Deinstitutionalization of Mentally Retarded Individuals: Controversy and Facts." *American Psychologist* 22 (8): 809–816.

Larson, Edward J. 1995. *Sex, Race, and Science: Eugenics in the Deep South*. Baltimore: Johns Hopkins University Press.

Larson, Sheryl, and K. Charles Lakin. 1989. "Deinstitutionalization of Persons with Mental Retardation: Behavioral Outcomes." *Journal of the Association for Persons with Severe Handicaps* 14 (4): 324–332.

———. 1991. "Parent Attitudes about Residential Placement before and after Deinstitutionalization: A Research Synthesis." *Journal of the Association for Persons with Severe Handicaps* 16 (1): 25–38.

Laughlin, Harry Hamilton. 1922. *Eugenical Sterilization in the United States*. Chicago: Psychopathic Laboratory of the Municipal Court of Chicago.

Lavigne, Muffi. 2004. "In Profile: Dr. Al Condelucci." UCP Press Room, November 4. Available online at http://www.ucp.org/ucp_generaldoc.cfm/1/9/10438/10438-10438/5875 (accessed May 2007).

Laws and Liberties of Massachusetts, 1641–1961, The. 1976. vols. 1–3. Wilmington, Del.: Glazier.

Lazerow, Herbert I. 1967. "Mental Incompetency as Grounds for Annulment." *Journal of Family Law* 7 (1): 442–464.

Leonard, Thomas C. 2005. "Protecting Family and Face: The Progressive Case for Regulating Women's Work." *American Journal of Economics and Sociology* 64 (3): 1–35.

Levy, Joseph H. 1951. *Parent Groups and Social Agencies: The Activities of Health and Welfare Agencies with Groups of Parents of Handicapped Children in Chicago.* Chicago: University of Chicago Press.

Lichtenwalner, Muriel. 1979. "Original Plaintiffs in Pennhurst Lawsuit Give Ultimatum to Attorney." *Reporter* (Royersford, Pa.), July 18.

Lindenmeyer, Kriste. 1997. *"A Right to Childhood": The U.S. Children's Bureau and Child Welfare, 1912–1946.* Urbana: University of Illinois Press.

Linton, S. 1998. *Claiming Disability: Knowledge and Identity.* New York: New York University Press.

Lipsky, Dorothy K. and Alan Gartner. 2004. "Equity Requires Inclusion: The Future for All Students." Pp. 45–55 in *Special Educational Needs and Inclusive Education: Major Themes in Education, Volume 2, Inclusive Education,* ed. David Mitchell. New York: Routledge.

Lister, Ruth. 1993. "Tracing the Contours of Women's Citizenship." *Policy and Politics* 21:3–16.

———. 1997. *Citizenship: Feminist Perspectives.* Basingstoke: Macmillan.

Lloyd, Margaret. 2001. "The Politics of Disability and Feminism: Discord or Synthesis." *Sociology* 35 (3): 715–728.

Longmore, Paul K. 2003. "The Second Phase: From Disability Rights to Disability Culture." Pp. 215–224 in *Why I Burned My Book and Other Essays on Disability.* Philadelphia: Temple University Press.

Louis Harris and Associates. 1989. *The ICD Survey III: A Report Card on Special Education.* New York: International Center for the Disabled.

Lowell, Josephine Shaw. 1879. "One Means of Preventing Pauperism." *Proceedings of the National Conference of Charities.* 189–200.

Luckasson, Ruth, Robert L. Schalock, Deborah M. Spitalnik, Scott Spreat, Marc Tassé, Martha E. Snell, David L. Coulter, Sharon A. Borthwick-Duffy, Alison Alya Reeve, Wil H. E. Buntinx, and Ellis (Pat) M. Craig. 2002. *Mental Retardation: Definition, Classification, and Systems of Support,* 10th ed. Washington D.C.: American Association on Mental Retardation.

Lumley, Vicki A., and Raymond G. Miltenberger. 1997. "Sexual Abuse Prevention for Persons with Mental Retardation." *American Journal on Mental Retardation* 101:459–472.

Lund, Alton. 1959. "The Role of N.A.R.C. in Advancing Horizons for the Retarded." *American Journal of Mental Deficiency* 59 (April): 1071–1077.

Lundberg, Ferdinand, and Marynia F. Farnham. 1947. *Modern Woman: The Lost Sex.* New York: Harper and Brothers.

MacKenzie, Donald. 1976. "Eugenics in Britain." *Social Studies of Science* 6:499–532.

Mackie, Romaine P. 1969. *Special Education in the United States: Statistics, 1948–1966.* New York: Teachers College Press.

Mamula, Richard A., and Nate Newman. 1973. *Community Placement of the Mentally Retarded: A Handbook for Community Agencies and Social Work Practitioners.* Springfield, Ill.: Charles C. Thomas.

Mandelbaum, Arthur, and Mary Ella Wheeler. 1960. "The Meaning of a Defective Child to Parents." *Social Casework* 41:360–367.

Maneely, Nancy. 1979a. "Pennhurst Appeal: AFSCME to Fight Judge Broderick's Phase-out Order." *Mercury* (Pottstown, Pa.), May 3.

———. 1979b. "Residents Skeptical of 'Idealistic' Pennhurst Plan." *Mercury* (Pottstown, Pa.), May 3.

Mann, Michael. 1993. *Sources of Social Power,* vol. 2. Cambridge: Cambridge University Press.

Mariner, Joanne. 2003. "Racism, Citizenship and National Identity." *Development* 46 (3): 64–70.

Marks, D. 1999. *Disability: Controversial Debates and Psychosocial Perspectives.* London: Routledge.

Marshall, T. H., and Tom Bottomore. 1992 (1950). *Citizenship and Social Class.* London: Pluto.

Martin, Edwin W., Reed Martin, and Donna L. Terman. 1996. "The Legislative and Litigation History of Special Education." *Future of Children* 6 (1): 25–39.

Martin, Robert, with Desmond Corrigan. 1996. "Self-Advocacy and the International League." Pp. 63–65 in *New Voices: Self-Advocacy by People with Disabilities,* ed. Gunnar Dybwad and Hank Bersani Jr. Cambridge, Mass.: Brookline Books.

Maryland Developmental Disabilities Council. Ca. 2000. "History of the DD Act." Available online at http://www.md-council.org/Resources/DD_Act/History/history.html (accessed September 2007).

Masland, Richard L., Seymour B. Sarason, and Thomas Gladwin. 1958. *Mental Subnormality: Biological, Psychological, and Cultural Factors.* New York: Basic Books.

Mason, Jennifer. 2004. "Personal Narratives, Relational Selves: Residential Histories in the Living and Telling." *Sociological Review* 52 (2): 162–179.

Mason, Richard G. 1986. "Rights of the Mentally Disabled." *Annual Survey of American Law* 1:195–219.

Massachusetts Province Laws, 1692–1699. 1978. Wilmington, Del.: Glazier.

Mattaei, Julie A. 1982. *An Economic History of Women in America.* New York: Schocken Books.

McAdam, Doug. 1982. *Political Process and the Development of Black Insurgency.* Chicago: University of Illinois Press.

McCabe, Marita P., Robert A. Cummins, and Shelly B. Reid. 1994. "An Empirical Study of Sexual Abuse of People with Intellectual Disabilities." *Sexuality and Disability* 12 (4): 297–306.

McKeon, Rebecca M. 1946. "Mentally Retarded Boys in War Time." *Mental Hygiene* 30 (1): 47–55.

McKesson, William B. 1956. "The Needs of the Mentally Retarded in Our Community." *American Journal of Mental Deficiency* 61 (2): 309–316.

McKnight, John. 1995. "Regenerating Community." *Social Policy* 25 (4): 54–58.

McLaren, Angus. 1986. "The Creation of a Haven for 'Human Thoroughbreds': The Sterilization of the Feeble-minded and the Mentally Ill in British Columbia." *Canadian Historical Review* 67:127–150.

Meekosha, Helen, and Leanne Dowse. 1997. "Enabling Citizenship: Gender, Disability and Citizenship in Australia." *Feminist Review* 57:49–72.

Mesibov, Gary B., Becky S. Conover, and William G. Saur. 1980. "Limited Guardianship Laws and Developmentally Disabled Adults: Needs and Obstacles." *Mental Retardation* 18 (5): 221–226.

Metcalf, Steven K. 1989. "The Right to Vote of the Mentally Disabled in Oklahoma: A Case Study of Overinclusive Language and Fundamental Rights." *Tulsa Law Journal* 25 (1): 171–194.

Meyers, Robert. 1978. *Like Normal People.* New York: McGraw-Hill.

Mickelson, Phyllis. 1947. "The Feebleminded Parent: A Study of 90 Family Cases." *American Journal of Mental Deficiency* 51 (1): 644–653.

———. 1949. "Can Mentally Deficient Parents Be Helped to Give Their Children Better Care?" *American Journal of Mental Deficiency* 53 (3): 516–534.

Miller, James A. 1994. "The Disabled, the ADA, and Strict Scrutiny." *St. Thomas Law Review* 6 (2): 393–418.

Miller v. Rutledge et al. 1887. 82. Sup. Ct. VA. 863.

Mills v. Board of Education of District of Columbia. 1972. 348 F. Supp. 866 (D. DC 1972).

Mink, Gwendolyn. 1990. "The Lady and the Tramp: Gender, Race and the Origins of the American Welfare State." Pp. 92–122 in *Women, the State, and Welfare,* ed. Linda Gordon. Madison: University of Wisconsin Press.

———. 1999. *Whose Welfare?* Ithaca, N.Y.: Cornell University Press.

Minnesota Governor's Council on Developmental Disabilities. 1996. "Parallels in Time: A History of Developmental Disability." Available online at http://www.mnddc.org/parellels/index.html (accessed February 2007).

Minow, Martha. 1990. *Making All the Difference.* Ithaca, N.Y.: Cornell University Press.

Minow, Martha, and Mary Lyndon Shanley. 1997. "Revisioning the Family: Relational Rights and Responsibilities." Pp. 84–108 in *Reconstructing Political Theory,* ed. Mary Lyndon Shanley and Uma Narayan. University Park: Pennsylvania State University Press.

Morris, Aldon D. 1986. *Origins of the Civil Rights Movement: Black Communities Organizing for Change.* New York: Free Press.

Morris, Aldon D., and Carol M. Mueller, eds. 1992. *Frontiers in Social Movement Theory.* New Haven, Conn.: Yale University Press.

Morris, J. 1993. "Feminism and Disability." *Feminist Review* 15:15–70.

"Motion for Modification," *Wyatt v. Aderholt.* 1978. Cited in Roos 1980.

Mount, Beth. 1992. *Personal Futures Planning: Promises and Precautions.* New York: Graphic Futures.

Murray, Dorothy G. 1956. *This Is Stevie's Story.* Elign, Ill.: Brethren Publishing.

Murray, Max A. 1959. "Needs of Parents of Mentally Retarded Children." *American Journal of Mental Deficiency* 63:1078–1088.

Myerson, Abraham. 1938. "Summary of the Report to the American Neurological Association Committee for the Investigation of Sterilization." *American Journal of Medical Jurisprudence* 1 (4): 253–257.

NAACP v. Allen. 1974. 493 F. 2d 614, 621.

"NARC: A Look at the Record." 1969. *Children Limited* 18 (6): 5.

"National Association for Retarded Children." 1959. *Marriage and Family Living* 21 (1): 47.

National Association of Superintendents of Public Residential Facilities for the Mentally Retarded. 1974. "Contemporary Issues in Residential Programming." Report to the Presidents' Committee on Mental Retardation. Washington, D.C.: U.S. Government Printing Office.

National Council on Disability (NCD). 1986. "Toward Independence: An Assessment of Federal Laws and Programs Affecting Persons with Disabilities—with Legislative Recommendations." NCD, Washington, D.C. Available online at http://www.ncd .gov/newsroom/publications/1989/stand.htm (accessed February 2009).

———. 1989. *The Education of Students with Disabilities: Where Do We Stand?* Washington, D.C.: NCD.

———. 1997. *Equality of Opportunity: The Making of the American with Disabilities Act.* Washington, D.C.: NCD.

———. 2001. *Righting the ADA.* Washington, D.C.: NCD.

———. 2003. "Statement by the National Council on Disability on MiCASSA." NCD no. 03-437, Washington, D.C., February 14.

National Organization on Disability. 2000. *2000 National Organization on Disability/ Harris Survey of Americans with Disabilities.* Washington D.C.: National Organization on Disability.

Nebraska Board of Examiners of Defectives. 1922 (1916). "Biennial Report of the Board of Examiners of Defectives, Nebraska." In *Eugenical Sterilization in the United States,* by Harry H. Laughlin. Chicago: Psychopathic Laboratory of the Municipal Court of Chicago, 1922.

Nelis, Tia, and Nancy Ward. 1995–1996. "Operation Close the Doors: Working for Freedom." *Impact* 9 (1): 12.

Newman, Herman. 1915. "The Unmarried Mother of Border-line Mentality." *Proceedings of the National Conference of Charities and Corrections.* 117–121.

New York State Association for Retarded Children, Inc., v. Rockefeller. 1973. 357 F. Supp. 752.

New York State Asylum for Idiots, 1852. "First Annual Report." Disability History Museum. Available online at http://www.disabilitymuseum.org (accessed January 2007).

Nielsen, Kim. 2006. "Historicizing Public Notions of Competency: Adult Guardianship Hearings." Paper presented at the annual meeting of the Society for Disability Studies, Washington, D.C.

Nirje, Bengt. 1969. "The Normalization Principle and Its Human Management Implications." Pp. 181–195 in *Changing Patterns in Residential Services for the Mentally Retarded,* ed. R. B. Kugel, and W. Wolfensberger. Washington, D.C.: President's Committee on Mental Retardation.

Nixon, Richard. 1971. "Statement about Mental Retardation." American Presidency Project. Available online at http://www.presidency.ucsb.edu/ws/index.php?pid=3219 (accessed June 2007).

———. 1978. *The Memoirs of Richard Nixon.* New York: Grosset and Dunlap.

Nolan, Blaine. 1955. "And for the Child Who Is Mentally Handicapped: A Story of the Renaissance in the Educational Program of the Winfield State Training School." *American Journal of Mental Deficiency* 60 (1): 30–40.

Noll, Steven. 1995. *Feeble-Minded in Our Midst.* Chapel Hill, N.C.: University of North Carolina Press.

Noll, Steven, and James W. Trent Jr. 2004. *Mental Retardation in America: A Historical Reader.* New York: New York University Press.

North Carolina Eugenics Board. 1942. "Biennial Report of the Eugenics Board of North Carolina." Raleigh, N.C.

Nosek, Margaret A. Steven D. Jones, and Yilin Zhu. 1989. "Levels of Compliance with Federal Requirements in Independent Living Centers." *Journal of Rehabilitation* (April–June): 31–37.

"Not Like Other Children." 1943. *Parents Magazine* 18 (October): 34, 98–102.

Nussbaum, Martha C. 2006. *Frontiers of Justice: Disability, Nationality, Species Membership*. Cambridge, Mass.: Harvard University Press.

Obering, William F. 1935. "Authority Says Alabama Sterilization Measure Is Declaration of Slavery." *Catholic Week*, May 5, p. 7. Cited in Larson 1995.

Obermayer, Liz. 2004. "Choices." In *"Community for All" Tool Kit: Resources for Supporting Community Living*. Syracuse, N.Y.: Human Policy Press.

Oberti v. Board of Education of the Borough of Clementon School District. 1993. 995 F.2d 1204.

O'Brien, Gerald. 2006. "War and the Eugenic Control of Persons with Disabilities: Metaphor, Rationalization and Point of Contrast." Paper presented at the Annual Meeting of Society for Disability Studies, Washington, D.C.

O'Brien, John. 1993. "Supported Living: What's the Difference?" Report prepared for the Center on Human Policy, Syracuse University, Syracuse, N.Y.

——. 1994. "Down Stairs That Are Never Your Own: Supporting People with Developmental Disabilities in Their Own Home." *Mental Retardation* 32 (1): 1–6.

——. 1995. "Principles for Individualized Services." P. 3 in *Individualized Services in New York State*, policy bulletin no. 4 (Winter), Research and Training Center on Community Integration, Center on Human Policy, Syracuse University, Syracuse, N.Y.

O'Brien, John, and Connie Lyle O'Brien. 2006. *Implementing Person Centered Planning: Voices of Experience*. Toronto: Inclusion Press.

O'Brien, Ruth, ed. 2004. *Voices from the Edge: Narratives about the Americans with Disabilities Act*. New York: Oxford University Press.

O'Connell, Mrs. Thomas. 1969. "Letter to the Editor." *Children Limited* 18 (9): 7.

Okin, Susan Moller. 1989. *Justice, Gender and the Family*. New York: Basic Books.

Olden, Marianne S. 1947. "The ABC of Human Conservation." Pamphlet published by Birthright. Archives of the North Carolina Human Betterment League, University of North Carolina, Chapel Hill.

——. 1974. "History of the Development of the First National Organization for Sterilization." Archives of the North Carolina Human Betterment League, University of North Carolina, Chapel Hill.

Oliver, Michael. 1990. *The Politics of Disablement*. New York: St. Martin's Press.

Olley, Gregory, and William J. Fremouw. 1974. "The Voting Rights of the Mentally Retarded: A Survey of State Laws." *Mental Retardation* 12 (1): 14–16.

Olley, Gregory, and Gregory Ramey. 1976. "Voter Participation of Retarded Citizens in the 1976 Presidential Election." *Mental Retardation* 16 (3): 255–258.

Olmstead, Commissioner, Georgia Department of Human Resources et al. v. L. C. 1999. 527 U.S. 581.

Olshansky, Simon. 1962. "Chronic Sorrow: A Response to Having a Defective Child." *Social Casework* 43 (4): 190–193.

Olshansky, Simon, Gertrude C. Johnson, and Leon Sternfeld. 1963. "Attitudes of Some GP's towards Institutionalizing Mentally Retarded Children." *Mental Retardation* 1:18–20, 57–59.

Osborne, Frederick. 1968. *The Future of Human Heredity: An Introduction to Eugenics in Modern Society*. New York: Weybright and Talley.

Oswald, Frances. 1930. "Eugenic Sterilization in the United States." *American Journal of Sociology* 36:65–73.

"PARC Asks Probe of Residential Facilities." 1970. *Pennsylvania Message* 6 (2): 1.

Parens, Erik, and Adrienne Asch. 2003. "Disability Rights Critique of Prenatal Genetic Testing: Reflections and Recommendations." *Mental Retardation and Developmental Disabilities Research Reviews* 9:40–47.

Pateman, Carole. 1988. *Sexual Contract*. Stanford, Calif.: Stanford University Press.

Patterson, Annette, and Martha Satz. 2002. "Genetic Counseling and the Disabled: Feminism Examines the Stance of Those Who Stand at the Gate." *Hypatia* 17 (3): 118–142.

Patterson, Gene. 1980. "Basic Principles and Philosophies for Developing Residential Services in the Community." Pp. 137–150 in *Shaping the Future: Community-Based Residential Services and Facilities for Mentally Retarded People*, ed. Philip Roos, Brian M. McCaan, and Max R. Addison. Baltimore: University Park Press.

Paul, Diane. 1995. *Controlling Human Heredity*. Atlantic Highlands, N.J.: Humanities Press.

Pearce, Diana. 1990. "Welfare Is Not for Women: Why the War on Poverty Cannot Conquer the Feminization of Poverty." Pp. 265–279 in *Women, the State and Welfare*, ed. Linda Gordon. Madison: University of Wisconsin Press.

Pearl, Raymond. 1927. "The Biology of Superiority." *American Mercury* 47:257–266.

Pedersen, Susan. 1993. *Family, Dependence, and the Origins of the Welfare State*. Cambridge: Cambridge University Press.

Pelka, Fred. 2004. "Pioneer in the Parents' Movement: The Campaign for Public Education and Deinstitutionalization of People with Developmental Disabilities." Transcript of oral interview from 2001 with Gunnar Dybwad, Disability Rights and Independent Loving Oral History Project, University of California, Berkeley. Available online at http://content.cdlib.org (accessed August 2007).

"Pennhurst Center Ordered to Close by End of 1981." 1979. *Mirror* (Altoona, Pa.), May 10.

"Pennhurst Closing Leader Now Voices Doubt over Ruling." 1979. *Times Herald* (Norristown, Pa.), June 2.

"Pennhurst Is Home." 1979. *Mercury* (Pottstown, Pa.), May 23.

Pennhurst State School and Hospital v. Halderman. 1981. 451 U.S. 1.

Pennsylvania Association for Retarded Children (PARC) v. Commonwealth of Pennsylvania. 1971. 334 F. Supp. 1257.

———. 1972. "Amended Consent Agreement." 343 F. Supp 279.

Pennsylvania Association for Retarded Citizens (PARC). Ca. 1977. *A Case Study of a Social Change Movement*. PARC Archives, Harrisburg, Pa.

Penry v. Lynaugh. 1989. 492 U.S. 302.

People First of California. 1984. "Surviving in the System: Mental Retardation and the Retarding Environment." Report commissioned by the State Council on Developmental Disabilities, Sacramento, Calif.

Pernick, Martin. 1996. *The Black Stork*. New York: Oxford University Press.

———. 1997. "Eugenics and Public Health in American History." *American Journal of Public Health* 87 (11): 1767–1772.

Perske, Robert. 1972. "The Dignity of Risk." *Mental Retardation* 10 (1): 24–27.

Phillips, Anne. 1991. *Engendering Democracy*. University Park: Pennsylvania State University Press.

Piccola, Frank (as told to Ralph Bass). 1955. "We Kept Our Retarded Child at Home." *Coronet* 39 (November): 48–52.

Pocock, J.G.A. 1992. "The Ideal of Citizenship since Classical Times." *Queen's Quarterly* 99:33–55.

Poolaw v. Parker Unified School District. 1995. 67 F.3d 830.

Popenoe, Paul. 1928. "Marriage after Eugenic Sterilization." *Proceedings and Addresses for the American Association for the Study of the Feeble-Minded* 33:62–76.

Popenoe, Paul, and Roswell Hill Johnson. 1918. *Applied Eugenics*. New York: Macmillan.

Potts, Blyden B. 2005. "Disability and Employment: Considering the Importance of Social Capital." *Journal of Rehabilitation* 71 (3): 20–25.

Pratt, Julie. 1998. "Introduction." Pp. 1–9 in *On the Outside: A Look at Two Decades of Deinstitutionalization through the Eyes of People with Developmental Disabilities*, ed. Julie Pratt. Charleston: West Virginia Developmental Disabilities Planning Council.

President's Committee on Mental Retardation. 1976a. *Mental Retardation: Century of Decision*. Washington, D.C.: President's Committee on Mental Retardation.

———. 1976b. *The Mentally Retarded Citizen and the Law*, ed. Michael Kindred, Julius Cohen, David Penrod, and Thomas Shaffer. New York: Free Press.

President's Panel on Mental Retardation. 1962. "A Proposed Program for National Action to Combat Mental Retardation." Report. Washington, D.C.: U.S. Government Printing Office.

Prichard, W. I. 1949. "Sterilization of the Mentally Deficient in Virginia." *American Journal of Mental Deficiency* 53 (4): 542–546.

Prince, Michael. 2004. "Disability, Disability Studies and Citizenship: Moving Up or Off the Sociological Agenda?" *Journal of Sociology/Cahiers canadiens de sociologie* 29 (3): 459–467.

Prouty, Robert W., Gary Smith, and K. Charles Lakin. 2003. "Executive Summary." Pp. iii–x in *Residential Services for Persons with Developmental Disabilities: Status and Trends Through 2002*, ed. Robert W. Prouty, Gary Smith, and K. Charles Lakin. Minneapolis: Research and Training Center on Community Living, Institute on Community Integration, University of Minnesota.

Pubantz, Jerry. 2005. "Constructing Reason: Human Rights and the Democratization of the United Nations." *Social Forces* 84 (2): 1291–1302.

Putnam, Robert D. 2000. *Bowling Alone: The Collapse and Revival of American Community*. New York: Simon and Schuster.

Racino, Julie Ann, Stephen Taylor, Pamela Walker, and Susan O'Connor, eds. 1993. *Housing, Support, and Community: Choices and Strategies for Adults with Disabilities*. Baltimore: Paul H. Brookes.

Rafter, Nicole H. 1988. *White Trash: The Eugenic Family Studies, 1877–1919*. Boston: Northeastern University Press.

———. 1992. "Claims-Making and Socio-cultural Context in the First Eugenics Campaign." *Social Problems* 39 (1): 17–33.

———. 2004. "The Criminalization of Mental Retardation." Pp. 232–257 in *Mental Retardation in America*, ed. Steven Noll and James W. Trent Jr. New York: New York University Press.

Ragsdale v. Overholser. 1962. 281 F. 2d 943, 950.

Rapp, Rayna. 1988. "The Power of Positive Diagnosis: Medical and Material Discourses on Amniocentesis." Pp. 103–116 in *Childbirth in America: Anthropological Perspectives*, ed. Karen L. Michaelson. South Hadley, Mass.: Bergin and Garvey.

Rapp, Rayna, and Faye Ginsburg. 2001. "Enabling Disability: Rewriting Kinship, Reimagining Citizenship." Pp. 511–531 in *Public Culture*, ed. Carol A. Breckenridge and Candace Volger. Durham, N.C.: Duke University Press.

Rauh, Joseph L., Mark S. Dine, Frank M. Biro, and Trudy D. Rauh. 1989. "Sterilization for the Mentally Retarded Adolescent." *Journal of Adolescent Health Care* 10:467–472.

Rawls, John. 1984. *Theory of Justice*. Cambridge, Mass.: Harvard University Press.

Raymond, Barbara Bisantz. 1986. "We're Family Now." *McCall's* (February): 333–334.

Reagan, Ronald. 1981. "Inaugural Address." Speech delivered January 20, Washington, D.C. Reagan Library. Available online at www.reaganlibrary.com/speeches/first.asp (accessed January 2008).

Rebenkoff, Marie. 1979. "Pennhurst Parent Group Organizes to Delay Move." *Suburban and Wayne Times* (Wayne, Pa.), June 28.

"Reflections of a Life at Pennhurst." 1979. *Mercury* (Pottstown, Pa.), September 12.

Reilly, Philip R. 1991. *The Surgical Solution: History of Involuntary Sterilization in the United States*. Baltimore: Johns Hopkins University Press.

Reindal, Solveig Magnus. 1999. "Independence, Dependence, Interdependence: Some Reflections on the Subject and Personal Autonomy." *Disability and Society* 14 (3): 353–367.

Reininger, Nancy M. 1986. "*City of Cleburne v. Cleburne Living Center*: Rational Basis with a Bite?" *University of San Francisco Law Review* 20 (4): 927–948.

"Report of the Committee on Classification of the Feeble-Minded." 1994 (1910). Pp. 87–88 in *Mental Retardation in America*, ed. Stephen Noll and James W. Trent Jr. New York: New York University Press.

"Residential Care Position Issued." 1969. *Children Limited* 18 (2): 1–2.

"Residents Oppose Closing of Pennhurst." 1979. *Mercury* (Pottstown, Pa.), May 7.

Richards, Margaret. 1953. "The Retarded Child in a State School and the Problems He Presents from a Parent's Viewpoint." *American Journal of Mental Deficiency* 58 (1): 56–59.

Richards, Penny L. 2004. "'Beside Her Sat Her Idiot Child': Families and Developmental Disability in Mid-Nineteenth Century America." Pp. 65–84 in *Mental Retardation in America: A Historical Reader*, ed. Steven Noll and James W. Trent Jr. New York: New York University Press.

Richardson, Angelique. 2003. *Love and Eugenics in the Late-Nineteenth Century: Rational Reproduction and the New Woman*. Oxford: Oxford University Press.

Richardson, Channing B. 1946. "A Hundred Thousand Defectives." *Christian Century* 63 (January 23): 110–111.

Riesenberg, Peter. 1992. *Citizenship in the Western Tradition*. Chapel Hill: University of North Carolina Press.

Robb, Kenneth. 1952. "Planning for the Feebleminded." *Today's Health* 35:54–55, 70–72.

Robbins, Margaretta D. 1957. "What Parents Expect the Institution to Do for Their Children." *American Journal of Mental Deficiency* 61 (3): 672–678.

Roberts, Christy D., Laura M. Stough, and Linda H. Parrish. 2002. "The Role of Genetic Counseling in the Elective Termination of Pregnancies Involving Fetuses with Disabilities." *Journal of Special Education* 36 (1): 48–55.

Robinson, Bruce B. 1928. "Problems of Community Management of Non-institutionalized Feebleminded and Delinquent." *Proceedings of the National Conference of Social Work*. 367–372.

Robitscher, Jonas, ed. 1973. *Eugenic Sterilization*. Springfield, Ill.: Charles C. Thomas.

Rogers, Dale Evans. 1953. *Angel Unaware*. Westwood, NJ: Fleming H. Revell.

Roos, Philip. 1976. *Trends in Education: Trends in Residential Institutions for the Mentally Retarded*. Columbus, Ohio: University Council for Educational Administration.

———. 1980. "Dealing with the Momentum of Outmoded Approaches." Pp. 11–20 in *Shaping the Future: Community-Based Residential Services and Facilities for Men-*

tally Retarded People, ed. Philip Roos, Brian M. McCaan, and Max R. Addison. Baltimore: University Park.

Roosevelt, Eleanor D. 1948. "The Promise of Human Rights." *Foreign Affairs* 26 (April): 470–477.

———. 1955. "Social Responsibility for Individual Welfare." In *Selected Writings of Eleanor Roosevelt*, New Deal Document Library. Available online at http://newdeal.feri.org/er/er03.htm#9 (accessed June 2007).

Roosevelt, Franklin D. 1935. "A Message to Congress on Social Security." In *Works of Franklin D. Roosevelt*, New Deal Document Library. Available online at http://newdeal.feri.org/speeches/1935b.htm#7 (accessed June 2007).

———. 1941. "The 'Four Freedoms.'" Address to Congress, January 6. Available online at http://www2.wwnorton.com/college/history/Ralph/workbook/ralprs36b.htm (accessed June 2007).

Roselle, Ernest N. 1955. "New Horizons for the Mentally Retarded When a State Looks at the Problem as a Whole." *American Journal of Mental Deficiency* 59 (3): 359–373.

Rosen, Christine. 2004. *Preaching Eugenics: Religious Leaders and the American Eugenics Movement*. New York: Oxford University Press.

Ross, Edward. 1914. *The Old World and the New: The Significance of Past and Present Immigration to the American People*. New York: Century.

Roth, William. 1983. "Handicap as a Social Construct." *Society* (March–April): 54–61.

Rothman, David J. 1971. *The Discovery of the Asylum*. Boston: Little, Brown.

Rothman, David, and Sheila M. Rothman. 1984. *The Willowbrook Wars*. New York: Harper and Row.

Russell, Marta. 1998. *Beyond Ramps: Disability at the End of the Social Contract*. Monroe, Me.: Common Courage Press.

Sanger, Margaret. 1921. "The Morality of Birth Control." Speech delivered at the First American Birth Control Conference, Park Theater, New York, N.Y. Available online at http://www.americanrhetoric.com/speeches/margaretsangermoralityofbirthcontrol.htm (accessed September 2005).

Sarason, Seymour B. 1958 (1949). *Psychological Problems in Mental Deficiency*. New York: Harper and Brothers.

Sarason, Seymour B., and Thomas Gladwin. 1958. "Psychological and Cultural Problems in Mental Subnormality." Pp. 145–400 in *Mental Subnormality: Biological, Psychological, and Cultural Factors*, ed. Richard L. Masland, Seymour B. Sarason, and Thomas Gladwin. New York: Basic Books.

Schaaf, Valerie, with Hank Bersani Jr. 1996. "People First of Oregon: An Organizational History and Personal Perspective." Pp. 171–179 in *New Voices: Self-Advocacy by People with Disabilities*, ed. Gunnar Dybwad and Hank Bersani Jr. Cambridge, Mass.: Brookline Books.

Schalock, Robert L., Pamela C. Baker, and M. Doreen Croser. 2002. *Embarking on a New Century: Mental Retardation at the End of the Twentieth Century*. Washington, D.C.: American Association on Mental Retardation.

Schalock, Robert L., and Ruth A. Luckasson. 2004. "American Association on Mental Retardation's *Definition, Classification, and System of Supports* and Its Relation to International Trends and Issues in the Field of Intellectual Disabilities." *Journal of Policy and Practice in Intellectual Disabilities* 1 (3–4): 136–146.

Schalock, Robert L., Ruth A. Luckasson, and Karrie A. Shogren. 2007. "The Renaming of *Mental Retardation*: Understanding the Change to the term *Intellectual Disability*." *Intellectual and Developmental Disabilities* 45 (2): 116–124.

Scheerenberger, R. C. 1976. *Deinstitutionalization and Institutional Reform*. Springfield, Ill.: Charles C. Thomas.

————. 1983. *A History of Mental Retardation*. Baltimore: Brookes.

Schonnell, Fred J., and B. H. Watts. 1956. "A First Survey of the Effects of a Subnormal Child on the Family Unit." *American Journal of Mental Deficiency* 61 (1): 210–219.

School District of Wisconsin Dells v. Z. S. 2002. 295 F.3d 671.

"School for a Different Child." 1941. *Parents Magazine* (March 16): 3, 79–81.

Schumacher, Henry C. 1946. "A Program for Dealing with Mental Deficiency up to Six Years of Age." *American Journal of Mental Deficiency* 51 (1): 52–56.

Schwartz, Louis. 1959. "Student Government." *American Journal of Mental Deficiency* 64 (3): 574–577.

Schwartzenberg, Susan. 2005. *Becoming Citizens: Family Life and the Politics of Disability*. Seattle: University of Washington Press.

Scotch, Richard K. 1984. *From Good Will to Civil Rights: Transforming Federal Disability Policy*. Philadelphia: Temple University Press.

Scott, Nicholas R. 2005. "John D. Rockefeller, Jr., and Eugenics: A Means of Social Manipulation." *University of Maine at Farmington Historian* 2 (2). Available online at http://studentorgs.umf.maine.edu/~aio/historian/vol2iss2/vol2iss2.html.

Scuitto, Barbara. 1974. "Letter to the Editor." *Mental Retardation News* 23 (3): 8.

Scull, Andrew T. 1977. *Decarceration, Community Treatment and the Deviant: A Radical View*. Englewood Cliffs, N.J.: Prentice-Hall.

Segal, Robert M. 1970. *Mental Retardation and Social Action*. Springfield, Ill.: Charles C. Thomas.

Seguin, Edward C. (Edouard Séguin). 1856. "Origin of the Treatment and Training of Idiots." *American Journal of Education* 2:145–152.

————. 1866. *Idiocy and Its Treatment by the Physiological Method*, rev. ed. New York: W. Wood.

Seldon, Steven. 1999. *Inheriting Shame: The Story of Eugenics and Racism in America*. New York: Teachers College Press.

Self-Advocates Becoming Empowered (SABE). 1999. "Strategic Plan." Available online at http://sabeusa.org (accessed April 2007).

————. 2000. Newsletter (Spring). Available online at http://www.sabeusa.org/sabenews/spring2000.html (accessed April 2007).

————. Ca. 2005. "SABE Summit Statement." Available online at http://sabeusa.org/documents/SABE%20Summit%20statement.pdf (accessed April 2007).

Sevenhuijsen, Selma. 2003. "The Place of Care: Relevance of the Feminist Ethic of Care for Social Policy." *Feminist Theory* 4 (2): 179–197.

Shallit, Joseph. 1956. "Hope and Help for America's Retarded Children." *Parents Magazine* (July): 42–44, 64–66.

"Shame of Pennsylvania, A." 1968. *Children Limited* (newsletter) 17 (4): 1–3.

"Shocking Decision." 1979. *Mercury* (Pottstown, Pa.), May 3.

Shorter, Edward. 2000. *The Kennedy Family and the Story of Mental Retardation*. Philadelphia: Temple University Press.

Shoultz, Bonnie, and Nancy Ward. 1996. "Self-Advocates Becoming Empowered: The Birth of a National Organization in the U.S." Pp. 216–236 in *New Voices: Self-Advocacy by People with Disabilities*, ed. Gunnar Dybwad and Hank Bersani Jr. Cambridge, Mass.: Brookline Books.

Shriver, Eunice Kennedy. 1962. "Hope for Retarded Children." *Saturday Evening Post* 235:71–75.

————. 1964. "Introduction." In Maria Eggs, *When a Child Is Different*. New York: John Day.

Silverstein, Pamela H. 1979. "Vermont's Voluntary Sterilization Statutes and the Rights of the Mentally Handicapped." *Vermont Law Review* 4 (2): 331–351.

Simons, Marten, and Jan Masschelen. 2005. "Inclusive Education for Exclusive Pupils: A Critical Analysis of the Government of the Exceptional." Pp. 208–228 in *Foucault and the Government of Disability*, ed. Shelley Tremain. Ann Arbor: University of Michigan Press.

Skinner, George T. 1934. "A Sterilization Statute for Kentucky?" *Kentucky Law Journal* 23 (1): 168–174.

Skocpol, Theda. 1992. *Protecting Soldiers and Mothers: The Political Origins of Social Policy in the United States*. Cambridge, Mass.: Harvard University Press.

Skolnick, Arlene S. 1987. *The Intimate Environment*, 4th ed. Boston: Little, Brown.

Slaughter, Stella Stillson. 1960. *The Mentally Retarded Child and His Parent*. New York: Harper and Brothers.

Slobogin, Christopher. 2004. "Is Atkins the Antithesis or Apotheosis of Antidiscrimination Principles? Sorting Out the Groupwide Effects of Exempting People with Mental Retardation from the Death Penalty." *Alabama Law Review* 55:1101–1107.

Smith, Groves B. 1922. "Practical Considerations of the Problems of Mental Deficiency as Seen in a Neuro-Psychiatric Dispensary." *Proceedings and Addresses of the American Association for the Study of the Feeble-Minded*. Quoted in Janice Brockley. "Rearing the Child Who Never Grew," in *Mental Retardation in America*, ed. Stephen Noll and James W. Trent Jr. New York: New York University, 2004.

Smith, J. David. 1994. *Pieces of Purgatory: Mental Retardation in and out of Institutions*. Pacific Grove, Calif.: Brookes/Cole.

————. 2000. "Social Constructions of Mental Retardation: Impersonal Histories and the Hope for Personal Futures." Pp. 379–393 in *Mental Retardation in the 21st Century*, ed. Michael L. Wehmeyer and James R. Patton. Austin: Pro Ed.

Smith, Jessie Spaulding. 1914. "Marriage, Sterilization and Commitment Laws Aimed at Decreasing Mental Deficiency." *Journal of the American Institute of Criminal Law and Criminology* 5:364–370.

Smith, Mark M. 2005. "Finding Deficiency: On Eugenics, Economics, and Certainty." *American Journal of Economics and Sociology* 64 (3): 887–900.

Smith, Rogers M. 1997. *Civic Ideals: Conflicting Visions of Citizenship in U.S. History*. New Haven, Conn.: Yale University Press.

Snow, David A., E. Burke Rochford, Steven K. Worden, and Robert D. Benford. 1986. "Frame Alignment Processes, Micromobilization and Movement Participation." *American Sociological Review* 51 (4): 464–481.

Snyder, Sharon L., and David T. Mitchell. 2006. "Eugenics and the Racial Genome: Politics at the Molecular Level." *Patterns of Prejudice* 40 (4–5): 399–412.

Sobsey, Dick. 1994. *Violence and Abuse in the Lives of People with Disabilities: The End of Silent Acceptance?* Baltimore: Paul H. Brookes.

Soloway, Richard A. 1995. "The 'Perfect Contraceptive': Eugenics and Birth Control Research in the Interwar Years." *Journal of Contemporary History* 30 (4): 637–664.

Somers, Margaret. 1992. "Narrativity, Narrative Identity, and Social Action: Rethinking English Working-Class Formation." *Social Science History* 16 (4): 591–630.

————. 1993. "Citizenship and the Place of the Public Sphere: Law, Community, and Political Culture in the Transition to Democracy." *American Sociological Review* 58 (5): 587–620.

————. 1994. "Rights, Relationality, and Membership: Rethinking the Making and Meaning of Citizenship." *Law and Social Inquiry* 19 (1): 63–112.

————. 1995. "Narrating and Naturalizing Civil Society and Citizenship Theory: The Place of Political Culture and the Public Sphere." *Sociological Theory* 13 (3): 229–274.

Soysal, Yasemin N. 2000. "Citizenship and Identity: Living in Diasporas in Post-war Europe." *Ethnic and Racial Studies* 23 (1): 1–15.

Spencer, Steven M. 1952. "Retarded Children Can Be Helped." *Saturday Evening Post* 225 (5): 25–26, 107–108, 110–111.

Spock, Benjamin, and Marion O. Lerrigo. 1965. *Caring for Your Disabled Child*. New York: Macmillan.

"Spotlight on Basic Aims and Prime Objectives." 1966. *Children Limited* 15, no. 1 (February–March): 7.

Spudich, Helmut. 1996. "'In Their Best Interest': How Self-Advocacy Came about in the ILSMH." Pp. 69–74 in *New Voices: Self-Advocacy by People with Disabilities*, ed. Gunnar Dybwad and Hank Bersani Jr. Cambridge, Mass.: Brookline Books.

Stancliffe, Roger J., and K. Charles Lakin, eds. 2005. *Cost and Outcomes of Community Services for People with Intellectual Disabilities*. Baltimore: Paul H. Brookes.

Stern, Alexandra Minna. 2005. "Sterilized in the Name of Public Health." *American Journal of Public Health* 95 (7): 1128–1138.

Stickney, Carol. 2001. "*Wyatt v. Stickney*." *Harbinger* (Mobile, Ala.), April 10.

Stoddard, Lothrop. 1922. *The Rising Tide of Color against White World-Supremacy*. New York. Charles Scribner's Sons.

Stone, Deborah A. 1984. *The Disabled State*. Philadelphia: Temple University Press.

Stone, Marguerite M. 1948. "Parental Attitudes to Retardation." *American Journal of Mental Deficiency* 53 (October): 363–372.

Stout, Lucille. 1959. *I Reclaimed My Child*. Philadelphia: Chilton.

Striker, Henri-Jacques. 2000. *A History of Disability*. Ann Arbor: University of Michigan Press.

Strode, Aubrey E. 1927. "Council for John H. Bell, Superintendent of Virginia's State Colony for Epileptics and Feeble Minded, for Defendant in Error." In *Buck v. Bell*, 274 U.S. 200. Louisiana University Law Center Web site. Available online at http://www.biotech.law.lsu.edu/cases/psyc/buck-v-bell.html (accessed August 2006).

Stroman, Duane F. 2003. *The Disability Rights Movement: From Deinstitutionalization to Self-Determination*. Lanham, Md.: University Press.

Stromsness, M. M. 1993. "Sexually Abused Women with Mental Retardation: Hidden Victims, Absent Resources." *Women and Therapy* 14:139–152.

"Study Legal Action." 1969. *Pennsylvania Message* 5 (2): 1, 3, 8.

Switzer, Jacqueline Vaughn. 2003. *Disabled Rights: American Disability Policy and the Fight for Equality*. Washington, D.C.: Georgetown University Press.

Szasz, Thomas S. 1974. *The Myth of Mental Illness: Foundations of a Theory of Personal Conduct*. New York: Harper and Row.

Taft, Jessie. 1918. "Supervision of the Feebleminded in the Community." *National Conference of Social Work*. 543–550.

TASH. N.d. "What Does TASH Stand For?" Available online at http://www.tash.org/WWA/WWA_what_acronym.html (accessed May 2007).

Taylor, Steven J. 1988. "Caught in the Continuum: A Critical Analysis of the Principle of the Least Restrictive Environment." *Journal of the Association for the Severely Handicapped* 13 (1) 41–53.

―――. 2001. "On Choice." *TASH Connections* 27 (2): 8–10.

Taylor, Steven J., Douglas Biklen, and James Knoll, eds. 1987. *Community Integration for People with Severe Disabilities.* New York City: Teachers College Press.

Terman, Lewis. 1916. *The Measurement of Intelligence.* Boston: Houghton Mifflin.

Thomas, Alexander, and Samuel Sillen. 1979. *Racism and Psychiatry.* Secaucus, N.J.: Citadel.

Thomas, Lorrin. 2004. "How They Ignore Our Rights as American Citizens: Puerto Rican Migrants and the Politics of Citizenship in the New Deal Era." *Latino Studies* 2 (2): 140–159.

Thomson, Rosemarie Garland. 1997. *Extraordinary Bodies: Figuring Physical Disability in American Culture and Literature.* New York: Columbia University Press.

Thurston, John R. 1960. "Counseling of Parents of the Severely Handicapped." *Exceptional Children* 26:351–354.

Titchkosky, Tanya. 2003. "Governing Embodiment: Technologies of Constituting Citizens with Disabilities." *Canadian Journal of Sociology* 28 (3): 517–542.

Toyota Motor Manufacturing, Inc. v. Williams. 2002. 534 U.S. 184.

Tremain, Shelley. 2005. "Foucault, Governmentally and Critical Disability Theory: An Introduction." Pp. 1–26 in *Foucault and the Government of Disability,* ed. Shelley Tremain. Ann Arbor: University of Michigan Press.

Trent, James W., Jr. 1993. "To Cut and Control: Institutional Preservation and the Sterilization of Mentally Retarded People in the United States, 1892–1947." *Journal of Historical Sociology* 6:56–73.

―――. 1994. *Inventing the Feeble Mind: A History of Mental Retardation in the United States.* Berkeley: University of California Press.

―――. 2001. "Who Shall Say Who Is a Useful Person? Abraham Myerson's Opposition to the Eugenics Movement." *History of Psychiatry* 12 (45): 33–57.

Tune, Lewis C. 1951. "Kansas Sterilization Law as It Applies to the State Training School." *American Journal of Mental Deficiency* 55 (3): 381–383.

Turner, Bryan S. 1990. "Outline of a Theory of Citizenship." *Sociology* 24:189–217.

―――. 1993. "Contemporary Problems in the Theory of Citizenship." Pp. 1–18 in *Citizenship and Social Theory,* ed. Bryan S. Turner. London: Sage Publications.

United Nations Office of the High Commissioner for Human Rights. 1959. *Declaration of the Rights of the Child.* Available online at http://www.unhchr.ch/html/menu3/b/25.htm (accessed June 2008).

U.S. Department of Commerce, Census Bureau. 1926. *Feeble-Minded and Epileptics in Intuitions, 1923.* Washington, D.C.: U.S. Government Printing Office.

―――. 1935. *Mental Defectives and Epileptics in Institution, 1933.* Washington, D.C.: U.S. Government Printing Office.

U.S. Department of Labor, Children's Bureau. 1930. *White House Conference on Children in a Democracy.* Washington, D.C.: U.S. Government Printing Office.

Vischi, Gabriel J. 1951. "A Treatise of Sterilization." *American Journal of Mental Deficiency* 55 (3): 366–369.

Vitello, S. John. 1978. "Involuntary Sterilization: Recent Developments." *Mental Retardation* 16 (6): 405–409.

Voice of the Retarded (VOR). 2008. "VOR Chronology: Milestones, 1983–Current (25 Years!)." Flyer, VOR, Elk Grove Village, Ill.

Wack, Henry Wellington. 1913. "Rational Eugenics." *Lawyer and Banker* 6 (1): 143–150.

Wald, Patricia M. 1976. "Principal Paper," in Chapter 1, "Basic Personal and Civil Rights." Pp. 3–30 in *The Mentally Retarded Citizen and the Law*, ed. Michael Kindred, Julius Cohen, David Penrod, and Thomas Shaffer. New York: Free Press.

Walker, Lisa J. 1987. "Procedural Rights in the Wrong System." Pp. 97–116 in *Images of the Disabled/Disabling Images*, ed. A. Gartner and T. Joe. New York: Praeger.

Wallin, J. E. Wallace. 1916. "A Program for the State Care of the Feeble-minded and Epileptic." *School and Society* 4 (98): 723–731.

Walzer, Michael. 1991. "The Idea of Civil Society." *Dissent* (Spring): 23–70.

Ward v. Dulaney, 1852. 23 Miss. 410.

Waskowitz, Charlotte H. 1959. "The Parents of Retarded Children Speak for Themselves." *Journal of Pediatrics* 54:319–329.

Watson, N. 1998. "Enabling Identity: Disability, Self and Citizenship." Pp. 147–162 in *The Disability Reader: Social Science Perspectives*, ed. Tom Shakespeare. London: Continuum.

Weaver, Thomas R. 1946. "The Incidence of Maladjustment among Mental Defectives in Military Environment." *American Journal of Mental Deficiency* 51 (2): 238–246.

Weber, Max. 1978 (1968). *Economy and Society*. Berkeley: University of California Press.

"We Committed Our Child." 1945. *Rotarian* 67 (August): 19–20.

Weidensall, Jean. 1917. "The Mentality of the Unmarried Mother. *Proceedings of the National Conference on Social Work*. 287–294.

Weingold, Joseph T. 1950. *The Formation of Parents' Groups and the Relation to the Overall Problem of Mental Retardation*. New York: Association for the Help of Retarded Children. Cited in Levy 1951.

———. 1954. "Discussion of Paper by Dr. Joseph Wortis, towards the Establishment of Special Clinics for Retarded Children." *American Journal of Mental Deficiency* 59 (January): 479–480.

Weingold, Joseph T., and Rudolf P. Hormuth. 1953. "Group Guidance of Parents of Mentally Retarded Children." *Journal of Child Psychology* 9 (2): 118–124.

Wendell, S. 1996. *The Rejected Body: Feminist Philosophical Reflections on Disability*. London: Routledge.

Wenocur, Stanley, and Michael Reisch. 1989. *From Charity to Enterprise: The Development of American Social Work in a Market Economy*. Urbana: University of Illinois Press.

"What Is the Community?" 2004. In *"Community for All" Tool Kit: Resources for Supporting Community Living*. Syracuse, N.Y.: Human Policy Press.

Whitehead, I. P. 1927. "Brief for Plaintiff in Error." In *Buck v. Bell*, 274 U.S. 200. Cited in Cynkar 1981.

White House Staff. 1995. *Affirmative Action Review: Report to the President*, July 19. Washington, D.C.: U.S. Government Printing Office.

Whitney, E. Arthur. 1945. "The Retarded Child in the Post-War World." *American Journal of Mental Deficiency* 11 (January): 98–99.

———. 1955. "Current Trends in Institutions for the Mentally Retarded." *American Journal of Mental Deficiency* 60 (1): 10–20.

———. 1959. "Present Day Problems in Mental Retardation." *American Journal of Mental Deficiency* 63 (January): 387–395.

Wickham, Parnel. 2001. "Idiocy and the Laws in Colonial England." *Mental Retardation* 39 (2): 104–113.

Williams, Harold J. 1915. "Feeble-mindedness and Delinquency." Pp. 57–62 in "Report of the 1915 Legislature Committee on Mental Deficiency and the Proposed Institution, ed. California Legislature Committee on Mental Deficiency and the Proposed Institution, State of California.

Williams, Paul, and Bonnie Shultz. 1982. *We Can Speak for Ourselves.* Bloomington: Indiana University Press.

Wilson, James R., Jr. 1980. "Reaching for the Last Straw." Pp. 75–81 in *Shaping the Future: Community-Based Residential Services and Facilities for Mentally Retarded People*, ed. Philip Roos, Brian M. McCann, and Max R. Addison. Baltimore: University Park Press.

Wilson, William Julius. 1978. *Declining Significance of Race.* Chicago: University of Chicago Press.

Winzer, Margaret A. 1993. *The History of Special Education: From Isolation to Integration.* Washington, D.C.: Gallaudet University Press.

Wolfe, Mary M. 1924. "The Relation of Feeble-mindedness to Education, Citizenship, and Culture." *American Association for the Study of the Feeble-Minded* 30:124–135.

Wolfensberger, Wolf. 1972. *Principles of Normalization in Human Services.* Toronto: National Institute on Mental Retardation.

Woodside, Moya. 1950. *Sterilization in North Carolina.* Chapel Hill: University of North Carolina Press.

Woodward, C. Vann. 2001 (1955). *The Strange Career of Jim Crow.* Oxford: Oxford University Press.

Wyatt v. Stickney. 1972. 344 F. Supp. 387.

Yates, Scott. 2005. "Truth, Power, and Ethics in Care Services for People with Learning Difficulties." Pp. 65–77 in *Foucault and the Government of Disability*, ed. Shelley Tremain. Ann Arbor: University of Michigan Press.

Youngberg v. Romeo. 1982. 457 U.S. 307.

Zenderland, Leila. 2004. "The Parable of *The Kallikak Family*: Explaining the Meaning of Heredity in 1912." Pp. 165–185 in *Mental Retardation in America*, ed. Steven Noll and James W. Trent Jr. New York: New York University Press.

Zigler, E. 1969. "Developmental versus Difference Theories of Mental Retardation and the Problem of Motivation." *American Journal of Mental Deficiency* 73:536–556.

Index

Allison C. Carey is an Associate Professor in the Department of Sociology and Anthropology at Shippensburg University.